Bauwelt Berlin Annual

Bauwelt Berlin Annual

Chronology of Building Events 1996 to 2001: 1998

Edited
by Martina Düttmann
and Felix Zwoch

Bauwelt Berlin   Birkhäuser Publishers
Basel · Berlin · Boston

The Bauwelt Berlin Annual is indebted to a number of persons and firms working in Berlin
and commited to the city. Through sponsoring and advertising they contributed to the making
of this Berlin chronology. The editors would like to thank

BAAG Berlin Adlershof Aufbaugesellschaft mbH
Bauwelt, Bertelsmann Fachzeitschriften GmbH, Berlin/Gütersloh
BAUWERT Allgemeine Projektentwicklungs- und Bauträgergesellschaft mbH, Berlin
BEGA Gantenbrink-Leuchten, Menden
Berliner Wasser Betriebe
Birkhäuser – Publishers for Architecture, Basel, Berlin, Boston
Bouwfonds – Bauentwicklung GmbH, Berlin
CCS Schöning & Ruh GmbH, Berlin
Dresdner Bank AG in Berlin
ERCO Leuchten GmbH, Lüdenscheid
FSB Franz Schneider Brakel
Gira – Giersiepen GmbH & Co. KG, Radevormwald
GROTH + GRAALFS Industrie- und Wohnbau GmbH, Berlin
GSW Gemeinnützige Siedlungs- und Wohnungsbaugesellschaft Berlin mbH
IHK Industrie- und Handelskammer zu Berlin
ITAG Immobilien Treuhand- und Vermögensanlage AG, Berlin
Jagdfeld FriedrichstadtPassagen Quartier 206 Vermögensverwaltung KG, Berlin
Jung, Schalksmühle
KME Europa Metal Aktiengesellschaft, Osnabrück
MetaDesign Berlin
OTIS GmbH, Berlin
Readymix AG für Beteiligungen, Ratingen
Wasserstadt GmbH, Berlin
WBM Wohnungsbaugesellschaft Berlin-Mitte mbH
WENDKER GmbH - Fertigfassaden, Herten und Berlin
WIR Wohnungsbaugesellschaft in Berlin mbH
WoGeHe Wohnungsbaugesellschaft Hellersdorf mbH, Berlin

Editorial Staff	Martina Düttmann, Hildegard Loeb-Ullmann, Christoph Tempel with Leni López, Simone Reichel, Susanne Schöninger
English Editor: Translations into English	Alexandra Staub
	Victor Dewsbery (p. 8,9, 72–91, 150–152, 155–159, 161), Jeremiah M. Riemer (p. 122–150, 153), Alexandra Staub (p. 10–31, p. 92–111), Melissa Thorson Hause (p. 32–71, p. 112–119, 121, 154–155, all quotes), Hans Unverzagt (p. 54, 55, 123, 127)
Design	MetaDesign Berlin and Beate Brauner
Lithography and Printing	Ruksaldruck, Berlin
Binding	Heinz Stein, Berlin

Deutsche Bibliothek – Cataloging-in-Publication Data
Bauwelt Berlin Annual : Chronik der baulichen Ereignisse 1996 - 2001 /
hrsg. von Martina Düttmann und Felix Zwoch. - Basel ; Berlin ; Boston : Birkhäuser.

[Englische Ausg.]. Chronology of building events 1996 to 2001
1998. / [Transl. into Engl. Victor Dewsbery ...]. - 1999
ISBN 3-7643-6015-1 (Basel...)
ISBN 0-8176-6015-1 (Boston)

This book is also available in a German language edition (ISBN 3-7643-6014-3).

World distribution by Birkhäuser Publishers.

© 1999   Bertelsmann Fachzeitschriften GmbH, Gütersloh, Berlin, and
            Birkhäuser – Publishers for Architecture, P. O. Box 133, CH 4051 Basel, Switzerland

Printed on acid-free paper produced from chlorine-free pulp. TCF ∞

Printed in Germany
            ISBN 3-7643-6015-1
            ISBN 0-8176-6015-1

            9 8 7 6 5 4 3 2 1

See Berlin before they finish it off completely.

Motto of the Berlin page 1998 in the Suddeutsche Zeitung

Content

In Its Third Year

of documenting Berlin's conversion into the German capital, the Bauwelt
Berlin Annual is proud to present the first undulating blocks which will make
up the Federal Chancellery. Appearing at the edge of Tiergarten, they will
be ready in about a year's time. Democracy has a different timetable from
the builders, so a new Chancellor will reside in the building that the old
Chancellor longed for. Nobody knows why his view to the east will be
obstructed by unreasonably high newcomers. And anyway, hardly anyone is
permitted to enter the building site. The people of Berlin, future citizens of
the capital, are forbidden to go there for a Sunday walk, as they would, if
they were allowed to. They flock to see anything they are offered in the way
of new buildings, trying them out like a new toy. Thus, the investors on the
new Potsdamer Platz have no cause to complain. The Berliners come by day
and they come in the evening, feeling as if they were away on holiday, and
so do people from elsewhere who may or may not want to settle in Berlin.
They marvel a little and buy a lot, they play in the casino, graded by their
suits and the size of their bets. Around Oranienburger Strasse the same
people – or different people – can be found sitting in the new cafés and galleries and, more rarely, in the old Tacheles art house, where the autonomous
republic is still holding out. The investor of the year, Anno August Jagdfeld,
finds no peace. Hardly anyone speaks of Alexanderplatz, so we asked planners and enthusiasts about it. Meanwhile, in the original center of Berlin, on
Schlossplatz, Italian mobile-home drivers camp out as if they were on the

beach. The best addresses on Friedrichstrasse and Pariser Platz are in a state of calm before the storm. Life has not yet moved into the "palaces from the readymade palace shop". In 1998, Berlin saw a number of prominent address changes. The Federal President's office has followed its leader, thus honoring the pioneer who was the first to move his official residence irrevocably to the banks of the Spree. The Chamber of Commerce and Industry has also moved, to the Ludwig Erhard Building planned by the English architect Nicholas Grimshaw. It still rebels somewhat, although it has been tamed by building regulations, which is not really a credit to Berlin. Berlin's famous paintings have also moved; they were long separated and kept apart in the Bodemuseum and their domain in Dahlem, but now they can begin life as a family in their first light-flooded house. A small move even took place in Wilmersdorf: the main pump station moved from its beautiful, old, Neo-Gothic home to an equally beautiful new building next door.
The Annual shows the building events singly and in large-format pictures, because nobody can foretell where and how Berlin will find itself. Before you is a numbered variety theatre in which each individual – whether architect or client – tries to defend their glorious role. Only the urban railway, linking all the places together, restores the democracy of the buildings which determine Berlin's identity.
Martina Düttmann

Felix Zwoch
Building the Chancellor's Office Building
An Interim Report From October 1998

Architects	Axel Schultes Architekten
	Charlotte Frank, Axel Schultes, Christoph Witt, Berlin
Project Managers	GBB Projektmanagement GmbH, Frankfurt M./Berlin
General Planer	Ingka – Ingenieure Kanzleramt GbR, Berlin
consisting of	
Construction	
Management	Diete + Partner GmbH, Kaarst/Berlin
Statics	GSE, Ingenieurgesellschaft mbH Saar,
	Enseleit + Partners, Berlin
Technical	
Installations	SRP, Schmidt Reuter Partner, Cologne
ARGE Rohbau	Wayss + Freytag AG, Frankfurt M./Berlin
	HMB, Hallesche Mitteldeutsche Bau AG, Halle
	Cubiertas y Mzov, Madrid/Berlin
Client	Bundeskanzleramt
	represented by Bundesbaugesellschaft Berlin mbH (BBB)
Address	Willy-Brandt-Straße 1
	Berlin-Tiergarten

The beginning and the end, urban wasteland and architectural vision, as schematic overlays: a wide, flat, stretched-out field, site of the chancellor's office, appears mirrored in the glass facade of the model office, a future workspace which functions as a house-within-a-house to create well-proportioned seclusion while allowing for vistas of a green courtyard. Recognizable at the edge of the field are: the Swiss embassy, the Charité hospital, Moltke Bridge. We are in a bend of the Spree, not far from the Reichstag.

The office model to a scale of 1:1 makes important design characteristics visible. The filigree facade lies exactly on the outer contours of the house. That is unusual, but characteristic for this architecture, in which different levels and layers are independent of one another. The single pane of glass is possible, because all of the offices are oriented to winter gardens. The office interior, a wooden cell which is independent of the bearing walls, admirably shows how the architects created bodies out of different materials and with different functions, and placed them one within the other to create three-dimensional layers, layers of space. They, who one day shall pass through these corridors, will first experience the division between the service track and the office groups. When they enter an office, they will find themselves in surroundings adapted from Dürer's painting of Hieronymus in the Hermitage, who, seated in expansive monastery halls, at work, removed from the world. This painting is like a key to the architecture. As in the painting, the chancellor's office building has an outer, bearing, structure which is smooth and cool, whereas the interior office walls will be paneled in warm, orange-varnished beechwood.

"The Band or Trace of the Federation" is the apt name for the large urban form with which Charlotte Frank and Axel Schultes won the competition in 1992. A 102-meter-wide strip begins at the Moabiter Werder, crosses the Spree twice, clasps the bends of the river, and, so the original design, only ends at Friedrichstrasse railway station. In order to orient oneself within the now ensuing arrangement, the order from west to east: On Moabiter Werder the Chancellor's Park, a hortus conclusus on a four-meter-high plateau, whose semicircle begins the 1,200-meter-long chain of buildings. From the garden, a bridge leads over the Spree to the chancellor's office building in the bend of the Spree. The forum adjoins, the forum, whose exact use and eventual buildings have as of yet not been determined. Then comes the Alsen block, which will house a part of the parliamentary offices. At the provisional end of the chain, again beyond the river, rises the parliamentary library.

The view due east shows the heterogeneous socialist capital with the high slab of the foreign trade center at Friedrichstrasse Station, and, peeking out behind, the Berlin cathedral. In the foreground, the apartment buildings from the final years of the GDR. The red house to the right is the new ARD (First German Television) building. The construction site in the foreground is the neighboring Alsen block, which will one day obstruct this view. The Alsen block will be six to eight meters higher than the wings of the chancellor's office building, an interference in the continuous Federation Band, an interference which in this form was not intended in the original design.

The building grew this summer, and reached the third floor. The wide-swept view from the top of the site, from where the viewer is on a level with the tops of the trees in Tiergarten, precisely locates the viewer within the city. The location is ideal, at once in the center and yet completely aside. The Berlin of stone, so expansive in its surface area, still has bare patches in which nothing has happened for a very long time. And on one of these patches, formerly occupied by birch trees, the chancellor's office building is taking shape. If one stands on one of the cranes today, or on one of the huge terraces tomorrow, and looks out as far as the eye can see, then Berlin appears spread out, staggered into the distance, and yet close enough to touch.

The first wave is under construction: it will top off the main building at a height of 18 meters, the height of the office wing. A second, similar, but more undulant wave will provide a roof for the building at a height of 36 meters. In order to divert the forces of the second wave's fresh concrete into the foundations, a forest of solid steel temporary supports has been planted. These supports will have to stay in place until the building is almost finished, while the three-dimensional scaffolding in the background can be removed much earlier.

To the north and the south, the wave joins up with a two-and-a-half-story-high wall while its weight is, via transverse walls, bounced back to and taken up by the building's core. For this complicated deflection of forces, a simple explanation exists: the architect's formal will requires an all-out effort on the part of the statics. The architect doesn't let physical forces determine his decisions, he sends them take off on a hike. Where forces are to be transferred, the building visibly jerks back and avoids all contact, for example via angular parapets, which complicate the transference of forces. The building's apparent lightness, a desired effect which has been brought about with many ingenious methods, has been bought with an astounding quantity of heavy steel.

The wave is a stubbornly curved shell. Its form is a hanging arch and this hanging arch has to be pre-stressed with several hundred tension cables, such as are used in bridge construction. The wave, in and of itself free-standing, is supported to the east and the west on eight supports respectively. These are located in the facade. The supports are about 1.50 meters wide and 13 meters high. In plan they have an irregular form. They were developed from large, door-like sun-protection elements, and even now, having become compact and bearing, they take over this original function. The glass between them has become unimportant – and thus transparent. The odd shape of the supports has earned them imaginative names, like amoebas, potatoheads, or chunky children.

Opposite side: The odd-shaped supports are delivered in prefabricated pieces a half-story-high. Since the glass facade cuts them in two, the outer and the inner half are precast seperately. View into the bearing core of a "potatohead" support. The reinforcement has already been inserted. When the concrete is poured, connection pockets for the glass facades are created.

The photo at the very bottom shows the main facade as it will be. The inner half of the potatohead supports grow under the rim of the large wave. In order to build the wave, a huge system of scaffolding with integrated supports is necessary.

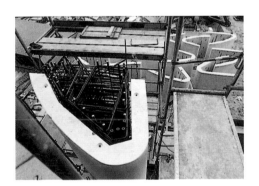

To the south Is the slte's actual attractlon: Tlergarten park begins at the building's front door and West Berlin's downtown neighborhoods are lined up just beyond. The main building is taking form, one can recognize the contour of the first wave, lying like an open hand, which a second hand, palm down, will cover three floors higher up. Also recognizable is the contour of the square main building and the circle inscribed in its middle. The corners between square and circle are cores which stem the total 55 x 55-meter area two and a half stories into the air. Further circles are inscribed into these cores: the elevators glide within round shafts. The main building will house central functions: the main foyer, international conference room, cabinet room, banquet and reception room, the chancellor's office and the chiefs of staff.

The office wings occupy the outer edge of the Federation Band, and with their 18-meter eaves level remain three meters under the traditional Berlin roofline. The otherwise so rigid design becomes humble here, and pays its respect to Tiergarten park. The offices form the long sides of an "н", with each of these sides divided into three blocks. And yet, because of the absolute uniformity of their dimensions, the wings, with a total length of 200 meters, will appear as one homogenous building. On the inside, functions will be strictly separated and have been planned as separate building parts: service tracts run the whole of the length along the courtyard or the garden side, respectively.

Opposite side: The office wings, which on their own cannot find an end, are, if they must be cut off, cut at the axis of a central corridor which then has to be completed by one half width. The wall slab which thus ensues is, for all practicality, windowless. Three small window slits per floor, so-called embrasure windows, located directly opposite the office doors across the hall, provide daylight. The light is collected outside in its full breadth, and distributed inside to ceilings and floors. The window detail demonstrates the plasticity of the building once again.

The building's planned vertical transparancy is already visible in the photos of the construction site. Light boxes trace a path, a perforation from above. The installation shafts which pierce the building from top to bottom are joined from east to west from the hollows of the light traces. Recognizable in the photo below is that the office clusters were designed apart from the service functions and as such are growing on-site at different rates.

Opposite side:
In order to allow the concrete ceilings to remain exposed, media canals have been developed as a series of floor canals. A ca. 60-cm-deep concrete canal runs down the middle of the corridors, which run off the main circulatory route. On the underside of these media troughs, lamp cavities have been formed. The now open and still empty concrete structure will later be closed by non-bearing plasterboard or wood-panel walls. Six individual offices will form a cluster. The 200 m long office wings will be clad in sandstone, while their cut-open surfaces will remain white exposed concrete. This is in keeping with the design decision which stipulates that all east-west facades in the Federation Band consequently be held in white exposed concrete.

An architecture based on a graphic fascination and developed with the help of countless models, an architecture for which the X, Y, and Z axes are one and the same, leads to displacements and unexpected cutouts, as in this stairwell window. A glass window, in and of itself vertical, scoots to the side a bit over the ground floor and with it scoots the upper building, optically. Behind the slit is the eye of a staircase at the edge, or more exactly, in the corner of the landing, which transverses the building from bottom to top. The architects avoided having floors directly join the facade. At each point, they searched for the connection-free layering of autonomous systems.

Architects	Gruber + Kleine-Kraneburg, Frankfurt/Berlin
Project Management	Bundesamt für Bauwesen und Raumordnung
Cost and Project Control	ibb Ing.-Büro Prof. Burkhardt GmbH & Co., Berlin
Structural Design	Polónyi und Fink GmbH, Berlin
Client	Bundesrepublik Deutschland, represented by Bundesministerium für Bauwesen, represented by Bundesamt für Bauwesen und Raumordnung
Opening	November 23rd, 1998
Address	Spreeweg 1 Berlin-Tiergarten

Heinrich Wefing
The Federal President's Office in Tiergarten

All photos:
Stefan Müller

Darkly, darkly the new federal president's office shimmers through a net of branches and leaves. For an instant it appears both strange and festive, a gray-green shadow in Tiergarten. The cool object resting upon its oval plan seems to recede from the viewer, no matter what the perspective. The park's trees are mirrored in the building's smooth surface; windows and frames shine in a blackened polish. It is a self-confident, in its introverted stance almost chilly solitaire which Martin Gruber and Helmut Kleine-Kranburg have placed at some distance to the white Bellevue Castle.

The Castle has been the federal president's official Berlin residence since 1959. For the six presidents before Roman Herzog it was little more than a symbolic dwelling, used now and again for receptions. It was Richard von Weizsäcker who, in the winter of 1993, pointedly moved his primary residence to the palace on the Spree. Weizsäcker had initially played with the idea of setting up house in the Kronprinzenpalais Unter den Linden, which would have given united Germany's head of state a representative spot in the heart of the nation's capital. This plan proved to be too difficult, both because of the rebuilding and security issues involved, and so Weizsäcker contented himself with Schloß Bellevue. In 1994, his successor Roman Herzog moved in and found that there was, of course, too little room for the staff coming in his tow.

The task of designing new quarters for them was in itself unspectacular enough. The main issue and special problem, however, was to design an office building which is in close proximity to while still observing a respectful distance from the early classicist castle itself. A fine line between closeness and remoteness had to be maintained, as the 1785 building by Michael Philipp Daniel Boumann called for spatial and architectonic distance which was difficult to reconcile with the desired connection between the president's office and the new civil servants' building. The three winged castle with a square cour d'honneur draws its life from its clear symmetry; any extension would have proven fatal. So the two buildings, old and new, play what for me is an impressive dialectic game of approach and withdrawal.

The architects placed their ellipse amongst the trees and took pains to keep damage to the Tiergarten, a park much loved by the Berliners, to a minimum. The "president's egg" pays no heed whatsoever to the castle's axiality. It does not play a subordinate role but instead—an only seeming paradox—pays respect to the existing structure by demonstrating its independence: it is dark rather than light, polished rather than matte, smooth rather than stuccoed. The two solitaires meet only at the junction, actually a narrow gap, of their outbuildings, two guard houses where material, stance, gestures and design philosophy of old and new come into direct contact with each other. There are, nonetheless, references to the old structure, for example in the ellipse's proportions, with a long axis of 83 meters and a short axis of 41, proportions which allude to the cour d'honneur of

A stone skin of dark impala wraps itself around the building in an endless loop and would make it appear impenetrable, were it not for the outer casements of the wooden-framed windows, which open outwards

Bellevue Castle. The new building's plan cites the oval ballroom which Carl Gotthard Langhans had put into the castle's piano nobile in 1791. And the two buildings' eaves are at least at the same height. Naturally the gaze wanders from here to there, broken again and again by the green tangle of the tree-tops; wanders from the civil servants' offices, across the president's private garden, and on to the south wing of the castle with the chief of state's official residence. This part of Bellevue is not exactly of classicist severity. After being damaged during World War II, it was restored in 1954–59 by Carl-Heinz Schwennicke and saw later changes in the form of a 1987 restoration which left it exuding the charm of staid respectability. To maintain that the hand which designed the interior was not always guided by the epitome of tastefulness would not be overly unkind.

The other extreme is represented by the new building. Its stone skin made of "impala dark" encloses a surprisingly light interior. The oval is roomy enough for 138 offices, a total of 9.000 sq. m., and the necessary service areas. A garage is below. It is a considerable program for the small office, which calls itself the most distinguished of the German authorities. The activities of the civil servants who work here are not especially earth shaking. They read dossiers, write letters, hold conferences, use the phone, send faxes, or type data into their computers; bureaucratic tasks which appear to be no different from those found in any insurance agency. Gruber and Kleine-Kraneburg very dexterously

An elliptical floor plan
surrounded by galleries,
on which the offices are
gathered. On the long
axis, the slab, as high as
the building, for the vertical circulation and service areas. The grid of
the light ceiling, above,
is answered by the light
marble floor with its
artistic inclusions

took the functional repetition, the almost endless
addition of office cubicles, and translated them
into a form which never seems to become mono-
tonous. The offices, lined up on an endless oval
corridor, all have a wonderful view of the park. The
interior space holds promise of a somber stillness
which in its own way continues the exterior's solem-
nity. Four stories of offices lie, neatly stacked, in an
oval ring around a glass-roofed hall as high as the
building itself. This central space demonstrates
what "poetic rationalism", in the best sense of the
word, can be. A grid of white supports and galleries
circles the expansive foyer. It is an airy screen, behind which lie the offices. Their doors lie embossed
into the wall, the different intervals being account-
ed for by the changes in the oval's radii. This irre-
gularity is one of the irritations in the otherwise
perpetual order. A four-story, smoothly cut off rectangular slab stands on the long axis of the hall. The
juxtaposition of curved and straight, of continuing
and abruptly cut-off walls, allows for an interesting
and yet clearly legible spatiality. Only light and air
lie between the outer ring and the inner slab. Rays
of light and shadows of cloud paint ever-changing
murals upon the walls.

Four bridges, arranged like the arms of a wind-
mill, connect the central core to the outer galleries
at each level. In fact, the centrally placed slab, with
its walls of a tender yellow hue, presents itself more
like the standoffish container for something like
the crown jewels. If there were something of the
sort, one could imagine the state gold reserves or

The house reflects the Tiergarten trees

the president's insignias, something very precious and valuable, in this large deposit box. Our expectations are, of course, too far-flung. The slab's function is rather profane: this is not the republic's softly gleaming Kaaba, it is merely the central office's service core. The heart of the building houses kitchenettes, file rooms, copy closets, stairwells and elevators. With a generous dose of benevolence, one could discover here an ironic comment on the state of our regulated world, a play on the dossier as the focus of the world of power. But that would refute the architecturally serious tone with which this building otherwise speaks.

The dream of a purified architecture, of a play between two stereometric bodies in light, of a modern classicism; this dream has for once been realized to the tune of 90 million marks. Naturally, doubts are raised as to the everyday utility of this ideal design, when the lucidity of the building and its almost flawless detailing are considered. Scrutinizing gazes dwell on every electrical outlet and are much more irked by the electronic garbage of air conditioning, lights, and smoke alarms which snakes its way along the ceiling than they would be in other buildings. The bureaucratic penchant towards advising and directing at every turn via hand-drawn or photocopied placards, preferably tucked into plastic sheet protectors and fastened onto doors and walls with scotch tape, a trait which in normal buildings is hard enough to endure, would have horrible consequences for this carefully calculated gesamtkunstwerk.

Oswald Mathias Ungers' influence on the new building can hardly be overlooked. It was in his office that Martin Gruber and Helmut Kleine-Kraneburg first met before winning the 1994 competition for the federal president's office. Naturally, the two young architects allow themselves the luxury of the curved line, and every once in a while they break out of the square detailing. But such liberties remain exceptions. There is a discernible strong will to keep the reins firmly grasped, with a resulting form which is clear-cut, almost monumental, in any case not free from pathos.

Such a house would never have been awarded a prize, let alone been built, in the now almost distant days of the Bonn republic. It would have elicited a well-trained defense and allergic reactions against symmetries, ideal solutions and grand gestures. Banned after 1945 in the wake of national socialist architectural propaganda, whose dull echo reverberates to this very day, every column seemed contaminated and every stone-sheathed wall suspicious.

Bonn embraced the aesthetic of the transparent thorough-quarter. Transparent pavilions, loosely strewn between trees and shrubs, like Sep Ruf's chancellor bungalow in the palace park of Palais Schaumburg, taking pains to retain their self-confidence behind filigree walls of steel and glass, were seen as architectural equivalents of the "transitorium" which, according to Theodor Heuss, described the essence of the old federal republic. Since Germany's history was itself dark enough,

the buildings were, above all, to appear light. The buildings on the Rhine had something ephemeral about them, always ready to move on, their charm emanating from something seemingly improvised. Now, however, with Bonn's move to Berlin, the buildings which the republic is newly commissioning or at least having reworked into comfortable adobes are being built to last a lifetime. What the Bonners' luxurious stance, their refusal to move into provisional buildings in Berlin, actually means, hasn't hit home yet. This stance declares: we want to stay, settle down, plan for the long term. This is the caravan's final stop. Instead of the short while, the longue durée. That is the novelty of the new Berlin architecture: this is architecture that wants to be permanent, wants to weather, wants to survive the moods of fashion.

It is for this reason that the federal president's office has dispensed with false ceilings, why the building consists solely of solid stone walls and wood-framed windows. Every stone of the facade is tailored and, according to the architects, meant to last at least a hundred years. Have they considered how incredibly long such a span of time is, in the flow of history?

The abrupt change of five political systems in only three generations meant that sudden change became a dependable constant, one which also left its mark on the architecture. Symbols of stone hardly had a chance to establish themselves. Whereas the political center of the United States has retained its well-known face for almost 200 years in the form of the classicist facade of the White House, the German chief of state has sent out "change-of-address" cards again and again. "Schloß Bellevue" is the sixth in the row in the course of hardly a hundred years. As far as the architects are concerned, he should keep this house for ever.

Cross section and ground floor plan, longitudinal section, and typical floor plan, scale 1:500

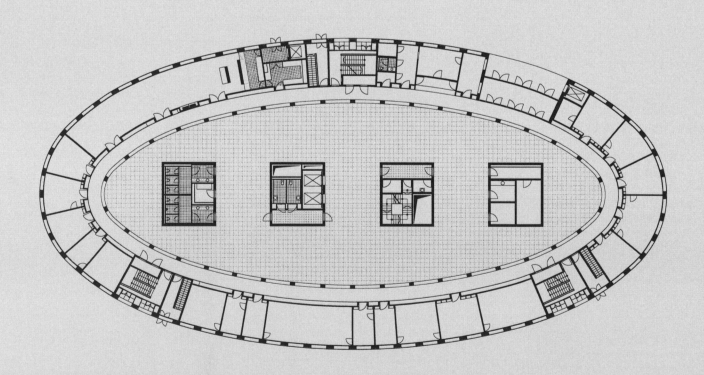

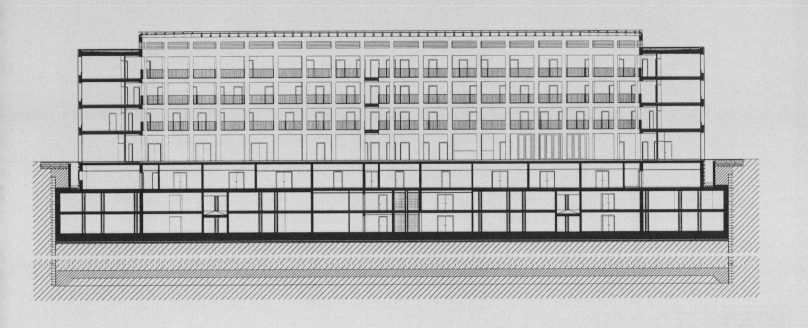

5 m   10 m

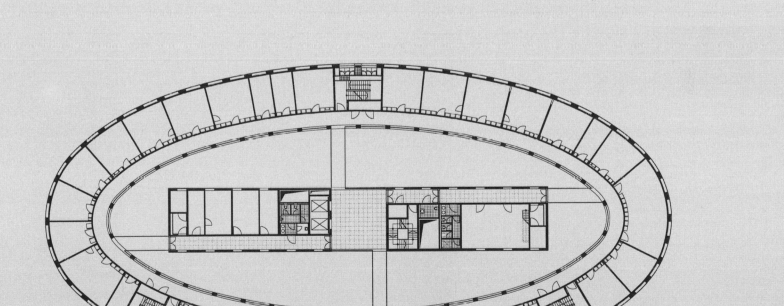

Architects	Nicholas Grimshaw & Partners, London/Berlin
Project Management	Neven Sidor
Project Control	BURO FOUR – SMV Project Management, Berlin/London
Structural Design	Whitby & Bird Engineers, London
Structural and Steel Works	Krupp Stahlbau Berlin GmbH
Interior Design of ABI	Nany Wiegand-Hoffmann, Berlin
Client	Industrie- und Handelskammer zu Berlin IHK
Opening	September 21st, 1998
Address	Fasanenstrasse 85 Berlin-Charlottenburg

Martina Düttmann
The Ludwig Erhard House

for the Berlin Chamber of Industry and Trade and the Association of Businesspeople and Industrialists

All photos:
Werner Huthmacher

The curved roof's vertex under its stainless-steel skin. The notched atriums between the arch segments follow the vault's curve. The glass panes, each differently dimensioned, are custom-cut.

During its long planning period, this building had to put up with a series of changes. In the process, it almost lost its particular qualities. It raised high expectations, dashed them, and then reversed the process, changing disappointed voices into ones of amazed approval. Now, at the writing of this text and with the building almost completed, the positive feelings predominate.

When the competition was decided in 1991, connoisseurs looked forward to a real Grimshaw, a free, light building evoking movement and emphasizing the construction (which is not to say that it was always easy to construct). It was to be a momentary respite from a Berlin otherwise cast in stone. Back then, the site stretched all the way to Kantstrasse. Plans were for a building which wound its way along a curved line beginning at the main entrance of the existing IHK building and touching down in the front yard of Delphi Cinema. The building wound its way beneath arches, whenceforth came the association, oft repeated, of an armadillo or a fish. The front of the building, located along Fasanenstrasse, was conceived as one big atrium, its hanging supports suspended from cantilevered beams. There was so much room that the Association of Berlin Businesspeople's headquarters building, recently put under historical preservation, would have fit under the new roof. This idea was dropped in a later phase, when a study showed its financial unfeasibility.

Intents were changed. The newly-awakened Hobrecht streetfront alignment plan demanded sac-

rifices, one side of the animal was trimmed down, the fish was pressed, its belly flattened, against the side of the aquarium. And its ends, front and rear, were cut back. The atrium front behind the reaching expanse of glass, perhaps an overly generous interpretation of the client's desire for "an emblem of Berlin's economy" had to make way for the understandable demand for more leasable office space. A simpler form of the arches remained, as did the hanging floors. Meanwhile, all sorts of fixtures began to populate the ground floor. Why then the hanging floors, why the arches, the visitor to the site queried well over a year ago.

The latter continue to define the house, even if they were unwanted and can hardly be seen above the Fasanenstrasse glass facade. On the northern and southern ends, the last arch in the series can clearly be perceived framing the glass front. The arches are also visible from the urban rail lines. A 4-mm-thin, stainless steel skin of scales covers the stabilizing concrete shell of the animal's back, on the side turned away from the street. Curved glass surfaces between the arches provide for the appeal of the notched atriums.

The shimmering green glass front extending along the street—the solar protection is also of glass—signals a return to the promised lightness and luminosity; from the outside you imagine it, from the inside you feel it.

The interior street is 7,50 meters high and around 100 meters long. The two entrances, one from the north and one from the south, are almost

The house on
Fasanenstrasse as
seen from the south.
The greenish-white
shimmering facade
with its glass sun
protection elements

Grimshaw extras, that
is to say, characteristic
episodes in an architec-
tural chronic which was
stretched out and watered
down by building codes:
The claws around the
slender supports
*Middle photo above:
Andreas Muhs*

on an axis. The soaring glass surfaces hardly separate the interior space from the sidewalk. The suspended upper floor surges into the space, as does
the parapet. The restaurant, which has been set on
a low platform, is part of the interior street. At the
northern end, the main room for the Association of
Berlin Businesspeople and Industrialists isolates
itself on an oval plan as if it were a detached building within the lofty space. The wide stairs to the
conference room below hang from a room-wide
parapet. These broad stairs visually add a further
floor to the already doubled height of the interior
street.

Up to now, the building has made amends to
the visitor. And so, he makes his way to the elevators, two batteries of three cabins each at the end
of one of the atriums. But wait, haven't we seen
these elevators before somewhere? The silvery
capsules with their panorama window out of the
Yellow Submarine, with two yellow wheels on
crossed bars below and a silver, stopperless chain
dangling from the center speak the futuristic language of Archigram. A dream, a child's toy, a unique
and technically highly-complicated piece. The
world-rank firms Flohr Otis and Schindler produced
three each in a sort of competition. We are enthusiastic, but could easily do without the detailed
wooden interiors with their highly complicated
sprinkler system. The thing begins its shaftless
glide, held only by guide rails and a cable. Try to
avoid already getting off on the second floor, at the
base of the atrium; instead, catch the view from the

middle or from the very top. There, the strange,
38-meter-high light courts under the curved glass
skin, one stretched out, one compressed, can be
seen to their best advantage. Too bad that the
larger atrium is somewhat spoiled by the flat oval
lid of the stock exchange.

The glass bridges where one gets off are part
of the inner circulation axis which runs parallel to
Fasanenstrasse. The corridors leading into the
wings run off perpendicularly. The construction
grid of the offices is 1,35 meters. At this point,
nothing much can be said about the offices' final
disposition. At the northern, narrower, end of the
building the plans call for open-plan office spaces,
and on the 7th and 8th floor, where the floor space
recedes as the building curves inward, there are
only large units with double-story offices, at the
end of the building with a magnificent view.

All of the building's windows can be opened.
The floors are made of precast waffle slabs and re-
maine unclad almost throughout. Installations are
in the raised floors. The first lamps are in the process of being installed, design by Renzo Piano. An
observation: the position of the arches, all of which
have different spans and vertex heights, is determined by axes which are at right angles to the street
facade. Since the building is curved, the clad arches
—one has to imagine their section as about two by
barely one meter and slanted—are a bit staggered
by the time they jut into the interior spaces of the
upper floors. The much more pronounced dynamism
of the original plan can be discerned once again, if

one is in the know. That the stories actually do suspend from the arches may easily be discerned when the gaze meets those filigrane round posts poking through the floors. You could, Grimshaw ponders in his opening speech, even imagine hanging anything else from this (almost) independent arched structure, or placing a huge skating arena underneath.

Back to earth. A few words remain to be said about the stock exchange on the ground floor, a rectangular unit around an oval core. A glass wall separates the stock exchange unit from the interior street; the glazed oval pierces the ceiling and protrudes into the atrium above. Visitors can follow the activities either from the ground floor or from the atrium level above.

And then there's the interposed realm for the Association of Berlin Businesspeople and Industrialists, which may be reached from the gallery level. Here, the club, bar, service kitchen and wine storage area will find their homes. Before the ambitious oval space was finished, the visitor could imagine a veritable smoking club for distinguished gentlemen here, but on opening day the room, ready and waiting and wood-paneled, seems to have lost its peculiarity to overabundance of flavours: a smack of stateroom, a whiff of Four Seasons, and a smattering of Grimshaw reminiscence in the hanging flight of stairs. The space is slightly sunken relative to the gallery floor, leading to a gain in height. A ramp provides the link between the two. Above, on the third floor, an elegant, curving, internal stair-

case leads to offices for the president, the manager and others. The conference room underneath, belonging to the same elliptical building-within-the-building, is likewise oval, and likewise wood-paneled, but has been equipped with sliding walls cutting the room into thirds. The egg has been beheaded at both ends, its stand-alone geometry chopped into pieces. On one side, a row of windows opens onto a basin of murky water, an architectural calamity in the basement of an otherwise sucessful house.

And with that, almost everything has been listed. But as this is an unusual house, it has its own stories to tell. Especially where the frozen movement of the building's form has to take up real movements which result from the play between the hanging floors and the elements which stand on the ground. Wonderful: the base of the stairs. The lower flights hang from the suspended floors and thus can't really set foot on the ground. In order to find their footing, they need highly complicated buffers which take up, ball-bear, cushion and who-knows-what-else them. The building is very much alive at the base of the stairs. The connection between the glass facade, which pours light onto the interior street, and the suspended floors is another such point of movement, since the floors can shift vertically up to five centimeters. The facade is stabilized via aluminium fins, which are attached to the ceiling in closely knit rows like precious handles. Or another detail: Between the suspended floors and the independent glass landings in front of the

The interior circulation axis, parallel to Fasanenstrasse, with its moving bridges between the hanging offices and the conventionally supported elevator platform

Grimshaw extras: The cladding for the base of the arches, like the paws of some great animal

elevators, hinged bridges are needed to lead across. The whole building reminds one of an upside-down ship's hull; the top is floating, the bottom docked.

The eye discerns an exception to the rule when resting upon the curved glass facades over the atriums. The original plans called for the glazing to overlap like the scales of a fish, not in order to take up, but to signal the possibility of movement and to solve the problem of the many irregularly-shaped glass formats. Then the Fischer Company offered to provide any desired glass shape at no additional cost and now the thousands of different formats are fixed.

In the adequately enthusiastic description of the elevators, one thought is still missing. At points, the visitor thinks, the technoid qualities of the original design, which were so watered down in the final version, come through as an exaggeration in the detailing. The elevators are a case in point, but the voluminous claws on the skinny poles in front of the north and south facades seem to be a reminiscence of the original design which I would wholeheartedly defend, in contrast to the organic swings of the gallery and the overabundance of ovals. These are only surrogates for the movement which the design once aspired to. The unnecessarily effusive cladding at the base of the arches, which were originally meant to be of concrete, call for an enthusiastic response.

The arches have their own story which one no longer sees, but which one must be told. Each arch has a different span, a different height, and a different inner and outer ellipse. The vertex height ranges between 31,20 and 38,60 meters and the span between 33,70 and 61,20. The plan was for the arches to be of concrete, but the Krupp Company's design, which was adopted in the final run, called for steel.

The first problem was getting the arches from the shop in Berlin to this slender patch of ground, since Fasanenstrasse is narrow and the urban rail bridges low. The arches were dismantled into seven parts which were each no more than 4,70 m high and thus, if inclined, could just fit through. The arch segments were calculated with a computer, worked out as a drawing, put back together in the computer and at its command, cut from steel plates. Finally, they left the shop, complete with all the fittings needed for the suspended posts, the floors, the arches' cladding and the facade. So far so good. Now they only have to be mounted.

First phase: The floor over the basement is finished, now the first arch segments can be raised. At this point, they still have to be held by special supports and use what will later be a hanging support as a conventional support. This calls for additional bracing along the supporting axes and temporary torsion braces between the supports. After the floors have been poured, helping stiffen the structure, everything moves up a level. The second arch segments are mounted, then the second set of supports plus torsion braces, then the third arch segments and finally the last segments. In the upper levels, where the floors have not been poured

The 100 meter long interior street, parallel to the sidewalk outside. Above, the surging parapets of the suspended mezzanine floor

yet, tie rods are temporarily affixed. To sum up: In order to mount 1,400 tons of steel for the first building phase, 350 tons were used as a temporary construction. Or, stated differently: In order to come into its own, the dynamic suspended construction, which one feels rather than sees, needs about 25 % extra steel as crutches. But finally, the fascinating switch of forces: The stabilizing compression members turn into suspended supports. In order to allow them to transfer their load onto the arches, the unfinished building is raised, arch by arch, and the temporary supports are lowered in 15 mm increments. After that, the building hangs from the arches, as planned.

The two building phases were necessary because the stock exchange building had to be torn down without hindering business at the exchange through a move or delay. That's why the new IHK building had to be partially finished before dismantlement of the old stock exchange building could be begun.

The advantage for the second building phase: The following six arches now have something that they can lean on, namely, the stable composition of the first ten arches. The arch segments can be laid out on the first floor and welded together. Then, the suspended supports can be mounted and the whole thing can be raised. In the early summer of 1997 two arches were mounted every two weeks. The raising of arch number 15 can be read up on in a protocol written by Thomas Gregull of Krupp Stahlbau Berlin:

"The vertex lay under the roof of the old IHK building and the rear base was directly next to the crane. With these two fixed points as givens, there was only one possibility to raise the arch: it had to be twisted out from beneath the already mounted construction in order to place it onto the proper bearings. Exactly as we had planned it on paper, the workers, using three cranes, threaded the final arch out, centimeter by centimeter. The last arch was righted."

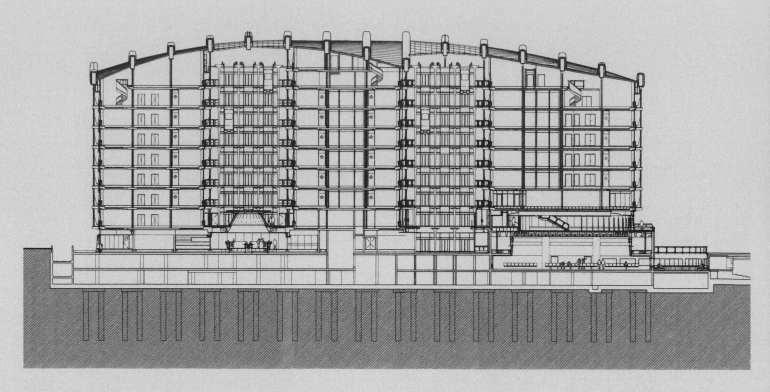

**Longitudinal section,
plans of
ground floor
1st upper level
4th upper level,
all to a scale of 1:750**

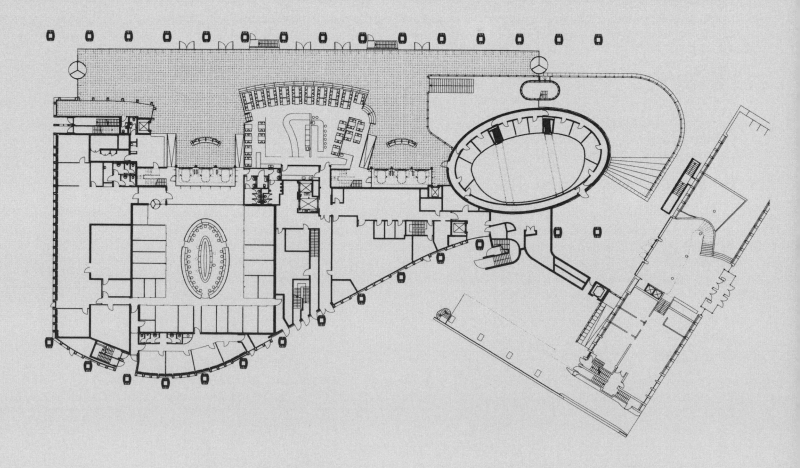

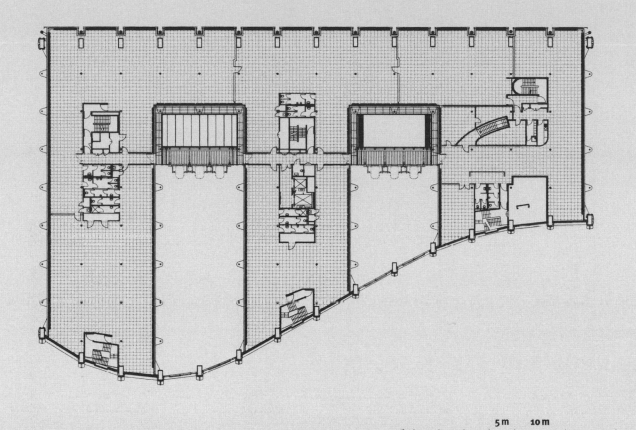

5m   10m

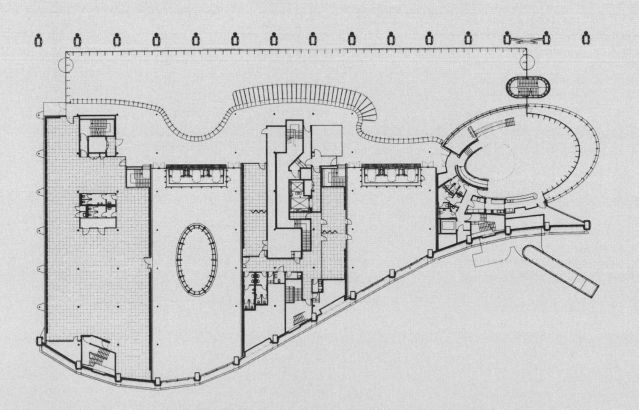

31

4

Architects · Hilmer & Sattler, Munich/Berlin
Partner · Thomas Albrecht, Berlin
Project
Management · Peter Dörrie, Berlin
Client · Staatliche Museen zu Berlin – Preußischer Kulturbesitz
Daylight · Institut für Tageslichttechnik, Dr. Hanns Freymuth, Stuttgart
Artificial Light · Lichtdesign Ingenieurgesellschaft mbH, Cologne
Wall Covering · Anton Buchele Raumgestaltung GmbH, Munich
Opening · June 12th, 1998
Address · Matthäikirchplatz 8
Berlin-Tiergarten

Philipp Moritz Reiser
The New Painting Gallery at the Kulturforum

Photos of the New Painting Gallery: Stefan Müller
Photos while moving in: Erik-Jan Ouwerkerk

You set out to visit the new Gemäldegalerie a day after the opening (to which it was impossible to get an invitation); for three weeks now, the newspapers have been anticipating the event, making your mouth water with interviews where the director explains what an art it is to hang the paintings in such a way as to bring out the kinships among them. The newspapers have published photos showing the sealed crates rolling through the streets with their secret and fragile contents, the careful process of unpacking and measuring the frames, a flood of paintings on casters in the still-empty spaces—photos you aren't really even supposed to see, for the Gemäldegalerie wants to and will open with a crescendo. To meet this surge of expectation, the directors of the Staatliche Museen have prepared two sensations: the new building, shrouded in secrecy and completely closed toward the exterior, and the unveiling of the two Berlin picture collections, now reunified. You wait, meanwhile taking a look around outside. The Kulturforum is familiar enough to West Berliners; they've watched it grow very slowly, always waiting to see what would become of it. They were promised another Museumsinsel, but over the years all the newspapers could report was continual conflict, with each of the factions advocating an equally convincing concept. Gutbrod's concept with Gutbrod's buildings—the winning project from a 1968 competition—wasn't even begun until 10 years later. As architects say, the leaves wither and fade when that happens. Still in 1985, the Kunstgewerbemuseum was built, opened—and immediately condemned. Straightaway, the next generation—the architects Hilmer & Sattler—were commissioned to polish and modernize Gutbrod's architecture and create new facades for the half-finished buildings on the edge of the Piazzetta. Yet the Piazzetta still slopes slightly upward, just as it did 30 years ago when it was first drawn, and the arrangement of the surrounding buildings still follows Gutbrod's design. Gutbrod's concept was preceded by that of Scharoun, which many people apparently think is still worth fighting for. Scharoun's gift to the Kulturforum—as start-up capital, so to speak—was his Philharmonic Hall; Mies van der Rohe's was the New National Gallery. The State Library, located on the other side of the wide bypass road, is an almost-Scharoun, while the chamber music hall is a no-longer-Scharoun. Beyond the Staatsbibliothek, however, a new city is in the making, and on October 2nd, its largest project—the debis site on Potsdamer Platz—was inaugurated. Why bother with an overall concept anymore, says the visitor, looking around from the highest point of the

The new Gemälde-
galerie, framed by
Mies van der Rohe's
Neue Nationalgalerie

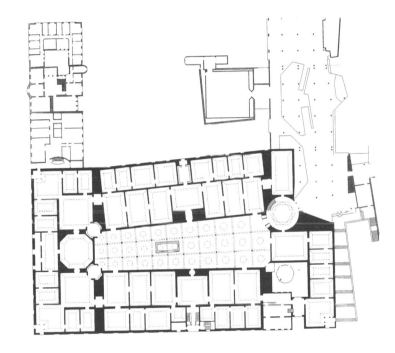

so called Plazzetta, protected from rain by the project-
ing roof; why bother, when
the history of the city itself
already presents a fine
exhibition in which the
fragments of incomplete
projects suffice to explain
themselves. At your feet are
the final, self-confident
performances of two epoch-
making architects: both the
Neue Nationalgalerie and
the Philharmonie were their
creators' last masterpieces. Next to you, Gutbrod's taciturn structure exemplifies the
unemotional austerity of the 1960s, when decoration meant nothing, not even on a
museum building. The chamber music hall before you is pure epigone, representative
of no time in particular, or at most the one that permitted such things. Finally, across
the street, the brand-new Potsdamer Platz awaits the turn of the millennium, allying
itself back to back with the Staatsbibliothek. Only the Gemäldegalerie is still missing,
as something different and possibly unique; as yet, no one can say how it will fit in,
since no one was allowed to see it until the architecture of the building and the hanging of the pictures had been completed down to the last jot and tittle. And so you set
out to enter the sacred halls from the broad entrance level, a space confusing to the
first-time visitor, because you think you've already arrived. But no, you find yourself in
a prosaic distribution hall for which no architect would want to take credit — neither
Ralf Gutbrod, who wasn't allowed to finish it, nor Hilmer & Sattler, who didn't design it.
The Gemäldegalerie, the new heart of the ensemble, adjoins it diagonally. Go left,
through the rotunda and the open door, and the doorman will whisper to you where to
go next. If you already have a ticket, the approach is easier via the very broad, shallow
stairs leading from Sigismundstrasse to the side entrance, with Mies at your back.

Plan of the main floor
(north at top) on a
scale of 1:1500.
To the right is the
adjoining distribution
hall; the wing to the
left is the director's
building

Entrance through the rotunda

From here, it's only another step or two into the rotunda, a space that signals the transition from one world to another like a spandrel. The rotunda is empty and high, surrounded by a narrow gallery; above it, staggered window levels on a hexagonal plan, growing smaller as they near the top, set the mood for a unique, unpracticed sense of light. You try to walk inaudibly; the passage to the Elysian Fields lies in the diagonal. You enter and feel a sense of relief: there is nothing intimidating about the large central hall with its two rows of pillars and three bays. It becomes a little narrower toward the rear, thus appearing even deeper; when the sun shines, the shallow oculi cast spots of light on the floor. It is reminiscent of an enclosed Moorish garden, of a railway station hall, of a... No pictures here. The fountain in the middle is negligible. The floor is covered with light parquet; the walls are lined with bright benches. You walk normally again. You don't whisper. You take a deep breath; now comes the art. Three entrances on each side and three entrances on the diagonal. The ground plan, if you haven't already studied it beforehand on paper, opens up to you of its own accord. The central hall is surrounded by an ensemble of large, high cabinet spaces with smaller, lower ones behind. The light comes exclusively from above—or almost exclusively: although most of the building is closed off toward the exterior like a jewelry box, tiny spaces set apart by thick piers are inserted on three of its corners. Here, picture windows permit a frugal side-light to enter. Having reached

these corner spaces, the view of the normal, exterior surroundings comes as almost a shock, for what you have experienced until now is a museum so museum-like that you can't even imagine the outside anymore. Here, there is a different sense of time—and not merely because you are surrounded by nearly a thousand pictures from the beginning of the 13th to the end of the 18th century. The classical proportioning of the cabinets remains that of the early 19th century, as developed by Leo von Klenze for the Pinakothek in Munich in the interest of optimal lighting. But because these spaces, with their velvet-covered walls and high haunches, appear so new, so perfect and unused, they seem to you like a quotation from the past; only the archaic spelling has been amended. All the spaces—the large, nine-meter-high and the smaller, six-meter-high ones—have exactly the same proportions. The light-absorbing velvet covering the walls in light green, pale blue, blue-rose, and light gray extends two-thirds of the way up the wall; above it, a curvilinear cornice accommodates artificial light and hanging devices, surmounted by the white plaster haunches. At the very top, rectangular glass skylights collect light from all points of the compass and filter it several times—though only those wavelengths that could harm the pictures and hinder their perception are removed. The changes in light caused by the seasons, the position of the sun, and the shadows of the clouds remain

Pillared hall at the center of the cabinets

perceptible; it is an animated light. The curvature of the haunches serves for the optimal diffusion of the light and maintains a virtually constant intensity of illumination from top to bottom. The velvet-covered walls conceal all manner of equipment for climate control, capable of attuning the interior temperature and humidity to the number of visitors with the greatest possible precision. These rooms will never be cold or musty. Now you realize: within and behind the classical shell is an ultramodern technology that makes it as easy as possible to view the pictures and enjoy the art. Now, finally, you can surrender yourself—wait, not quite yet: the oversize baseboards with their ventilation slits, so prefabricated-looking, are foreign bodies that attract far too much attention. Sometimes they

even expand into a kind of misshapen, fireplace-height pedestal beneath a triptych. But you are quickly reconciled again: looking at the floor, you discover the narrow metal strip in the wonderful dark oak parquet, serving in place of heavy cordons to discretely signal the appropriate distance from the pictures. Finally, you look up—and there is a Canaletto, and another one. You were so caught up in the architecture that you have already traversed a whole series of rooms, unaware of your passage into the cisalpine 17th century. And now, to your amazement, you realize that it is not only the classical proportioning of the rooms that seduces you away from your own time, but also the revival of the gallery tradition of the 19th century. As you approach from the rotunda, the transalpine paintings are located on the long side to the right and the cisalpine to the left, while the 17th-century Flemish and Dutch paintings are found in the transverse wing at the end of the hall—quite without regard to which artists influenced whom, or who traveled to Italy when, as an art historian who doesn't like the arrangement points out. You can't decide whose view you think is right. "Pictures only feel at home among their own kind," says museum director Jan Kelch, who agonized over the arrangement in an endless series of experiments. The care taken in the placement of the pictures becomes obvious when the Madonna with Child in a Rose Garden appears through the series of rooms, framed by the doorways. And yet, you wonder what inspired Kelch to wrest so many symmetrical arrangements from the walls, whether framed by doorways or not. In principle, one thing is clear: the excellent light, consistent throughout the museum, knows no privileged or disadvantaged places, and even the selection of close to a thousand pictures from the now overflowing collection of almost 3,000 paintings from East and West Berlin yielded only masterpieces. There is no hierarchy among the pictures, and no hierarchy of places within the museum. With its well-placed passages, never linking more than three rooms in a row and usually less, the architecture enables you to find any picture quickly. Still, couldn't the works have been hung in configurations other than the quasi-triptych scheme you encounter again and again? Once again, you've allowed yourself to be distracted from the concentrated enjoyment of art made possible by these pleasantly climate-controlled and naturally lit spaces—indeed, above all by the lively and consistent illumination. Now, at last, you can say it: once the occasional obstacles presented by the historicizing architecture are surmounted, all that matters are the pictures, with their individual layers of color that practically jump out at you. Pleasure. Surfeit! The light makes the pictures speak; they narrate, they intoxicate and overwhelm you, they insulate themselves from their neighbors, they glow, they laugh. And you pity the few, very small ones behind glass that have no chance at all. With sated eyes you return to the large,

bright, empty central hall, which proves itself for a second time: having received you with a friendly and composed mien at the beginning of your stay, it continues to do so at various points throughout. Somewhere, about halfway down, must be the stair to the lower story, to the actual ground floor. Originally—i.e. in the competition phase, before reunification—this level was meant to accommodate workshops; now it is a study gallery. The swell of pictures from the reunified collection was so great that the directors of the Staatliche Museen were justifiably unwilling to consign the paintings to either a splendid presentation on the main floor or a shadow existence in the warehouse. The study gallery is a compromise between the two: here a cross section of art from the Middle Ages to ca. 1800 is once again displayed, but this time quite unpretentiously, in a long, shallow-vaulted hall with meandering rooms on the street side. Here, pictures hang next to and above one another, as in the ancestor gallery of a castle, where good and bad, beloved and less-cherished relatives take their place alongside one another, whether with dog or horse, before an ideal landscape, or in a veduta. The study gallery seems almost to embody a collector's personal passion—unlike the main exhibition above, whose aspirations to perfection do little to ease the encounter with the pictures, for you at least. Maybe it will be difficult, even for those who come to view their old familiar friends from the Dahlem holdings or the Bode Museum. Certainly, very few will have known the entire collection from the period before the war. At that time, it hung in the Kaiser-Friedrich-Museum; only in 1904 had the paintings been separated from the collection of antiquities in the Altes Museum, where they had counted as the modern section. When war broke out, the paintings were divided up: one half, possibly the more important, was placed for safekeeping in the flak tower on Friedrichshain, while the other half was hidden in magazine cellars in the north wing of the Pergamon Museum. In March 1945, around 1000 pictures from Friedrichshain were transported to safety in the mines of Kaiserroda-Merkers; supposedly, the largest of the pictures would not fit into the tun-

nels. In May 1945, two fires in Friedrichshain destroyed 434 masterpieces, among them works by Rubens, van Eyck, and Caravaggio. The pictures in storage were returned to West Berlin in 1957 after the founding of the Stiftung Preussischer Kulturbesitz, and were subsequently exhibited in the Dahlem museums. The other group of paintings survived the war behind the thick walls of the Pergamon Museum, nursed through the earliest post-war years with special allowances for ovens and heating material. Together with sculptures, these laid the foundation for the collection of the Kaiser-Friedrich-Museum in East Berlin, since 1956 the Bodemuseum. Now the two collections are once again reunited in their house at Kemperplatz, and, as paintings, have a building to themselves for the first time in their history.

All has been subordinated to their needs; the architecture has been cut to fit them like a glove. Nowadays, architecture can do anything: it can put on a show with costly facades that deny everything taking place behind them; it can make itself almost invisible with self-supporting glass; it can imitate the historical and perfect it technically. Biased though it may sound, the Gemäldegalerie at Kemperplatz in fact epitomizes the architecture of the 1990s in Berlin. It submissively — even perfectly — adopts a design solution from the 19th century, transplants it from Munich to Berlin, works with its designated functionality, and at the same time uses it as an excuse to linger in a classicistic vein. Always the servant, it treats the paintings as its clients, investing the

whole with a generous measure of those high-tech conveniences — concealed, of course — that our era takes for granted. Its no-risk approach to form, its extreme care in the treatment of the historical, and its high level of technical achievement makes this architecture unassailable. The architects have provided a costly, expensive, and self-effacing frame for self-confident pictures. The text presented here imitates them, winding around the photos, showing the paintings in their dark and golden frames on the velvet walls with their curving cornices.

Pierre Rosenberg, General Director of the Louvre Museum, Paris, 1998 In its present form, the collection is admirable, though not without its lacunae: only a few early Spaniards, a single Goya, one El Greco and no Fragonard, no Hogarth, no Leonardo. On the other hand, there is a wonderful and diverse assortment of Flemish and Dutch paintings—still lifes and portraits, landscapes and genre scenes, often in perfect condition. All, or almost all the early Italians and masters of the Renaissance are represented: Giotto and Masaccio, Piero and Antonello, Fra Angelico and Domenico Veneziano, Simone Martini and Sassetta, Bellini and Mantegna, the Lippi and Botticelli,

the Vivarini and Pollaiuolo, Sebastiano del Piombo and Correggio. To say nothing of the five Madonnas by Raffael, the equally impressive Cosimo Tura, Ercole de' Roberti, and the large Marco Zoppo, which was already stunning in the Bodemuseum. The high quality of the Mannerists is a pleasant surprise—Fontana, Vasari, Sabbatini; one tends to forget about them. As far as German Renaissance masters are concerned, only Munich can compete with Berlin (and Basel, for Holbein). But more than ever, Berlin asserts its absolute superiority with respect to early Flemish and Dutch painting, with its Robert Campins and van Eycks, with Rogier van der Weyden and Petrus Christus, Hugo van der Goes and Geertgen tot Sint Jans, to say nothing of Ouwater and Brueghel. That is Berlin's triumph.

Leo von Klenze, 1826 A painting gallery should be built on an open site, secure from the danger of fire, dust and reflected light. It should encompass the entire range of graphic art, and offer significant effects to the visitor on both interior and exterior, capable of instilling his soul with a fitting mood: for such a collection should be intended and calculated more for the nation than for the artist, in whom this mood is innate. The paintings should be arranged and exhibited according to the sole, historically grounded system of schools; yet one should be able to proceed directly to each section without being distracted or wearied beforehand by the sight of other pictures.

Large and small pictures do harm to one another; the large ones stifle the small, which seek the uniform north light. For the preservation of the pictures and the comfort of the viewers, it is recommended that the premises be moderately heated.

Study gallery in the basement level, where workshops were originally planned. Once again, a brief tour through five centuries of painting

Bernhard Schulz
Restoration of Berlin's Urban Railroad and Its Stations

The 24th of May, 1998 was a day to remember. Actually, it should have been the day on which a wholly new chapter in Berlin's rail history was launched; the day on which the urban rail line, which transverses the city from west to east, was festively reopened to inter-city rail traffic. Yet, as fate would have it, the day also brought the change from the winter to the summer train schedule, turning celebration into chaos. Nearly all trains stood stranded in open fields, passengers were cooped up in wagons for hours on end, and those at the stations had to wait for their connections, sometimes for days.

The bungled startup masked what the city had regained in terms of mass transit, architecture, urban planning and urban design. No other building and engineering ensemble has played such an important role in defining the city's structure and none comes close when considering frequency of use. The railroad snakes along, six meters above the ground, along a viaduct of more than 700 brick arches which plow their way

through the inner city from Westkreuz Station in Charlottenburg all the way to Ostbahnhof in Friedrichshain. Since 1882, the year it was opened, the urban rail line has been the backbone of the city's mass transit system. It cuts through the city at its "diameter" and unites inner and inter-city railways in parallel track systems. Eleven urban rail stations and five long-distance stations are strung along this route.

During the days of the city's division, the potential of this urban mass-transit element remained largely unused or underused. Since September 1994, Deutsche Bahn (German Rail), with aid from the federal government, has invested more than 2 billion marks to restore, electrify, and modernize the 8,8 km segment between Zoo and Ostbahnhof stations as well as to prepare the stretch for the high-speed InterCity Express (ICE) trains. For trains arriving from the west, Zoo station is no longer the terminal station. Now, trains continue, as if it were the most normal thing in the world, on into the eastern part of the city. From the south, an airport express train brings passengers from Schönefeld Airport

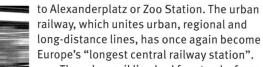

to Alexanderplatz or Zoo Station. The urban railway, which unites urban, regional and long-distance lines, has once again become Europe's "longest central railway station".

The urban rail line had four tracks from the start, two for the S-Bahn, the inner-city line, and two for long-distance trains. The S-Bahn tracks, on the northern part of the line, were electrified via a direct-current "third rail" in 1928. A lot more has been changed with the latest remodelling. The long-distance tracks have been conspicuously electrified via an overhead cable. Since the urban rail viaduct couldn't handle this new load, the 410 masts, up to 12 meters high, had to be placed on a separate steel construction which was fastened onto the side of the viaduct. Even more of an engineering feat, the top of the viaduct itself was widened and reinforced and turned into a "firm road", an 18-m wide and 25-cm thick concrete slab which juts out 60 cm on both sides of the viaduct, continuing on over the line's 52 bridges. Reinforced concrete troughs were mounted onto this slab, serving as the base for the tracks on their concrete ties and replace the usual gravel. The "firm road" stabilizes the difficult geometry of the urban rail line with its many curves, it promises greater durability and easier maintenance, and, by way of insulation slabs around the

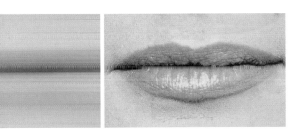

tracks, will lessen the rumblings generated by the 800 trains and 360 regional and long-distance trains which pass over the viaduct daily.

Twenty-five of the 52 bridges between Zoo Station and Ostbahnhof were entirely rebuilt; the rest restored. Thoroughly restored were also the Tiergarten, Bellevue, Fried-richstraße, Hackescher Markt, Alexanderplatz and Jannowitzbrücke stations. Train service was not interrupted. Instead, the S-Bahn was, from time to time, diverted onto the long-distance tracks, allowing the heart of Berlin's rail system to beat on.

Some day in the future, the urban railroad will no longer be the backbone of Berlin's rail system but rather the rim of what has been called a "mushroom" concept for Berlin's trains. Even if the now-under-construction north-south tunnel, the "stem" of the mush-room, should one day provide transportation for more passengers than the east-west route; with the exception of the huge Lehrter Central Station complex, it will still not compare to the old urban rail route in terms of its impact on the city.

A ride along the old line allows us a closer look at the changes. From Zoo Station, partly modernized in 1987, newly restored in 1993–94, and slated for a further renewal which will provide yet more light and amenities (architects: AS Architekten Societät, Berlin), we move on to Tiergarten station, by Strasse des 17. Juni, an unassuming station recently redone in light wood (architects: Dörr, Ludolf, Wimmer; Berlin) with only a roof

**S-Bahn station Bellevue.
S-Bahn arches on
Flensburger and
Lüneburger Strasse.
Old-established using
mix: Restaurants,
bookstore and furniture**

over the platforms. From there, we go on to the Bellevue Station, built in 1881 by Johann Eduard Jakobsthal and now under historical preservation. With its 1987 renovation, it regained the old charm of its Wilhelminian origins.

The graceful little Lehrter Stadtbahnhof station, next in line, was also pepped up for the festivities surrounding Berlin's 750th birthday in 1987, but will fall victim to the

yet to be finished design by the large Hamburg office gmp (von Gerkan, Marg and Partner). Their new central station is under construction just south of the bend Lehrter Stadtbahnhof lies on today.

For those who saw a voyage to and through Berlin as inevitably ending under digny brick arches, the new Friedrichstrasse Station will literally seem like an "illumination". The station's state before its renovation was not the original one from 1880, but dated from 1919–1925, in the time of the S-Bahn's electrification. This newer state was declared worthy of historical preservation status. The current renovation strove to retain the huge, double-naved hall and the plain facade with its expressionist touches. Added to this was a desire to admit as much light into the halls as possible, through skylights and clerestory windows (architect: Werner Weinkamm).

Daylight, and plenty of it, in any case enough to also illuminate any underground stories, was not only a major consideration when planning Friedrichstrasse Station. Just about all of the new stations saw roofs being torn open and facades turned into glass. In the Friedrichstrasse project, the architects were able to completely retain the primary construction consisting of steel beams. That the original putty-held panes were traded in for windows held by rubber profiles is hardly noticeable, since the original dimensions and thus the most characteristic features of the facade were retained. The skylights

Lehrter Stadtbahnhof. Last S-Bahn arches before reaching the construction site of Central Station. S-Bahn line passes a row of houses

were made larger and the roof truss infill was adapted to the original, whitewashed, lightweight concrete. Even though all of the reconstructions are true to the building's historical state, a contemporary aspect is evident. Friedrichstrasse Station shines like a freshly restored painting. As soon as passengers leave the hall and reach the circulation area, they are on the new mezzanine floor, which, following Deutsche Bahn's new market-

ing concept, is full of shops. The maze of additions and partitions with which visitors using this former border-crossing point were shunted about have disappeared, much to the advantage of the building's interior. Friedrichstrasse Station now presents itself as an open field. Even the huge columns which support the concrete rail troughs and the hall's construction have been made to disappear behind matte glass, in order not to disturb the spacious impression. Only the northern facade, with its two portals and decorative sculptures, was reconstructed strictly to historical specifications. To achieve this, 133,000 special-order bricks had to be fired. They have the old, "reichsformat" measure of 25 by 12.5 cm, their coloring reveals irregular variations in hue, and their glazed surface even sports inclusions. The facade's decorative elements of molded, glazed terracotta were recreated after historical originals.

The architects were not able to recreate the southern facade's history in the same manner. The extensive alterations which had to be made when the underground S-Bahn station was built in 1934–36 were not documented in detail, and no photographs were made in the long span of time between this first rebuilding and the second, partial, restoration during GDR times in the early 1960's. Thus, the architect designed a facade which recalls the historic northern facade while taking into account the new entrance on the level of the subway entrance in the middle of Georgenstrasse. For the first time,

Bahnhof Friedrichstrasse.
Bridge over the Spree
Georgenstrasse.
The viaduct extension
and the electricity masts
are clearly visible

a lateral path has been provided through the station. Only on the short ends of the building, the unspectacular facades under the enormous arches of the railway bridges facing the Spree in the west and Friedrichstrasse in the east, did the condition of the original structure allow for simple restoration and completion. The reconstruction does not deny the station's complicated history, it only smoothes it over in order to present a mostly

homogenous, light-colored building. Restorations cost 113 million marks, with 21 million going to square footage for Deutsche Bahn services and shops.

The Hackescher Markt station, built in 1882 by Johannes Vollmer and reconstructed based on his designs (architects: AS Architekten Societät, Berlin), once again shows us what the urban railroad once must have looked like. The richly ornamented facade is subdivided through piers, and big-city life is once again moving in under its brick arches.

The historical phases of Alexanderplatz station have been extensively documented. Built after the plans of Johann Eduard Jacobsthal, opened in 1882, sensationally modernized in 1886 through the addition of a new central market hall with a direct connection to the tracks, and perfected through the addition of the subway with its famous underground system of passages in 1927–30 (architect: Alfred Grenander), Alexanderplatz Station was a hub for long-distance and inner-city trains, three subway lines and several bus and streetcar lines. After its partial destruction during World War II, the station was reconstructed and expanded by Hans Joachim May and Günter Andrich in 1963–65. The architects retained the characteristic murals from 1926 and added a generous expanse of glass. With the latest and, for the time being, final reconstruction in 1995–98, architects Rebecca Chestnutt and Robert Niess used a concept they call "visualization", in order to uncover the historical layers of the station. Several additions from 1965,

S-Bahnhof Hackescher Markt. Line over Kupfergraben between Bodemuseum and Pergamonmuseum. Brick facade on Hackescher Markt

which presented the station as a solitaire and made it part of the then-contemporary vision of a modern socialist city, had to be removed. The original architectonic and functional spatial division was restored and the grand brick viaduct arch construction made visible. Because the route to the station itself was widened, three parallel spans, and not the viaduct, bear the platform construction. No mean feat: The architects managed

to both present these rows of 18 arches in their own light, while at the same time making them available for commercial use.

The station's interior harbors further historical layers. In the western part, remnants of the arches' abutments from the 1882 structure can be seen along with decorative elements on the brick vaults. Even their ingenious reinforcements, carried out during the first electrification of the S-Bahn, are visible. At the time, all of the urban railway's arches had to be reinforced, making bracing of the foundations and lateral anchoring necessary. The later, receding, vaults are made of brick in the western portion of the station; everywhere else they have been stuccoed over. The rhythm created by alternating exposed brick and stuccoed surfaces was intentional. The historical citations can also be found in the various frame and window types used to convert arches into shops. Some of the shop windows have inserted, bent-metal frames, while some have straight-edged boxes set before the actual vault. Deutsche Bahn has gained 3,360 square meters of marketable space, of which 2,900 square meters will be occupied by a carefully thought-out mix of 41 stores. A circular stairwell serves as the difficult connection between the commercial zone and the Alexanderplatz subway station. The differently oriented up and down stairways have been dexterously placed between the huge substructure of the actual station. The need for a large circulation hall on the ground floor, thwarted because the vaults had

Bahnhof Alexanderplatz. To the west: a maze of booths instead of the market hall next to the rail lines. Bridge over Karl-Liebknecht-Strasse. Rolling on at Diercksenstrasse

to be placed under the parallel running tracks, is thus circumvented. The station hall itself was restored by the Deutsche Bahn railway company in the course of the 1963–65 renovation.

Chestnutt and Niess used their "layering concept" on the exterior surface as well. This concept makes it possible to see, at a glance, what an enormous variety there was in

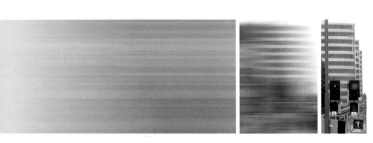

the station's design in the course of its 120 year history. Of the 125 million marks total cost for the latest renovation, 64 million are for the commercial areas. Twenty-seven million marks were provided by the community traffic financing law for the S-Bahn entrances.

After this last stop, the train glides on to the final portion of the viaduct. Here we pass over the wonderfully rational, angular, steel-and-glass hall which is Jannowitzbrücke Station, built in 1927–32. The interior of this station has seen a reconstruction of its great skylight as well as a taming of the commercial areas by placing them behind a cool steel-and-glass construction. The special attraction of this station: the viaduct arches reach into the water, where they have been gutted and their water side glazed. Five S-Bahn lines use Jannowitzbrücke Station along with subway line 8. A stop for steamships is next door on Rolandufer. On the other side of Holzmarktstrasse, which is crossed by the railroad via one of its 25 new bridges, the uniform, four-track railroad viaduct comes to an end.

Since May 1998, Ostbahnhof Station has once again become a stop for five regional express lines. In all, 360 regional and long-distance trains as well as the S-Bahn bring around 100,000 passengers daily to this station. Ostbahnhof Station was once the famous "Silesian Station," where immigrants from the east disembarked into a new life. Almost nothing remains of the original building from 1842 or the reconstructions and

S-Bahnhof Jannowitzbrücke. Alexanderstrasse crossing with Jannowitz Center behind. The viaduct's arches have glass fronts to the Spree. Trias in the background

renovations from 1869, 1882, 1926 and 1937. The reason for this is that under GDR reign, this station, then "Hauptbahnhof", the central railway station, was rebuilt for the city's 750th birthday in 1987. The station was given its former name of "Ostbahnhof" only in 1998. An "archeological" approach for its reconstruction is thus unfeasible and the historicizing, fake facade of 1987 impossible to retain. The architects (Becker, Gewers,

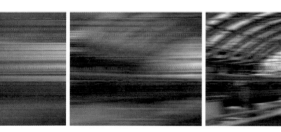

Kühn, and Kuhn, Berlin) have suggested a steel-and-glass architecture which is founded on the 1987 supporting structure. The station has seen its track area widened, the platforms have been extended to 420 meters, in order to accommodate InterCity Express (ICE) trains, and roofs with glass barrel vaults have been added. The interior of the spacious double hall has remained pretty much the same, though fixtures were removed, the interior was renovated and, as was the case with all the renovated stations, a new lighting system, directional signs, and design elements to conform with Deutsche Bahn's new corporate identity were installed. Around 12,700 square meters of service and shop areas will be ready by the year 2000. They will provide amenities, not just for

**Ostbahnhof
(before Mai 1998
Hauptbahnhof)**

travellers but for the community at large. The area in front of the station will probably be an eyesore for some time to come, at least until the "general plan for the banks of the Spree" has been realized. This plan calls for

Ostbahnhof Station and the area in front of it to be connected to the Spree River, which at this point is especially wide, bringing together the two now-far reaches which comprise the banks of this river in the Kreuzberg and Friedrichshain neighborhoods.

The urban railroad ends at Ostbahnhof. Farther east, the immense expanse of a classic track system opens up, with countless switches, and sidings, and track changes. The trains, by the way, are back on schedule and the ICE and ICE 2 as well as the AirportExpress and the normal regional trains feel quite at home on the new tracks.

Florian Profitlich
Voices from Alexanderplatz

An Interim Report

All photos:
Florian Profitlich

Actually, the idea practically suggests itself: Alexanderplatz could and should become Berlin's "Gateway to the East." Just as the city as a whole needs a new strategy for its mediating role in the heart of Europe—one that overcomes established patterns of thought and embraces unconventional political approaches—a prominent urban space like Alexanderplatz needs to expand its conceptual horizons as well. The urbanistic idea of a "Gateway to the East" points to a future as yet discernable only in outline. Completely new kinds of conflicts loom, especially in Berlin. And if traditional demonstrations of the self-glorification of wealth have triumphed once more on Potsdamer Platz, the city must find another prominent place to show itself equal to the conflicts that will arise from the future. Why not Alexanderplatz?
Wolfgang Kil, 1992
architecture critic

The creative process of the architects and engineers of Berlin is aimed above all at making decisive progress in the development of socialist architecture. The construction on Alexanderplatz presents a tremendous opportunity to achieve an artistic statement that constitutes a genuine reflection of the humanistic principles of our socialist order, extending from the vital and impressive composition of building masses, to the plasticity and differentiated articulation of the structures, to a careful and loving attention to detail. All these efforts are oriented to the goal of achieving a genuine synthesis of economy, modern technology, and artistic design. Without doubt, the construction on Alexanderplatz represents a high point in the socialist redesign of the city center.
Joachim Näther, 1967, Chief Architect for Greater Berlin, GDR

In GDR times, Alexanderplatz was the center, the pivot and fulcrum of the "capital city." Here people met friends and acquaintances, here they brought guests from out of town. Here, around the "Weltzeituhr," the whistle demonstrations heralded the political change, and here the people gathered on November 4th, 1989, to laugh their bankrupt government out of town. With reunification, the one-time center of East Berlin received an overpowering competitor, and an aura of shabbiness promptly descended on the erstwhile first class area. The colossal high-rises stand around like boulders; suddenly everything seems a little too big and a little too crude. Suddenly, a harsh wind seems to blow across the square.
Wolfgang Kil, 1992
architecture critic

From whatever direction we come—whether by car from the west and south or from the northern and eastern arteries, whether on foot, descending from the S-Bahn, ascending from the U-Bahn, or through one of the underpasses beneath the inhumanly broad thoroughfares—we will never be able to say with conviction that Alexanderplatz is here.
Lore Ditzen, 1998
architectural writer

Alexanderstrasse

The design is a continuation, not only of Martin Wagner's vision as interpreted by Peter Behrens, but also of the composition of the capital of the GDR with its pedestrian square, Forum-Hotel, and television tower.

Both are subsumed into a new unity intended to overcome the division of the city, a division incipient long before the Wall was built. Martin Wagner's urbanism was intended to achieve the same effect, to shape the city of Berlin as a whole, to create an image of Berlin at Alexanderplatz that was more than the sum of its parts.
Hans Kollhoff, 1993, winner of the urban design competition

The competition announcement of 1993 called for something like a critical reconstruction of the fragmented city plan. The urban network was to be brought closer to the square again, with the structures at its immediate edge oriented to the scale of the Behrens buildings, and the square itself kept free for pedestrians. Blocks towering up to a height of 150 m would be permitted only in a second tier, along the U-shaped street behind the buildings at the edge of the square. On June 7th, 1994, the Senate approved the winning design by Hans Kollhoff as the basis for the mandatory building guidelines for Alexanderplatz and its immediate surroundings.
Hans Stimmann, 1997

Alexanderplatz always was the prototypical square for the city's drive toward modernization. This was true in the late 19th century, when the construction of the Ring- and Stadtbahn after 1876 established the Alexanderplatz station as a node of local public transportation, and with it the central market hall of Berlin, the main police station, the department store Hermann Tietz, the teachers' association, and numerous new hotels and office buildings. It was equally true in the 1920s, when Martin Wagner sought to realize his vision of a dynamic metropolitan square on Alexanderplatz (competition 1929), even if Peter Behrens' "Alexander" and "Berolina" ensemble tends to contradict the desired architectural dynamic in material and articulation.
And it was true of Alexanderplatz in GDR times. One need only recall the 1964 competition (capital city center with new city crown) and the exhibition "Results of Urbanism and Architecture" in honor of the 20th anniversary of the GDR in 1969, with the accompanying manifestos.
Hans Stimmann, 1998, Senate Building Director until 1996, now Secretary of State in the Senate for Urban Development, Environmental Protection, and Technology

For me, the historic city lies between Schlossplatz and Brandenburger Tor. The old city isn't
around the Rathaus anymore. That was earlier.
And that's why Alexanderplatz will continue to
be a second-rate location for the next 20 years.
Alexanderplatz is and will long remain a wasteland.
*Klaus Landowsky, 1998, leader of the CDU frac-
tion in the Berlin house of representatives*

**House of Travel
and House of the Teacher**

In the beginning, after 1989, Alexanderplatz was all there was. The
people from the east, where else could they go? Only to the Alex.
Of course it's different now. The people from Hohenschönhausen
don't come to us anymore for their daily errands. But we have a
large Russian-speaking clientele. I don't know whether they're all
Russians. But usually anyone who comes from the former East Bloc
also speaks Russian. That's why we make our announcements in
Russian too; Russian was always the first foreign language of our
store. English came later. As far as the development on Alexanderplatz is concerned, I can only welcome the concentration of building
activity on Potsdamer Platz and Friedrichstrasse. Linked up with this
"central axis," Alexanderplatz is the best thing Berlin will have—
prime real estate, Mr. Landowsky. There he's dead wrong, there he
shows a lack of knowledge of the commercial landscape. We have
20–30 thousand customers in our store every day, and every day
100–200 thousand people pass Alexanderplatz. We are the second
busiest department store in Berlin, after KaDeWe. But KaDeWe isn't
even really a department store—it's a legend.
*Günter Biere, 1998, business manager of the department store
Kaufhof*

Ain't much to say about the Alex, what with
all the building going on everywhere in the
city, up and down Friedrichstrasse, nah,
nothing's going on here, they say the hotel
ain't the best either, but to be honest, I don't
live here, so what do I care if they put up a
bunch of high-rises. Everything here is a
little strange anyway, if you ask me.
Taxi driver, West Berlin, 1998

View from Alexanderhaus
to Alexanderplatz

My desire and goal is for the building plan for Alexanderplatz to be resolved before the end of this legislative period.
The last chance would be early 1999. Two political forces, however, stand in the way: the PDS party wants to preserve the modernizations from the GDR, and the Greens will support them, from what in my opinion is a misguided sense of tact. For the CDU, on the other hand, everything beyond Schlossplatz is terra incognita and arte povera, and they refuse to concern themselves with it. If we don't do something now, this attitude will become ingrained, and the city will begin to manifest a new political, economic, and topographical division.
Hans Stimmann, 1998

High-rises on the Alex? Well, if that's what the real estate market wants, why not. The modern buildings here aren't exactly great, architecturally speaking, and it's supposed to be more of the same, but in my humble opinion it would be better if they built a whole lot more apartments, 70 %, I'd say. That'd be a good mixture, but no architect would ever think of that nowadays. The old Alex is gone anyway, and when people come and ask me where old Berlin is, I have to tell them it's gone too. You want to see old Berlin, I'll take you to Wilhelminenhofstrasse in Oberschöneweide.
Taxi driver, East Berlin, 1998

We have serious objections to the building plan, above all to the high proportion of dwellings. Around the Alex it's so loud and dirty that according to EU norms, it's not an appropriate residential area. Yet estimates call for an average of 30 % dwellings, with some blocks totaling up to 64 %. Accordingly, the building plan calls for air conditioning in the apartments. Just imagine: air-conditioned children's rooms with very little sunlight, to say nothing of the traffic situation. That's cynical and irresponsible. The federal government is a 100 % partner of the TLG (Trustee Real Estate Management); it has valuable property at its disposal here, value that is being jeopardized by the planning. A total of 1.25 million square meters of floor space is projected for construction. The plan assumes that almost nothing will remain of the existing architecture, and ignores the fact that demand for housing in this area is decreasing. Our objections have received no response. Instead, the building plan has simply been divided up in order to avoid endangering the entire project and throwing it off schedule.
Andrea Sölle, 1998, Trustee Real Estate Management (TLG)

Next Station ...
Alexanderplatz

I think it is completely unrealistic to imagine that we could take the urban design, start at one corner, and literally complete it piece by piece. Buildings are still standing on most of the site; for now, wholesale demolition and reconstruction would be unthinkable.

What would work would be to realize a few sections of the design. It's no tragedy if the TLG doesn't participate now. The construction on the neighboring sites of Hines Immobilien and Deutsche Interhotel would close one whole side of the square. Nor is there any need to reroute the Memhardtstrasse, just because the overall plan calls for it. The traffic administration is prepared to agree to intermediate solutions as well. Nevertheless, we have a clear statement of the Senator's intent to stick to the overall plan in the long term. The investors have been busy: they have continued to develop their individual projects, reached agreement among themselves in regard to housing distribution, retail trade, and parking, and have calculated the cost, above all the cost for the infrastructure that they will have to provide, since the city has no money. A reduction in the price of the property on the part of the city would be the only fair response. We are banking on the good will that has characterized negotiations between the investors and the State of Berlin for years. Each individual investor will now draw up an urbanistic contract. If, as we hope, the building plan—or rather, the partial building plans—are resolved in due time, the actual planning phase can begin in 1999. I'm not at all worried about Alexanderplatz. The old visions—city crown, gateway to the East—still hold, especially since time is on our side: Kollhoff is right to speak of a completion date around the year 2020. When the federal government moves to Berlin, the demand for commercial areas and housing will increase, and international investors might well be drawn to just this kind of emerging metropolitan square.

Bodo Fuhrmann, 1998, Investors' Association Alexanderplatz

This is the Alex lying there
in silence. No, he doesn't care.
This house or that one? Honor? Shame?
To him it's seemingly the same—

not so to us. The place? The space?
The railway station's brand new grace—
a looking glass so neat and clean—
get out and look at this Berlin,

just for a minute leave the train,
enjoy the famous view again:
the center of metropolis!
O what a metamorphosis!

A center of the highest rise
and of despicable despise,
restored, recovered and redressed,
but freezing on and overstressed,

Pages 52/53
Karl-Marx-Allee looking
towards Alexanderplatz

Karl-Liebknechtstrasse
with Berliner Verlag

divided, unified, and still
missplanned, misshaped and looking ill –
A square? A sort of area,
of whereabouts, of tralala –

the Alex does no more exist,
the Alex of the novelist
Döblin, his figures do no more
invigorate the city's core –

metropolis of fish-and-ships,
of shop-in-shops, of teasing-strips,
of everywhere and everyone
and everything and everynone – – –

*This is the Alex lying there
in silence. No, he doesn't care.
This house or that one? Honor? Shame?
To him it's seemingly the same –*

Hans Unverzagt, 1998

**Crossing
Alexanderstrasse/
Karl-Liebknechtstrasse**

It is widely suspected by the general public that the urban design for Alexanderplatz is more of a vision than a fact. That is incorrect. Admittedly, at Alexanderplatz, we had to subject the entire, densely built area to careful examination, commission a series of expert opinions, and conduct investor and citizen surveys for the whole district. You remember the exhibition in May 1997? By now, evaluation and consideration of all the proposals and objections have been concluded.
In June of this year, the parliamentary building committee was informed of the result, and gave it their provisional approval. The public presentation of the three partial building plans A, B, and C is still to come. The TLG will remain in its quarters; Gruner und Jahr have invested in their holdings and are not interested in building for now. That means nothing is going to happen in the area around Karl-Liebknecht-Strasse. The remaining investors are Interhotel with three plots on the south side, Hines Immobilien next to it, Alexanderplatz 5 GbR, the Berliner Volksbank, and the DeGeWo, though here it functions as more of a project developer on behalf of the state of Berlin, responsible for a large portion of the housing. Unlike other core areas, the goal is to make the complex around Alexanderplatz up to 30 % residential—realistically, probably ca. 17–20 %. I make no bones about the fact that every step in that direction required an enormous amount of discussion. It has been decided that there will be 10 high rises instead of the original 13, that only 50 dwellings will be demolished instead of the original 1,000 called for in the competition design. The next step will be the building plan and its public presentation. The plan defines a block structure with a maximum ground area (specification of building boundaries and, more restrictively, building lines) and a height of 30 m plus a maximum of two attic stories, towers with a maximum height of 150 m and the obligation to plan the foundations in such a way that towers can be built, if not immediately, then at some point in the future, etc. Whether design principles should be stipulated as well, is still open to discussion. The investors have submitted statements of their intention to provide infrastructure ranging from sewers to streets to daycare centers. In view of the long history of cooperation between the City of Berlin and the Investors' Association Alexanderplatz, one that already began with the competition process, we hope for the best. But the tension that has marked the entire procedure will continue throughout the next stages as well...
Heinz Schildt, 1998, Senate Administration for Building, Housing, and Traffic

Kaye Geipel
Potsdamer Platz

The great tumult of the opening has subsided. The smoke from the fireworks sparkling up through the rain on October 2nd has dispersed, the building-high facade decorations have been rolled up, and the visitors—all 1.5 million of them—have gone home. The orchestra that played Mendelssohn's Italian Symphony in honor of the architect Renzo Piano has long since returned to its own building to rehearse comic opera. Around Potsdamer Platz, too, the still unfamiliar rhythms of every-day life have begun to set in. The new cinemas are showing Götz George, the 120 stores in the shopping passage are open late, you can gamble at the roulette tables without a tie, and even the Grand Hyatt Hotel, which wasn't finished in time, is no longer offering its "soft opening" deal, but a room with a bath like any other fine hotel.

But there is another, public side to Potsdamer Platz where normalcy has not yet set in. The opening apparently disquieted many commentators even more than was expected. In the ongoing industry of journalistic curiosity, the plaza is illumined with a tracer bullet of universalistic discourse, one variation after another. There is hardly a profession that won't have its say: the Berlin publisher Wolf Jobst Siedler describes the new

October 2nd, at night, October 3rd, in the morning

urban quarter as a Phoenix thrown down into the sand; the theater critic Benjamin Henrichs characterizes Potsdamer Platz as "the stone colossus of Daimler City"; the archbishop Georg Sterzinsky discerns the undisguised "power of capital" at work, while Frédéric Edelmann, architecture critic for Le Monde, speaks of a veritable "révolution urbaine."

Presumably, Potsdamer Platz and its creators are unimpressed by such comparisons. By the same token, however, the influence that the plaza exerts on its commentators is undeniable. In one respect, at least, Potsdamer Platz imposes its will on the critics: the words used to describe it have to be big.

Yet now that the tumult of festivities has subsided, things could take a different turn. The plaza could be subjected to a simpler gaze, a view of its architecture and streets, free from the baggage of big metaphors. Here is an opportunity to take the architect at his word when in 1992, shortly after the beginning of the competition, he formulated two rather modest maxims for his own urbanistic approach. With regard to the existing city, he stated: "The city is a fragile body that must be preserved at all costs"; regarding his master plan for Potsdamer Platz, he said: "I want to build something in this place

that is very corporeal, that is not… overwhelming." A body with nothing overwhelming, a body that is very fragile? This metaphor, with its overtones of a complicated prosthesis but also of a graceful dance, rings truer with respect to the first statement. It is a commentary that shows the Genoese architect's subtlety, his ability to win over the parties involved with the elegance of his ideas rather than with radical innovation. Above all, however, it represents Piano's response to the controversy played out in Berlin since the sale of the property in July 1990. Architecturally and urbanistically speaking, a responsibility was forced upon this project, a burden that no building site in Europe could bear uninjured: here, at the meeting of East and West, on a site swept clean of almost all historical traces, a piece of "European city" was to be built.

Implicit in this term was a diffuse, ill-defined concept of the city, in which elements ranging from the Greek agora and Roman forum to the medieval market square to the 19th-century block were mingled into a vague overall image. Piano wanted to steer clear of this overcharged, only seemingly "European" universalism. And so he replaced it with a vocabulary more indicative of the provisional and the fragmentary, the combination of "many

Streets:
one is glass-roofed and
serves as a shopping
mall, the other widens,
forming an urban space

**View from the Casino roof
towards the east, via the
old tree-lined Potsdamer
Strasse, towards the ori-
ginal and farther-away
Potsdamer Platz.
To the left: Hyatt Hotel by
Rafael Moneo,
to the right: apartment
house by Piano/Kohl-
becker**

images" into a fragile unity; this is the
vision to which he wanted to obligate himself and all the other architects involved.

Was this aspiration—the desire to
plan "ruptures" into the urban image from
the beginning—adequately fulfilled? Even
now, shortly after the realization of the
six-year-old master plan, it sometimes
seems difficult to reconstruct the origin of
the ideas from a single concept. From a
bird's-eye view, especially, there are some
surprising juxtapositions of contradictory
elements, a device Piano has used to
counteract an artificial uniformity. The
inner area of the quarter, for example, is
given a narrow, compact appearance
through the reduction of street widths,
while the few genuine high-rises are
positioned in two separate locations at
the edge of the district. Also unusual is
the addition of public street spaces com-
plemented by large atriums at ground
level, as well as an incision in the form of
a large triangle, creating a wide opening
in the block structure toward the Landwehrkanal—even though here, no building exists to "respond" to this opening.

Not all of these unexpected gestures
are convincing. Already in the winter of
1992, when Renzo Piano's winning plan
was first presented to the public, the
nonchalant use of expanses of water as a

Marlene-Dietrich-Platz, an urban square of proper dimensions where all the alleys and streets meet. The actors: left Rafael Moneo with his Hyatt Hotel, to the right Piano/ Kohlbecker with their apartment house and the Imax Cinema.
Below and left: Piano/ Kohlbecker again with the debis headquarters and the Musical Theater

space-defining element in the southern part of the quarter elicited surprise. Piano justified the creation of a large pond in front of the musical theater with a biographical reference: trees and water, he said, evoke "a glittering feeling of buoyancy" as in the harbor of his home city of Genoa. But here, Berlin has no harbor, even if in former times a few ships dropped anchor along the banks of the Landwehrkanal, firmly ensconced between its quay walls. The wide-open flanks facing the Schöneberg district to the south, moreover, seem somewhat exaggerated, particularly in view of the fact that this expansive gesture embraces nothing but a new parking garage on the opposite bank.

Alte Potsdamer Strasse: Today, the criticism of the open south side of the quarter seems less of a concern than when the plan was originally presented. The deficiency is compensated above all by the design of the street that begins at the canal and passes through the entire quarter like a backbone. If one had to identify a single stage of planning as Piano's answer to the challenge of creating a new urban quarter, it would be this street. Bending in the middle, it leads namelessly northward from the Landwehrkanal, metamorphosing into Alte Potsdamer Strasse at the halfway point as it moves

toward Potsdamer Platz itself. With its highly nuanced execution and five buildings designed by Renzo Piano—their facades growing increasingly compact toward the center of the quarter—this street eclipses the "acte gratuite" of the deep incision. On a smaller, more contemporary scale, it evokes something of the atmosphere of the corniches of Cannes and Nizza, maybe even a trace of Lake Shore Drive in Chicago.

In about the middle of the quarter, Alte Potsdamer Strasse takes its surprising turn, transforming itself into a narrow, compact street space. While toward the canal everything seems new and traditionless—the renovated Canaris House in the middle of the pond notwithstanding—here at this bend "history" begins to emerge. It was a marvelous idea to effect this transformation with an element easily overlooked at first glance: the surviving trees of Potsdamer Strasse, which provide a spatial point of reference for the new street on the site. In a very real sense, these trees are history—a reminder not only of the Potsdamer Strasse of the 1920s, cut off once and for all by Scharoun's building of 1963, but also of the final dissolution and disintegration of the post-war remains in the period after the construction of the Wall, when

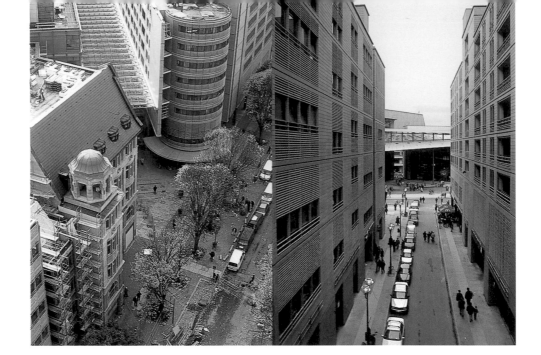

Last witnesses of
Potsdamer Platz:
Weinhaus Huth and the
old trees of former
Potsdamer Strasse.
Characteristics of the
new Potsdamer Platz:
varied terracotta facades
and deep, narrow streets

Dialogue between two
of Piano's buildings:
Musical Theater and
debis Headquarters,
reflected in the
water basin

Mendelsohn's Columbia-Haus was finally
torn down. What was left was nothing
more than an overgrown moor landscape
with a double row of trees, transforming it
into a place of secluded poetry. Amid the
chest-high grass, with the old Weinhaus
Huth left behind on the green plateau, the
sight of the Wall at the end of the row of
trees was not even necessary to evoke the
sense of a street without a goal, an image
of the stagnation of Berlin's urban history.
Something of this transformation is still
visible in the new street, exposed on one
side to a large urban space while dis-
appearing on the other into the dense
structure of the city.

Facade faces: As far as architecture is
concerned, the terracotta facades give the
street space a legibility that continues
from block to block and results above all
from the rod-shaped elements, reminiscent of French baguettes, that form a more
or less open structure in front of glass
walls. Apart from the architectural volume
itself, the design variations from building
to building are limited to the differing
coloration of the baguettes and the play
of densities in the horizontal articulation.

On the east side of the quarter as
well—on Linkstrasse, where buildings by
Isozaki and Lehmann, Lauber and Wöhr,
Richard Rogers and Renzo Piano line up

The public spaces on the ground floor: transparent and welcoming. Above: Entrance of the Musical Theater of Piano/Kohlbecker; below: foyer of CinemaxX Cinema by Lauber + Wöhr

side by side—the architects in question agreed on the materials of terracotta and brick for their facades. Still, the optical connection between the buildings is less convincing here; the street image disintegrates into individual blocks, and only the new park and the neighboring ABB buildings, scheduled for completion in a few years, will alter this impression.

Also on Alte Potsdamer Strasse, incidentally—to the right-hand side as you approach from Marlene-Dietrich-Platz—is the building that Renzo Piano considers his best. To be sure, the debis tower on the south side of the quarter, with its unusual double facade, is more spectacular. Yet it is here, in the residential and commercial building next to the renovated Weinhaus Huth, that the not uncomplicated facade system appears at its most convincing. The relation between openness and closure is in balance, yet without a loss of tension. Only upon closer examination does the "mechanism" that gives rise to this impression become clear: the facade conceals just enough to elicit curiosity concerning the "inside" of the building, while at the same time revealing enough to satisfy initial expectations.

With his facade concept, it appears that Piano has outsmarted the "sexier," more immediate appeal of the architecture

otherwise espoused by commercial enterprises from the American Imax Cinema to the musical theater. The elegant relation between concealing and revealing is continued on a larger scale, as well, in the relation between the closed street facades and the glimpses of small side streets or interior courtyards, incisions that split open the homogeneous street fronts in a number of places.

Two of these situations manifest this quality with particular clarity. One is the steep exterior staircase, narrowing toward the top, that suddenly appears on the west side of Marlene-Dietrich-Platz between two facade fronts, opening up a view of the elevated residential courtyard. The other is the view through narrow Ludwig-Beck-Strasse. Here, within the narrow framework of a side street, the seemingly impossible is achieved: the autistic form of Helmut Jahn's Sony Center on the north side of the quarter is domesticated and integrated into the new street system— still blockish and oversized, to be sure, but laterally framed by the slender perspective of the street passage.

The artificial "piece of city," designed by Renzo Piano and constructed here in record time, thus shows two completely different faces. Inside of the quarter, the impressiveness of the diverse urban

The edge of the new Potsdamer Platz is already visible, the silhouette not yet complete. The two towers at its eastern border are still growing higher and higher. Below: The sphere of the Imax causes the glass facade to swing outward

Architectural triplicity at the real Potsdamer Platz: Left Piano/Kohl-becker's highrise, neighboring that of Hans Kollhoff. To the far right, almost invisible, the edge of Helmut Jahn's swinging tower signaling the passage to Sony's side

Photo below:
Friederike Schneider

situations, all of which can be traced back to a common idea of the city, is amazing. The astonishment is all the more justified when we remember that every one of the commercial investors, in view of the enormous expense involved in building here, naturally wanted as loud and conspicuous a structure as possible. Piano was able to persuade even the managers of the musical theater to do without the large poster walls and neon signs that would have disfigured the new bronze-colored building —a reference to Scharoun's Staatsbibliothek.

"Something very corporeal, that does not seem overwhelming"—that is what Piano wanted to create with his new urban quarter. The adjective "overwhelming" was inspired by the massive aggregation of commercial uses that have heretofore played almost every architect into the ground; Piano, however, has mastered the self-imposed challenge with bravura.

Less positive is the verdict regarding the outer areas. The cityward facade, where the property lines of the new quarter cut into the existing urban structure, appears overdone with its expansive opening toward the south, and resembles a stage set toward Linkstrasse in the west. Admittedly, much is still unfinished, and the connecting structures to the out-side still remain to be built. The true test will be the three high-rises in the northeast—where Hans Kollhoff emulates Louis Sullivan, Renzo Piano imitates Mies van der Rohe, and Helmut Jahn vies with his colleagues in a half-round structure reminiscent of the 1970s.

This node will be the real challenge —not because this is where the "real" Potsdamer Platz will be, but because here, where the Wall once stood, a spatial connection between east and west must be established. A barely visible octagon, traced into the sand by the remaining fragments of sidewalk pavement, is all that remains of neighboring Leipziger Platz.

In a few years, when the lengthening arms of new construction join the blocks of Potsdamer Platz with the high-rise apartment buildings of Leipziger Strasse, we will know how well the challenge was met.

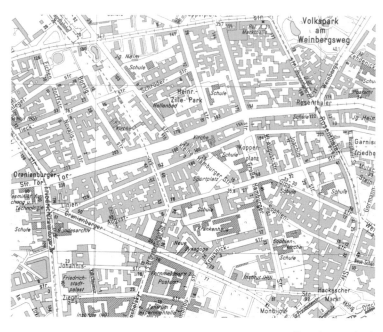

Daniela and Hans Düttmann
Linienstrasse, Seven Years Later

The beginning: a run-of-the-mill brokerage deal for Linienstrasse 160 — a house like a lot of others on Linienstrasse, built ca. 1820–30, amazingly small and daintily proportioned compared to the familiar Kreuzberg tenements, and in absolutely abysmal condition. A building in desperate need of help, with a run-down little carriage house in the back. But the beginning of the beginning was even earlier: our impulsive emigration from Germany in the spring of 1989 was followed by an even hastier return to Berlin after the fall of the wall in early 1990. We rode the S-Bahn to the East, curious and self-conscious like everyone else, ready, impatient to do something. At some point, we discovered to our amazement that there was a genuine piece of old city left in the Scheunenviertel and the Spandauer Vor-

stadt, completely untouched by the Hobrecht plan. We saw these beautiful, utterly dilapidated houses and went straight to the land-registry offices and municipal building authorities, uncertain, confused, and always with the same question: What about these houses, what's going to become of them, doesn't anyone want to redevelop them? At first, incomprehension; maybe we were the first to ask. Or almost the first — a "Verein zur Gründung einer Stiftung zur Rettung des Scheunenviertels" (Society for the Establishment of a Fund to Save the Scheunenviertel) had already been founded, on a strictly socialist basis… Jürgen Stoye was the one who got us involved in the project Linienstrasse 160, since the house had once belonged to his grandmother. Together we renovated this first building, then a second,

*All Photos:
Florian Profitlich*

Wolfgang Braatz
Old Suburb, Up to Date

All Photos: Hendrik Rauch
Photo Scholz & Friends:
Florian Profitlich

"Every day I find it more difficult to live at the high level of my blue porcelain." Oscar Wilde on a wooden gate on Linienstrasse. Linienstrasse: excise boundary, north part of the palisade line erected in 1705 just outside the fortification wall. It kept deserters from escaping the garrison and guarded the citizens in a stiffly controlled consumer ghetto—you know how that goes.

The settlement of the area outside the Spandau Gate already had its history. 1668: Frederick William, Elector of Prussia, married his second wife, Dorothea. In 1670 he conferred upon his "beloved spouse" the farmland outside the Neues Tor north of the Spree. The princess—energetic, enterprising, and disliked; "favored with certain privileges"—founded Dorotheenstadt and conceived the idea of developing the farmland on the other side of the Spree, where wine and beer were traded and the wagon drivers were allowed to sleep, in order to increase her tax revenue.

1671: Jewish families, driven out of Vienna, were allowed to settle in the city "for the furtherance of trade." For protection, they paid eight talers a year. The community was founded. Already the next year, they acquired a plot on the Grosse Hamburger Strasse for use as a cemetery. Building began.

Rummaging around in a 300-year-old urban structure—do the pieces still fit together? Who assesses their value? Döblin's Biberkopf wanders down Rosenthaler Strasse, "turning right into narrow Sophienstrasse; better to be where it is dark." The guide of the city with his entourage approaches from the left, from the Hackesche Höfe. Now as everyone knows, "the courtyards (Höfe) on Hackescher Markt were named after the city commandant, Lieutenant-General Johann Christoph Friedrich Graf von Hacke, who served at the time of Frederick II. They are surrounded by a commercial and residential complex built in 1905–07." "Der lange

then a third... since then we've done a total of nine. Almost of its own accord, our redevelopment model grew into a service for others. The area appealed to a lot of people, and the reasons to invest there as opposed to anywhere else were the same for everyone: enthusiasm for this unusual quarter of the city and for the restoration of old houses, as well as an undeniable tax benefit. That basically already sums up the two aspects of what we do. Each of these houses is a commodity, and has to be developed according to the rules of the market— and each is an individual building, not originally intended to be rental property, and has its own architectural character. You have to take that into account. First the cold-blooded part. We work with two models. The investment model means that a number of interested parties come together to invest their money in the building, but don't want to live there themselves, or at least not right away. They buy shares that are held by a legal partnership known as a Gesellschaft bürgerlichen Rechts (GBR), and we regulate these shares in such a way that they are always equivalent to one or more dwellings which the investors or their children may want to use someday. One such GBR was founded for every house, and the model requires the founding members of the partnership to hold shares. In the other model, the houses are transformed into purchased condominiums. In this scheme, the buyers purchase the dwellings in non-renovated condition, though at a price that reflects the value of the dwelling after it has been renovated. There are tax reasons for this arrangement. Both

Sophie Gips Höfe

Art(ificial) lawn

Hacke" had already been close to Frederick's father. Now he called for the fortification to be demolished and new streets laid out. And—in accord with a cabinet order issued in 1751 by his well-affectioned king—he settled builders from the Voigtland outside the Rosenthaler Tor, where they were exempt from the excise tax.

1786: By now the former fortifications are built over; about 80 m in front of Linienstrasse is a "real" wall. Friedrich Nicolai counted 1,394 houses in the suburb Spandauer Vorstadt; 374 of them in the rear courtyards.

Franz Biberkopf "stood in a courtyard and sang." Today, 70 years later, the charm of the courtyards is being restored, and the entrance gates receive new locks.

Sophienstrasse 21 (1): eleven elegant company signs, the Silent Porter hangs by the street, and a camera waits behind the array of doorbells. How do you follow the information of architects? The transformation of a sewing-machine factory into an ensemble to house contemporary art? In the first courtyard, a list of opposites as high as the building mocks the rules of elementary education.

In the second courtyard, the scent of coffee lures you into a frugally lit modular restaurant. How did the city smell in 1989? Brick walls and windows give evidence to the appropriate handling of the building's substance. But beyond the edge of the roof, a new world begins. Here the client lives in his collection. A gentleman about six feet tall, who succeeds in making older people involuntarily remember the life and times of the amazing Mr. Howard Hughes —the producer who rode into American film history with the unacceptable woman-or-horse question. Enough, the city has its

models demand an extraordinary amount of trust in advance, both on the part of the investors, who want to see their dwellings rented to the right tenants, and the buyers, who have to trust that the renovation they paid for will be realized just as it was promised. And so, at first we worked with friends, but the basic advantage, even for outsiders, lies in the fact that the entire enterprise is a cooperative one: the services of depreciation contractor, investor, architect, and landlord are all in one hand. The special tax deduction "Aufbau Ost" for the reconstruction of the East will be in effect until the end of this year. It allows 100 % of the redevelopment costs for an old building—i.e. the building itself without the cost of the property—to be deducted over a period of 10 years, with up to 40 % the first

year. That provided the basis for the restoration of the houses. The rental income could never bring in as much money as the houses swallow up. Renovation costs can be as much as 2,500 DM per square meter, and up to 3,500 to 3,700 DM if you include the price of the property and other additional costs. The rent controls, on the other hand, are set by the district, independent of the cost of the building. Depending on size, the apartments rent for around 8–9 DM per square meter. Even though about half the total costs are paid from the investors' own pockets, there are huge budget gaps everywhere. I often think I have to explain why this or that had to be done the way it was. We work with the most inexpensive firms, we save money by renovating quickly, i.e. about 12 months per house, we invest all our

At Koppenplatz

Kunst-Werke
Auguststrasse 69

Construction site Rosenthaler Hof

own stories. Far below, in the third courtyard, lies a sharp-cornered, green, garage roof, a children's playground, art in grass. Moving on to the new exit onto Gipsstrasse — between No. 11, the Institution for the Blind of 1806, and plot 12a, where the "Rabbinical Seminary for Orthodox Judaism" began its work in 1873. The "Sophie-Gips-Höfe" are open from 9 a. m. to 10 p. m. The project's name evokes memories of Queen Sophie Luise — patroness of the parish church in the background, built 1712–14 — and the former plaster kiln "Gipsküche" at No. 18. The stumps of

the supports for the new "Rosenthaler Hof" have stood on this site for a long time. The project includes a renovated Wertheim department store, an office and commercial building, and "99 v.i.p. apartments" — quoting the sign literally .

On to Koppenplatz. Should the silent tribute to Christian Koppe, who embodied "care for the poor" around 1700, give occasion for a designer of residential architecture to trot out antipathy? Linienstrasse. Where was the little

green walk-signal man when the concrete street lamps were invented? Dusty facades: the royal pawn shop, the deaf-mute institute — no passion for use?

Auguststrasse 69 (2): The building dates to 1794, exemplifying the careful transformation of a margarine factory into a place for the protection of contemporary art. The "Kunst-Werke" give evidence to the spectacular career of a very young and subtle managing director. On the plaster of the side wing, a sentence from Walter Benjamin adorns the Art-Works; it increases the "cult value." The new architectural event is the "Café Bravo" in the shade of a walnut tree, following a proposal by the artist

energy in the houses and still have to cut corners. The houses were originally built by relatively affluent people for their own use; little townhouses, a trifle rough since they were built somewhat at random, but relatively spacious inside. In the late 19th century, additional structures were built within the plots, factory buildings or carriage houses. The rapid growth of the city soon turned the area into a slum, and with the social decline, the dwellings were reduced to a couple of rooms each. What we find today are tiny apartments of about 30–40 square meters in almost totally dilapidated houses that have been altered again and again. It's one thing to turn the dwellings behind the old facades into spacious, livable floor plans again; it's another to reconstruct what little remains of facade ornamenta-

tion and interior details in order to even begin to discover what was there in the first place. Only on this basis can we carefully start to improvise. It's a strange form of historic preservation we're engaging in here. First we had a lot to learn about the architectural history of the houses. For example, the early classicist decorations are handcrafted in lime mortar, quite unlike the mass-produced ornaments of the 1870s. Or the stairs: Schinkel designed a stair type that required only a single cast-iron support. The small-time architects here liked the stair type and used it, but replaced the cast-iron supports with wooden ones. Or the porches in the upper stories, added later, probably around 1870, when break-ins and crime began to be a problem. The frames themselves are relatively coarsely built, but if you're

Every Wednesday Ladies' Choice

Tucholskystrasse

KuLe in Auguststrasse

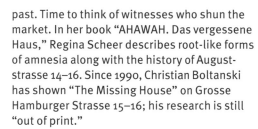

Prefabricated Houses

Dan Graham, whose one-way-mirror pavilions eloquently point to the distant future and to biblical times.

Auguststrasse 10: KuLe, a colorful nine-year-old spectacle of art and life, historic preservation and elite dwelling. The squatters, on their way to becoming veterans, seem to tolerate the new owners' applause. Behind No. 9, the "Heckmann Höfe" are being plastered. "The prime location with historical flair" extends to Oranienburger Strasse. But the small pub, "At the Underground Aunt. All different

kinds of beer," has finally gone under. They say it never existed, only as a backdrop for a DEFA film. Next door, on Tucholskystrasse, a comforting graffito from the squatters: "Profit addiction is curable." "Nice people," says the investor. The facades haven't been painted yet.

"Art" and "courtyard" stabilize the real estate jargon, as if the late prefabricated apartments at the edge of the district and the sports field on Kleine Hamburger Strasse were already a thing of the

past. Time to think of witnesses who shun the market. In her book "AHAWAH. Das vergessene Haus," Regina Scheer describes root-like forms of amnesia along with the history of Auguststrasse 14–16. Since 1990, Christian Boltanski has shown "The Missing House" on Grosse Hamburger Strasse 15–16; his research is still "out of print."

Auguststrasse 24: "Clärchens Ballhaus," a rudiment since 1913. Lost and gone are the "Palast des Centrums," the "Altes Ballhaus" — and the ladies with the large hats and doubtful reputations. Let's do away with the "pleasure barracks" and nocturnal impressions. Around 7,300 people live in the suburb and everyone

lucky, you might still find an original door, and then it's the finest craftsmanship. No matter what board you lift, there's always a surprise. Either you find a layer of straw in the ceiling space or carved door capitals, like on the second floor of Linienstrasse 153. When we cleaned the ceilings, we also discovered classicist paintings in bright turquoise, blue, red, and emerald green — that famous, poisonous emerald green. Actually, each of the little houses is a monument in itself. The whole area is under historic preservation, the resolution dates from 1992. At some point, we realized that the actual renovation was less trouble than getting the bureaucrats to cooperate. We have to juggle the claims of the historic preservation agency — whose demands are based on

investigations that show up in our budgets to the tune of 8,000 to 10,000 DM — and the redevelopment administration, which broods over its statutes, keeps close contact with the residents, conducts extensive tenant surveys, and negotiates the renovation contract, which in turn is part of the building permit. Still, these tenant consultations are an important thing, regardless of how they turn out. It's important to remember that in the seven or so years we've worked here, the residential population has changed radically. Not entirely, but at least partially due to our efforts. We have even renovated a few houses occupied by squatters. The people who move in are often artists, musicians, art dealers. We don't seek them out, they come of their own accord. Recently we were at a fashion and art ex-

The Missing House

finds his pub, and whoever wants to, his gallery as well. Where are the old people?

"Franz pays attention, wanders through the Auguststrasse hostel 'Das Christliche Hospiz'." To the left, No. 83, "Marotte," vaguely reminiscent of a puppet theater. The facade calls for the Dahnberg'sche Institute of Architectonic ornamentation. How do you renovate a historic area? One architect is satisfied to leave his calling card, at Krausnickstrasse 23 (3). Other investors follow the beck and call of a

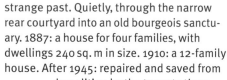

strange past. Quietly, through the narrow rear courtyard into an old bourgeois sanctuary. 1887: a house for four families, with dwellings 240 sq. m in size. 1910: a 12-family house. After 1945: repaired and saved from demolition by the tenants themselves. A spacious, leafy place, the site of annual parties: Linienstrasse 147. Now under renovation.

The goals of the renovation include the "protection of the resident population" and the "preservation of the established social structure." In the Spandauer Vorstadt, the average household

income is DM 3,093 a month; beyond the city wall, torn down in 1868, it is DM 2,352.

About 130 m between Kleine Hamburger Strasse and Tucholskystrasse (4). How do you calculate in a historic area? Unhurried, for example. Eviscerated antiquities don't need any special costume to evoke a mood. Moreover, everyone knows that a white wall arouses the imagination, and color makes it cozy. Old supports, new balconies. In the courtyards, the somewhat uncomfortable pavement, and granite flagstones from the street, green from the garden of a country house. The subtle will find how an art shop can take up residence in a gate path, and that a somewhat clumsy original

hibition at the Guggenheim Museum here in Berlin, and suddenly it turned out that a third of those participating were residents of Linienstrasse... What excites us is that people immediately know how to take what we offer and use it to enhance their own lives. Almost all the shop owners in the neighborhood live in our houses — the people who run the health food store, the travel agency, the various pubs. One person is planting a garden on the roof of the carriage house. That sounds so offhand, "renovated a few houses occupied by squatters." Since 1991, we've seen four generations of squatters. First it was the young artist-types who established studios, workshops, galleries; they were driven away by the militant French, who in turn were scared off by the more rabid Polish alcoholics. Finally,

right at the end, the house was taken over by wandering Russians. Each group was replaced by a rougher one; the groups became smaller and more violent, cats were skinned in the courtyard, there were drummers playing night and day, you couldn't even get rid of the rats, the houses were barricaded like forts. One morning a young man was found dead in the courtyard. At that point, even the squatters were shocked, and the house was vacated within a few hours. In another case, it turned out that for a long time the house was occupied by only four people. In another house, where the squatters long enjoyed the protection of a city councilwoman, there was a wonderful stairwell with a square oculus, something quite rare in Berlin. Five years later, the stairwell had disappeared along with

Scholz & Friends

Kunsthof (Artyard)

craftsmenship can be renewed and transformed into a motif. In the shops there is Spanish furniture and Greek wine. Aristocratic residents? Normal people in artistic professions. "Kunsthof," Oranienstrasse 27. The artful handling of the real estate reveals routine. The givens: a self-contained dwelling and commercial complex from the middle of the previous century, and an "identity-creating" neighborhood. A mixture of artistic and cultural production and presentation is the goal; workshop spaces described as "art-friendly" are pro-

vided, along with dwellings, shops, and exemplary hospitality ventures. Comforting signs of bygone days are conserved with careful craftsmanship (5).
Who would want to speak lightly of "Her Royal Majesty's Garden Mombejux," of the Neue Synagoge, the Postfuhramt, of Tacheles? Their histories are in good hands.

300 m to Chausseestrasse 5 (6). Here, the iron foundry "Egells Eisengiesserei" operated after 1827; after 1836 the machine shop "Borsigs Ma-

schinenbauanstalt" as well. Soon, 24 factories were to be seen in "Feuerland." "Work hails industry." Heinrich Seidel works at Wöhlert's. He builds the roof of the Anhalter Bahnhof, and later writes the novel Leberecht Hühnchen. Noise and idyll. Second rear courtyard. Close to the wall of the building is a city-proof tree. Its offspring sway in all corners of the suburb. It grows on Pfaueninsel and in the garden of the Charité, thanks to Lenné? A tree of the gods. Machines and locomotives are followed by sarcophagi and pianos.

In 1995, in light of its "outstanding urban location," the piano factory was transformed into, "a spacious, prestigious office complex."

the squatters—either chopped up as firewood or hawked at the market. Well, so we persist in our Sisyphean task; we buy back the doors from the antique building market, we repair the old double windows or have them reconstructed by the carpenter next door, a master at copying historic moldings, we scour the flea market and tell our old friend at the Palestinian booth to start collecting, we need 200 old window latches, those shallow ones where you can still close the second window. No problem, he says, I'll get them for you. It would never occur to our tenants that they were anything special; when the window latches are installed, they just look like they belong there. Amazingly, the district offices and the redevelopment administration have no idea about all this, and no idea of the cost. They exhaust

Besides the roof supports, there is a bearing system for two steel galleries; parts of the roof were glazed. House and courtyard say "workshop." The young team from the advertising firm Scholz & Friends seems relaxed.

"And he trotted briskly down Elsasser Strasse," i.e. Torstrasse. Each new generation changes the street signs. Past the site of the Wülcknitz family houses and on to the Neu-Voigtland of spinners, weavers, and day laborers. "Mietshausgeschichten", Berlin block history built over and crowded out. Berg-

strasse 12: in 1752 a colonists' house, now No. 22, an outpost of the redevelopers (7). Behind the slick front house, two zinc drinkers greet us from the cherished gable of the former Josty brewery; they've been there since 1890 and would be worth keeping. In former days, the Café Josty flourished on Potsdamer Platz amid the "feverish bustle of life." It is quiet on Bergstrasse. An art-courtyard remains to be developed here. The art of cooking is on the menu. As they say in Cologne, the palate becomes a cathedral.

Architects

(1) **Eike Becker, Georg Gewers, Swantje Kühn, Oliver Kühn, Heike Haack Lauerbach, Wolfgang Gasde**
(2) **Johanne Nalbach, Gernot Nalbach**
(3) **Hinrich Baller**
(4) **Daniela Düttmann, Hans Düttmann**
(5) **Büro civitas, Rüdiger Reisig**
(6) **Carlos Zwick**
(7) **Klaus Lattermann**

themselves In regulating the rents. A mere profit-loss statement, no more than a page, would be enough to show that the investors can expect no profits for the first five years. But the houses are going strong again. When the redevelopment administration helps us relocate tenants — for example when someone can't tolerate the construction activities due to health reasons — we pay for it by relinquishing the right to choose our own tenants for ten years. Why do we put ourselves through all this? Well, the area really is quite nice. Of course we're not the only ones here. Fortunately, there are others who have come to appreciate the area too, so that by now a lot of ambitious renovations are underway in Mitte district. An investor from Hamburg is involved in our neighborhood; he's going to remodel the nice little clinker factory on Linienstrasse along with the Sophiensäle, but probably on other models. He works more expensively and more slowly, and probably won't break even. The architect Fridolin Weber has also established himself here as a building patron. But what will happen when the tax benefit is eliminated at the end of this year, no one knows... Least of all the residents' committee, an institution awarded great power by the urban development code and which, though composed very randomly, can decide whether a project stands or falls. A committee of around 30 people, where you never know exactly who's going to be there, makes decisions for about 8,000 residents... At the rate we're going, pretty soon we'll be able to put together our own residents' committee...

Hildegard Loeb-Ullmann
From Checkpoint Charlie to Pariser Platz

The Latest New Buildings at the Best Addresses

*Photos of the
new buildings:
Christian Gahl
Photos while
strolling along:
Erik-Jan Ouwerkerk*

The second walk through the new center of Berlin, along Friedrichstrasse from south to north with views into the side streets, a short detour across Gendarmenmarkt and then back to Charlotten-strasse. Briefly touching and crossing the street Unter den Linden. Two stopping points on Reichs-tagufer. And then at last Pariser Platz, the edges of which are gradually being completed. As in 1996, when the first new buildings arose along this route, the Bauwelt Berlin Annual has again waited until shortly before going into print in order to present the 1998 buildings in completed form. That was not possible everywhere. The bank building by Frank Gehry, which everybody is so eager to see, is still enclosed and boarded up. And the facade of the office and shopping building at the start of Friedrichstrasse, although it looked perfect in September, was scaffolded once again in October. To help the reader to shorten the distances bet-ween the new buildings, complete or nearly com-plete, Erik Jan Ouwerkerk has photographed the views in between, views of shop windows and curbs, of the caravan colony on Schlossplatz and the boules players on Unter den Linden. These pictures are at the foot of the pages next to the floor plans to a scale of 1:1000 which are oriented to the north, but which have only a limited significance: the reader may observe that where space can be rented, the floor plans are flexible, and that almost all of them offer extraordinarily large entrance halls. Building in superlatives makes the buildings similar to each other. All of them offer luxurious foyers, communication zones, glass-covered atriums, roof terraces—in marble, granite, bronze, stainless steel or behind a double-layered glass shell. At first glance the buildings appear to be brothers and sisters, and it takes longer to understand the differences that nevert-heless exist and to discover the personal "hand-writing" of the architects.

There is, however, one obvious exception. This time there are three new buildings along the route which follow the urban development regulations like all the others, but not the fashions of the time. Or which simply chose to follow the fashions of a different era. They are called "Kronenpalais", "Charlottenpalais" and "Dompalais"—and they look like palaces too. They are made up of pillars, columns and mouldings, they interchange be-tween noticeable imitations of historical styles and simplified adaptations of these styles to modern fashion. They are built on narrow vacant plots, and when the beholder looks along the frontage line on the streets and sees the pillars in a perspective view, the illusion is complete: a historical street front has been historically sup-plemented. In the chain of ever more similar new buildings of the 1990's they appear like figures against a background. Nobody would wish the whole inner city to be restored in this way, but in individual buildings here and there, as they can now be seen, they are not only tolerable to the eyes—although it is difficult to comprehend why —they are reconciling.

9.10 ARD Hauptstadtstudio
Architects:
Ortner & Ortner Baukunst

9.9 Federal Press and
Information Office
Architects: KSP
Engel Kraemer Zimmermann

9.12 Office, Commercial and
Apartment Building
Pariser Platz 6a
Architect: Bernhard Winking

9.11 Eugen Gutmann House
Architects: von Gerkan,
Marg and Partners

9.14 House Liebermann
Architect: Josef P. Kleihues

9.14 House Sommer
Architect: Josef P. Kleihues

9.13 DG Bank
Architect: Frank O. Gehry

9.8 Deutsche Bank
Architects: Novotny, Mähner & Assoziierte

9.7 Charlottenpalais
Architects: Patzschke, Klotz and Partners

9.5 Rosmarin Karree
Architects: Jürgen Böge
+ Ingeborg Lindner-Böge

9.6 Rosmarin Karree
City-Apartments
Architects: Petra und
Paul Kahlfeldt

9.4 Science Forum Berlin
at Gendarmenmarkt
Architect: Wilhelm Holzbauer

9.7 Dompalais
Architects: Patzschke,
Klotz and Partners

9.3 Kronenpalais
Architects: Patzschke,
Klotz and Partners

9.2 Office, Commercial and
Apartment Building
Quartier 108
Architect: Van den
Valentyn – Architektur

9.1 Office and Commercial
Building at Checkpoint Charlie
Architects: Lauber + Wöhr

9.1

OFFICE AND COMMERCIAL BUILDING AT CHECKPOINT
CHARLIE

Architects	Lauber + Wöhr Architekten, Munich
Project Manager	Manfred Walter
Structural Design	LAP Ingenieurbüro, Berlin
Mechanical	INTEG, Berlin
Client	Checkpoint Charlie KG, Berlin
Opening	End 1998
Address	Friedrichstrasse 50
	Berlin-Mitte

The office and shopping building at Friedrichstrasse
No 50 is part of the American Business Center group
of buildings at Checkpoint Charlie. It covers one
complete side of a block on Friedrichstrasse, and its
sides reach asymmetrically into Schützenstrasse and
Krausenstrasse. On the corner of Schützenstrasse
the building has a curved facade which breaks up the
severity of the edge of the block. The solid, load-
bearing, reinforced-concrete structure is covered
with white aluminium panels and narrow window
bars. The ground floor has two reception foyers.
Some of the shop units span two stories. The office
zones in the upper stories are arranged on both sides
of long corridors, and face either the street or the
inner courtyards. The uppermost stories contain
residential units, and the staggered roof means that
they have terraces all around the building.

Non-load-bearing, lightweight, glass walls
permit flexible office use. The building has double
floors throughout and a light deflection system
integrated into the facade. Air conditioning can be
fitted retrospectively.

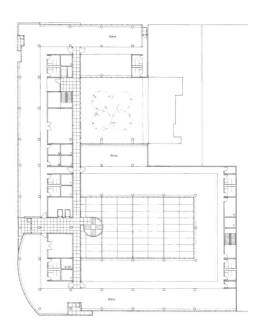

**Typical floor plan
to a scale of 1:1000**

9.2

OFFICE, COMMERCIAL AND APARTMENT BUILDING
QUARTIER 108

Architect	Van den Valentyn – Architektur, Cologne
Client	DIFA, Deutsche Immobilienfonds AG, Hamburg
General	
Contractor	Unternehmensgruppe Roland Ernst, Heidelberg
Completion	End 1998
Address	Friedrichstraße 191–193a
	Berlin-Mitte

The nine-storey building at the junction of Friedrich-
and Leipziger Strasse is part of "Quartier 108," which
remains to be completed and, like all the new buildings, follows the edges of the block.

Until the middle of the 19th century, "Quartier
108" was a purely residential area with loosely-
spaced, three-story buildings, but it was then built up
in a five-story block structure. From this period, only
the "WMF" building on Leipziger Strasse and two
residential buildings on Kronenstrasse survived the
war — one of them adjoins the new building. The
black granite facade of the new structure, with its
greenish glazing and stainless steel window frame
bars, fits in with the new stone tradition of Friedrichstadt. The facade is made up of several levels. On the
ground floor are shops facing the street, with an
arcade along Leipziger Strasse. The upper stories
contain offices (almost 10,000 m²), and there are
apartments and more offices in the staggered roof
stories. The central entrance from Friedrichstrasse
leads to halls of red marble and separate reception
areas on the upper stories. Two basement stories
contain underground parking facilities.

Facade: granite, Nero Assoluto, polished, stainless steel metal cladding, polished with 240 grain.
Foyer: marble, Rosso Carpazzi, polished. Arcade:
granite, Serpentino di Sonfrio, sand-blasted; foyer:
marble, Rosso Carpazzi, polished.

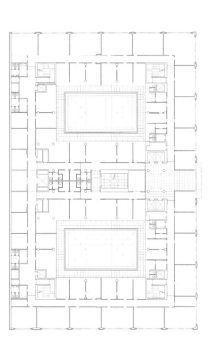

1st upper floor plan
to a scale of 1:1000

9.3

KRONENPALAIS

Architects   Patzschke, Klotz and Partners, Berlin
Structural Design   Müller Marl, Marl/Berlin
Mechanical   INTEG, Ottobrunn
Client   GbR Dr. Leibfried und Patrick Reich, Berlin
Opening   April 1998
Address   Kronenstrasse 8/10
                    Berlin-Mitte

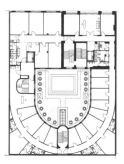

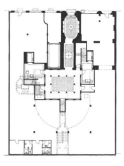

**Plans of ground floor
and 1st upper floor
to a scale of 1:1000**

By combining Kronenstrasse 8 and 10, a historical building with a natural stone facade that is a protected monument has been extended by the addition of a new seven-story building covering the rear of Kronenstrasse 8 and the whole of the Kronenstrasse 10 plot. Deviating from the current fashion, the architects and client selected a traditional facade design: a pedestal with window arches spanning two stories and a rendered middle zone with a shallow tectonic relief pattern. The facade with its mouldings, pilasters and wall slabs is in dialogue with the lavishly decorated adjoining old facade.

The small, inner, ground-floor courtyard was designed as a classic atrium with colonnades. The ground floor and the stories above it are used by the Deutsche Kreditbank, and the two top stories contain residential units.

9.4

SCIENCE FORUM BERLIN AT GENDARMENMARKT

Architect   Wilhelm Holzbauer, Vienna
Project
Developer   ICM Center- und Facility-Management, Düsseldorf
Client   IVA Immobilien-Verwaltungs- und Anlagen-
                          gesellschaft Dr. A. Steiger KG , Düsseldorf
Completion   November 1998
Address   Markgrafenstraße 37, Taubenstraße 30
                          Berlin-Mitte

To the north and east, the 1,140 m² plot borders on
the building of the Berlin-Brandenburg Academy of
Science, which describes a U-shape on Jägerstrasse,
Markgrafenstrasse and Taubenstrasse and, with the
new building, forms an inner courtyard. The Science
Forum closes the block at the southwestern corner
and completes the structure facing Gendarmenmarkt.

   The facade proportions and roof structure follow the forms of the adjacent historic buildings,
transformed by the use of modern materials. The
slope of the tiled roof is matched by metal louvres,
the rows of mouldings of the old building are transformed into pillar structures in an otherwise even
and regular facade-grid pattern. The main entrance
is on Markgrafenstrasse, and internal access is via
an entrance hall spanning all stories, equipped with
panoramic lifts. The glass roof provides natural light
to the hall, which is designed as a meeting place in
conjunction with the adjoining foyers. Next to the
entrance hall on the ground floor are a restaurant
and a number of shops. The six upper stories provide
about 3,500 m² of office space.

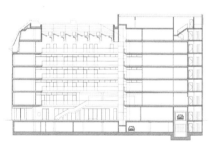

**Typical ground floor plan
and longitudinal section
to a scale of 1:1000**

9.5

ROSMARIN KARREE

Architects	Jürgen Böge + Ingeborg Lindner-Böge, Hamburg
Working Drawings	Meyer-Haake + Munzig, Stuttgart
Project Management	Büll u. Dr. Liedtke + HINES, Berlin
Facade	IFFT, Institut für Fassadentechnik, Frankfurt/M.
Lobby Design	Hachtmann + Pütz, Hamburg
Statics	Ingenieurbüro Weiske and Partners, Stuttgart
Client	Rosmarin Karree Grundstücks GmbH + Co., Berlin
Completion	July 1998
Address	Friedrichstraße 82
	Berlin-Mitte

The office-and-shop building is part of "Quartier 209 A" between Friedrichstrasse, Rosmarinstrasse and Behrenstrasse, which also includes the protected architectural monument of the Commerzbank and the slab-type building on the right with city apartments. The entrance to all offices is on Friedrichstrasse — because of the address this confers — and the offices, which can be subdivided into five units per story, are reached via the two-story reception lobby. There is a horizontal ribbon-type story between the ground floor arcades and the regular grid pattern of the middle band of the facade. This device reveals the modern natural stone facade as a thin facing layer. The upper facade consists of two layers. The inner layer is made up of floor-to-ceiling wooden windows. The outer layer consists of frameless single glazing with moveable glass louvres, and is mounted flush into the natural stone facade. Large winter garden windows on the corner of Friedrichstrasse illuminate the building at night-time. The staggered upper stories also have floor-to-ceiling windows.

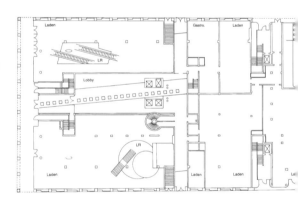

**Ground floor plan
Rosmarinkarree
(with City-Apartments)
to a scale of 1:1000**

9.6

ROSMARIN KARREE – CITY-APARTMENTS

Architets	Petra and Paul Kahlfeldt, Berlin
Structural Design	Ingenieurbüro Weiske and Partners, Stuttgart
Client	Rosmarin Karree Grundstücks GmbH + Co., Berlin
Completion	July 1998
Address	Behrenstrasse 47 / Rosmarinstrasse 9
	Berlin-Mitte

Photo to the left:
Stefan Müller

The narrow plot spans the small distance from Behrenstrasse to Rosmarinstrasse. The old building of the Sparkasse Association, with its continuous fire wall, forms the eastern boundary. The U-shaped building structure is subdivided into three parts. On the street sides facing north and south are two almost identical ten-story residential buildings. They are linked by a lower, transverse building with apartments which face west onto an inner courtyard. The courtyard, in turn, borders on the transverse wing of the adjacent office building. Along the streets, the building reaches a height of 30 meters without recesses, thus forming a break between the staggered upper stories of the adjacent office building (see left-hand page) and the roof structure of the old building. Above the ground-floor shops and the first-floor offices, the steel structures of the winter gardens overhang slightly. The street facades have a modular structure of equal-sized slabs of Sellenberg shell limestone. The slabs are left rough-hewn and show the uneven deposits within the stone. In the courtyard, the load-bearing structure and ceilings are shown by narrow white stucco strips, and large wooden windows are inserted into the square grid which is so defined in order to give as much light as possible to the apartments overlooking the courtyard. Access to all apartments is via corridors which link the two vertical access shafts. Spatial zoning is marked by supports and ceiling joists.

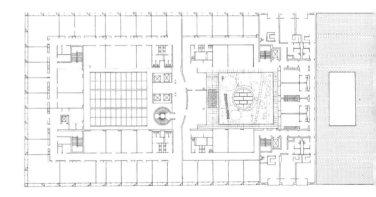

Typical floor plan
Rosmarin Karree
with City-Apartments
to a scale of 1:1000

9.7

DOMPALAIS

Architects   Patzschke, Klotz and Partners, Berlin
Statics   Leonhardt, Andrä and Partners, Berlin
Client   GbR Dr. Leibfried / Bauwert GmbH, Berlin
Opening   July 1998
Address   Charlottenstraße 62, Berlin-Mitte

CHARLOTTENPALAIS

Architects   Patzschke, Klotz and Partners, Berlin
Foyer Interior   von Wecus and Baumann, Munich
Statics   Leonhardt, Andrä and Partners, Berlin
Client   GbR Dr. Leibfried and Patrick Reich, Berlin
Opening   May 1998
Address   Charlottenstrasse 35/36, Berlin-Mitte

**Plans of 1st and
2nd upper floor
to a scale of 1:1000**

Dompalais and Charlottenpalais, both situated in Charlottenstrasse, are examples of historicist architecture which represents an alternative to the standard designs of the new buildings in Berlin-Mitte, and reflect the preference of many people for traditional forms.

The Dompalais is a solitary building between two vacant plots over a two-story underground parking garage. On the ground floor and first floor it uses the depth of the plot (26 m) for shops and a conference room. Above are office stories (14 m building depth). The staggered stories on top contain apartments with roof gardens.

Charlottenpalais is situated between two old buildings which are protected monuments: the Deutsche Bank on Unter den Linden and the building of the Senate Department of Construction and Residential Development on Behrenstrasse/corner Charlottenstrasse. The pedestal is faced with Wartau sandstone and accentuated by a traditional column finish and ribbon-type moldings up to the lower edge of the windows on the first floor. The shop windows of the two shops on the ground floor contain classical-style floor-to-ceiling cast-steel supports. The four-story middle part of the facade is subdivided by protrusions and recesses, two side risalites and one middle risalite. The pillar structure is emphasised by columns spanning several stories. The entrance hall spans two stories and has an open-plan staircase to the first story. Shops on the ground floor, offices in the upper stories, apartments with outdoor terraces on the two staggered top stories.

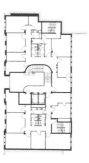

**Plans of ground floor
and 1st upper floor
to a scale of 1:1000**

9.8

DEUTSCHE BANK

Initial Concept	Benedict Tonon, Berlin
Design and Working Drawing	Novotny, Mähner & Assoziierte, Offenbach/Berlin
Interior Design	ECART, Paris
Project Management	Eitelbach Consult GmbH, Koblenz
Realization	Arbeitsgemeinschaft Unter den Linden 13–15, Berlin
Statics	Ingenieursozietät BGS, Frankfurt/M.
Facade Technic	Ingenieurbüro Schalm, Mörfelden-Walldorf
Client	Deutsche Bank AG, represented by DEBEKO-Immobilien GmbH, Eschborn
Opening	March 1997
Address	Unter den Linden 13–15, Berlin-Mitte

Photos: Deutsche Bank

The Deutsche Bank has set up a new central building on Unter den Linden in two historical buildings which were once owned by the company. Building Unter den Linden No. 13, of red sandstone, was built in 1889 by the architects Ende and Böckmann; the adjacent corner building of yellow sandstone was built in 1922 to 1925 to plans by Bielenberg and Moser. Large parts of the buildings are protected architectural monuments.

Access to the renovated building complex is now from three points. Most impressive is the main entrance in building No. 15, which has been moved into Charlottenstrasse and appears behind the historic column facade. It is emphasized by the glass facade, which is suspended above it in front of the historic column facade, integrating the new, two-story upward extension. The corner entrance to building No. 15 from Unter den Linden has become the portal for the hall, which now houses the annex of the Guggenheim Museum. The entrance to building No. 13 on Unter den Linden leads through the former coachman's entrance into the restored, richly decorated, 19th-century staircase. Behind the windows of the staircase is the smaller green courtyard, which is almost Italian in its atmosphere. The larger courtyard, which is shared by both buildings, connects to the main entrance area in Charlottenstrasse. It is covered by a curved glass roof, and wide wooden landings. The covered courtyard is suitable for a wide variety of uses.

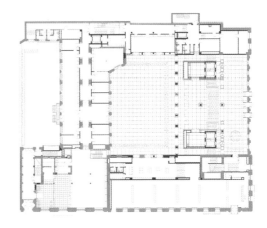

Ground floor plan to a scale of 1:1000

9.9

PRESS AND INFORMATION OFFICE OF THE FEDERAL GOVERNMENT

Architects	KSP Engel Kraemer Zimmermann, Berlin
Landscaping	WES & Partner, Hamburg
Project Management	HPP Gesellschaft für Projektmanagement mbH, Berlin
Statics	CBF – Berlin Bauconsulting
Opening 1. BP	October 1997
2. BP	October 1998
Address	Reichstagufer 12–14, Dorotheenstrasse 84 Berlin-Mitte

The site consisting of eight single plots lies in the northern part of Friedrichstadt, close to Friedrich-strasse Station. The historic block structure is large-ly preserved and extends to the river Spree. The ensemble, which is a protected architectural monu-ment apart from one prefabricated concrete build-ing, is being renovated, and new buildings are only being added on the vacant northeastern section. The project is designed to provide office space for 550 staff members and contains the press and visi-tor center with conference rooms to hold up to 800. In the first building phase the pavilion-type new building was built, which is linked to the bank of the Spree by a paved open space. This building contains the public rooms of the press and visitor center (PBZ). Its outer and inner shells consist of finely perforated, stainless-steel panels. In addi-tion, the eastern fire wall of the former postal check office has been extended by a narrow build-ing with a depth of only six meters. This enabled the existing rooms on one side of the corridor to be supplemented on the other side of the corridor. The new glass building structure, which is 120 metres long and about 20 metres high, penetrates the block and links the different buildings which will be con-verted in further construction phases. The last phase will complete the block facing Neustädtische Kirchstrasse. This edge of the development will meanwhile be marked by trees.

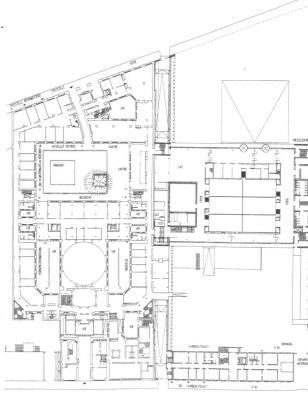

Ground floor plan to a scale of 1:1500

9.10

ARD HAUPTSTADTSTUDIO

Architects	Ortner & Ortner Baukunst, Vienna/Berlin
Project Management	Hanns Peter Wulf, Berlin
Client	Bauherrengemeinschaft ARD Hauptstadtstudio
Statics	ARUP, Beratende Ingenieure, Berlin
Mechanical	Zibell Willner & Partners
Completion	September 1998
Address	Wilhelmstrasse 67a (Studio), Reichstagufer 7–8 (Apartment Building), Berlin-Mitte

The new buildings supplement the existing block of the old institute buildings of the university and the Charité Hospital between Dorotheenstrasse, Bunsenstrasse, Wilhelmstrasse and Reichstagufer, and at the same time they form a transition between the different heights of the buildings. On Wilhelmstrasse, the end structure of the new studio building restores the symmetry of volume on both sides of the framed courtyard entrance, and on Reichstagufer the step structure of the residential building acts as a buffer between the studio and the existing lower building on the corner of Bunsenstrasse. The new buildings retain a special feature of the historic block: the surrounding 80-cm-wide ditch, which is only bridged at the pedestrian and vehicle entrances.

The facade consists of two layers. In front of the inner facade, with windows which can be opend, and roller blinds, an outer facade has been placed, out of reddish concrete blocks between large flush-mounted glass panels.

Studio A with a panoramic view, situated above a large foyer marks the corner of the block close to Marschall Bridge. Connected to it facing Reichstagufer is a single-story area with a lobby and a conference room. Between the galleries of the two five-story side wings with the editorial offices is a broad hall with a glass roof to allow in light. The single-flight staircase along the southern wall and the narrow landings link the stories and the side wings.

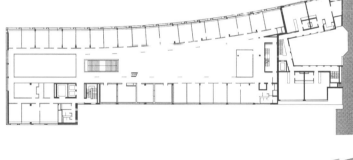

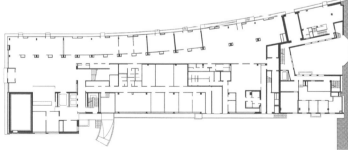

Plans of ground floor and 1st upper floor to a scale of 1:1000

9.11

EUGEN GUTMANN HOUSE
HEADQUARTER OF DRESDNER BANK AG IN BERLIN

Architects	gmp, von Gerkan, Marg and Partners, Hamburg
Design	Meinhard von Gerkan
Project	Volkmar Sievers
Management	Ingenieurgemeinschaft Rauch, Wiese and Partners, Berlin
Projektsteuerung	CBP Cronauer, Munich/Berlin
Statics	Waagner-Biró, Munchi/Vienna
Roof	M. Schweitzer Grundbesitz- und Verwaltungs
Client	GmbH & Co KG, Berlin, vertreten durch DRESDNER BANK AG, Konzernstab Immobilien und Verwaltung, Bauabteilung Berlin
Opening	December 15th, 1997
Address	Pariser Platz 6, Berlin-Mitte

Photo to the right:
Dresdner Bank

The building contains the main headquarters of the Berlin branch of Dresdner Bank. The southern facade facing Pariser Platz is made of stone to conform with regulations. Above a low pedestal of matte granite, the main stories rise in light-coloured sandstone with upright windows, and the top of the building consists of a staggered story with inlaid bronze panels. A two-story portal with an outdoor staircase leads into the building: first into a rectangular foyer which also spans two stories, then into a cylindrical hall with a diameter of 29 meters which reaches to the top of the building and around which all the inner rooms are arranged on five stories. The hall has a glass-roof dome because the surrounding buildings —the residential and shopping building by Bernhard Winking and the future French embassy—make it necessary to provide daylight from above. The uppermost stories are reached via an exposed spiral staircase or two glass lifts. The exclusive suites for staff or visitors to the Dresdner Bank are situated in the staggered top story, and the lined-up terrace in front gives a fine view of Pariser Platz and the downtown area.

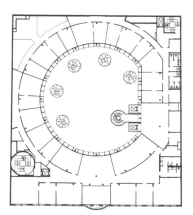

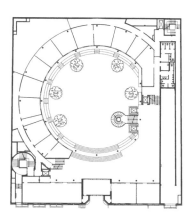

**Plans of ground floor and
a typical upper floor
to a scale of 1:1000**

9.12

OFFICE, COMMERCIAL AND APARTMENT BUILDING
PARISER PLATZ 6A

Architects	Bernhard Winking, Hamburg/Berlin with Martin Froh, Berlin
Project	HANSEATICA Unternehmens Consulting GmbH, Hamburg and
Development	Deutsche Immobilien Anlagegesellschaft mbH, Frankfurt/M.
Project	
Management	HANSEATICA Projektsteuerungs GmbH, Hamburg
General	
Contractor	Arge Pariser Platz 6a Hochtief, Berlin
Statics	Leonhardt, Andrä and Partners, Berlin
Client	TASCON Zwölfte Beteiligungsgesellschaft mbH & Co KG,
	Hamburg/Berlin
Completion	June 1998
Address	Pariser Platz 6a/ Ebertstrasse 24, Berlin-Mitte

The setting at Pariser Platz 6a in the corner between Dresdner Bank and Haus Sommer determines the concept of the residential and commercial building. The frontage on Pariser Platz is narrow and adheres to the height of the other buildings, but behind the corner the building extends three stories higher.

The facade facing Pariser Platz and Ebertstrasse consists of stone, with solid Silesian sandstone set in a pedestal of kernel granite. The ground floor on Pariser Platz is heightened by a solid cornice. The entrance loggia has slightly recessed soffits, which are also of granite. The subdivisions and size of the windows are classical, and follow the historic buildings of Stüler and the other new buildings on Pariser Platz, with window frames of oak and stainless steel. Contrasted with the closed facades on Pariser Platz and Behrenstrasse, the rendered, light-colored courtyard facades open up with large windows. In the tower structure between Pariser Platz and the wing along the street is a spacious staircase. The open inner courtyard, with shops and restaurants, provides a connection to Ebertstrasse. The typical stories have offices on both sides of the corridor on Pariser Platz and Ebertstrasse, and on one side along the fire walls. The required 13 apartments have been created in the tower and on the third and fourth floor overlooking Ebertstrasse.

**Plans of ground floor and
a typical upper floor
to a scale of 1:1000**

9.13

OFFICE AND APARTMENT BUILDING PARISER PLATZ 3

Architects	Frank O. Gehry & Associates Inc., Los Angeles, Planungs AG Neufert Mittmann Graf Partners, Cologne
Project Management	Tensho Takemori, Michael Heggemann
Statics	Ingenieurbüro Müller Marl, Marl/Berlin, Schlaich, Bergermann and Partners, Stuttgart
Client	Pariser Platz 3 Grundstücksgesellschaft mbH + Co Bau KG, Berlin
User	DG Bank Frankfurt/M.
Completion	End of 1998
Address	Pariser Platz 3 Berlin-Mitte

The new DG-Building houses a bank on Pariser Platz and a residential building on Behrenstrasse. The demands on the design are met on Pariser Platz by a perforated facade of Italian limestone with automatically-operated casement windows framed by stainless steel. A glass canopy held by invisible supports is suspended 1.50 meters above the main entrance. The apartments facing Behrenstrasse are provided with wooden winter gardens which are inserted into the facade as prefabricated boxes, and faced with stainless steel. The office and residential section each have a glass-roofed atrium. The atrium in the office section measures approximately 60x20 meters and has an irregularly curved roof of stainless steel and glass, with triangular latticework consisting of star-shaped knots and straight bars. In the middle of this atrium a conference room is placed, which was modeled as a free shape, revised in a 3-D model and is being implemented with computer assistance. Its structure is based on shipbuilding. Welded steel ribs form a basic framework which bears the outer stainless steel and the inner wooden facing.

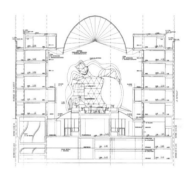

Plans of 2nd upper level and longitudinal section to a scale of 1:1000

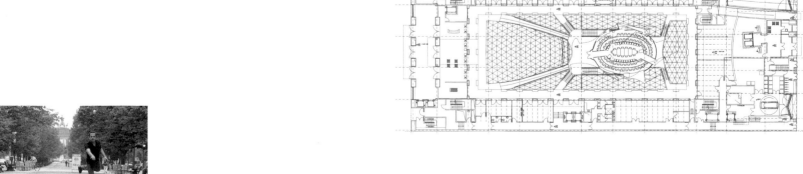

9.14

HOUSE SOMMER

Architects	Josef P. Kleihues with Norbert Hensel, Berlin
Project Management	Matthias Koch
Client	Rheinische Hypothekenbank, Franfurt/M.
Completion	February 1998
Address	Pariser Platz 1, Berlin-Mitte

HOUSE LIEBERMANN

Architects	Josef P. Kleihues with Norbert Hensel, Berlin
Proj. Management	Matthias Koch
Client	Harald Quandt Grundbesitz KG, Bad Homburg
Completion	December 1998
Address	Pariser Platz 7, Berlin-Mitte

Photo:
Andreas Muhs

The main dimensions of the two buildings follow the volume of House Sommer and House Liebermann as they were after being converted by August Stüler in 1844–1846. The vertical dimensions of the facades are aligned with the cornice heights of the two gatehouses and the Brandenburg Gate. But by contrast with their precursors, these new buildings are not directly linked with the gatehouses, thus leaving the gate ensemble as a free-standing unit. The floor plans are subject to a strictly modular structure, but no further requirements were placed on their use. Both buildings have a facade of Portuguese sandstone, a particularly hard and resilient stone with a light color which shines almost white in the sun. The banks, which are the users, will put life into their buildings at this prestigious address by staging conferences, lectures, meetings and occasional art exhibitions.

House Sommer
ground floor plan and
1st upper level
to a scale of 1:1000

House Liebermann
ground floor plan and
1st upper floor
to a scale of 1:1000

Investing in Berlin

Interview with Anno August Jagdfeld on September 3rd, 1998

Your name first became known in Berlin when it was linked with the Hotel Adlon. Preceding this engagement, what experiences did you have? I began as an investment consultant. Initiating closed-end real estate funds was a logical consequence. We sold finished properties until we realized that we could perhaps do some of the interesting projects better ourselves—or even do projects which nobody else wants to get involved in. As you see, we started from the investment side and gradually grew into the role of a project developer with an interest in projects that are somewhat out of the ordinary—and we had a willingness to carry them out.

What projects resulted from this approach? First of all the "Adlon". "Quartier 206" on Friedrichstrasse followed. Nobody else would have done in the way we did it, and nobody else would have chosen this particular form. The next projects were Heiligendamm, the "Tacheles" in Berlin and the Wustrow Peninsula. They, too, are projects that no one else would have even touched.

Why and when did you come to Berlin? It happened very quickly. In West Germany, where we come from, practically every good plot has already been built on. And here in Berlin there are lots of splendid sites and building opportunities. Berlin is like a magnet, it has attracted all the interesting building developers and investors. And where else in the world can you meet the architectural elite? Berlin definitely is becoming a metropolitan city. In the cultural field, Berlin is absolutely competitive with any other world metropolis: theater, opera, museums, the philharmonic orchestra, concert houses, cabaret; even London and other major cities don't have more. What is missing is the well-to-do middle class that has long existed in places like Munich, Hamburg and Düsseldorf. On the whole, I believe that Berlin will be for Europe what New York is for America. An American investor once said to me: "Berlin is magic." We Germans are more sober and cautious, but you can believe me as an investor and a rational accountant, that even we approach such an investment with our emotions—with pride and a feeling of gratitude. One reason why we invest is that great memories might otherwise grow pale and be lost. Friedrichstrasse was once the most exciting street in the largest and greatest city in Germany. The name Friedrichstrasse stands for a particularly creative, revolutionary and tense phase in the history of Berlin, but the name is also a reminder of destruction, collapse and the futility of war. Checkpoint Charlie—just a few yards farther on—became a location and a concept that fascinated and shocked artists and authors of detective stories, politicians, and tourists. The chance of constructing a new generation of buildings here inevitably gives cause for optimism—who could have hoped for this opportunity in view of the history of the last 40 years?

What makes you really enthusiastic about a project? First and foremost, an exceptional location. That's the main factor that characterizes all of our projects, the location. And then, an exceptional aesthetic standard, which always integrates history. I took my inspiration for all of my projects from pictures; pictures of old Berlin or of Soho in New York for the Tacheles, the outstanding beauty of Heiligendamm, and for Wustrow the unspoiled nature which reminds me of certain parts of Long Island and the American East Coast in general.

And the Adlon? Of course I was inspired by pictures of the old Adlon. The old Adlon was a hotel that had never before been seen in Europe. Modern, in step with the latest technology, a sensation not only in the extravagant luxury of its fittings but also because of its address: Unter den Linden 1, the most exclusive location in Berlin, even in the whole of Germany.

When you set up investment funds or advertise in West Germany for Berlin as a location, do you not often hear that much too much money is being invested here? Couldn't they aim a bit lower in Berlin? The situation was actually rather favorable for the investors. Just think of the varied subsidies which investments in Berlin provided. Nowhere else were more subsidies paid.

But they're running out now... Yes, but they've achieved their purpose. Berlin is well supplied with dwellings, that was the aim of residential policies, and now that the supply is there and location disadvantages have disappeared, it is absolutely correct to break off. Berlin no longer needs subsidies in the property sector.

Is that really your opinion? Yes, of course, I'm a market economist. When there was a supply shortage and a high political risk for investors, subsidies were sensible and right. But now, in a phase in which Berlin is the city with the greatest possible potential — there is no place with greater prospects for property investment than Berlin — we no longer need any subsidies.

Do people in West Germany in general think like that? Well, you can't judge things well, if you don't live here and if you don't participate in or see the day to day development. Ten years ago, I didn't even know what Friedrichstrasse was. I didn't even know anything about the Hotel Adlon. But if you live here and watch things develop and have a bit of imagination...

It seems that you really need imagination... It's interesting to observe what happens in Germany when you decide to do something new or out of the ordinary. In Heiligendamm, for example, we had nothing but opposition at the beginning. In America they would have said; "Great that somebody is coming to modernize Heiligendamm." Here you start out with three hundred misgivings, objections and doubts. As if for one reason or the other, it just can't work! That's been true of all inventions — from the steam machine, X-rays, the railway to the Transrapid magnetic railway today. It's a very German phenomenon.

And you're willing to put up with it? It's just the way things are. With the Adlon, for example, there were fierce discussions about reviving the traditional architecture. That's died down now. You would no longer find a majority for a modern steel-and-glass facade. A few weeks ago I read in the newspaper "Süddeutsche Zeitung" that even such a man as I. M. Pei, who is absolutely above suspicion, said that our gamble of building in a traditional style had paid off. And "Die Welt" recently asked in an article: What will be more interesting, Kurfürstendamm or Friedrichstrasse? For the first time, the people of Berlin said Friedrichstrasse. But the best thing was the headline: "They are against everything new until it arrives."

Will Friedrichstrasse overtake Kurfürstendamm in popularity? Why should it? Kurfürstendamm was always the shop window of Berlin's West, and such it will remain. What interests me personally is not what is tried and tested, but movement; not what is, but what could be; not "the West" or "the East" but the dynamism of the city as a whole. I'm certain that a productive mixture of commerce, art, journalism, trade and politics in a new capital city of Berlin is not just a beautiful dream. When we began, it was really just a vision, but today, it's plain for all to see that the central district of Berlin-Mitte is where the future lies. It thrives on the vitality of a clientele that exists all over the world and that simply looks for an ideal place to communicate, enjoy, work and stroll. And for Berlin that place is the new, respectively the old center.

If you were a reader of our interview and finding out about yourself, what would you like to read? What information on you as a person and about your work would be important to pass on? I'm not really the sort of person who pushes to get into the newspaper. But there's quite a lot of reporting about us, sometimes critical and sometimes positive. It's full of ups and downs, but you get used to it. Being a project developer simply means that you enter into a problematical situation and solve it step by step. That's what we live with every day, but for outsiders, and even for the press, its seems as if the project developer has a problem. All I can say is, it's his job to solve problems. Each project is the sum total of many solutions for many problems. Being a project developer and investor has an unbelievable number of facets. You have to have ten or more heads on your shoulders. You have to think like a banker, like a tenant, like a hotel keeper, like a retailer, like a planner, and you have to have a vision that holds it all together. "All of life consists of solving problems," that's my favorite sentence from my favorite philosopher, Karl Popper. Of course there have always been building owners who have lived quite well without a vision. Having problems is a typical characteristic of investors. But when the press report on them, hardly anybody understands that problems are actually quite normal. If it were possible to buy finished projects, what would be the need for project development? My professional colleagues sometimes ask me why I do such difficult projects. It might be much easier to do three easy ones, and I'd earn much more in the process. But these unusual projects — they're just my very personal passion.

But it's a game with high risks.
Yes, but that's just part of our job. Since we are always working on a whole series of projects, some go well and others take a little longer. But there hasn't been a single project yet that we've failed with. Our job is to make a success of projects that need a little longer. At the moment we're in a phase of unoccupied premises and a surplus of properties, so there are sure to be a few disappointments. In the office market we're experiencing the same situation as anyone building office spaces does. When it rains, everyone gets wet. But here you can't build on the basis of short-term speculation or profit expectations. After a difficult starting and transition phase, our gamble is that Berlin will again become the economic, political and cultural center of Germany, and that an investment here will, in the long term, find its demand and its approval. The locations on Friedrichstrasse are becoming more valuable with every new inhabitant who moves to Berlin, with every hotel, with every step which brings us closer to Eastern Europe and with every new job that is created in Berlin. This process, by which a strong center is developing in a polycentric city, takes time but it is just as sure as the economic development of Germany as a whole. And because we bank on this optimistic long-term expectation, we're trying, in conjunction with others, to make Friedrichstrasse a boulevard of variety, a boulevard of luxury shopping as well as one answering to the demands and wishes of wide sectors of society, a boulevard for the rich and the not-so-rich. And we hope that the proximity to the museums, to the Reichstag, and to the important government ministries will also benefit our investments.

The Tacheles is one of the projects that need a little longer. Why are you holding on to it so persistently? I believe that the part of the city around Oranienburger Strasse between the "Spandauer Vorstadt," Friedrichstrasse and the central government district is an absolutely unique phenomenon, and that it will become the most fascinating residential area in Berlin. It is a mixture of informal culture, museums, politics, and creative artists, all in one area. And we will make something special of it. At present, our actions have to stay limited because we only have possession of some of the plots; other parts of Tacheles are still occupied and declared an autonomous republic. In this respect, the seller must help us to clarify the situation and speak to the people. As for us, we want to preserve the cultural location of the Tacheles on a long-term basis come what may, i.e. the protected monument of the Tacheles art building as an open, innovative and international cultural center. We want to give a real chance to the mixture and urbanity that are appealed to in many projects and to the promised integration into a fully functional neighborhood. A particularly dense mixture of shopping and residential accommodation is planned. Large parts of the ground floors of the residential buildings should be used commercially. No solitary or tall buildings are planned, only smaller building units. Numerous variants were developed and discussed with all parties before our project was agreed on by the urban district, the Senate Building Department, the Senate Cultural Department and the Revenue Board. Continuing to develop the city in the same way that it has grown historically, to keep historic memory alive, is a concept that has been admirably proven in the example of the Hackesche Höfe on Hackescher Markt.

The rebuilding of the Hotel Adlon is something that everybody can understand. But what led you to get involved so early on Friedrichstrasse, which at that time was more or less terra incognita? How would you define your architectural approach?

There was the image of a unique classiness, that can only be achieved by a cosmopolitan city like Berlin— the only such city we have got in Germany. We wanted to bring an international trend to Berlin, a trend that had until then not been reflected anywhere in Germany. We wanted to transport the energy and imagination of other international cities to Berlin and to cultivate shopping as a personal source of pleasure. For me, luxury does not consist of a greater volume of goods on offer— on the contrary, it consists of a range of goods that help people to find their own personal style. Here, we have a unique setting with Unter den Linden, Gendarmenmarkt and Museum Island, and we wanted to add something new that will perhaps one day be compared with Fifth Avenue. I believe that in "Quartier 206" we've succeeded in doing something that many try and few achieve: bringing real cosmopolitan architecture to Berlin. I'm grateful for the allusions to the architecture of Gendarmenmarkt and Unter den Linden, which the architects of "Quartier 206", Cobb, Freed & Partners, have been able to create. They decided on a type of rationalization of Classicism. The building itself is fundamentally classicist, but its styling contains references to Art Deco.

Let's move away from Berlin for a moment to your Heiligendamm project. How did you come to do it?
In the magazine "Focus" I saw a full page photograph, a view from the sea, and was fascinated. It's a real gem of nature, scenery, and architecture that's without match in Germany.

Photos:
Erik-Jan Ouwerkerk

So you went there and said, "I've got to try this?"
Yes. A year and a half later, we had created the conditions to set up an investment fund. The fund is on the market now, and after the fund has been placed we'll begin construction.

Who will be your architect?
Robert A. M. Stern. Meeting him was one of those chance biographical encounters that seem to follow a pattern. A friend who is a jeweller in New York had engaged him for the interior design of his shop. We met Stern in New York and he showed us his books. It was only much later that I learned that he has a reputation in America of being the most important modern architect for classical buildings.

So here again, pictures seduced you?
Yes, I've always made my decisions on the basis of pictures.

How would you define your personal responsibility for Berlin when investing here?
The fact is, that for our own success we need a vigorous and varied city, in which tourists and the people of Berlin can feel at home. We also need a permeable government district, not sealed-off office blocks isolated by safety zones. The inner city has to remain open and permeable. That's why we believe that a close link between Friedrichstrasse, the Spandauer Vorstadt and the adjacent areas is so important. Investors must build a bridge between visions and what is feasible. They can't hide behind lofty words. Our language is construction, and we express ourselves through building. That's the standard we are judged by. Our ideal is not an isolated island of luxury. Every city needs friction and contrasts. In spite of the compulsion to invest profitably, it's possible to create a wide range of quality, experience and utilization in Berlin-Mitte. But this requires a close and trusting cooperation with the public authorities—and in Berlin we've always found this atmosphere.

If you had to make recommendations for Berlin, what would you advise?
The city and its people exude a great energy of their own. And their agility will grow. There's no advice needed. I'm very optimistic.

You really think that? Berliners are known to be doubters...
Listen, no place is as interesting as Berlin—not Cologne, not Munich, Stuttgart or Frankfurt. Visitors from abroad, be it from New York, Paris, London or Madrid, see things the same way. Nowhere else are such interesting people moving to as to Berlin, and the city will benefit. Throughout history, Berlin has always consisted to a large extent of people who have moved here from somewhere else. That hasn't always been comfortable for the people of Berlin, but in hindsight it was a great gain. What's missing, of course, is a traditionally wealthy middle class in the German capital. And the Jewish society is still lacking—and there is nothing to replace it.

If you could choose a project, solely for pleasure?
I would love to set up the best and most extravagant Chinese restaurant in Germany. In Berlin-Mitte of course.

Architects	Ackermann und Partner, Munich,
	Eoin Bowler, Heinz Riegel and Christof Simon
Client	Berliner Wasser Betriebe
Opening	September 1998
Address	Hohenzollerndamm 208
	Berlin-Wilmersdorf

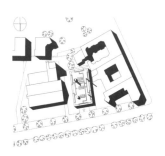

Christoph Tempel
The Wilmersdorfer Water Works

All photos:
Christian Gahl

The location could hardly be more exclusive: a site in verdant Wilmersdorf, Hohenzollerndamm 208, in close proximity to Fritz Höger's expressive dark brick church on Hohenzollernplatz, framed by mature trees and fire walls steeped in history. A few feet down the road: glimpses into small courtyards, a freestanding apartment building for civil servants, and, at a respectful distance, a 1950's building which creates the border to Bundesallee. In the midst of this tranquillity two halls stand facing each other, lined up as if they were an exhibit of sewage technology then and now.

Parallel to the street is the old Wilmersdorf pump station by Hermann Müller, which began operation in 1906. Built in a brick-gothic style, it has fields of white stucco framed by decorative red gables, large arched windows and a high, pitched red roof. The ensemble, consisting of machine hall, extensions, and the dwelling house for civil servants, has just recently been put under historical preservation.

Ackermann and Partner of Munich have erected their new main pump station perpendicular to both the street and the old hall. Their building, a smoothly-surfaced rectangle of metal and glass, is both distant and close enough to mirror the neighboring historical gem. Three 35-meter-high, technoidly shining smokestacks jut through the roof.

The green island, now open to the street, was contained within a large block structure before the destruction of World War II, with the surrounding firewalls and courtyards standing witness to the fact. Heavily damaged during the war, the old pump station was rebuilt during 1947–49 and has demonstrated its worthiness as a block edge, visible from the street. In its new position, the pump station, technically renewed in the late 1950's, has since served in noble reserve.

"Howe'er may it be put to use / This water with no energy / For toads, serpents and snakes produced / By our distinguished citizenry," asks an inscription in the machine room. The answer, so easy today, was more difficult around 1870. Up until this time, the distinguished citizenry closed its eyes and nose to the sewage problem. The first water works, which began operation in 1856 outside the Stralau Gate, and the introduction of water closets led to an increase in sewage, which was simply dumped into the Spree River or which flowed, untreated, through open gutters into cesspits and canals. The memory of the unbearable stench which arose as the temperatures rose led August Bebel to comment in hindsight, "Berlin, as a major city, only really went from barbarism to civilization after 1870."

In 1871, James Hobrecht, who had for two years been the royal building advisor, presented his canal project bases on the "radial system". In his mixed-sewage system, feces, rainwater, and other waste water flowed into one canal, in contrast to the more ecological but more elaborate and expensive separation system. Realization of the project was begun a year later. The city was divided into 12 areas, each containing a sewage pump station.

After 1874, it was mandatory to hook up to the sewage system if a canal was present. Twenty-two years after the first water works, the sewage system was officially opened. By the end of the 19th century, almost every household was hooked up to the central water and sewage systems.

Then, as now, a sewage pump works is a monofunctional structure. Its one and only task consists of pumping waste water, the volume of which varies along with the weather, into a pressurized pipe system. The pipes run under the whole city and end at the municipal sewage treatment plant, where their contents run through a series of treatments before they are dumped into rivers, canals or sewage farms.

Continuous technical difficulties with the old pumps and the condition of the suction room under the building had been a problem for some time. A first idea, to expand and modernize the existing works, was dropped in view of the difficulties which would have arisen because of the stipulation that sewage continue to be pumped during construction. Because the plant is on the lowest point of the area it serves, and because the sewage pipes all lead to it, the new building had to be in direct vicinity to the old.

Its position was carefully calculated. There was a minimum required distance to be kept with respect to the housing to the west, in order to prevent tremors resulting from the diesel pumps. To the south, the civil-servants' housing belonging to the old pump station demanded respectful

treatment, and to the east lay the existing sewage canals, which had to be kept in operation during construction of the new building. The new glass structure, measuring 40 by 20 meters, stands well positioned in the midst of these demands from all sides. Its height of 8.4 meters takes up the eaves-level height of the old building.

The starting point for Ackermann and Partner's design work was a preliminary technical plan by the Berlin Water Works, for which an architectural form had to be found. This preliminary design stipulated how much space would be required for the pumps, as well as their position 14 meters underground. In section, three zones are discernible. To the right—seen from Hohenzollerndamm—is the suction room, where all the canals end and out of which the pumps, on the same level and in the middle, pump sewage. To the left is a room for the diesel engines, which are needed in case of a power outage. The above-ground portion of the building took up this division into thirds and continues with a basilica section: a taller central nave with cranes to lift the pumps, and two smaller naves which flank the central space. These contain electrical and ventilation rooms and two tall waste-air smokestacks, one on either side of the central nave. Continuously occupied work areas are not planned, which is why daylight throughout is not a necessity. Those with an eye for pump works can find many such closed structures in Berlin: hermetically sealed buildings, most done in brick. One of the best known is surely the building by Oswald

The double glass facade's transparency allows views through, into, and out of the building. Right: the central machine room with its cranes. Distorted only by the stairs and the catwalk, the view onto the civil servants' apartment house to the south

Mathias Ungers and Stefan Schroth, which was built next to the old Tiergarten sewage pump works in Alt-Moabit for the 1987 International Building Exhibit.

The new pump works in Wilmersdorf dispenses with this idea. The large arched windows of the old building already allow one a view of the mechanical world within, and the new pump works is entirely of glass.

The design strictly separates load-bearing elements from the enclosing skin. A fascinating contrast is created between the large, tranquil glass form of the building, or rather, the outer skin's frameless glass fields, lying rather than reaching, and the dynamically reaching, filigree construction, bordered in white, which stands extended like a spreadeagle figure. The bearing construction consists of four autonomous blocks, each one stabilized independently of the others, which rest on the subconstruction. A 20-meter-long, three-truss beam with extensions spans the whole upper structure of the pump works. The central and lateral naves have a common, airy, upper level and roof.

On the ground floor, the construction is less visible as such. The round, charcoal-gray supports which stand in eight double rows, 3.50 meters apart, directly behind the inner of the two glass skins, take up the color scheme of the muted, gray-black-charcoal fixtures.

The double glass skin is "conditionally intelligent". Spring and fall and on sunny winter days it allows for additional heat gain. Ventilation windows

in the upper part of the inner facade allow the air warmed between the facade's layers to reach the interior of the building. The openings for cold air in the lower part of the outer facade allow fresh air into the space. During the summer, blinds prevent overheating.

Between the two glass facades, between outside and inside, are two catwalks, one directly over the other. The walkway which is on the level of the second floor circles the whole building; a wonderful place for performances of all sorts, thinks the visitor. But the reason for the catwalks, which were not anticipated in the first, competition, design, are sobering: "In order to ensure the maintenance of the glass surfaces, appropriate measures are to be taken," counseled the jury.

The floor plan is, in keeping with the preliminary, technical design, divided into three parts. In the middle part is the 9 meter wide machine hall, which is as high as the building. It contains a yellow crane, which follows the length of the building. Three large floor openings used for the assembly of the pumps allow a view into the lower levels. The sides of this space are closed. Behind the walls there are one-story rooms of different sizes with apparatus which provide and regulate electricity and ventilation. In addition, there are areas for circulation and a shop. These side rooms are reached from outside via glass doors in the double-layered facade; from within, dark doors with large bull's-eye windows lead to the central machine hall.

In the building's belly: six electrically driven pumps, and two fueled by diesel

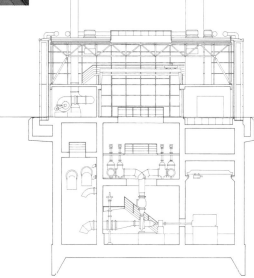

The spaces on the upper level are dominated by the four white spread-eagle supports.
The section, scale 1:400, shows the contrast between the mighty building underneath and the filigree building above the ground.
Close enough to have its handsomeness mirrored: the old pump station

The upper-levels, reached via stairs and a walkway to the south, have no function. They have an air of church galleries on a weekday; empty, but with a first-class view of the construction and the central nave. The architects had planned rooms for employees' breaks here which, because of the noise level, were not realized.

A stairway in the southeastern corner leads down into the actual heart of the building, to the eight rotating pumps, of which six run on electricity and two, in case of power outages, on diesel fuel. They stand lined up, connected by silvery tubes, four stories, or 14.6 meters under the earth, on the building's sole. They sit on the same level as the suction room, where all gathers that goes down the drain in Wilmersdorf and nearby Schöneberg. Why this room is still called suction room is unclear. In the old building this room is under the level of the pumps, but in the new building there is no suction. One can only imagine the capacity of 1.25 cubic meters per second, which translates to 4,500 cubic meters an hour. The pipes which lead in and out of the building are invisible to our eyes. Loud it is, but much to see there's not and that, despite the glass shell. The technical happenings on the pressure pipe stages or the service walks are no more spectacular. But the visitor is flooded by a feeling of experiencing an extraordinary underground world when his gaze is directed from the depths of the pit to the sunny heights of the glass building, from which mirrors mounted on the ceiling cast artificial light into the levels below.

A glance back into the machine hall of the old pump works makes the relationship between the two buildings evident. The lofty space with the old pumps, which seem incredibly large, has a tranquil, and almost exalting aura about it. The much smaller space of the new pump works instills this festive atmosphere through remaining practically invisible and by leading the gaze directly into the loud, underground world of machines, a world which seems steered by invisible forces.

According to the competition text of 1991, the old pump works was to be converted into a sewage museum. One of the large pumps will remain where it is, although the museum idea has been dropped, as the museum in the Friedrichshagen water works will take over this role. The historical preservationists have agreed to transform the old hall into a public space for exhibitions or performances. Nobody has yet decided about the use of the magnificent gallery spaces in the new pump station. Though the population at large will be waiting for the next open house.

12

Photo essay by Erik-Jan Ouwerkerk

Mathias Remmele
Adlershof, the Science City

A strange emptiness surrounds this promised land in the far south-eastern reaches of Berlin. The Science City of Adlershof appears suddenly, seemingly a bit lost, surrounded by a barren landscape far from Berlin's contourless suburbs, and yet related to them in bits and pieces. What for years has been talked about as an ambitious development, a future-bound base for science and economics, and a ray of hope for the city, presents itself, at first glance, as tristesse on the outskirts. And yet, rumblings of movement are discernible on both sides of Rudower Chaussee: a renovation here, a new building there, both ambitious and perhaps even following some master scheme. Interests are roused, and enquiries made.

The science city's surface area, 180 acres large and once used by the Science Academy of the GDR for a research center, is a part and the showpiece of the long-term "Development Project Adlershof," a tract which consists of the city district around the former airport Berlin-Johannisthal. Whereas the "Science and Economics Base Adlershof" is planned, marketed and managed by WISTA Management GmbH, development of the rest of the area, including the "MediaCity Adlershof" among others, is the responsibility of the BAAG (Berlin Adlershof Advancement Group mbH). The BAAG's task is to "build a city" – with everything included. Its fields of activity are, as a result, far-flung. Naturally, aside from a painstaking planning stage, not much has happened yet. The science city is Adlershof's showpiece, its attention-getter.

The concept of the sciences-and-economics city is to bring together, within a clearly defined area, non-university research institutes, firms specialized in technology (for whom special "subject innovation centers" were set up), and those Humboldt University departments focused on the natural sciences and technology. The term "science city" stands for the idea of creating a research, technology and commercial park with a clear-cut, (big)-city character. A district which, for lack of any allure coming from the surrounding landscape, draws its particular attributes from civic qualities: urbanity, a mixture of uses, and physical density. The necessity of giving Adlershof a quality of its own results from the global competition of such science city areas. That explains why the question of architecture and urban design was so important at Adlershof. The buildings were not just meant to provide a utilitarian framework for their specific functions. Much more, they were meant to—a mission as vague as it is meaningful—document modernity through technically and aesthetically outstanding buildings; buildings which are to lead into the future, provide their inhabitants with an unforgettable "address", and finally, serve as an image and a bearer of advertisement.

No one has met those demands as perfectly as Sauerbruch and Hutton. Thanks to their "optical quality", praised by many as being inaugural, their design for a part of the innovation center for optics, optoelectronics and laser technology (photonic center) is considered to be the most striking and most popular new building in Adlershof. Their two colorful amoebas, in whose glass membranes the sky is reflected, are a real feat, and the undulating space between them a wonderful experience. Remarkable for their oscillating color scheme and their softly curving outlines, they are something completely different and yet don't seem out of place. The smaller of the two amoebas, a steel hall for scientific experiments with large machines, is, with the exception of a glass wall which creates the interior boundary for a clean room, a real protozoa. Color and sun protection is provided by blinds located behind the glass skin, just as in the big brother next door. In the bigger of the two buildings, the three story high laboratory and office building, slender pairs of concrete supports between the semi-permeable double membrane set additional accents with their colorful glaze. The two main entrances are at the point where the smooth outer skin breaks open in a zigzagged fold. Their expressive design leaves no wishes for identity through architecture unanswered.

Seen from the edges, Adlershof looks a bit like a colonial city. The borders between built and unbuilt are often abrupt and hard, especially to the north, where the overgrown airfield lies. The newly laid-out path, smoothly paved, suddenly breaks off and loses itself in sand. A few trees hide behind piles of rubble and builders' wagons; behind them are sparse shrubs and heath. The airport has been shut down for a long while. Berlin-Johannisthal, the first regular airport for motor planes in Germany, was closed shortly after the Great War. The rather unsightly moor, correctly classified as half-sandy-dry lawn, worthy of protection for its rare herbs with such pretty names such as "Lying Veronica" and "Thrift", will have its status raised to a landscape and nature park soon, providing that it doesn't remain a building land reserve.

At the edge, just a few steps away from the amoebas and also used by the photonic center, are two sand-colored boxes dressed in small-format ceramic panels. Impeccable in their urban design and well adapted to their orthogonal surroundings, these buildings by Ortner & Ortner remain comparatively inconspicuous. The architects from Vienna, perhaps out of respect for the sober field of science, seem to have imposed an almost Prussian severity on themselves here. And yet the first glance is misleading. Asymmetrically divided windows with light aluminium frames, arranged in a rhythm which skips back and forth from story to story, liven up the facade.

Too bad then, that the graphics of the facade are so totally unrelated to the spaces behind. In order to encourage "face to face contacts" and especially in order to "give the buildings an identity", both buildings were planned with transparent "termini" at their short ends. They are home to the main staircases as well as generously proportioned, purposely restrained communication areas. That the square grid which protects the glass termini from all too much sunlight and heat gleams golden is, after the manner of the Ortners, probably not without deeper meaning.

Synergy is the key word, which planning of the science city was based on and which gives the city a deeper significance. The physical proximity of the institutions is meant to develop into a closer relationship in the course of time, a relationship which will lead to a bundling of energies and an acceleration in the development of new products and processes. Aside from the planable, technical-functional synergy effects (money-saving joint use of laboratories and other research resources) and the hoped-for, as it were idealistic-humanistic effects (a stimulating and fertile working environment), Adlershof has produced a special interwoven environment; one could say, a synergy on the building level, an exciting play of old and new, of historical and contemporary architecture. On the everchanging WISTA site, where permanent structures exist next to painfully provisional ones and where carefully planned structures stand cheek-to-cheek with haphazard ones, an impression of the unfinished and disparate predominates. But beyond the contrasts, emphasized by the changes, the relics of the past and the new buildings which have grown up between them treat each other with a respect which is almost quaint.

That holds true even for the Innovation Center for Environmental Technology (UTZ). At first, the building just seems too large. With its endless wings (200 meters) the U-shaped, four-story building (an additional wing can extend the building into a meander) seems too big for the site. Why Eisele + Fritz, Bott, Hilka, Begemann of Darmstadt planned such a massive building in this park-like environment characterized by its one-story barrack-like buildings seems, at first, difficult to comprehend. The fact is, however, that with their richly varied facade they reduce the magnitude of the structure considerably. Wooden panels, light concrete, a lot of glass, and silvery shimmering, vertical sun-protection blinds bestow an almost domestic grace upon the building. And in the stretched-out courtyard, whose atmosphere profits immensely from the trees which

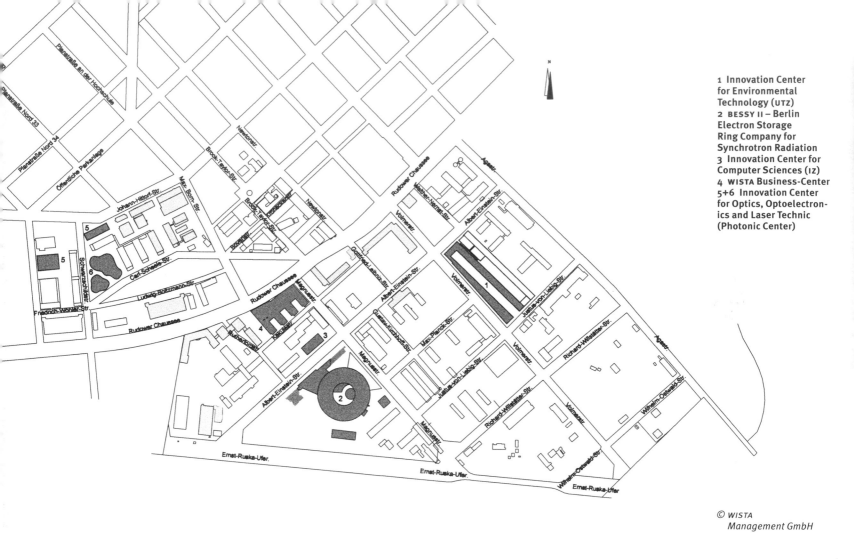

1 Innovation Center
for Environmental
Technology (UTZ)
2 BESSY II – Berlin
Electron Storage
Ring Company for
Synchrotron Radiation
3 Innovation Center for
Computer Sciences (IZ)
4 WISTA Business-Center
5+6 Innovation Center
for Optics, Optoelectron-
ics and Laser Technic
(Photonic Center)

were retained, the individually adjustable "sun protection systems"
provide for an ever-changing facade composition.

Thoughts of synergy, both functional and architectonic, are
behind the WISTA business center as well. Conceived of for services
close to the fields of science it is, for the present and until their own
building is completed, being used by the Computer Sciences Department of Humboldt University. The building's long, concave facade
follows the curve of Rudower Chaussee. Berlin architects Dörr,
Ludolf, Wimmer organized the complex as a comb form in plan. On
the side facing Rudower Chaussee the spaces between the legs of
the building are, principally for acoustical reasons, filled in with
glass halls. At the rear, there are three differently planted garden
courts. The facade's red-clay brick panels refer, if one wishes to read
it that way, to the older buildings nearby, for example the two airplane hangars, which are architectural highlights of Adlershof. The
new building appears light in both senses of the word, the organization of the building is clear and easy to comprehend; everything
here is comme il faut—contemporary to the point of being inconspicuous.

The overly large halls with their glass facades, halls in which
trees grow, and the wide flights of stairs, announce to the visitor at
the WISTA business center in no subtle terms what is also valid for the
other new buildings: Here, spaces were created with dimensions as
if they were spaces for some certain function, spaces with a myriad
of different zones. And yet these spaces have no other function than
to create a good atmosphere. The spaces between, which were
created for the breaks between bouts of highly concentrated work,
are meant to further random meetings, talks, and friendships which
are so important for the hoped-for synergy between the scientists
and between the sciences and technical fields.

Directly next to BESSY is the Innovation Center for Computer
Sciences (ITZ), originally planned by the Dutch office CEPEZED bv,
with the Berlin office DGI Bauwerk taking over the working drawings.
Askew, V-formed steel supports; eight bundles of four each, lift
the building off the ground; the back half only a floor, but the front
half all of 14 meters. The intended effect of a floating building doesn't
seem to want to materialize and so the impressive tour de force
lacks the necessary motivation. In the air space between the bundled
supports, three ellipsoid platforms, which can be reached via narrow bridges, hang at different heights: They are for "get-togethers",
panorama and spatial excitement included. With the four steel-
panel-clad office floors, located above the glassed-in supports, the
zest for design seems to have suddenly fizzled. Ribbon windows
divide the facade into strips.

Possibly, the "vision of a science city," with so many development planners and project managers, scientific organizations and
marketing strategists, all of them working in a confusing array of
institutions, is slowly coming into being. And yet the tirelessly
produced concepts, expert reports, brochures and press releases,
all of them mirroring the planning stages, seem to lack vigor when
one reaches the site. Despite the catchy phrases, despite the means
to an end, the language used by the planners and image builders
seems suddenly imprecise, one-dimensional, and as if they could be
describing anything. The site doesn't play along.

The claim is often made that in Adlershof, science is a tradition.
And yet the site doesn't merely have tradition, it also has a past. It
tells a story. That's what makes it so many-sided, so contradictory,
so surprising. A construction sign on a dirty, gray-beige wall defiantly announces: "Berlin is building a future in Adlershof." There's
a story about the "securing of technical monuments in the field of
aviation research." And, lo and behold, the 1930's wind tunnel, a
mighty, sharply-folded concrete tube whose expressive form wholly
follows the demands of function and construction, a tunnel erected
by the "German Center for Aviation Studies", just recently received

a new, lead-gray coat of paint. The nearby spin tower, a longish, almost archaic and very secretive appearing concrete egg, awaits similar treatment. Another older building, this one next to the wind tunnel, is probably waiting for its final demolition. It's too bad for the building with the symmetrical front facade, its glass hall, strapped like a backpack onto its square base. Next door, a sign of the future: piles of sand mark the pit which was bulldozed for Humboldt University's new Chemistry Institute building.

BESSY II is the pride of Adlershof. The funny, friendly name stands for Berliner Elektronenspeicherring-Gesellschaft für Synchrotronstrahlung mbH (Berlin Electron Storage Ring Company for Synchrotron Radiation), a firm which built a new third-generation high brilliance radiation source for vacuum, ultraviolet and soft x-rays here. Experts judge BESSY's scientific importance to be exceptionally great, fueling the hope that the world-renowned device could become a magnet for Adlershof. Of the new buildings at Adlershof, the complex planned by Brenner & Partner of Stuttgart is the only one whose outer design corresponds with its inner function, like in the technical monuments. The experimental hall, a large circle with a 120-meter diameter, ring shaped in plan, takes its form from the electron storage ring of the radiation source. Whereas the hermetically closed-off ring with its aluminium cladding emits a cool, high-tech aura, the attached four-story office and laboratory building, which, because of urban planning constraints, had to be placed at the edge of the street, definitely appears friendlier. Of course, this building tries to please, what with its myriad of color applications and its array of materials. The sometimes bizarre dialectic of building up and tearing down, of restoration and neglect which characterizes Adlershof today will, if everything goes according to plan, fade away with time. But the Science City of Adlershof will never be a test-tube high-tech park. The Adlershof canteen "Am Windkanal" (At the Wind Tunnel) invites those who, let's say leave

their ultramodern crystal-cultivation laboratory for a half-hour break. The restaurant defiantly and yet quite charmingly challenges fast changes and styled modernity. The menu, prettily decorated with all sorts of historical flying machines, sticks to the tried-and-true, and offers hearty Berlin fare at moderate prices. In the restaurant space itself, the tone is even clearer. Relief panels on the walls, the neon tubes which, in do-it-yourself manner, have been arranged into chandeliers, the dark green oilcloth on the tables, and the carefully cultivated potted plants on the window sills demonstrate a undaunted ability to hold out in the face of time.

12.1

INNOVATION CENTER FOR
ENVIRONMENTAL TECHNOLOGY (UTZ)

Architects	Eisele + Fritz, Bott, Hilka, Begemann, Darmstadt
Project Management	Fraunhofer Management GmbH, Munich, with Bauplanung Stoessel, Munich
Client	WISTA-Management GmbH
Opening	Oktober 5th, 1998
Address	Volmerstrasse Berlin-Adlershof

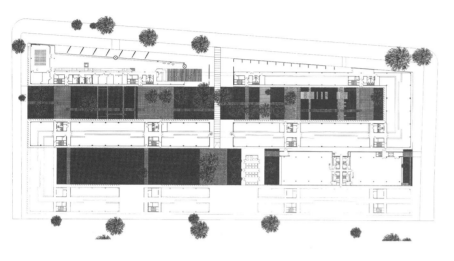

The 200-meter long southwest wing of the UTZ and its courtyard with the vertical brise-soleils.
Ground floor plan, scale 1:2000

Old laboratory building from the 1950's before its renovation; unconvincing land art in one of the courtyards

Former shop building with a dark green glass facade across from the Innovation Center for Environmental Technoloy

12.2

HIGH BRILLIANCE SYNCHROTRON RADIATION SOURCE – BESSY II

Architects   Brenner & Partner, Stuttgart,
with Building Department of Max-Planck-Gesellschaft, Munich

Client   BESSY II – Berliner Elektronenspeicherring-Gesellschaft für Synchrotronstrahlung mbH

Opening   September 4th, 1998

Address   Einsteinstrasse
Berlin-Adlershof

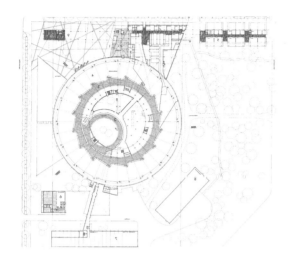

Bessy II, the new electron storage ring with the 4-story building for offices and laboratories on Einsteinstrasse. Ground floor plan, scale 1:3000

The heating plant in Adlershof, restored and with a new skin of aluminium and glass

The 20-meter high, egg-shaped spin tower is from the early days of military aviation research. A vertical stream of air was created here, airplane models were hung in the space, and then their free fall was studied

12.3

INNOVATION CENTER FOR
COMPUTER SCIENCES (IZ)

Architects CEPEZED bv, Delft, Netherlands
Working Drawings DGI Bauwerk, Berlin
Client WISTA-Management GmbH
Opening January 1999
Address Einsteinstrasse
Berlin-Adlershof

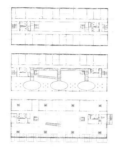

12.4

WISTA BUSINESS-CENTER (WBC)

Architects	Dörr, Ludolf, Wimmer, Berlin
Project Management	Drees & Sommer GmbH, Berlin
Client	Objektgesellschaft WISTA Business-Center mbH & Co. KG
Opening	August 26th, 1998
Address	Rudower Chaussee Berlin-Adlershof

Four wings, three glassed-in atriums and a concave facade facing Rudower Chaussee join to create the WISTA Business Center.
Floor plan, second floor, scale 1:2000

On the Kekulestrasse side, the building separates into four wings and three green courtyards

Left side: the ITZ opens its facade to BESSY II, across the road. Ellipsoid platforms for all sorts of encounters are hung into the 14-meter-high air space.
Floor plans, scale 1:2000

12.5

INNOVATION CENTER FOR OPTICS, OPTOELECTRONICS AND LASER TECHNIC (PHOTONIC CENTER)

Architects
Project
Management
Client
Opening
Address

Ortner & Ortner Baukunst, Berlin/Vienna
Fraunhofer Management GmbH, Munich,
with Bauplanung Stoessel, Munich
WISTA-Management GmbH
September 24th, 1998
Etwaldstrasse
Berlin-Adlershof

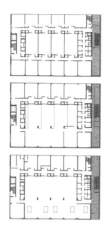

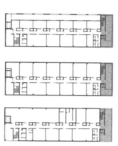

Twin buildings on the outside, different floor plans on the inside: the Photonic Center. The ends of the buildings, covered by a golden, small-format grid, provides spaces to meet people.
Floor plans to a scale of 1:2000

The resemblance to the machine hall, not far off and threatened by demolition, is not to be overlooked

The wind channel, new and silvery on the outside, is under historical protection. A slit in the long side allows a view of the technical fixtures on the inside

12.6

INNOVATION CENTER FOR OPTICS,
OPTOELECTRONICS AND LASER TECHNIC
(PHOTONIC CENTER)

Architects	Sauerbruch Hutton Architekten, London/Berlin
Project Management	Fraunhofer Management GmbH, Munich, with Bauplanung Stoessel, Munich
Client	WISTA-Management GmbH
Opening	September 24th, 1998
Address	Etwaldstrasse Berlin-Adlershof

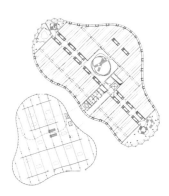

Right nearby, two more buildings for the Photonic Center, this time on an amoeba-shaped plan and with glass facades.
Ground floor plans, scale 1:2000

The former airplane hangar of the German Aviation Institute is under historical protection. It was once also used as a maintenance shop for locomotives. Now, rebuilt into a center for technical gasses for the Messer Company, it keeps the memory of the airfield alive.
How closely together old and new coexist here is once more visible through the window of the Photonic Center

Foto: BitterBredt

The building's color scheme results from the colorful supports in the facade and the sun protection shades

13

Architects BP. 1, 2	O. M. Ungers, Cologne/Berlin with Walter Arno Noebel
Architects BP. 3, 4	O. M. Ungers with Jörg Lenschow, Karl-Heinz Winkens
Client	Land Berlin
Project Management	SBWV Projektgruppe Messe
Prefabricated Facade Systems	WENDKER Leichtmetall- und Leichtbauweise Gmbh, Herten/ Berlin
Project Control BP. 1, 2	Gruppe 80, Wohnungs- und Industriebaugesellschaft
Project Control BP. 3, 4	Hanscomb GmbH/ Hartnack GmbH
Opening BP. 1, 2	Internationale Funkausstellung, IFA 1995
Opening BP. 3, 4	IFA 1997 (3. BP.), IFA 1999 (4. BP.)
Address	Messedamm 22 Berlin-Charlottenburg

Paula Winter
New Halls for the Funkturm Fairgrounds

All photos: Stefan Müller

Almost unbeknownst to press and public, Berlin has bought itself a ca. two-billion-deutschmark new trade fair building. In order to accommodate it, the course of Jafféstrasse was changed and a new urban railway station exit, Eichkamp, created. The statistical record cites for the third and fourth building stages alone: 3,000 plans from the office of O. M. Ungers, 1,200 construction workers under 21 cranes, 17,000 tons of steel, and 133,000 cubic meters of concrete. In short: building activity to the tune of about a million marks a day. A gross of 60,000 square meters was built over the course of the past eight years. With no one taking notice. Because, this building remains an understatement. Despite its 255 x 270 meter dimensions, it remains utilitarian architecture, refuses to become a form, and presents itself as a built spatial system which is limitlessly, mix-and-match expandable.

The "Southern Trade Fair Extension" is a complex make up of three parallel, double-loaded wings spanning east-west, and one wing spanning north-south as a border to Messedamm. The courtyards between the east-west wings are linked at each end by mechanical stories above the driveways, an approximation of the completely closed block with which Ungers originally won the competition. The visitor doesn't notice the block structure at first; instead, he is confronted with a modular structure which is too huge to take in all at once. The architecture, he says to himself, allows for everything, for every sort of use, even for distortion or decoration.

The building complex has been, without exception, written over with a three-meter square grid divided into fields of 2.50x2.50 meters and bands of 0.50 m width. This grid becomes visible on ceilings, interior walls, floor coverings and facades. On the facades it is ubiquitous. A net of steel lesenes covers the building and borders the square, brick-red ceramic panels, white stucco panels in the courtyards and the dark window surfaces. And yet the square's demands, often enough celebrated in Ungers's facades, have been rescinded by almost endless interconnections. Stated differently: the square, immeasurably repeated, could have been any other form. And since here different functions are not equalized behind large squares, but rather a neutral box had to be perfectly clad, Ungers has created a notably pure building.

The new trade fair buildings exclaim that they are no more than a backdrop, one which effectively forms an urban border for the oval of the Summer Garden, allows Richard Ermisch's buildings to stand in the foreground, emphasizes the Marshall House as a 1950's jewel, and leaves the existing trade fair extensions additions to, and bearing the signature of the International Congress Center, untouched as witnesses of the 1970's.

Hans Poelzig and Martin Wagner had demanded that their 1929 design for the display forum at the foot of the radio tower make an "unforgettable impression". Ungers has done the opposite. He holds back, even as far as height is concerned. The halls make use of the site's northeast-southwest

Mechanical stories run perpendicular to the wings and close off the block. Views through the ca. 250 meter long courtyards. Although the red ceramic fields were, for financial reasons, replaced by white stucco panels in the courtyards, the building has profited from the change

The exhilarating
view from the upper
driveway to the lower
level and vice-versa

Hall 7, urban border
of Messedamm,
east facade

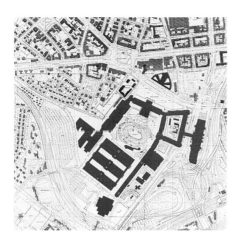

Site plan:
Remnants of the complex
by Martin Wagner and
Hans Poelzig encircling
the summer garden; the
ICC and the connecting
halls. Minuscule at the
edge of the summer gar-
den: the Marshall House.
The new complex creates
a terminal point for the
summer garden. Hall 7
extends the urban border
to Messedamm

Floor plans of halls 1–6
(called Building A) and
of hall 7 at the +/- 0.00
level to a scale of 1:3000

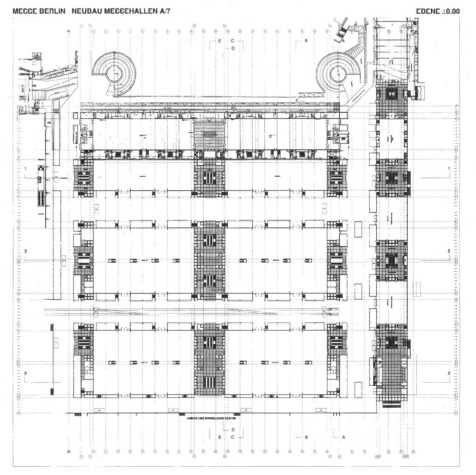

The black boxes of an exhibition hall. Below, the light stairwells

slope and practically burrow themselves into the terrain. The result is two exhibition levels and two circulation levels, at 48,60 m and + 57,60 m above datum level. They are served by two double spindled ramps, one entry and one exit. The height of + 57,60 m corresponds with the pedestrian level of the old exhibition area. Here, the motor lane serves as a wide bridge, from whose parapet the visitor can gaze down and witness the whole of the building's height.

This sleight of hand, combined with the incredible expanse of the grounds, adds drama to the sober lineup of identical halls. Another sensational vista awaits those who visit the trade fair halls when there is no exhibition on. When the halls' axially-located gates are all open, the visitor sees a fivefold repetition of four square panels surrounded by six glass fields, all perspectively diminished. Then, something like trompe l'oeil takes hold, something unreal which makes orientation difficult and which, if one has a feeling for that sort of thing, heightens the impression of a stage set. The empty halls, and that is how those who write about architecture see them, and the empty courtyards, allow a sensation of film sets to arise which is hardly present when trucks are being unloaded or fair visitors make their rounds.

The rounds have been prepared for. When visitors leave the 9-meter high black boxes, they find, in the buildings' axis, daylighted foyers, painted white and, of course, square. The large, light stairwells, with two escalators and two stairs each, not

only serve the two main levels but also mezzanine levels at 53,10 meters. Here are the restrooms and small cafeterias, as well as suspended, not terribly hospitable bridges, over which one can crisscross the whole of the huge building without having to cross the motor lanes.

An expansive "forum", provided that the ice sports stadium be torn down, was planned as the main entrance from the south on the middle circulation axis. With its position perpendicular to the halls, the forum was meant to be their prelude. Realization of the forum has been postponed, whereas the fourth building phase of the halls will be completed this year, earlier than expected. The exhibition area in the trade fair halls at the television tower will than have increased from 100,000 sq. m. to around 160,000 sq. m.

The enormous need for additional space was given from the start. In autumn of 1989, before the fall of the Berlin wall, Oswald Mathias Ungers and Walter Noebel were asked to prepare a study. This was followed by a competition, one of the first after the wall came down, and the same office won over Sir Norman Foster's transparent triangle and eight other designs. It was decided to build a neutral, almost impersonal structure instead of something flashy. The trade fair commission had insisted on a serial architectural system which could be continuously worked on, even during exhibitions, and so be put into use bit by bit. The domino game stipulated for the design was cleverly adopted by the city for its "forfeiting" financing concept, as

Mounting the prefabricated ceramic facade: a total of 64,000 m² of ceramic and stucco facade, 2,000 windows, 400 gates and 14,000 meters of lesenes. Walls, windows, doors and lesenes are all fastened to the subconstruction with the same system. The prefabricated elements are hung into place and fastened without screws. Insulation panels were first affixed to the subconstruction with plugs

Photos:
Erik-Jan Ouwerkerk

costs could not be covered all at once. The city and the trade fair commission would have had to defer construction, which would have threatened their position in the competition with other cities. Forfeiting means that the client lets a bank pay the day-to-day bills as they come in, and that after construction is completed, the bank collects an annual sum consisting of the yearly costs plus interest. These terms made it possible to begin construction of the halls in 1990.

The system of order's ultimo ratio running through design, plan and realization, is the prefabricated ceramic facade. It guarantees the exactness of the 10 mm joints between walls, windows and lesenes, and more than halved the time of assembly. The ceramic tiles measuring 115 x 240 mm with 10 mm joints are factory-mounted on fiber concrete panels in aluminium profile frames. While they are being assembled, insulation panels and aluminium subconstructions can be mounted on the building's concrete or brick walls. To complete the facade, a mobile crane picks the finished panels out of a container and hoists them onto the subconstruction, which can even out differences of plus or minus 5 cm. The laser measurements guarantee the precise 10 mm grid, which in turn guarantees the watertightness and durability of the profiles and, what is more important, the effect of the architecture. Without this astounding precision, the building's order and rationality, two qualities which in this case almost replace the design, would not manifest themselves so conspicuously.

Watching the light-footed construction of the facade, one could imagine that instead of ceramic panels, the square fields could be used for all sorts of information, art and commercial panels. The serial facades make such images easy to envision and the system which allows panels to be mounted without screws would, at any rate, allow for it. The building remains open for further conjecture.

14.1

URBAN DEVELOPMENT STORKOWER STRASSE

Architects	Hascher + Partner, Berlin, with:
Clients	Markus Häffner, Steffen Keck,
	Dorothee Küttner and Nikolaus Tennigkeit
Project	Jost Hurler Beteiligungs- und Verwaltungs-
Management	gesellschaft KG, Munich and
	Drees und Sommer, Cologne
Structural Design	Pirlet und Partner, Cologne
Completion	March 1998

Ulrich Brinkmann
In the Heart of the Urban Development

All photos:
Werner Huthmacher

"Critical reconstruction", "Planwerk Innenstadt", "Berlin style", "The new suburbs", "IBA single family house" —the slogans of recent years indicate the most hotly debated flowers in the blossoming urban garden of Berlin. Large-scale developments, on the other hand, have tended to play a secondary role, graced only with the neologism "heterotope." 3:2:1—a clear disproportion, measured against the total number of Berliners who live—or at least sleep —in the legacy of industrialized urbanism.

No one doubts the need for action. Maintenance projects like the renovation of buildings and the improvement of residential environments and infrastructures are legitimate, but for all their necessity they belong to the realm of the mundane. The breakdown of economic and conceptual frameworks, on the other hand, poses more fundamental questions: how should we approach residential complexes that were projected 20 years ago on fields and swamplands, what conventions should we adopt? Does the perpetually invoked ideal of the "European city" extend to the periphery of the "Berlin of stone," or are isolated architectural events more to the point? Does the credo of "urban diversity" still hold, or is the implantation of large-scale structures our only hope?

The results of the urbanization process are beginning to appear in places like Lichtenberg and Hellersdorf. Statistically, the new centers "Storkower Bogen" and "Hellersdorf Mitte" are about as comparable as a mosquito and an elephant; in

terms of the ideas which shaped their inception, however, they serve well to exemplify the range of urbanistic and architectural possibilities.

Storkower Bogen

"'Wohnkomplex Pfennpfuhl,' large-scale residential development with complex facilities for ca. 46,500 inhabitants, built 1970–80 under the direction of Joachim Näther, Heinz Graffunder, and Roland Korn on a 346-acre site. Residential buildings with 15,518 dwelling units include: 10- and 11-story structures, series QP 71, P 2 Berlin, WBS 70; 5- to 6-story structures, series WBS 70; 14-story residential slab with built-in commercial units; 24-story high-rises with restaurants, and 12-story high-rises, Frankfurt (Oder) type... Community center Storkower Strasse accented with high-rises, serial buildings grouped into a plaza-like configuration, shopping center, service building with youth club, indoor swimming pool, and restaurant "Lichtenberger Wappen" with café, ballroom, and bowling alley; in front a fountain by Rolf Winkler."

Ten years later, Joachim Schulz and Werner Gräbner's dispassionate description of the new development between Leninallee, Ho-Chi-Minh-Strasse, and Storkower Strasse, published in a 1987 guide to Berlin, still suits the residential buildings, but everything else has changed: Leninallee is now called Landsberger Allee, the streets Ho-Chi-Minh-Strasse and Jaques-Duclos-Strasse have become Weissenseer Weg and Möllendorfstrasse, and of the erstwhile community center, only the

The architecture was the basis for the name "Storkow Bow". A square with mature trees is encircled by the new houses; the bus station is on the exterior, shops are within. Aluminium and glass in the midst of prefabricated concrete

indoor swimming pool remains. External changes, to be sure.

Admittedly, in those days I never bothered to stop at the old community center, even on the rare occasions when I found myself traveling along the interrupted north ring of the Stadtbahn. But not to worry—despite all the changes, the ubiquitous ascent from the S-Bahn station still leads to the longest pedestrian bridge in Berlin: 520 m of central perspective opens up along the path leading from the late 19th-century district of Friedrichshain to the prefabricated housing complex in Lichtenberg.

Where Paris would save time by automating forward motion, Berlin lets you walk. Below me, extending far to either side, is the massive slaughterhouse complex, partly decayed, partly still in use, partly already demolished. Still remembering the passage from Döblin's "Alexanderplatz" — "this is light, my dear pigs, that is the ground, just snuffle and root, a few minutes more" — looking, musing, I inadvertently cross over into new territory and suddenly notice the 13 stories rising up to greet Friedrichshain. With the extension of the pedestrian bridge, the passage between the district center "Storkower Bogen" and the S-Bahn station could hardly be more unobtrusive.

Then comes a fork in the road: further along the bridge to the new office towers on Franz-Jacob-Strasse, or to the right and down a few steps to the plaza? I choose the plaza. It provides access to all the consumer amenities the center has to offer: the stores "Connys Container" and "Plauener Spitze,"

the familiar chains Foto-Quelle and Lotto-Toto, a post office and theater box office. Two curved buildings provide the inspiration for the name "Storkower Bogen" (The Storkow Bow): the larger of the two, an office building, marks the edge of the plaza on the busy thoroughfare Storkower Strasse and the bus station to the rear, while the smaller one, on Rudolf-Seiffert-Strasse, accommodates 14 dwellings. Businesses occupy the ground floors of each, as well as the ground and upper stories of the office towers. Only the full-grown chestnut trees contrast with all the newness. They are leftovers "from before," and their preservation was one of the explicit goals of the architectural firm Hascher, winner of the competition for the new sub-center in 1992; a sensible idea, for they give the plaza an air of the old and well-established.

Accepting the invitation of lawn, water, and wooden terrace to tarry a while, one notices that the bridge and trees are not the only elements that integrate the large complex into its environment. First of all, there are adept transitions of scale. From the 22-story residential tower on the west side of Franz-Jacob-Strasse, the silhouette drops to the 13 stories of the office building, falling again to the 6-story structures at the edge of the plaza; east of Seiffert-Strasse, it rises once more to the 11-story residential buildings. Further down Franz-Jacob-Strasse, the rows of offices correspond to the 5-story residential buildings behind the high-rise, but remain a unified form in their monotactic rhythm.

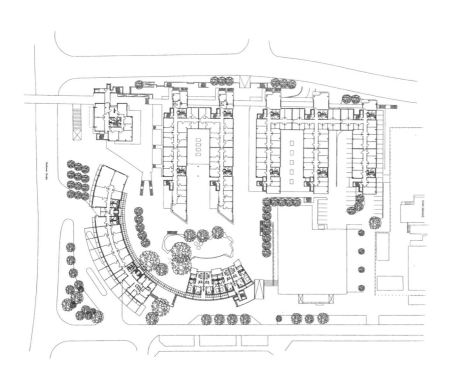

The integration is successful at the spatial level as well. The plaza is unconstrained by any geometric ideal; the autarky of the circular form is diffused by the rows of buildings, and is only suggested anyway (outer radius = residential building, inner radius = offices). The plaza holds its own almost casually: gaps in the office structure open up passages to the bus station, while the rows of buildings lengthen the paths leading from the residential area to the plaza; the small residential building seems almost like an accessory. The indoor swimming pool, a single-story structure left over from the original development, serves effortlessly as a northern boundary for the plaza, without sealing off the adjacent open space connecting "Storkower Bogen" with the former main center on Anton-Saefkow-Platz. And, just as the office complex seeks a link with the larger urban context via the extended pedestrian bridge, so the plaza level is integrated into the surrounding structure in a self-evident, even elegant way.

Such interconnections not only provide structural benefits for Storkower Bogen, but also visually strengthen its identity. The omnipresent view of the prefabricated residential buildings counterbalances the "southern German"-seeming architecture of the new buildings; the grayish brown of the older residential towers reflects in the aluminium and glass of the facades, relieving them of their cool neutrality. The carefully stacked buildings shun visible contact with the ground, as if they could rethink their position at any time. In and of

itself, the high-rise may represent the weakest member of the ensemble: its proportion and functionalistic dismemberment refuse to exploit the expressive potential inherent in a building of that size. Its reserve is conducive to friendly relations with the much taller residential tower behind, but also juxtaposes an "architecture of detail" to the latter's ungainly form. On the whole, it seems to me that with its clean structure, careful detailing, and differentiation of scale, "Storkower Bogen" profits in a double respect from the neutral backdrop of the 1970s high-rises: it needs them as a contrast in order to show itself to advantage, but also as a calming influence. Under the circumstances, a more felicitous, symbiotic partnership could hardly be imagined. The same holds true for the elaborate circulation system between the rows of offices: considered in isolation, the plethora of bridges, catwalks, ascents, and descents may recall the urbanistic ideals of the 1970s, but the austere slabs around confine this eloquence to the limited area of the sub-center.

Economically, the 120 million DM investment doesn't seem to have paid off yet: the sixth edition of the neighborhood magazine "Bogen" trumpeted the call for a "commercial offensive in Storkower Bogen," noting: "We need entrepreneurial daring!" In its efforts to boost the latter, the management is willing to go to unusual lengths: three storefront locations will soon be awarded to candidates with unusual business ideas—at first rent-free, later scaled to profit.

The visitor, however, notices nothing of the necessity for such involvement. Inimitably and affectionately nicknamed "Storki," Storkower Bogen's function as an urban center is already unmistakable: in the afternoons, older people rest on the benches while younger ones linger on the wooden platform by the water; in the shops and on the plaza, the generations and intentions mix.

Storkower Bogen represents an urban development cast from a single mold and realized by a single investor — a concept perhaps little suited to current ideals of incremental urban growth. As a public space, however, it holds its own, integrating this built alternative to the "official" architecture of Berlin into the surroundings more effortlessly and unpretentiously than the photos may suggest.

14.2

HELLERSDORF MITTE

Clients   MEGA Entwicklungs- und Gewerbeansiedlungs - AG
                  Partners:
                  ITAG-Immobilien-Treuhand- und Vermögensanlage AG
                  Dr. Görlich GmbH
                  Rentaco-Unternehmensgruppe
                  R&W Immobilienanlagen GmbH
                  Otremba Unternehmensgruppe
Urban Design   Brandt & Böttcher, Berlin
City hall
Hellersdorf   Brandt & Böttcher, Berlin
Multiplex-Cinema Jürgen Sawade, Berlin
Alice Salomon
Fachhochschule   Bernhard Winking, Hamburg
Mark(t)
Brandenburg   Walter A. Noebel, Berlin
Shopping Center   Monika Krebs, Berlin
Private
Medical Center   Monika Krebs, Berlin
Apartment and   Liepe & Steigelmann,
Office Building   Schattauer & Tibes, both Berlin
Apartment and   HPP – Hentrich, Petschnigg & Partner KG,
Office Building   Hielscher & Derksen, both Berlin
Apartment and
Office Building   Christine Jachmann, Berlin
Apartment and
Office Building   Dorner & Partner, Nagold

Hellersdorf Mitte

Continuing on the S-Bahn to Frankfurter Allee and changing lines eastward, we arrive in another world: the Hellersdorf center elevates East-Berlin's newest large-scale development to the status of "European city." A mere look at the Falk supplemental city map II, d/e 19, is revealing: the dense configuration north of the Hellersdorf subway station leaves no room for street names and has to be numbered; the legend appears on the Hönow fields. Even Berlin's marvel of historic urbanism behind the Hackescher Markt seems loosely woven in comparison.

Another analogy suggests itself: like the more or less contemporary debis project on Potsdamer Platz, the differentiated street and plaza spaces cut the coherent "pochée" into blocks of varying geometry. The dimensions of the project, marketed under the name "Helle Mitte" (Bright Center), are smaller than those of Potsdamer Platz, but dizzyingly large in comparison to Lichtenberg—for those who prefer solid data to mere appearances, the 14 dwellings of quiet "Storki" contrast with a total of 1,000 in Hellersdorf, while the line for "area in sq. m." bears the number 320,000 instead of 35,000. The overall volume of investment is 20 times as great. For 2.2 billion DM, 76 acres of fallow land will radiate urban splendor—coming in second after Potsdamer Platz in the battle of the Berlin construction sites.

From 1986 to 1990, the East German government built 42,000 dwellings here in a new, special-ly-founded district. Time ran out for the completion of the district center, however, and when the Wall fell, a veritable small city had to travel 15 km to Alexanderplatz to run its daily errands. The resumption of building opened up the opportunity to expand the new ideal of the "European city" beyond the one-time reconstruction of the historic city center and adapt it to everyday life. Down with cityscape and functional monoculture, was the call; give us streets instead of transit lines, houses instead of meanders — in short, give us a city, not a housing project.

Accordingly, in their design, Brand & Böttcher, winners of the 1992 competition, invoked every conceivable image to breathe life into the abstract ideal. A finely articulated structure of "boulevards" and "ring avenues," "gallery streets" and "alleys," an "Italian quarter" and a "French quarter," "open-air and flower market" mingled Milan with the Middle Ages, Paris with Vienna, the bistro with the coffee house—a double- and triple-exposed tour of "The City Image." The monumental high point was the "Spanish plaza" inspired by Salamanca: opening toward the large park in the south and accessed by irregularly spaced streets, a homogeneous enclosure was to maintain its spatial potency. The structure of the complex concealed this plaza setting, but two high-rises on the "Rathausplatz" and the "Pariser Platz" were to signal the "hidden" districts. Despite the idealization, the jury deemed the extension of existing streets and the addition of two diagonals an adequate

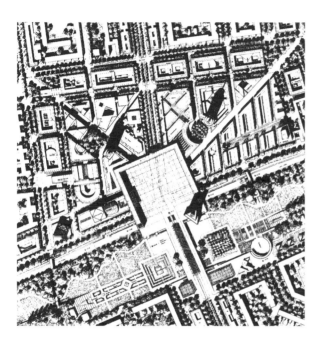

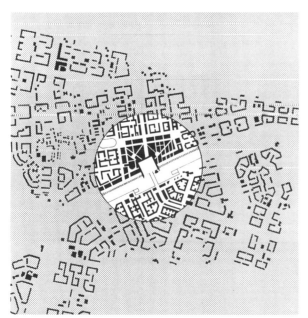

Lil Dagover Lane:
Atrium/Cinestar and
Mark(et) Brandenburg;
Fritz Lane Square:
the new town hall.
Alice Salomon Square:
colonnades with the
neighboring doctor's
offices.
Below: isometrical plan
and site plan showing
urban design

approach to the scale and structure of the existing residential areas — the squaring of the circle, as it were; simultaneous renunciation and completion.

"Public-private-partnership" was the catchword for the realization of the design; the private developer was Entwicklungs- und Gewerbeansiedlungs-AG, fittingly abbreviated MEGA AG. Controlled by a steering committee led by the Senate Building Direction, MEGA AG relieved the city of responsibility for all circulation measures and in return was compensated with plots in the planning area, whose total current market value corresponded to the expenses incurred. These parcels could then be built on or sold at will by MEGA AG; a similar measure was suggested for Potsdamer Platz as well, but never put into effect.

"Helle Mitte" promises a kind of "instant urbanism": not just shops and leisure facilities, but also dwellings, offices, and public buildings—none of it strictly segregated, but combined and layered at close range. Does the function of such a "center" automatically change with the ideal that informs it? By now the first pieces of the mosaic have been put into place; prominent and not-so-prominent architects have been allowed to make their contribution, and the Hellersdorf population has been given opportunity to familiarize itself with the new amenities on its doorstep — see for yourself.

For a while yet, the first impression will be sobering. The hoped-for perspectives from the 100 m square "Plaza Major" can be set aside for the moment, for as yet no Spanish plaza greets us with

Alice Salomon Square,
still unfinished. The
Alice Salomon Vocational
School was opened in
October 1998.
Far left:
view of the housing
complex north of Janusz
Korczak Strasse

the open arms of its three sides. The east and west edges of the Alice-Salomon-Platz show only fragments, while Stendaler Strasse plows eccentrically through the north side—at about the place where the town hall stands in Salamanca. Another public facility enlivens the space: in the winter semester, the 1,000 students of the "Alice Salomon School of Social Work and Social Education" moved into their new building, planned by Bernhard Winking. The neutral segment of wall though, facing the plaza, is identifiable as a vocational school only to the initiated. A different site, or at least visible articulation as a public building, would have done greater justice to the institution's significance for Hellersdorf — as well as the Salamancan model.

But when will the subway tunnel be covered over? And when will the proposed triumvirate of high-rises begin to provide orientation? A realization assessment recommended the completion of the large plaza in the first building phase, and rightly so. Morosely, I note the delay and slip through the western diagonal to Fritz-Lang-Platz — to the city hall, one of the projected towers.

Instead of metropolitan visions, I find a 7-story cube — built not by a public agency, but by MEGA AG: the district occupies "its" town hall as a tenant. What architectural symbols Berlin will still need after the district reform is anybody's guess. Yet there is comfort in the fact that the stump can grow: the option of increasing the height to 14 stories was included in the building permit. In any case, Brand & Böttcher did succeed in smuggling in a council

chamber, and despite the austerity of the means the bullish cube still asserts its presence on the plaza as a public building. Urban culture has yet to make an appearance, but a library and cultural center are promised for the site opposite—clearly privileging the small square over the "Plaza Major."

Thanks to these facilities, Hellersdorf Mitte is frequented not only by customers, but also by citizens, elevating the traditional urbanistic spatial typology out of the quagmire of profit-enhancing Romanticism. Fritz-Lang-Platz has already proven its suitability for district festivals; the first demo will dignify it as a "genuine city square."

But is there a "spiritual center," a "city crown" or comparable ornament? One hesitates to ascribe such qualities to the town hall. But no church is planned, and the high-rises are still unbuilt; nor can traces of a "temple of consumerism" be found. One may apostrophize Berlin's first new multiplex movie theater as a "cathedral of leisure": while the CineStar is only one of a number of five-story buildings, the contemplative tranquility of the block, planned by Jürgen Sawade, gives it a sense of scale that distinguishes it from its surroundings. Here, more than a cinema has been created. Too bad it's invisible from Alice-Salomon-Platz, concealed by the structures surrounding the plaza.

Almost all the other buildings follow the urban streetfront scheme: shops on the ground floor, dwellings above. This arrangement serves not only to banish the "downtown ghosts" that turn Friedrichstrasse into a ghost town after closing hours,

The cultural heart along Stendaler Strasse. In its midst, the covered atrium. Below left: the shopping mall within the block, parallel to Fritz Lang Strasse

but also to functionally integrate the city center into the residential blocks surrounding it. The interconnecting paths, much-praised in the competition design, do in fact contribute to this integration; one strolls almost inadvertently into neighboring quarters. The response to the existing five-story panel buildings is successful in terms of scale as well: the new blocks confront the older structures self-confidently, but unobtrusively.

Finally, "diversity" was supposed to place the constraints of urbanity on commerce as well: the department store at the northeast corner of Alice-Salomon-Platz is supplemented by smaller shops east of Stendaler Strasse, a market hall with Brandenburg wares in Block 11, and chain stores on the ground floors of the other blocks. Block 18, however, fell prey to the enemy: the investors placed greater faith in the Berlin weather forecast than the Mediterranean promise of the site names, and built — a mall. Predictably, since the businesses only want a single entrance for security reasons, the streets are nearly empty of passers-by, and even Alice-Salomon-Platz finds itself at the rear of this urbanistic "prime location." Meanwhile, the shops in Block 24 hope to be able to profit from the attraction by pasting their display windows onto the plaza and opening their entrances to the mall. Maybe, just maybe, the urban spirit will prove itself stronger and the completion of the plaza will correct this situation.

Yet an indisputably urban atmosphere prevails in Hellersdorf, one that—perhaps on Lil-Dagover-Gasse, between the "big-city" buildings of Sawade and Noebel—evokes the atmosphere of places in downtown Berlin. Following Stendaler Strasse a few hundred meters to the north, however, the visitor stops thunderstruck in his tracks: here, right at the edge of Berlin, the tiny community of Eiche approved a gigantic shopping center several years ago. The belly of this whale, swimming amidst of a giant sea of sheet metal and parking lots, houses the buying frenzy that reduces the human being to a "consumer"—and for which the shop owners of "Helle Mitte" perhaps also yearn. Now it is up to the inhabitants of Hellersdorf themselves to weigh the alternatives and vote for one solution or the other.

Chronology

of Building Events from January to December 1998

All In all, the past year was not an especially remarkable one. If you think about it, 1998 was the last year before the very last year before the turn of the millennium, and as Alfred Kerr noted in 1898 — exactly one hundred years ago — such years tend to be marked by "the presence of a flourishing backwardness." There was, of course, the momentous decision to reduce the number of districts in Berlin from the current 23 to a total of 12 at the turn of the century; in the year 2001, this will presumably lead to all kinds of marriages of convenience and compulsion. Not so in Lichtenberg and Hohenschönhausen, where the mayors — both from the PDS party — betrothed their respective districts already in August of this past year. There are no other weddings to report, but we did observe an increase in memorial celebrations. Whether cause for joy or lament, this was the year of Fontane (the 100th anniversary of his death), Brecht (his 100th birthday), and those fallen in the revolution of 1848, as well as Münchhausen twice over and a number of new monuments and busts. The nicest of the monuments are the benches. In February, the first of the fine little bank buildings opened at Pariser Platz. February also saw the students' futile attempt — after the failure of their winter strikes — to take over the Berlin FDP party by joining it en masse. In March, Christoph Schlingensief founded his "Last Chance Party," and Berlin and Brandenburg took their chances with a shared development plan.

This was election year in the Federal Republic of Germany. Late March saw a mild conflict over whether those killed during the revolution of 1848 should be appropriated for the plaza in front of Brandenburg Gate or the one behind the Maxim-Gorki-Theater. From April through the entire summer, the good and bad news accumulated regarding the building activities, the federal eagle-to-be, and the representatives of the German federal states, all of whom have now arrived on the scene in Berlin. Already Augustine knew that "all this is true in a certain way because it is false in a certain way," and now, in our third year, the writers of the chronology know it even better than before.

November and December may seem like the most peaceful and uneventful months of the year, but this is true only in part. Of course Berlin does quiet down a little when the first snow falls early, as it did this year. On the other hand, it may also have something to do with the weariness of the chroniclers as we approach the end of this year; presumably, the really important events have long since cast their shadow in the form of project approvals, contract signings, ground-breakings, cornerstone-layings, chancellor's visits, client bankruptcies, etc., and have already forced their way into the previous months of the chronology.

The only real news is the falling glass facades of the Galeries Lafayette. Furthermore, deadlines loom. All reports — even those from December 31, 1998 — are due at the publishers in flawless, proofread form, in both German and English, promptly on Monday, January 4, 1999.
The Editors

What is Berlin? The sculptor who at three o'clock in the morning, after his fourth bottle, smashes a chair against the wall and falls to his knees sobbing, wanting to know how he can become a Jew this very second. Berlin is the journalist who hugs you because next to him, you are the only person left on earth who knows that in Hamsun's "Mysterien," Nagel carries dirty laundry around with him in his violin case. Berlin is Osram, where the technical writer Artur Fürst was received by the notables of the firm during his visits there and where his wife Gertrude, my mother, was a slave laborer ten years later. Berlin is a sudden gust of wind, whose stench makes your stomach double up in anguish. And Berlin is every gray tenement with bullet holes that resembles my parents' house on Kaiserallee…

Peter Fürst, 1998

1-1-1998

8 million guests were accommodated in Berlin in 1997, which comes to an average of 21,917,81 guests per day, corresponding to an increase of 8.18 % compared to last year, which converts into 1,638,83 additional guests daily.

1-1-1998

Bonn gets a new government office: a "Federal Office for Construction and Regional Planning" was created in order to unite the former office of Federal Construction Management (Berlin) with the Federal Research Institute for Regional Study and Planning (Bonn) in Bonn. The new office has 560 staff members, of which 180 may work in Berlin. Just who gets to do this is now under negotiation.

January 1998

Ambitions reciprocal: The Berlin Senate Building Administration is going to supplement the design statutes and rendering regulations for "Unter den Linden" Street with a new system of rules intended to lay down the

1-1-1998

The German Conference of Cities (DST, for Deutscher Städtetag) is moving back to Berlin, where it was founded in 1905 and had its seat until 1933. After had been refounded in 1946, the headquarters for the DST was set up in Cologne; since January 1, the main business office is operating again in the newly renovated Ernst-Reuter-Haus in Tiergarten. Staff members (according to unclear, but hopeful, reports) will orient themselves to the rhythm of the federal government's moving schedule, so that the lot of them will gradually wind up in Berlin. The German Conference of Cities represents the interests of 5,600 cities (with more than 50 million inhabitants) vis-a-vis the federal government and both houses of parliament.

1-2-1998

Thirteen years of "Scheinbar Varieté" ("Shine Bar Varieté"), at Monumentenstrasse 9 in Schöneberg. Jugglers, mimes, clowns, chansoniers, cabaretists, and artistes arrived as youthful talent, worked their way to stardom, and (starting today) return to Berlin for a one-month ceremony.

1-4-1998

Dr. Hermann Stöhr, one of the quiet heroes of the Resistance, is honored; on the occasion of his hundredth birthday, the square at the main railway station in Friedrichshain is given his name, and a porcelain plate embedded in a boulder chronicles the main points of his life story. Hermann Stöhr worked in the International League of Reconciliation and in the eastern Berlin section of the Social Welfare Working Group. He lost his job in 1931, and in 1939 he was sentenced to one year in prison as a conscientious objector. Since, even there, he was not prepared to take the "Führer's Oath" of allegiance, he was hanged at Plötzensee in 1940.

Early January

Balance sheets: DM 170 million flowed out of the property sales made by Berlin's municipal districts. To whom? And where did the money go? According to the Finance Senator's regulations, half should go to the districts and half to the city. That is, unless one of the recurring budgetary freezes is imposed, as happened last autumn; in that case, the city gets everything… that is, unless the district has already spent the money quick and proper or issued a proper declaration to that effect by December 31, 1997 (First Circular), or by January 31, 1998 (Second Circular) or by March 31, 1998 (option of the Mayor's advisers), but then only as per cash receipt. The district could do even better by avoiding any statements in its budget draft entering the proceeds of property sales on the books as "additional unanticipated revenues," that is, unless…

1-1-1998

Debit and Credit in the Berlin Zoo—the annual balance sheet at the start of the year. The aggregate of animals is the zoo's capital, so they—like in any other stock company's assets—have to be counted, entered into the books, and inspected by auditors. Errors in the aquarium (2,924 fish, 433 reptiles, 412 amphibians, and 6,374 invertebrates) cannot be ruled out…

stipulations governing how competitive designs for street furniture should be submitted. The primacy of the historical is undisputed. At the same time, Berlin's kiosk king Hans Wall is presenting his new collection of street furniture with the "Thinking Waiting Hall 2000" (design: Josef Paul Kleihues), using this furniture to equip his subsidiaries in London, Paris, Rome and Tokyo, signing a contract with St. Louis, and baiting New York with a promise to exhibit his ready-to-use street furniture in Harlem at first. After that he is marketable at the stock exchange.

January 1998

Reported late: The tradition-rich Berlin cinema "Colosseum" on Schönhauser Allee reopened last December, after a year-and-a-half renovation, with ten theater halls and 2,814 seats. Architects: Architektengruppe medium, Hamburg. Initiator and developer: Artur Brauner; cost: DM 56 mill.

1-6-1998

Prelude to the series of events commemorating the 50th anniversary of the Free University of Berlin. American ambassador John Kornblum speaks about "Berlin and the Completion of Europe."

1-6-1998

Mission possible: The City Mission inaugurates the "Hotel Atrium" at the Friedrichstrasse railway station. 79 rooms were set up in the remodeled building that formerly accommodated the "Headquarters for the Guest House Mission" (through 1933), the "Christian Waiter's Home Association" (until 1945), the officers of the Red Army (after 1945), and the state-owned collective enterprise "VEB Gaststätten HO-Berlin" (through 1989). The house itself dates back to 1861.

1-7-1998

Contract negotiations have been concluded for the Theater am Schiffbauerdamm as a performance site for the Berliner Ensemble. Rolf Hochhuth, representing the Ilse Holzapfel Foundation as owner, has conceded an annual lease of DM 360,000 to the Berlin Senate (and withdrawn his demand for DM 1.3 million). The city of Berlin is responsible for building maintenance. The rental agreement is valid until 2012, and it will be possible to extend the contract through 2027. The Foundation maintains the right to use the theater when the Ensemble is on vacation. In 1998 in order to commemorate October 16, 1943, the day the transport of Berlin's Jews to concentration camps began — Hochhuth's "The Deputy" will be staged. According to its statue, the Berliner Ensemble will perform works by politically engaged or socially critical 20th century authors. Negotiations with Claus Peymann, whom Berlin

1-9-1998

Federal Presidential renunciation. No bungalow in the Schlosspark. Apparently (at least this is how one must interpret the otherwise so modest Federal President's immodest wish), he does not feel comfortable in Schloss Bellevue. Readers of Tagesspiegel are familiar with the groundplan of the residential wing. It seems long and narrow. Too few baths. Renovation and remodeling are required. Where should the Federal President go in between? Today, any plan to build an interim bungalow in Tiergarten was filed away for good. The Presidential wishes remain the same.

1-10-1998

"Münchhausen. From Tall Tales to Global Bestseller," two exhibits and a symposium, put on in the two library buildings (east and west) housing the Staatsbibliothek. The library at Unter den Linden is exhibiting the most comprehensive collection of Münchhausen editions so far; at the library on Potsdamer Strasse, Münchhausen illustrations are on exhibit (woodcuts by Doré, melancholy drawings by Kubin, picture sheets from the "Gründerzeit" of the 1870s, cigarette and margarine albums from the Thirties and Fifties).

1-11-1998

Last day for the exhibit "Pictures of Germany — Art in a Divided Country" in the Martin-Gropius-Bau. Over four months the visitor count came to 150,000, and in its final days the exhibit was open until midnight. To conclude the exhibition, a lecture series — "Prospects for Dealing with Cultural Difference" — whose final evening was again supplied with persons who, by virtue of the power they wield and the offices they hold, are supposed to be developing and implementing just such prospects: Christoph Stölzl, Director of the German Historical Museum and entrusted with the birthday exhibition for the Republic, "Unity and Right and Freedom;" Ulrich Eckhardt, Festival Director and Commissioner of Festivities before, during, and after the turn of the millennium; Bernd Kauffmann, General Agent for Weimar as a European Cultural City in 1999; Martin Roth, EXPO-2000-Manager.

It's Got an Air *Hans Unverzagt*

It's got an air, a kind of global touch
about its being bent and stretched, a vision
of calm, composed rapidity — and much
of modern energetic repetition.

It's got an air of being light, *légèr*,
though firmly standing up: a sort of rental
accomodation shelf — yet, as it were,
a house, a place, and nothing incidental.

It's got a moderate monomanic air,
a flexibly disposed ability
for change and permanence and seems aware
of self-reducing self-esteem. — To me

it's got an air of being well prepared
to presence in *Marzahn*. It does'nt play
a futurism game for being stared
at. — *Assmann, Salomon & Scheidt* will stay.

would like to see as director of Brecht's old theater beginning with the 1999/2000 season, will be continued.

1-7-1998

Seventieth birthday of the Comedian Harmonists, celebrated at the Komödie am Kurfürstendamm with the show "Veronica, Spring Is Here." Standing ovations. Boisterous house. Since december 25, 1997 the film "Comedian Harmonists" with Meret and Ben Becker has been showing in cinemas. The members of the famous Berlin sextet of the Twenties supposedly never saw each other again after their group was forcibly split up in 1935 (performance ban for the three Jewish members). Longtime visitors to "Zwiebelfisch" on Savignyplatz know Robert Biberti, the bass, who could always be found up front on the righthand side of the entrance.

1-9-1998

As of today, a Japanese macaque monkey is lodging at his swinging bachelor pad in Biesdorf-Süd. He does not hail from the zoo (according to the zoo's annual balance sheet) and local keepers of "dangerous animals from wildlife species subject to compulsory registration" are also not acquainted with him. For the duration of his stay, Constable Peter Zurko from Police Section 72 has been put in charge of the "primate directive" and released from his other daily duties.

1-10-1998

Attempt at getting a higher assessment of the big housing projects around the edge of Berlin by loosening non-occupancy charges, in other words, by bringing rents for small, medium, and high incomes closer in line. The goal is mixed-income housing, which is supposed to be fortified by improvements in the residential environment and security measures. The entire package is called "integrated promotion".

Through March 14th. Münchhausen shorthand: In Berlin in 1781 there appeared the "Vade Mecum [Handbook] for Merry Folk," a first collection of Münchhausen stories, followed by a Berlin pirate edition, then by "Baron Münchhausen's Narrative of His Marvellous Travels and Campaigns in Russia," written by a man who had been driven into destitution by his wife and into exile in England, one Rudolf Erich Raspe, whose version was then expanded and re-translated into German by Gottfried August Bürger. The Baron — having thus been propelled to world-wide fame — died as an embittered man in 1797. Enough Berlin connections? Not quite. Wilhelm Hausenstein is missing ...

The Martin-Gropius-Bau will be closed for eleven months owing to renovations, and it will then reopen with "Unity and Right and Freedom." The Berlinische Galerie, temporarily without a home, is taking its precious collection on tour to Brussels, Geneva, Edinburgh, Porto, Madrid, and other places. Cf. BBA '97, July 2 and beginning of December.

1-11-1998

As of today, Berlin's public museums have a new schedule of opening hours: daily, from 10 a.m. to 6 p.m., Sunday until 5 p.m. The balance sheet for last year sounds positive; in Berlin, the visitor count went up by 10 per cent, while elsewhere (according to the comparative study of 5,040 German museums), it declined. Favorite of all: the Pergamon Museum.

1-13-1998

Developer's prize for "High Quality" goes to the low-energy house of architects Assmann, Salomon, and Scheidt, Berlin, which they built in cooperation with the engineering firm ARUP GmbH. The 20 m high and 85 m long building behind a glass front facing south contains two- and three-room apartments. Client: Wohnungsbaugesellschaft Marzahn.

For here, once, in the fateful moment when it was decided whether Berlin would exist or not, the fable of the Baron of Münchhausen came true: it pulled itself out of the swamp by his own pigtail. And that's not all: it wasn't even there to begin with, but had to put itself there in the first place.
Wilhelm Hausenstein, 1932

1-13-1998

Construction start for expanding the Rudower Chaussee with a 1,700 m long segment stretching through the Adlershof Business and Science City (Wirtschafts- and Wissenschaftsstadt Adlershof, or wista for short). The 17 m wide street will be broadened to 44 m, a medium strip for two streetcars is envisioned, and construction work will go on until the year 2000 (though without otherwise impairing use of the street).

1-13-1998

Once more, the memorial for the murdered Jews of Europe (cf. Holocaust Memorial, bba '96, June 25, 1995) is contemplated, discussed, written up, but not resolved. Four designs are still up for debate. They will be exhibited starting today in the Marstall-Galerie, where the artists will explain their concepts. Peter Eisenman and Richard Serra propose a walkable labyrinth made

1-14-1998

...Abandoning Berlin with its thick sand: Klaus Töpfer, Federal Building Minister and the federal government's commissioner for the move from Bonn to Berlin, takes leave. He assumes the post of Executive Director for the un environmental organization unep and will be in charge of the un Secretariat for Urban Development and Housing Questions. His successor will be Eduard Oswald, formerly parliamentary manager of the Bavarian csu state delegation in the Bundestag. Oswald promises that he, with a staff of 460 (or roughly 80 per cent of the personnel working for the Federal Building Ministry) will move to Berlin, that he will see to it that the move takes place in a timely fashion, that he also wants to be a reliable partner for Berliners, and that "the whole country will profit from Berlin's role as capital city."

1-14-1998

Opening of the exhibit "Cost- and space-saving construction" in the daz (Deutsches Architekturzentrum — German Architecture Center) Berlin. For exemplary objects of private developers there is a dm 100,000 promotional prize awarded by home savings bank badenia Bausparkasse ag.

1-16-1998

Two hundred years ago on this day, on January 16, 1798, the numbering of houses in Berlin was ordered by cabinet decree. The system went: Consecutive numbering, from the vantage point of the city center, moving upward on the right and downward on the left. Kurfürstendamm heeds the regulation to this day, even if the operative rule has become, in the meantime, "even numbers on the right and odd numbers on the left, alternating and across the street from each other, moving outward from the historical urban core," supplemented by the rider "properties on the remaining streets are to be numbered clockwise with the urban core as pivot."

Through January 31

Two exhibits by the American photographer and Berlin connoisseur Will McBride in the Gallery "argus fotokunst" on Marienstrasse 25 and in "argus II" at Sophienstrasse 32, both in the Mitte district. During the Sixties, Will McBride was part of Berlin society and photographed friends, everyday life, festivals, the city. His first famous photoessay (never individual pictures, always picture series) from 1959/1961 registers the feeling of the time: economic miracle, incipient rebellion, the Berlin Wall. "twen," the most spectacular German periodical of those years, was his forum.

out of countless, narrowly placed squares concrete columns (lecture 1.13); Jochen Gerz lines up 39 steel masts with the inscription "Why" in all the languages spoken by the persecuted Jews of that era, with the aim of transforming the visitors' answers into a conceptual and daily changing form of commemoration (lecture 1.16); Daniel Libeskind varies his design for the Jewish Museum and erects a high wall interlaced with empty spaces (lecture 1.19); Gesine Weinmiller attempts to articulate emptiness and silence on an oblique plane with scattered wall panes (lecture 1.23). The decision in favor of one of the designs, slated for January 27, is being postponed.

January 1998

Further symptoms of a long but steady development: Synthélabo, a French pharmaceutical firm, is moving its Germany headquarters from Munich to Berlin; Nishiden, a Japanese technology firm, will open an office in Berlin; the Berliner Bank's bb-Mobilien-Leasinggesellschaft (Property Leasing Company) was set up in Berlin on January 1 of this year.

January 1998

A lease on life has been secured for the "Gründerzeitmuseum" with the Charlotte von Mahlsdorf collection. The manor house on Hultschiner Damm will be purchased by the Hellersdorfer Förderverein (Hellersdorf Promotional Association) and refurbished bit by bit. The Promotional Association had already acquired the collection for the stately sum of dm 523,000.

1-14-1998

Opening night for a series with the highly promising title "Space for Language — Language in Space." Encounters between architects and writers, sponsored by literaturWERKstatt and the Federation of German Architects under the auspices of "For a Modern Berlin: Homeland in the Metropolis." Efforts to cross literature as the interpretation of architecture with architecture as the interpretation of past and present — efforts always undertaken at the very sites being debated. First showplace and theme: the tv tower on Alexanderplatz. Protagonists: the architect Wolf. R. Eisenraut and the author Jens Sparschuh, in whose novel "Der Zimmerspringbrunnen" ("The Indoor Fountain") the miniature tv tower sinks into a mass of water and is then resurrected as a symbol of the East. Next scheduled event: February 26.

1-16-1998

"Schauplatz Museum" ("Showplace Museum") opens in the Knobelsdorff Wing of the Charlottenburg Palace. "Dichtung und Wahrheit" ("Poetry and Truth") is the theme around which roughly 200 events will be organized by Berlin's forty public museums. The Alte Nationalgalerie, for example, has issued an invitation for three evenings under the motto "The Brief Departure" so it can exhibit the most beautiful pieces in its collections — because, immediately afterward, the building will be shut down for three years. "Showplace Museum" ends on February 15 with a "Long Night of the Museums."

1-16-1998

Rapid transit travelers can take the S-Bahn to Pichelsberg again. The important thing about this is that the new, old, 4.8 km long stretch (S 5, S 75) from Westkreuz station can now reach the Olympic Stadium in 9 minutes, and just at a time when the Herta bsc soccer team is playing in the first division of the Federal League. "Never again u 2" is what the fans were singing on Saturday, January 31, before and after the match Hertha against Vfl Wolfsburg, and "S-Bahn Passes the Hertha-Test" was the headline in "Der Tagesspiegel" the next day. For 17 long years, there was no rapid transit access to the Olympic Stadium, the Deutschlandhalle, and the Waldbühne. Now, the new trade fair convention halls can easily be reached via their own exit in Eichkamp, and even the Deutschlandhalle enjoys a top-flight transit link for the first time. For major events, the S-Bahn can move 21,500 people per hour in 3.3 minutes' time.

1-18-1998

Heinz Hajek-Halke, artist and seaman, photographer and collagist, was rediscovered by the Haus am Waldsee. The exhibit, which opened on December 12, 1997, displays (among other things) his meticulous documentation (previously unknown to many) of the growth of buildings in the Hansaviertel during the Interbau in 1957.

1-19-1998

It's happening today: Demolition work begins on the Victoria Area. Helmut Jahn's long-controversial, 160 m long, 16-story glass bolt at the beginning of Kurfürstendamm, behind Kranzler-Eck-Ensemble (1958 by H. Dustmann) will be built. Offering an open market and an aviary of 700 sq. m the developers recommend their project to be benevolence to the Kudamm stroller. The Deutsche Immobilien Fonds AG (Difa) and Roland Ernst project management are counting on a construction time of 30 months and an investment of DM 650 mill.

1-21-1998

Festive presentation of the annual balance sheet: Building Senator Jürgen Klemann first invites journalists to tour the Reichstag cupola and then to the brand new Dresdner Bank on Pariser Platz. The tour, the food, the numbers—DM 970 mill. in investments, record residential construction (25,000 residential units) at lower prices, investments at the same level in the current year —everything was graciously received.

1-22-1998

Werner Knopp, President of the Prussian Cultural Property Foundation (Stiftung Preußischer Kulturbesitz) takes leave after 21 years. The name "Prussian" is deceptive, and "property" also raises doubts. The foundation is supported by the federal government and the states, and it encompasses leftover property (in other words, museums, palaces, libraries, archival holdings) from the state of Prussia following its dissolution in 1947. In 1989 it expanded to include two national galleries, two Egyptian Museums, two State Libraries etc. In the meantime, the selection of a

1-19-1998

Openings at Aedes East: Buildings by Gatermann + Schossig and ornaments by Thomas Weil.

January 1998

The Berliner Volksbank announces: Its headquarters with a staff of 750 will be installed on the debis Area at Potsdamer Platz, Eichhornstraße 1, in a wing of the building segment designed by Arata Isozaki. The move is planned for the third quarter of 1998. On December 19, 1997 the contract to buy the building with 38,000 sq. m of useable space was signed. Originally, a new building on the Messedamm in Charlottenburg was supposed to be built as headquarters. There is now an empty no-future property.

1-21-1998

Opening at noon: Two exhibits in the foyer of the Prussian Parliament building. They provide information, on the one hand, about the history of the house from 1898 through today, largely furnished from the personal collection of Klaus Friedrich, the manager of the parliamentary administration's technical service; and, on the other hand, about the work surrounding a plenary session, from invitation to recorded minutes.

1-21-1998

Opening in the evening: Exhibit in the Tiergarten's Berlin Pavilion on "Cities in the City, Prefab Construction and Large Housing Projects"—in the series of events sponsored by the Senator for Construction, Housing, and Transportation. Through March 15.

successor failed to happen for the second time. The federal government's choice is the director of the German Historical Museum in Berlin (DHM), Christoph Stölzl, while a majority of states favors the general director of the German Library (DB) in Frankfurt am Main, Klaus-Dieter Lehmann.

1-23-1998

Interim assessment of the master plan. At a meeting of the City Forum, the working results of the "Inner City Plan" are discussed with district mayors and the environmental administration. Where the master plan (intended to prescribe 30 years of urban development) is concerned, there cannot be any expectation of bringing a bill before Berlin's legislative assembly, as was originally planned for 1998. The overarching city planning concept for "Berlin's historic center" is being contested from all sides and for various reasons. Fundamental points of criticism: the traffic concept, with its

narrowing of inner city streets to their historical widths. Or: the "primacy of the city center," in other words, a countervailing power against Berlin's existing structure as a city of many cities. Or: the compression of the inner city through residential property, that is, the sale of public greens and open spaces. The individual projects of the five planning workshops (at the Kulturforum, Molkenmarkt, Spittelmarkt, Breitscheidplatz and Lietzenburger/Schillstrasse) are supposed to be revised this year, with requests adjusted. Exhibit in the Staatsrat (former GDR executive council) building extended through February 13.

But Berlin is a special case. There are no moderate people there; distress has made the spirits restless and unquiet...in an instant, in the twinkling of an eye, they think something through, only to "cut it to shreds" again! There is no repose, no measure or purpose in the quickness of thought and construction of systems.
Sulpiz Boissere, 1815

1-23-1998

Berlin is the "City of Knowledge," the "City of Change," the "City of Logistics." That, at least, is how "Project Future," which is packaging "Berlin's Path Toward the Information Society," would like to see it. In plain language: Following a Senate resolution from last July, an initiative is being started uniting contributions from five circles of experts (in business, the university, and public administration) to work cooperatively on multi-media projects. The most concrete of these: The project "CidS – Computer in die Schulen" ("Computers into the Schools"). With the aid of DM 10 mill. donated by the German Class Lottery Foundation Berlin schools can buy the right kind of equipment to ease their way into the Internet.

1-24-1998

Hundredth anniversary of the German Oriental Society (Deutsche Orientgesellschaft or DOG), founded on January 24th, 1898 (on the birthday of Frederick the Great) in the colonnaded courtyard of the Neues Museum. They had catching up to do. The English and French had already been excavating for half a century. In 1898 it was decided: the DOG will excavate in Babylon. It did so, and it kept digging until 1917, with the active and financial support of Kaiser Wilhelm II.

1-25-1998

The Brecht Year has begun. In Berlin with an exhibit in the Academy of the Arts that is far more vital and Brechtian than the title's quote "...my work is the final song of the millennium, 22 attempts to describe a work." The manager of the Brecht Archive, Erdmut Wizisla, is owed a word of gratitude for the exhibit's structure and catalogue. All the commemorative speeches (of which there were many) are over the top; if just one could keep a distance from all the interpretations and simply let Brecht speak clearly for himself. As a preview of the jubilee year and maybe be the thing that Brecht would have liked most of all: The staging of Brecht's piece "The Bread Shop" by the homeless theater "Die Ratten 07" ("The Rats 07"). The very people who are in the know interpret a piece that interprets their existence. Sturdy. With a battle in the auditorium. A theatrical event.

Brecht makes his debut *Carl Zuckmayer*

And so they could afford to engage two dramatists, who themselves wrote plays and were therefore not ideally suited for mail duty or office work—namely, Bert Brecht and myself. In a theater like this one, the dramatist was either a low-level office clerk who administered the library and so forth, or a more or less intellectual ornament. We were neither. We wanted to make theater ourselves, new theater; we wanted to promote plays, to stage them—wherever possible our own. Brecht showed up only on rare occasions, looking like a cross between a truck driver and a Jesuit schoolboy in his loose-fitting leather jacket. He demanded absolute power, as it were, the right to organize the program according to his theories, to rename the stage the "Epic Smoke Theater," for he maintained that people might even be induced to think if they were allowed to smoke. But since this wasn't permitted, he confined himself to occasionally picking up his check.

1-24-1998

In keeping with the lukewarm January temperatures, an exhibit on "Berlin's Artistic Spring" is opening today in the Ephraim-Palais, in order to commemorate—a good quarter year before its actual anniversary at the beginning of May—the 100th birthday of the Berliner Secession. 220 paintings, prints, and sculptures by artists from the Secession, including Max Liebermann, Lovis Corinth, Oskar Kokoschka, Käthe Kollwitz, Walter Leistikow, Edvard Munch, and Franz Skarbina, were assembled chiefly from the collections of the City Museum.
Through March 23.

Still more important, however, was James Simon, a wealthy Berlin cotton dealer, philanthropist, and the heart of the DOG. After 1900, there were also excavations in Egypt, in the capital city Echnaton starting 1911, where in 1912 the bust of Nefertiti was discovered. The finds belonged to James Simon, the sole financier of the excavations; he donated them to the Neues Museum in 1920. In 1935 all Jewish members of the Society were forced to leave, many others had honor enough to follow, and membership of 1,500 (around 1914) shrank to 150. The commemorative ceremony for the Society's 100th birthday will take place on March 23.

1-26-1998

Just in time for—today's—deadline announcing the procedure for declaring an interest in "Building on the Berliner Schlossplatz," the "Association for the Preservation of the Palace of the Republic" takes its place among the total of 15 investors, including Roland Ernst, Hypo Real, the Fundus Group, the Deutsche Bank along with ECE, Hochtief, Deutsche Immobilien Leasing, and the Verein Stadtschloß e.V. (City Palace Association) with HANSEATICA. Also part of the action: The VDI or Verein Deutscher Ingenieure (Association of German Engineers), which (together with the Fraunhofer Institute and the Gedas automobile consortium) is contemplating a Berlin World Engineering Center.

1-26-1998

Opening of the France Center at the Technical University of Berlin. This implements a resolution passed by the Berlin Senate in January 1995 envisioning a new way of anchoring the city's nearly fifty-year relationship with the Western protecting powers—in the form of cultural-scientific partnerships with Berlin's universities. The John-F.-Kennedy-Institut at the Free University already exists, and a Great Britain Center at the Humboldt University is next.

1-29-1998

With a symbolic avalanche, work starts on renovating the Karstadt department store at Hermannplatz in Neukölln. Over the next two years, the building opened in 1929 will be thoroughly reshaped inside and out. Plans include glazing the facade, tearing down the parking deck on the roof at the corner of Hermannstrasse/Urbanstrasse in favor of two new floors, building a roof terrace, and redesigning the entrance from Hermannplatz subway station. In doing all this, the renovations will allude to the original shape of what was then the most modern department store in Europe (architect: Philip Schäfer). Architects for the remodeling: The firm of Landgraf and Kriegbaum, Berlin. Cost: DM 140 mill.

1-30-1998

Garden designer Hermann Göritz has died at the age of 95. The design that became famous was his Bornstedt garden (which has since come under the protection of landmark conservation laws), in immediate proximity to the palace and garden of Sanssouci, which he built up and cared for with his green thumb beginning in 1937.

1-30-1998

On the 65th anniversary of the National Socialist seizure of power: The premiere of "Speer," a two-person play by Esther Vilar about Hitler's master builder. The performance site: the rooms of the former "General Inspection" office designed by Albert Speer, now among the ruins of the Academy of the Arts on Pariser Platz. Klaus Maria Brandauer staged the piece and plays one of the two roles, but the main role here is performed by the site. Here is where Speer and Hitler kneeled before the monstrous models for rebuilding the Reich capital city

2-3-1998

The Marzahn district has become wealthier to the tune of one new attraction. In the Eisenacher Strasse, Deutsche Telekom puts its first telephone booth using solar and wind energy into operation. A congenial side-effect of this eco-commitment: In out-of-the-way locations, it will now become possible to dispense with costly power hookups.

2-5-1998

Modus, at Wielandstrasse 27–28, issues an invitation to its exhibit "Charles and Ray Eames." By Vitra, in Weil am Rhein, where Eamses' entire estate may be found, the show is restricted to works from the realm of furniture design between the Forties and Seventies. Through March 9.

2-5-1998

The information network linking Bonn to Berlin is put into operation with a video circuit. Over the next year, 100 sites at both seats of government are supposed to be networked with each other. Telekom will invest DM 400 mill. over the next ten years.

2-6-1998

Topping-out ceremony for the first "Courtyard by Marriott" hotel with 190 rooms in Köpenick. Until 2003 15 additional hotels in the American Marriott chain are will come to Germany. Architects: Auer + Weber, Stuttgart, opening: October 2, 1998.

For some twenty minutes or other
We walk around the corner and stroll
About the old churchyard and bother
No more about nothing at all
There's smelling and twitter and blooming
Though right in the City. You are
Just after a few steps assuming
There's not any noise so far

And as we take hold of each other
We stroll onto Bertold Brecht's grave
The gravestone of gray granite, brother
Not bad for the purpose and brave
And next to him lies Helene
The famous Weigel at last
Recovers. All theater playing
And cooking and washing have passed

And as we're going on we're being glad then
And keep in mind while kisses giving
How near to us are some dead, yet
How dead are some people living

There's lying all kinds of great people
There many a little man lies
There's giant plane-trees arising
Above us to please our eyes
We're just walking over, see Hegel
And near him we visit again
Hanns Eisler, Wolf Langhoff. John Heartfield
Lives right down the neighborlane...

Wolf Biermann, 1973

February

with a domed hall planned as the world's largest man-made building. Here is where the GDR border guards had their lounges, and the cell for "escapees from the Republic" still exist.

2-2-1998

Sir Norman Foster invites the Building Commission of the Bundestag to table and chair in the 1:1 model of the future plenary chamber. No ultimate decisions on the seating arrangements have yet been made, and even the form of the federal eagle is still up for debate. The Building Commission seems to act more decisively when it comes to naming the new Bundestag buildings: the Dorotheen Blocks going under the name of Jakob Kaiser (CDU, 1888–1961), the Alsen Block under that of Paul Löbe (SPD, 1875–1967), while the Luisenblock will carry the name of Marie-Elisabeth Lüders (FDP, 1878–1966). All three personalities played a prominent role in establishing democracy in the Weimarer as well as in the Federal Republic.

2-4 to 3-4-1998

In the seventh year of the program's existence, the calendar for "Black History Month" swells to 69 events. As at its founding in 1990, the "Initiative of Black Germans and Blacks in Germany" continues its effort to dismantle prejudice and misunderstanding, to combat (both "emotionally and intellectually") racist tendencies resulting from ignorance and incomprehension of the ostensibly alien.

2-4-1998

Final journeys for a border facility. At Checkpoint Charlie, the remains of the GDR border facilities are loaded onto trucks and brought to Schönefeld. There they await their reincarnation as museum, which is expected to be located not far from the old site at Friedrichstrasse 78. This last move will require that the Wall Museum and the investor, CEDC, agree on how to integrate the remnants of Checkpoint Charlie into their "Quartier 200".

2-6 to 2-8-1998

Let's have a Gedankenspiel. "Berlin: Fashioning a National Capital at the End of the Twentieth Century." Harvard's Center for European Studies and Graduate School of Design (where refugees Walter Gropius and Martin Wagner taught architecture and city planning) sponsor a forum giving Berlin's city and traffic planners, architects and writers, cultural policy and capital city mavens an opportunity to air their disputes before an American audience. Cultural historian Peter Jelavich's provocative "thought experiment" in the final roundtable: If aesthetic criteria alone — and not politics — were decisive in city planning, then the Berlin Cathedral (and not the Palace of the Republic across the street) would have to be torn down. None of the other participants — takes him up on this suggestion.

2-7-1998

The final chorus of Beethoven's IXth Symphony with Schiller's "Ode to Joy" rings in the conclusion to the celebration opening the XVIIIth Olympic Winter Games in Nagano, Japan. Intoned by five choruses from five cities representing the continents symbolized by the Olympic rings. The Ernst Senff Chorus from Berlin is carried thence via satellite at 4:44 a.m., in ice cold weather, from the Brandenburg Gate. 150 visitors are there to pass expert judgment on this nocturnal choral art, and the number of witnesses watching courtesy of the media is said to number a billion.

2-7-1998

Making Marriage Pretty, Part 2. André Barnowski (30), volleyball player and medical assistant Susanne Kusch (25) pledge their troth to each other from atop the Television Tower at a height of 203 meters. The manager of the registry office, Rainer Ahnert, thereby takes another important step toward his goal of eventful nuptials at unusual sites. The series is bound to be continued. Cf. BBA '97, August 18.

2-9-1998

Opening of a German office representing the American Jewish Committee (AJC) in the Mosse-Palais on Potsdamer Platz. The first AJC office in Europe will be managed by Eugene DuBow. It's assignment will be to initiate exchange programs for Germans in the USA and for American Jews in Germany and other European countries, and to facilitate conferences about German-Jewish relations, scholarly research on Jewry, and especially cooperation with the Jewish communities of Eastern Europe.

2-10-1998

Hundredth birthday of B.B. "Flowers for Brecht" at the Dorotheenstadt cemetery "next to the house where I live." Brecht has rested there since August 17, 1956, along with Helene Weigel, Hanns Eisler, Paul Dessau, Hegel, and Fichte. A bit further on: Ruth Berlau and Elisabeth Hautmann. Taking the guided city tour "With Brecht through Berlin", one passes by the "Haus Berlin" on Strausberger Platz with Brecht inscriptions from 1954, then past Bertolt-Brecht-Platz in front of the Theater am Schiffbauerdamm with its 1988 memorial by Fritz Cremer, continuing past the Brecht House on Chausseestrasse (a museum since 1978) etc. Organization: StattReisen Berlin.

2-10-1998

Pariser Platz—Banken Platz (Bank Square). In the wake of Dresdner Bank and the Allgemeine Hypothekenbank, today the Commerzbank is opening its office in the capital, right next to the Brandenburg Gate. The bank's office for lobbying the government and diplomatic representatives will be taking up its work in the newly rebuilt Haus Sommer (architect: J.P. Kleihues), which (just as in former times) sports the address No. 1. There will not be a service hall for tellers. Cf. BBA '97, April 18.

2-10-1998

Building Senator Jürgen Klemann approves Stuttgart architect Günther Behnisch's revised design for the building that will house the Academy of the Arts on Pariser Platz. Contrary to all of the Senate's historicizing design statutes, to which all the other architects for the surrounding buildings willingly submitted, the facade for the Academy of the Arts remains transparent. The Building Senator's finding is that incorporating new building segments into the interior lends the building as a whole a greater corporeality, so that it fits harmoniously into the overall stone ensemble at Pariser Platz. This autumn there will be a selection procedure for investors to come up with DM 80 mill. for the Academy's new building. Construction start planned for beginning of 1999.

2-11 to 2-13-1998

Three-day "Internationaler Plattenkongreß Berlin" ("International Prefab Convention") in the ICC, organized by the Senate Building Administration within the framework of "bautec Berlin '98." 400 residential construction experts, urbanists, and representatives of city administrations from 19 Central and Eastern European cities, Berlin, and the new eastern German states get together to share experiences about renovating their gigantic prefab housing projects. 170 million people in the formerly socialist countries of the Eastern Bloc live in large projects like these. Since it would be unthinkable simply to demolish them, there is a need to find models for preserving and renovating these prefab projects, to upgrade them architecturally and (above all) with a social conscience.

2-12-1998

On the occasion of the 100th birthday (and 50th anniversary of the death) of Soviet director Sergei Eisenstein (1-23-1898 to 2-11-1948), the Academy of the Arts (in cooperation with the Berlinale) sponsors an Eisenstein Symposium. On two different evenings, filmmakers and authors discuss "Eisenstein and Modernity" as well as "Eisenstein and the Art of Film Today." In addition, the publication "Eisenstein and Germany" is presented before this sympathetic public. The International Forum for Young Film shows Sergei Kovalov's version of the classic that Eisenstein himself never got to finish, "Que viva México."

February 1998

In an overzealous campaign against graffiti, a brigade of painters from Britz removes a two-and-a-half by four meter large section of a four-story mural by artist Werner Brunner. The whitewashed Ice Age rhinoceros, whose skull bones had been excavated a hundred years ago from the Körner gravel pit in Neukölln, will be replaced by head of the brigade.

February 1998

A decision on usage is reached: The Diplomatic School of the Foreign Office moves into the building adjoining the Niederschönhausen Palace, which Wilhelm Pieck, the first and only President of the GDR, used as a seat of office until his death in 1960. Future utilization of the actual palace building, which was later used as a guest house, remains unclear. Here is where Michael Gorbachev is supposed to have devised his dictum "Life punishes those who arrive too late." As the scene of the Two-Plus-Four talks between the Allies and representatives of the two German states, Niederschönhausen stood in the limelight of history for one final time in the summer of 1990.

Solutions have been sought since 1992. At the end of this year's convention, they announce the "Berlin Declaration: The Future of Prefab Housing Projects—A European Challenge." Social, technical, and ecological insights from the "best practice" model of Berlin-Hellersdorf are going to be passed on, and to this end there will be EU money flowing into self-renewing funds for local job creation.

2-12-1998

Topping-out ceremony for the conversion of the former Narva Factory Building Nr. 4 in the Oberbaum-City. The building, demolished except for its landmark-protected facade, is scheduled to be handed over in the third quarter of 1998: Developer: Sirius-Projektentwicklungsgesellschaft, architects: Reichel und Stauth, Braunschweig/Berlin.

2-14-1998

Hertha in a fever: 2:1 against the reigning German champion FC Bayern München in front of the hometown fans. The Berliner Zeitung reports: "After the whistle that ended the game, the buzz began, first in the stadium, then throughout Berlin: fireworks in Lichterfelde, urgent announcement and cheering at the Green Party convention in Kreuzberg, and the news even droned out of speakers by the kiddy pool in Charlottenburg."

2-14-1998

The third "Long Night of the Museums" marks the end of "Showplace Museum 1998." Record number of visitors! 75,000 people crowd into the thirty participating houses.

2-15-1998

"The Brief Farewell to the 19th Century" will be dragged out a bit longer, for not until the 21 century—more precisely, at the beginning of 2001—will the Alte Nationalgalerie reopen the gates that it is closing today with the aforementioned exhibit. Beginning in May 1998, it will be presenting its masterpieces in the Altes Museum at the Lustgarten. Renovation cost: DM 130 mill. Architectural reconstruction: Merz, Berlin/Stuttgart.

2-16-1998

After a long struggle the Radio Council for Sender Freies Berlin (SFB) agrees on a successor to Günther von Lojewski. The new station director, picked by a vote of 20 out of 29, will be Horst Schättle, 58 years old, member of the SPD, formerly the SFB's television director.

2-16-1998

Topping-out ceremony for the DM 31 million quality control laboratory building at Schering AG on Fennstrasse in Wedding. Architect: Ulf Hein, Schering AG, Berlin. Cost: DM 41 mill., scheduled completion May 1999.

2-18-1998

Open exchange of letters. After a year of uneventful peace and quiet, things are starting to fly fast and thick. An open letter of February 10th condemns the selection of the painter Bernhard Heisig to be part of the design team for the Reichstag building and accuses him of serious "state loyalty" to the GDR. This "salvation of Heisig's honor by post hoc recognition at

2-20-1998

Cornerstone laying for the "Marzahn Promenade Leisure Center" on one of the "prime filet properties in the district," as Marzahn district mayor Harald Buttler puts it. Architects: Müller and Reimann, Berlin. Construction cost: DM 56 mill.

2-20-1998

68th meeting of the Stadtforum. Theme: "Berlin—completely private," which translates as: real estate assessment, surface area management, and socially conscious urban development.

2-21-1998

Somewhat disoriented, sections of the board of directors of INIT (the Initiative to Promote Contemporary Art) present their new old rooms at Chausseestrasse 119–20. Just as is customary in the city nowadays, the newly founded art association has converted a slightly run-down eastern property (formerly a department store)   with all

2-24-1998

The last occupied house in Berlin is evacuated, at the behest of Interior Senator Jörg Schönbohm, and in opposition to other arrangements made with the district government of Lichtenberg. The western side of Berlin already became occupier-free in August 1996; the house at Marchstrasse 23 evacuated then remains vacant.

2-26-1998

A Berlin institution celebrates its birthday. The BeHaLa (Berliner Hafen- and Lagerhausbetriebe, or Berlin Harbor and Warehouse Operations), owner of both the western and eastern harbors and many warehouses spread across the entire city, turns 75.

Eight percent of the metropolitan area of Berlin is water. No other European city has so much water. Berlin grew up on its rivers—the Spree, the Havel, and the Dahme—on its canals and lakes, on 800 kilometers of waterways, of which 182 kilometers in the urban area are navigable to this day. There are 650 bridges leading over this network of waterways. There is more water and there are more bridges in Berlin than in Venice, Amsterdam, and Stockholm combined. And because the Spree has entrenched itself so deeply with its tributaries and canals, because it doesn't call attention to itself and doesn't have any grand promenades like those of the Seine in Paris, most inhabitants of Berlin are usually not even conscious of all that water.
Evelyn Roll, 1997

February

---

the neo-German level" is to be regarded (say the letter's signatories) not only as an error in art history, but also as a decision betraying a lack of political instinct. The counter-letter, displaying today's date and the signatures of 30 celebrities from both East and West, articulates the suspicion that the first letter's rejection of Heisig is tantamount to a "wholesale exclusion of the GDR East." Cf. BBA '97, March 17.

2-19-1998

The road to a home of your own leads through the lottery drum. Owing to the enormous interest in a prospective purchase, the first 31 options to buy a DM 300,000 house in the development region Biesdorf-Süd are raffled off. An additional 30 are to follow later. The Senate makes the investor, Veba Immobilien AG, guarantee that it will deliver the rowhouses planned for sites on state-owned properties (within the framework of the initiative "Berlin 2000") for no more than DM 350,000 (property included).

the charm that goes along with it—to its new use as temporary art hall. Beginning in April, four artists will be displayed in four individual exhibits: Albert Oehlen, Isa Genzken, Martha Rosler, and Heimo Zobernig.

2-22-1998

Beloved Chronicler's Duty! The somewhat offside winners of the 48th Berlin Film Festival: The Caligari Film Prize of the International Forum of Young Film: "Kasaba" by Nuri Bilge Ceylan (Turkey). Wolfgang Staudte Prize: "Xiao Wu" by Jia Zhang Ke (PR China). Gay Film Prize Teddy for best feature film: "Hold You Tight" by Stanley Kwan (Hong Kong). Unicef Prize: "The Climb" by Bob Swaim (Great Britain). Film Critics' Prize: "Sada" by Nobuhiko Obayashi (Japan), and finally the Peace Film Prize: "W Toj Stranje" by Lidija Babrowa (Russia).

2-25-1998

The Friedrich-Ebert-Stiftung, the political foundation with close ties to the SPD, returns to the site where it was founded. Today SPD Vice Chairman Wolfgang Thierse and the governing Mayor of Berlin, Eberhard Diepgen, lay the cornerstone for the foundation's new conference and seminar center between Hiroshimastrasse and Hildebrandstrasse in Tiergarten. The four-story building under construction, not far from the Konrad-Adenauer-Stiftung (the foundation close to the CDU), will be built by Offenbach architects Novotny, Mähner & Weber on a 3,720 sq. m. large property. Total cost: DM 53.2 mill.

2-26-1998

Finally, it will be possible again to look at the sky while walking: Environment Senator Strieder is testing one of 13 new dog excrement machines from the BSR (Berlin's Sanitation Department). The machines cost between DM 35,000 and DM 50,000.

2-26-1998

Provisional utilization of the Bodemuseum. Since renovations for the building keep getting delayed, the museum's management invites visitors into eleven cabinets on the upper floor formerly used as depots. The exhibit "Riemenschneider on the Museum Island" presents masterpieces from the collections (now united for the first time) of the Dahlem Painting Gallery (western Berlin) and Museum Island (eastern Berlin). Through June 1999.

2-27-1998

Fall in by order of rank for the "Thread Binding History and the Present" at the Lustgarten. Since this power move is blocked by 50 old linden trees standing in front of Schinkel's Altes Museum, they will be cut down today. In this way Environment Senator Peter Strieder is letting facts be created, and two unrealized competitive designs (Gerhard Merz 1996 and Gustav Lange 1997) will now be followed by the "restoration of the Lustgarten according to Schinkel's intentions." The landmark-protected pavement, which recalls the National Socialist marching grounds erected in 1933, will be removed, and 34 new linden trees, lawns, flower beds, and a fountain will move in. Landscape architect: Hans Loidl, Vienna/Berlin, scheduled completion autumn 1999, planned cost DM 7 mill.

3-2-1998

The decision concerning the undecided urban design competition for the Kulturforum is discussed at DAZ, the German Architecture Center. Some more information on this subject: The dedication of the picture gallery is scheduled for June 12, 1998; until then, the (media) world should be prepped to get a good impression of the Kulturforum's sandy environs, which go back 35 years. In February, the Senate of Berlin authorized DM 1,000,000 for provisional landscaping of the area, an authorization that the budgetary committee of the city parliament overturned at the end of 1997. Now, Munich landscape planners Donata and Christoph Valentien and Munich architects Hilmer & Sattler, responsible for the new gallery building, are receiving first prize to reorganize the Kulturforum. For landscaping, a little pine forest augmented by some oleaster trees has been proposed; Hilmer and Sattler are adding on a three-story rail

3-2-1998

The Council for the Arts invites participants to join the 16th public discussion in its series "Capital Culture Forum." Place: The Academy of the Arts. Under the moderation of Wolfgang Kil, those taking the podium include Cultural State Secretary Lutz von Pufendorf and "taz" editor Uwe Rada. Two basic moods are registered: on the artistic side, there is anxiety about "festivalizing the city," while on the sociological side, the fear is about erosive damage to abandoned sections of the city whenever artists on the lookout for cheap space start searching after what's new out in the great wide open.

2-27-1998

On the anniversary of the liberation of Auschwitz concentration camp, the Monument for the Deported Jews of Berlin is unveiled at Grunewald railway station. On track number 17, where the trains used to depart for the east, the dates of the transports are displayed on 186 steel construction components. Between 1941 and 1945, 56,000 Jewish Berliners were deported and murdered.

2-27-1998

Hostile takeover attempt. In line with the provision "why form a party when we can take one over," Berlin students submit 2,700 applications to join the F.D.P. After the failure of the recent student strikes, the strategy of the "absolute majority" now being put to the test was thought up. The applicants for party membership live all over the city, and their voting residences are distributed in such a way as to give them a theoretical majority in all 42 F.D.P. local associations. The F.D.P. is reserving the right to examine the applications.

2-28-1998

In the presence of Israeli ambassador, the exhibit "Longing for Zion: Towards the State of Israel" opens in the Academy of Arts. Through April 5.

3-1-1998

Of all the times for this to happen, on the anniversary of the Berlin Airlift: The "weakness of Berlin as a business location" prompts the last American airline company remaining in Berlin, Delta Airlines, to cancel its daily direct Berlin-New York flight. Instead, the airline is concentrating on "markets with higher yields from business travel," meaning Frankfurt, Stuttgart, and Hamburg.

3-1-1998

For the time being, a visitor's last chance to view the Arts and Crafts Museum in Schloß Koepenick. As of tomorrow, owing to reconstruction measures, the building will be closed for about 4 years. Renovating the 17th century facility has already been going on since 1995, and the cost is rising; the DM 50 mill. sum originally envisioned has, in the interim, turned into DM 74 mill. Reopening the museum could be in jeopardy. The federal government is interested in the Baroque palace along the Dahme river.

3-2-1998

Moving deadline for the Mitte District Office, which is switching from the Berolina-Haus on Alexanderplatz into the newly built municipal city hall on Karl-Marx-Straße. Cf. BBA '97, June 12. Investor: Trigon. Architects: Bassenge, Puhan-Schulz, Heinrich, and Schreiber, Berlin.

in place of the entrance rampsloping platform, together with two seven-story houses on either side of Potsdamer Strasse. The million marks allotted is not even enough for all the trees; furthermore, time runs short. In addition, there is an ongoing debate about the aesthetics of pine trees; the Matthäi-Kirche congregation continues to be incensed about the planting. A sod lawn is now being contemplated.

Early March

Construction start for an office and commercial building at Breite Straße 18-21a in Pankow. Completion is scheduled for September 1999. Client: Fundus Group, Berlin. Architects: EPA Architects, Volker Mayer and Partners, Stuttgart. Cost: DM 130 mill. Commercial space: 22.000 sq. m.

Early March

Now that the Shell House on Reichpietschufer in Tiergarten is ready for interior renovations (going back to the summer of 1997), the healing process is also discernable on the outside. This month, renovation of the exterior begins by scaffolding the object, whose remodeling concept had been the subject of dispute for 13 years. Client: Bewag. Architect: Hans Achim Grube. Cost: around DM 50 mill., sheduled completion: end of 1999.

3-3-1998

The Urania celebrates its 110th birthday. The first building stood on Invalidenstrasse and housed an observatory, a scientific theater with lecture shows, and experimental workshops. The idea of a "popular observatory for educating the public" goes back to the astronomers Wilhelm Foerster and Max Wilhelm Meyer. The current Urania was founded again in 1953; by getting high-ranking scientists to deliver lectures about the latest state of research in their respective fields, latching on to old tradition. Beyond that, it offers the public a colorful mixed program with movies, field trips, and slide lectures. Urania took up its current location on the street called "An der Urania" in 1962. And last but not least, it has been getting by without subsidies since 1993.

3-5-1998

The "Berliner Tafel" ("Berlin Table") celebrates its 5th year. The non-profit organization with around 300 volunteers organizes the collection and distribution of unspoiled food that has become leftovers for any number of reasons. Within a single month, 40,000 kg of food is accumulated this way and then distributed to social welfare facilities.

3-5-1998

After the six years it took to get approval, a 16 sq. m small bistro opens today in the landmark-designated "Café Achteck" (nickname for famouse public toilets, type "Octogon") on the Südwestkorso, corner of Wilhelmshoeher Strasse. The toilets imposed on the Café are next door.

3-6-1998

As of today, instead of advertisements on the U 2 line's subway platform at Alexanderplatz, there is something else to look at — namely, art. Or maybe advertisement after all, just different. For Renata Stih and Frieder Schnock (prizewinners in the contest "Art Instead of Advertisement" sponsored by the New Society for Fine Arts, NGbK) have taken over the subway platform's design for several months. On Stih and Schnocks posters mnemonic words appear to draw attention to self-help initiatives.

3-10-1998

An exhibit of photographs by Andreas Feininger has opened in the Bauhaus Archiv. The artist himself (born 1906) had a hand in selecting the pictures for this comprehensive retrospective.
Through June 1.

3-10-1998

The main work on converting the old Prussian House of Lords on Leipziger Strasse into the new seat of the Bundesrat (Germany's upper house of parliament, representing the federal states) commences today. Previously, cleaning the facade was what got special attention. By mid-1999, the first offices for staff are supposed to be completed, and by 2000 the committee rooms and plenary hall are to follow. Architect: Peter Schweger, Hamburg. Cost: around DM 194 mill.

3-11-1998

Announcement of the results in the competition to complete four buildings on Leipziger Platz. In order of numbers: Nr. 1: Office of Rave and Partners, Berlin, (owner: Deutsches Reisebüro); Nr. 4: Jan Kleihues, Berlin, (owner: DG-Immobilien-Management); Nr. 6: Walter A. Noebel, Berlin (for the Züblin-Projektentwicklungsgesellschaft); Nr. 7: two second prizes for Axel Schultes, Berlin, and Bellmann & Boehm, Berlin (for the Bauherrengemeinschaft Knauthe). Jury chair: Christoph Sattler. Inherent in all four objects is the stone severity that has been chosen as a hallmark of the "Berlin style." This common feature was brought to the immediate attention of the Canadian jury that will soon have to assess the competition for its own country's embassy on Leipziger Platz.

3-3-1998

A new item from the Bahnhof Zoo railway station: Here now hangs a punctuality board, telling how many trains have reached their destinations according to schedule. For, with 49 % of its trains arriving late, Bahnhof Zoo lies at the top of the tardiness scale, according to "Consumer Reports".

3-4-1998

At the Hamburger Bahnhof, a traveling exhibition has opened showing works that won the "ars viva 97/98" prize. The award is given by the Cultural Circle of the German Industry and is open to young artists working in new media. Through April 13th.

3-6-1998

Starting today, the long-term impact of the IBA (International Building Exhibition) is being put under the microscope for an examination taking place in three successive colloquia at weekly intervals and sponsored by the "Society for Careful Urban Renewal." Today the discussants include IBA architects Alvaro Siza Vieira, Oriol Bohigas and Josef Paul Kleihues.

3-7-1998

As of today, the Guggenheim branch on Unter den Linden is housing a monumental opus — specially tailored for the space available and almost 50 m long — by American Pop artist James Rosenquist. After June 14th, the good piece with the name "The swimmer in the Economist" will take to the road on a tour of Deutsche Bank branches abroad.

3-7-1998

A power move of political decision-making (done without putting it to a vote in the Senate) and a festival for the media: As of today, and for about the next 8 months, the Brandenburg Gate will be opened to auto traffic (not including trucks) heading from east to west, so that Dorotheenstrasse and its substitute road can be cordoned off. Buildings for the Bundestag are being erected here.

3-11-1998

At the Hamburger Bahnhof exhibition hall, Federal Building Minister Eduard Oswald presents the federal government's 150-page "art concept." The Arts Advisory Council, founded in 1996 as an outside independent review board of art experts to help federal authorities make recommendations for art at government buildings, has compiled a list of 36 possible sites calling for art; it is now anticipated that the first competitions will be held at mid-year.

3-12-1998

Inaugural ceremony for the Alexanderplatz rail station. In three years, the rapid transit platforms and facades were thoroughly renovated. In the process, previously walled-up arcades from the Twenties were opened, some of them clinker-clad in the old style and furnished with glass facades. On the ground floor and in the basement, two shopping arcades with a total of 47 shops on 3,500 sq. m have been installed. The building is not yet finished, and the new regional track hookup will not be opened until May. Client: Deutsche Bahn AG. Architects: Rebecca Chestnutt, Robert Niess, Berlin. Construction cost: DM 125 mill.

3-13-1998

Ulrich Schamoni—film director, author, media manager, and licensee of Berlin's first complete private television channel —dies at the age of 58 in Berlin.

3-13-1998

Electoral circus in the Prater circus tent. Christoph Schlingensief jumps over the barrier separating action art from politics by founding a "last chance party." Anybody can become a candidate, and everyone is supposed to vote for him- or herself. The technique of jumping over a 5 % hurdle (the barrier erected by German electoral law to deter extremist parties) is demonstrated by circus goats at appropriate barricades inside the tent.

3-13-1998

The 3rd International Festival "Film and Architecture" starts with 40 programs and over 50 international films. Even houses that are not classical sites for showing

3-14-1998

Cornerstone laying for the office of the German Bishops' Conference on the site of the former St. Hedwig Cemetery at Hannoversche Strasse in the Mitte district. A new building with a total of 8,200 sq. m is supposed to be built there, including (in addition to the Bishops' Conference) an auditorium and a new guest house for the Catholic Academy. A new church will also be built. Architects: Arge HOEGER HARE Architekten RKW. Completion: 1999.

3-18-1998

With a wreath-laying at the cemetery for the "Märzgefallenen" (those fallen in March"), the battles at the barricades where the populace was pitted against the royal army 150 years ago are commemorated. Plaques are placed at eleven public squares, and a number of scheduled events praise the '48 revolution as the beginning of the modern constitutional state. On May 18, 1848, the German National Assembly convened for the first time in Frankfurt's Paulskirche with 585 delegates; on December 27, the Assembly proclaimed the "Basic Rights of the German People." The Berlin Senate and the district governments are behaving less ceremoniously, though, when it comes to designating an appropri-

Berlin, early Thursday morning, March 23 *Adolph von Menzel*

How had I left Berlin, and how did I find it when I returned? Already on the way from the train station to my dwelling I passed the remains of four barricades. Berlin has saved face tremendously!!!—a thing no one would have believed, either in Berlin itself or abroad. Since Monday of the previous week, a state of alternation had persisted between isolated bloody skirmishes (in which the military was victorious), agitation, and quiet; by noon on Saturday, the coming storm announced itself as individual persons hurried back and forth through the street. Later, people of the most diverse rank and class appeared, at first equipped only with tools; they broke out the planks of the gutter bridges and carried off sentry-boxes (the sentinels had disappeared earlier); my landlord, for example, a master mason, immediately

movies get played: the Big Eden, the House of German Sport, the Hydraulic Engineering Experimental Station, and the Kreuzkirche, a church in Schmargendorf. Through March 18.

3-14-1998

The best of the national advertising campaigns are chosen by the Art Directors Club in Hangar 2 of Tempelhof Airport. A panel of 130 jurors in 10 separate groups is voting on 5,400 entries, divided into 25 categories, submitted by 485 participants. The winners include the Berlin branch of the Hamburg agency "Scholz & Friends" for their FAZ (Frankfurter Allgemeine Zeitung) ad campaign "Clever Mind." All of the entries are on exhibit March 13-16 in the Berliner Kunsthalle.

3-14-1998

At the Hamburger Bahnhof Swiss video artist Pipilotti Rist puts on an exhibition of her work, including an installation specially designed for this show called "Remake of the Weekend." Through June 1.

3-15-1998

Cornerstone laying for the annex to the Georgenkirchstrasse Lutheran Center (Evangelisches Zentrum) in Friedrichshain. The new building complements the Berlin Mission. In the Center and the St. Bartholomäus parish next door, the mission and Church's regional offices will be seated, including the Lutheran Radio Service, regional Synod offices, and consistory. Architects: Dieter Ketterer + Partners, Berlin. Construction cost: DM 87 mill.

ate public square that might carry the name of the March Revolution. The former has opted for the square in front of the Maxim Gorki Theater (behind Schinkel's neo-classical sentry house "Neue Wache"), while the latter is in favor of the square in front of the Brandenburg Gate; no agreement is in sight.

3-19-1998

Today, the Import fair is opening, though with the number of participants reduced. The trade fair has been around for 30 years, and it serves the goal of making it easier for Third World and Eastern European countries to gain access to the Western European market. Now the implementations of the Schengen accord is putting up bureaucratic hurdles for outsiders. 40 exhibiters have not even received visas.

3-19-1998

In front of the Ibero-American Institute on Reichpietschufer at the corner of Potsdamer Strasse, a statue of the South American freedom fighter Simon Bolivar is unveiled.

surrendered his tool shed to the barricades, and so forth. Finally, around four o'clock, the alarm bells began ringing from all the towers. In hopes of finding me, my sister started for the train station in order to make it back to the city in time. The street Hasenhegergasse was already closed, forcing her to go down the Feldstrasse, and even there she had to be lifted over the beginnings of a barricade; on the way, she frequently encountered coachmen with unharnessed horses and no wagons, as well as one who had kept only his whip. While all this was happening on the street, all the bakers (perhaps) had baked the whole night through as never before, and despite the long stretches occupied by troops, a way was found to transport large baskets of all kinds of bread into the barricades. No one provided for the soldiers. Since Sunday, the whole city has been armed and quiet. Everyone takes his turn at public security duty without regard to rank or class, both in the royal palace and at all the other sentry posts, empty barracks, etc. Most of the citizens have infantry rifles, while the students use cavalry swords and sabers, as do the pupils from the Gymnasium. The artists keep watch in the academy. In addition to tricolor and mourning flags, the (now former) palace of the Prussian prince bears three large inscriptions. The first, painted in white on the wall, reads: "Property of the Entire Nation." A large white flag spread out on the balcony bears the words: "The property of the nation stands under the protection of the citizenry," while a nailed-up board announces the construction of a workers' and complaint bureau with the words: "Here men of the people work for the people." Nothing has been damaged or even pilfered either in or on the building, and in general one hears of many examples of honesty and orderliness.

The Taming of the Stuffed Animals *Michael Jeismann*

When the stage sets are changed, the actors get a break. What is true for the theater, moreover, often applies to politics as well: the stage is dominated not by the actors, but by work on the set. New political landscapes and interiors are in the process of being created, and no one knows which play will be performed next. No wonder the politicians are having a hard time with the text. At present, the loudest hammering is being heard on the European stage. Chairs are being carried in and out, coins distributed, old pictures hung elsewhere or replaced. Nor is the chorus of interpreters idle as it rehearses its commentary on the European play. The most recent example is the exhibition "Mythen der Nationen" (Myths of the Nations) at the Deutsches Historisches Museum in Berlin, an institution under the sponsorship of the federal chancellor of Germany. An excerpt from a speech given by Helmut Kohl in 1995 to the parliamentary assembly of the European Council in Strasbourg, "Toward a shared Europe in peace and security," provides a preface to the catalogue: Europe is to serve as a bulwark against the national barbarism of previous eras. It is to outstrip the nations without overrunning them. The exhibition presents central myths from sixteen European lands; in the catalogue, the mythic treasures of the United States and Russia are included as well. Each country was allotted five such myths, resulting in a total of ninety myths. In view of this inflation, the national myth banks would have to reject the proposed common currency of myths, citing the monetary stability requirements of the Euro as a precedent. This accumulation of myths is divided into three thematic sections: "Freedom," "Faith and War," and finally "Where We Come From." The exhibition shows an impressive number of pictures as well as nationalistically decorated objects of everyday life. The viewer's curiosity and enjoyment of the myths, however, is soon spoiled by the increasing intru-

sion of another discovery as well. The fact that the exhibition is informed by a political agenda is not illegitimate; nor is the mixture of theoretical over-ambition and practical industry in the execution an unusual one. The fact, however, that the whole is presented with a gesture of superiority—as if a circus trainer had tamed all the national demons, lions, and eagles, as if all the while, we ourselves were standing safely on the shores of a comprehending rationality—is a joke…

3-19-1998

Opening of the Heinrich-Heine-Forum on the square named for the poet in the Mitte district. The core of the facility is the landmark-protected riding and drill hall from 1828/38. Around the hall, a new nine-story building has been built with 165 residences (using subsidies from the so-called second method of public funding) and retail space for around 30 shops and service businesses. Developer: HANSEATICA Unternehmens Consulting. Architects: Karl-Heinz Cammann, Barbara Weppler-Meier, Derlin. Cost: DM 140 mill.

3-20-1998

Retroactively as of January 1, the Berlin company Herlitz AG has sold its subsidiary McPaper to the Deutsche Post AG.

3-20-1998

Opening of the exhibit "Myths of Nations" in the German Historical Museum. Through June 9.

3-23-1998

Under the title "Concrete Germany," the "Theater am Halleschen Ufer" lets its actors perform the capital city's favorite play: construction. Concrete is mixed and transported, encased and torn down, and texts on the theme are recited. Through March 29.

3-23-1998

Dedication of a four-story office complex for the Berlin Union-Film company on Oberlandstrasse in Tempelhof. Developer: Deutsche Immobilien-Investierungs AG, Berlin. Architecst: Meyer, Ernst, and Partners, Berlin.

3-20-1998

At the Hamburger Bahnhof, film installations by the Belgian conceptual artist Marcel Broodthaers are presented. Through May 24.

3-20-1998

"How do societies transmit visions and intellectual leadership?" is the question prominent American and German politicians and scholars discuss at the second "New Traditions Conference." The conference is a framework for opening the "American Academy." As an "intellectual airlift from America to Berlin," the Academy is meant to be a site for conferences and a home to visiting fellows. The Villa Arnhold in Wannsee, Am Sandwerder 17–19, future seat of the American Academy, will be converted into a conference center by September. The villa is a donation of Anna-Maria Kellen, daughter of its Jewish owner, who had to flee to the US from the Nazis.

3-21-1998

Berlin and Brandenburg heading down the same pathways, even without a merger: As of today, a development plan for Berlin and 275 Brandenburg local governments surrounding Berlin become legally binding. In February, both state governments passed the appropriate legislation applicable to planning for both residential areas and open spaces. The common program is meant to prevent damaging competition and to secure a balance between the Berlin region and the structurally weak rural sections of Brandenburg. It is also to ensure environmentally protection in endangered areas.

3-25-1998

Opening of the first building segment for the Museum of Medical History at Charité hospital. On 350 sq. m of exhibit space, in a section of the Institute for Pathology, around 1,000 pieces relating to pathology and anatomy are on display. The original museum with its collection space and large lecture room, the result of an initiative by Rudolf Virchow, was destroyed in the war. Since 1990, work has been proceeding to rebuild a comprehensive medical collection (the only one in Berlin), which is ultimately intended to include all five floors. Heading up the collection: Dr. Peter Krisch. Open to the public on weekdays from 1 to 5 p.m., Wednesday till 7 p.m. In tandem with the museum, the ruins of the former lecture hall (nicknamed "Ruine") are being used for public events of all kinds. Remodeling: Schreiber. Egger Architects, Berlin.

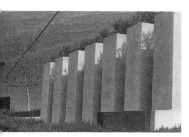

3-26-1998

Municipal district reform: By a tiny margin—140 out of 206, with solid support from the CDU, disunity within the SPD, and solid rejection by the Green Alliance and PDS—Berlin's Parliament votes out a reform package revolving around the reduction of Berlin's municipal districts from 23 to 12. In addition to a thoroughgoing administrative reform, the Parliament is to be shrunk to 130 delegates by 1999. The number of Senators in the cabinet will be shortened to 8 from 10, its current number. The district reform is meant to go into effect in 2001. The following precincts will be consolidated: Prenzlauer Berg, Pankow, and Weissensee; Mitte, Tiergarten, and Wedding; Charlottenburg and Wilmersdorf; Friedrichshain, Kreuzberg; Lichtenberg, Hohenschönhausen; Marzahn, Hellersdorf; Treptow, Köpenick; Schöneberg, Tempelhof; Steglitz, Zehlendorf. The districts of Reinickendorf, Spandau, and Neukölln will

Mid-March

Completion of the E.T.A. Hoffmann Garden, part of the Jewish Museum by Daniel Libeskind. The garden, a sloping area bearing forty-nine concrete steles with crippled oaks growing out of them, is a site commemorating the Jews of Berlin who were expelled, murdered, or never born. And yet it is not—at least, for the time being, according to what the architect and city cultural administration have declared—supposed to be viewed as a memorial of admonishment.
Cf. BBA '97.

3-27-1998

Cornerstone laying for a hotel on Budapester Strasse in Tiergarten. It is being built on the property of the former Hotel SchweizerHof. Client: Dorint Hotel Schweizerhof Berlin/Dr. Ebertz KG, Cologne. Architects: Architektengemeinschaft Bassenge, Puhan-Schulz, Heinrich, Schreiber, Berlin. Cost: DM 180 mill. Opening: September 1999.

3-27-1998

In person, Bundestag President Rita Süssmuth opens the federal parliament's very own souvenir shop on Unter den Linden 69b. Everything fans dream of is displayed across the shop's 90 sq. m:

3-27-1998

Today, 10 months after its cornerstone was laid, the Berlin branch of the Deutsche Genossenschaftsbank on Pariser Platz 3 celebrates a topping out ceremony. Architect: Frank O. Gehry, Los Angeles. Gross floor area: 20,000 sq. m. Investment volume: DM 250 mill. Completion: Early 1999. While the perforated facade behaves strictly symmetrically along all four sides, thereby corresponding to the official design stipulations for Pariser Platz, in the interior of the building things get wild. A 50x20x20 m courtyard is covered to make an atrium; inside there is (as if hung up) a sculptural and "biomorphic" construction frame that, covered with stainless steel scales on the outside and on the inside wood-paneled, will house a conference hall for 100 people as well as a small foyer.

3-28-1998

Shopping in the Kulturhaus Dussmann is now allowed until 10 p. m., and from Monday through Saturday. Approving this exception to the rule required extraordinary legal tact: First of all, the special dispensation was dependent on the range of merchandise; Dussmann sells "tourist goods." Secondly, it depends on the status of the shop's white-collar staff, for only executives are allowed to sell after 8 p. m. Dussmann made promotions across the board.

4-1-1998

Topping out ceremony at WISTA (short for Wissenschafts- und Wirtschaftsstandort Adlershof, or Adlershof Business and Science Site) for the Information Science Innovation Center. Architect: Cepezed bv, Delft. Client: WISTA-Management GmbH. Main useable space: 3,200 sq. m. Scheduled completion in autumn 1998.

4-1-1998

Today, for around 17,000 residences in Category I (areas severely at risk for social welfare), occupancy requirements for low-income tenants as well as non-occupancy charges for high-income earners are cancelled. By taking this measure, the Senate is trying to retain mixed-income rental occupancy and counteract the exodus of families with stable incomes.

3-25-1998

The Finland Institute opens an exhibit on Finnish architect Alvar Aalto (1898–1976). Main theme: the brick tile buildings of his "red phase." Through April 24.

retain their autarchy. À propos: A similarly narrow margin of victory led on April 27, 1920 to the consolidation of Greater Berlin from the merger of 8 cities, 59 rural communes, and 27 estate districts. Starting last year, a "Berlin Speech" commemorates this date.

Miniature editions of the Basic Law (postwar Germany's provisionally permanent constitution), ties and pencils and watches and so on, all decorated with the federal eagle. The shop is managed, outside the purview of the Bundestag, by the bookstore Bouvier.

3-30-1998

May we have a little more cinema, please? The municipal district office in Prenzlauer Berg resolves —after a dispute lasting months, and in spite of having rejected the same project once before—to approve a cinema multiplex at the Kultur-Brauerei ("Culture Brewery") and to conclude a contract with the TLG (Treuhand Liegenschafts Gesellschaft, the trustee real estate company managing the privatization of former GDR commercial properties). There is no end in sight to the discussions, however. Whatever happens, though, Arthur Brauner (owner of the nearby Colosseum) can be counted on initiate legal proceedings.

4-2-1998

Souvenirs the second: The Social Democratic Party of Germany (SPD) opens its very own party souvenir shop, "ROTE Beete" ("RED Beet"), in the Willy-Brandt-Haus on Wilhelmstrasse, thereby pulling even with the Bundestag. Unfortunately for the sorely tested SPD fan, some items the shop is selling, like its "games of patience" puzzles ("Geduldspiele"), come a decade and a half of political opposition too late.

4-3-1998

The Staatsbibliothek (German State Library) acquires the papers of actor and theater director Gustav Gründgens (1899–1963).

4-3-1998

Fluxus artist Wolf Vostell, whose Cadillacs poured in concrete on Rathenau Platz brought the popular soul of what was then West Berlin to a boil in 1987, dies at age 65.

The journalists were completely convinced that I was the right man to show them Berlin. After all, how could they know that we Wilmersdorfers, if we could possibly help it, never went further than the shoe repair shop on the corner in Wilhelmsaue, and that for us, there was no difference between Treptow and Teltow, since they sounded so much alike...
Peter Fürst, 1998

April 1998

Federal settlements: The sites for all the federal states' delegations to Germany's upper house of parliament have been determined for good: The Bavarian federal delegation is converting a bank building on Behrensstrasse 21/22, while Berlin is taking over the former house of the Charité hospital's board of directors on the corner of Wilhelmstrasse and Dorotheenstrasse. The Hanseatic City of Hamburg is moving into the former seat of the "Club der Kulturschaffenden" (the "Cultural Producers' Club" of the former GDR) on the corner of Jägerstrasse and Mauerstrasse. The Free State of Saxony will reside at Brüderstrasse 11–12, and Saxony-Anhalt at the former artists' club "Die Möwe" ("The Seagull") on Luisenstrasse. The federal states of Brandenburg, Hessen, Mecklenburg-Eastern Pomerania, Lower Saxony, Rhineland-Palatinate, the Saarland, and Schleswig-Holstein will erect new buildings in the

4-3-1998

The city's first public park, the Friedrichshain, celebrates its 150th birthday today.

4-3-1998

First day of school in the new school building at Predener Strasse 29 in Hohenschönhausen. The elongated building, covered with dark green-tinted concrete plates, houses an elementary school, a comprehensive secondary school, and two triple athletic halls. Architect: Max Dudler, Berlin. Developer: Hohenschönhausen District Municipal Office in Berlin. Construction costs: DM 92 mill.

4-4-1998

Berlin's public transit authority, the BVG (Berliner Verkehrsbetriebe), and the Senate Building Administration conclude a "Contract to Accelerate 26 Tram Lines." To this end, 200 traffic lights are being put into a new shift, so that the tram now gets the right of way. By 2001, the acceleration project will have been concluded.

In those days, all the world was watching Berlin. Some out of fear, others out of hope—for in this city, the fate of Europe would be decided for the coming decades. Everything was strange to me here: the houses, the customs, the meticulousness with which depravity was cultivated, the belief in numbers, screws, diagrams. And still I wrote. I have added so many repulsive details to my loving words about Berlin that you are probably glad not to be here. I implore you, believe me and grow fond of Berlin, the city of the atrocious monuments and the anxious eyes.
Ilja Ehrenburg, 1921-22

April 1998

The Great Elector rides onward for Charlottenburg. The giant statue by Andreas Schlüter will not be set up at its original site on the Lange Brücke (Long Bridge) in the Mitte district; instead, it will (as far as one knows) remain in the honor courtyard of Charlottenburg Palace.

4-20-1998

In the Galerie Aedes East, the Kingdom of the Netherlands and the Republic of Austria present the designs for their embassies. Within the framework of the Aedes Lectures series at the Technical University, Hans Hollein and Rem Koolhaas explain their projects before a packed house.
Cf. BBA '97, April 22.

4-22-1998

Presentation of the business "rental mirror" for Rosenthaler and Spandauer Vorstadt. The average "cold" rent (excluding heat and utilities) for the 1,200 businesses located there runs between DM 17.50 and DM 23 per sq. m. Pubs there are aplenty, and more are on the way. Over the next two years, 30 additional restaurants are expected to be added to the area's 100 gastronomic locations. That way, according to the prognosis for this section of the Mitte district into which everyone seems to be moving, 16,500 people can dine simultaneously.

former Ministerial Gardens. Baden-Württemberg will build at Tiergartenstrasse 15. Not far from there: the City of Bremen and the state of North Rhine-Westphalia, both in Hiroshimastrasse. With a new building on the corner of Mohrenstrasse and Mauerstrasse, the Free State of Thuringia returns to an historic site. Cf. BBA '97, September 8, 10, and 22.

April 1998

Construction start for the shopping and recreational Hansa-Center on Hansa Strasse at the corner of Malchower Weg in the Hohenschönhausen district. The complex will house specialty markets, fitness and bowling facilities, as well as a dance café on 24,000 sq. m. Architects: Firm of Hasselbach, Wiesbaden. Developer: BOTAG-Bodentreuhand- und Verwaltungs-AG. Investments : DM 100 mill. Scheduled completion June 1999.

4-5-1998

Streets, public squares, and their names.
As of today, the Philharmonie is on Herbert-von-Karajan-Strasse, no longer on Matthäikirchstrasse. On the occasion of the 90th birthday of the orchestra's long-time conductor, one half of the tiny street is renamed; the other, even smaller half now answers to the name Scharounstrasse.

4-6-1998

Today the Hellersdorf Municipal District Office is moving into the six-story city hall building on Alice-Salomon-Platz 3, in the middle of the newly created center for the Hellersdorf district known as "Helle Mitte" ("Bright Center"). Architects: Brandt & Böttcher, Berlin. Cf. main section.

4-7-1998

With the opening event for the festival "Picking Up the Trail from the Fair Hæth to the Industrial Site," the 100th anniversary of the industrial district Oberschöneweide is celebrated.

4-7-1998

At the Werderscher Markt, Foreign Minister Klaus Kinkel und Building Minister Eduard Oswald lay the cornerstone for the Foreign Office's extension to the Reichsbank building (Heinrich Wolff, 1932–38), which later became the Central Committee headquarters of the SED (Communist East Germany's ruling "Socialist Unity Party"). Three glass-covered interior courtyards will subdivide the building on rectangular plan. The design lends the construction a certain transparency unusual in a government building, which has given rise to the addition's designation in the Berlin vernacular as "Kinkel's tea house." Architects: Thomas Reimann and Ivan Müller, Berlin. Costs for conversion and extension: DM 540 mill. Scheduled completion: November 1999.

4-8-1998

Movie premiere in Friedrichshain. With the cloak-and-dagger epoch "The Man in the Iron Mask," the second cinema multiplex in Friedrichshain opens its gates. At Landsberger Allee 54, in the immediate vicinity of the Kosmos cinema (reopened in 1996), the new movie theater offers 2,099 seats in eight halls.

4-11-1998

The Velo-Taxis go into their second season with extended service. In addition to the three lines already offered last year, a new route through Oranienburger Strasse in Mitte is installed.
Cf. BBA '97, October 12.

4-17-1998

As of today, Aedes East is showing the exhibit "Public Squares—Interior Courtyards—Parking Lots from 1985–98. Recovered Spaces." Works by Berlin architect and landscape planner Regina Poly. Through May 17.

4-18-1998

The College of Arts (HdK) presents three museum designs for German cities by the Italian architect Giorgio Grassi. These include his winning design for the Museum Island from 1994, which was not granted approval by the Berlin State Museums. Through May 6.

4-19-1998

The America Memorial Library (AGB, for Amerika-Gedenk-Bibliothek) is merging with the Berlin City Library (BSB, for Berliner Stadtbibliothek) to become the Central and Berlin State Library (ZLB, for Zentral- und Landesbibliothek). As of May 5, an experimental bus shuttle offers service between the two houses; the user's fare is DM 1.

4-20-1998

Design for living, from the Fifties through the Eighties, is on display in the Fontane-Haus on the Märkisches Viertel today. Through May 24, furniture as well as music and film clips convey the residential feel of these four decades.

4-22-1998

Premiere of the new Botho Strauß play "Jeffers-Act I and II" in the Hebbel-Theater in Kreuzberg. Staged by the Schaubühne, and directed by Edith Clever, who also plays a role, with Bruno Ganz as the anti-hero.

4-22-1998

Wolfgang Branoner, Berlin secretary of state for economies, introduces 23 capital city projects that will be taking part in Hanover's Expo 2000. These include the "Info-Box" at Potsdamer Platz (Schneider and Schumacher, Frankfurt/Main), the Hellersdorf District Center (urban design concept by Brandt & Böttcher, Berlin), the ecological high-rise for the GSW on Kochstraße (Sauerbruch and Hutton, Berlin), the Tempodrom multi-functional performance tent (Frei Otto, Stuttgart), as well as the new building for the Technology Museum on Schöneberger Ufer (Ulrich Wolff and Helge Pitz, Berlin).

4-22-1998

Topping out ceremony for the Wilhelminenhof block heating plant in Oberschöneweide. Architect: Jörg Froemming (Berlin, manager of Gasag's construction division). Investor: BLEG, construction costs: DM 10 mill. At the same time, and in the presence of Berlin's Environmental Senator Strieder, 16 maple trees and 26 willows are planted along the banks of the Spree as a way of illustrating urban ecological renewal and its affinity to modern power plant technology.

4-24-1998

With a snow-white asparagus pyramid on the Gendarmenmarkt 2.5 meters high and weighing 300 kilos, the Beelitz Asparagus Association opens this year's season. Katrin Hocke, the reigning Asparagus Queen, assisted by Brandenburg's Agricultural Minister Gunter Fritsch, sells the first sticks to impatient connoisseurs. The season ends June 21.

4-25-1998

Some statistics on the "Day of the Tree": The lime tree, at 400,600 (36.4 per cent), is planted more than any other of Berlin's 80 species. It is followed in the rankings by the maple (28.5 %) and oak (8.4 %), as well as by the plane tree at 6.1 %. The wild pear tree became the "Tree of the Year," one of which now gets to be planted each year hence in the Technology Museum's newly designed Museum Park.

4-26-1998

In sports: By 1 to 4 in the hall of their opponents, the Berlin "Eisbären" ("Polar Bears") lose the playoffs in ice hockey and become Germany's second place team, just behind the Mannheim "Adler" ("Eagles").

4-26-1998

Following Roman Herzog (4-26-97), Finland's Premier Martti Ahtisaari delivers the second talk in the series "Berliner Rede" ("Berlin Talk") at the Hotel Adlon, on the topic of the future of Europe in times of globalization.

4-27-1998

First Inner City Conference under the aegis of Berlin's Mayor Eberhard Diepgen. The participants are district mayors of inner city wards, and the discussions have been occasioned by increasingly urgent social problems in this part of the contemporary city. This time, the focus is on education policy.

4-27-1998

"Claude Vasconi. architectures européennes" is the name of the exhibit that Aedes West is presenting as of today. It displays recent european projects, both planned and already built. Through May 14th.

4-28-1998

Bundestag President Rita Süssmuth and Building Minister Eduard Oswald lay the cornerstone for the "Bundesschlange" ("Federal Snake"). The site on Moabiter Werder between Paulstrasse, S-Bahn-line, and the Spree will absorb 718 residences for members of parliament and federal civil servants as well as an elementary school. Architect: Georg Bumiller, Berlin. Architects for individual buildings: Müller - Rhode - Wandert, Berlin. The Frankfurter Siedlungsgesellschaft (FSG) and the Deutschbau-Immobilien-Dienstleistungen GmbH are completing the project for the federal government. Construction costs: approx. DM 200 mill. Scheduled completion: End of 1999.

4-29-1998

Trial run for the new Pamukkale Fountain at Görlitzer Park in Kreuzberg. Wigand Witting's artistic interpretation of this Turkish miracle of nature still lacks a sponsor, which is why the test operation is being restricted to a single day. Client: Kreuzberg Municipal District Office. Construction time from October 1995 through June 1998. Cost: DM 3.8 mill.

4-30-1998

Topping-out ceremony in Charlottenburg. The shells are now standing for seven buildings with a total of 90 residences for Federal Defense Ministry staff; they will be ready for occupancy in December of this year. Address: Passenheimer Strasse at the corner of Scottweg. Developer: Deutsche Bau- und Grundstücks-AG (Baugrund), Bonn. Architects: Planungsbüro Schmitz, Aachen. Construction total: DM 13.4 mill.

5-1-1998

The month of May starts on a highly satisfactory note, culture-wise: Just as the "Theatertreffen" ("Theater Conclave") convenes, Claus Peymann announces that—beginning on August 1, 1999—he will be honoring the Berliner Ensemble and the city (that "barren desert") with his presence and his work. His Berlin debut from ages ago, as co-founder of the "Schaubühne am Halleschen Ufer," was short and to the point. Half a lifetime later, he returns with a knapsack full of well-tested true revolutions. Cf. BBA January 7.

April 1998

Last rounds using two wheels on the cycling race track in Weissensee. The track and stands at this popular athletic facility were put up in 1956 as part of the GDR's "National Building Works." Work on converting the arena into an athletic center for track and field begins this month.

April 1998

Next to the Infobox, Sony erects a 10 by 10 meter large model of the tent roof that will span the oval Forum on Potsdamer Platz designed by Helmut Jahn, Chicago. The model lets the viewer experience the interplay among fabric rails, steel beams and wires, and large glass surfaces. For the roof construction, developed together with the firm of Ove Arup, 600 tons of steel, 3,500 sq. m of glass, 150 tons of steel wire, and 5,200 sq. m of fabric rails will be used. Scheduled completion: End of 1999. Roof construction cost: approx. DM 20 mill.

5-4-1998

Candlelight dinner for Barbara Perplies and Catrin Peters, Quiz Queens, served by Jürgen Klemann, Berlin's Building Senator. The delicacies came from the KaDeWe department store, the table by crane, the Senator from a meeting, the ladies from Wilmersdorf. The guests were served dinner on the road in the ducts of the Tiergarten tunnel. Ambient temperature: dimly cold.

5-5 to 10-1998

"Fine little additions" is what the daily paper "Der Tagesspiegel" calls the theater and festival series "Rich and Beautiful '98," which is taking place for the third time alongside the "Theatertreffen" ("Theater Conclave"). Offerings for border crossers and denizens of the outskirts, this time in Podewil and the Parochialkirche.

5-5-1998

"Built in 1998—First Buildings by Berlin Architects," an exhibit of the Berlin Chamber of Architects, hosted for the first time by the Building Senator in the Berlin Pavilion. As of today, the following are on display: Buildings and designs scheduled for building, along with award-winning competition entries by young local architects (male and female).

5-6-1998

With a trial explosion, demolition work begins on the old Spandau sluicegate. The facility, built in 1911, had to be taken out of operation in 1993 because it was dilapidated. Now, demolition and rebuilding are proceeding in tandem. The locks, which connect the Havel-Oder and Lower Havel waterways, will contain a sluice chamber widened to 115 m from 67 m. In addition, a plant building, transformer station, and pumping works are supposed to be built. Completion is scheduled for the end of 1999.

5-6-1998

Today, in the Berlin Parliament's steering committee, implementation of a pilot project for leasing buildings is being considered, after the full Senate had already approved the trial program back in April. To test the "sale-and-lease-back" procedure, two public administration buildings were selected—Klosterstrasse 64 and Am Köllnischen Park 4. Both are in need of renovation. The fiscal advantage gained by going to a private developer—who can first purchase the houses, then renovate them, and finally transfer them back to the city via leasing—would derive from special depreciation regulations used in the eastern part of the city, rules that a private investor (as opposed to the public sector) is able to utilize to lower costs. Skepticism among the Greens, PDS, and Audit Division.

5-7-1998

Opening of a new permanent exhibit organized by the Stadtmuseum (City Museum) in the Ephraim-palais: "The Art from the times of Frederick the Great through 1945." 160 paintings and sculptures were selected from the City Museum's splendid collection, which includes 3,000 paintings alone (out of 1.5 million exhibit pieces overall). General Director Reiner Güntzer complains about the lack of space in each of his two houses, the Berlin Museum and the Märkisches Museum (by Ludwig Hoffmann, 1907). Something might be done expanding the latter, for it is already an elaborate architectural composite in all sorts of Maerkish styles (styles of the Brandenburg region).

May 1998

Decision in the competition for a new building to house the Institute for Physics at the Humboldt University in Berlin-Adlershof. First prize: Augustin und Frank, Berlin; 2nd prize: von Gerkan, Hamburg; 3rd prize; Abcarius & Burns, Berlin.

5-3-1998

The last auto race on the "Avus," after 77 years of making history in motor sports. "Nowhere else did you have such a long straight lane, nowhere such a sharp turn, such a blind passage as on the north curve. And hardly anywhere else were the fans so close to the action," said Peter Mücke (from the motor sports team of the same name). In 1959 the last Grand Prix race was held in Berlin.

5-1-1998

Decision on the location for the Cuban embassy. In Prenzlauer Berg, in the so-called "Stavanger Complex" where other diplomatic missions are also to be found, the Cuban Republic has acquired properties on Ibsenstrasse 12 and Stavangerstrasse 20, on a site whose overall size is 4,300 sq.m. Here is where the embassy's chancery and ambassador's residence will be built.

Today, Stefan Kissling wins both runs in the German Touring Car Challenge. The Avus road house from 1935 (formerly, the administration building for Avus GmbH) and the grandstands from 1937 are designated landmarks. In 1999, the Lausitz-Ring, a raceway near Berlin suitable for Grand Prix competition, is supposed to be dedicated.

5-4-1998

Chief Cantor Estrongo Nachama turns eighty. Berlin counts it as an honor to have him here for over fifty years. Congratulations!

Not a Prussian, but rather Greek by birth, to whom it was not sung at the cradle on May 4, 1918 in Salonica that he would one day become a pillar of Jewish life as reconstructed in Berlin. And the path leading here was the most horrible imaginable: Deported on Passover 1943 in cattle carts to Auschwitz, forced to work there in the quarry at the nearby camp of Golischau, survived because—as the "Singer of Auschwitz"—he entertained the guards with song, then liberated by the Red Army on one of those "Death Marches" out of Sachsenhausen. What he experienced then, he never told me. But when circumstances call for it, he will explain what happened to his grandchildren…
Andreas Nachama, 1998

5-6-1998

"Break-in-free plastering" is on the way. All around the Reichstag, the State Criminal Police (LKA, for Landeskriminalamt) recommends laying plaster that nobody can tear out. And other security measures to boot. However, Gerhard Schröder (the Social Democratic candidate hoping to unseat Chancellor Kohl on September 27) regrets this, saying that—when he arrives—he doesn't want to be holding office at a place "where the government and the governed could not really encounter each other."

5.6.1998

Special exhibition for Erwin Redslob (1884–1973) opens in the rotund of the Ephraim Palace. The art and culture historian served Berlin as the Reich cultural attaché during the Weimar Republic, and after what he called "Germany's most evil time" he became a co-founder of the Free University, the Tagesspiegel newspaper and the Berlin Museum.

5-7-1998

Cornerstone laying for the expansion of the Lindenschule in Staaken. The old schoolhouse located on what used to be the border strip, is being extended (by Berlin architects Dörr, Ludolf, and Wimmer) to include a four-track elementary school with athletic hall. Costs: DM 31.6 mill. (financed by the elementary school special funds).

5-7-1998

The joint estate of Inge Müller and Heiner Müller enriches the archive at the Academy of the Arts. Today, the acquisition was announced, with some of the finds displayed in cases. The material—consisting of manuscripts for plays, letters, documents on theater work, photos, videos, reviews, and a plethora of personal documents (130,000 pages overall)—is located in the archival building on Robert-Koch-Platz 10. It will take just a year to sift through the archive, and two and a half years to collate the archival material into a "book of findings."

5-7-1998

Ceremony marking the 50th anniversary of the state of Israel's founding, at the Berliner Schauspielhaus in the presence of the Federal President, Federal Chancellor, Bundestag President, and two thousand invited guests. In the Axel Springer publishing company's Berlin quarters, the exhibit "Israel: The First 50 Years—A Photobiography" by Magnum photographer Micha Bar-Am is opend. Bar-Am was born in 1930 in Berlin and has lived in Israel since 1936.

I can still remember how we planted the first tree-lined avenue on Tu B'Shevat, the Jewish new year festival of trees in the spring, little delicate saplings. And 50 years later, a journalist arrives from Egypt and says, "Interesting, how the Jews have settled in the most beautiful places." They always sold us the worst places, rocky deserts and swamps, but we made the best of it. Really and truly, I am not much of a Zionist. I live in Israel, I don't need to be a Zionist. But we cultivated the land, that's a fact.

The everyday language of the kibbutz was Yiddish, and so I learned Yiddish instead of Hebrew, which was more to my liking anyway. If someone spoke to me in Hebrew while we were working, I would always say, "Chaver, red' Yiddish!" (Friend, speak Yiddish). To work in that heat and then have to speak Hebrew was really asking too much. But Yiddish was easy. As they say, "You speak German, but Yiddish speaks itself."

One day, when some newspapers had just come from Germany, someone came to me and said, "Just look at what your Hitler is doing!" In Germany, I had been the filthy Jew; here, I was the representative of the German Reich.

Gad Granach, 1998

5-13-1998

Topping-out ceremony for the Forum on Landsberger Allee at the corner of Storkower Strasse, right next to the Perrault's Velodrome. On a 12,200 sq. m area, two new buildings with up to 11 stories are being erected, integrating an existing building already renovated. In addition to offices and retail shops, there will be a hotel with 161 rooms here. Developers: Bauwert, Allgemeine Projektentwicklungs- und Bautraegergesellschaft, and BB-Immobilien-Service GmbH. Architects: Rhode, Kellermann, Wawrowsky (RKW), Düsseldorf. Total rental space about 36,000 sq.m. Investment total: DM 288 mill. Scheduled completion in autumn.

5-14-1998

Topping-out ceremony for the new rapid transit garage in Grünau. The complex includes a workshop hall with two tracks and a maintenance hall with five service tracks, supplemented by a social and administration building with storage and technical rooms. Client: S-Bahn Berlin GmbH. Architect: Peter Altenkamp, Berlin. Construction cost: DM 50 mill. Opening: November 6, 1998

5-14-1998

A little revolution in the Mitte district. Karin Baumert of the PDS (successor party to the East German Communists), and City Councillor for Building in the Mitte district, a politician averse to architecture though (it is said) favorably disposed toward investors, is removed from office by a motion from her own party. She is succeeded on an interim basis by Eva Mendl, City Councillor for Culture and Education (likewise PDS).

5-8-1998

Cornerstone laying for a Gymnasium (secondary school) in the Hellersdorf district on Kyritzer Strasse. The building for 950 students and 80 teachers will cost only DM 55 mill. instead of the DM 75 mill. originally anticipated. Savings are coming at the expense of the main building and the athletic hall. Architects: MBM Arquitectes/S.A., Barcelona, with Klaus Kammann, Berlin. Scheduled completion: Mid-2001.

5-10-1998

Under today's dateline, "Karow Live '98 Highlights" reports: "Cornerstone laying for the Community Center on Achillesstrasse, corner of Bucher Chaussee. Architects: Lunetto and Fischer, Berlin. Scheduled completion: December 1998.

5-10-1998

The Jewish Cultural Association of Berlin (Jüdischer Kulturverein, or JKV) moves into its new quarters in the Jewish Communication Center (JCC) at Oranienburger Strasse 26 in the Mitte district. One floor above, the Anne Frank Center, a branch of the Anne Frank House in Amsterdam, will have its rooms.

5-11-1998

Conclusion of negotiations between the "Special Federal Office for Unification-Related Matters" and the German Civil Servants Federation over the sale of the "Haus der Demokratie" ("Democracy House") on Friedrichstrasse, once the seat of the SED (East Germany's ruling party) headquarters for the Mitte district. Purchase price: DM 14.7 mill. Politically, the negotiations were difficult, because the rooms used during the "Wende" (GDR's peaceful revolution) of '89 had been promised to the GDR's citizen movements (including the "New Forum"), whose impact on events emanated from these quarters. The current users are 41 political and social groups, though only 4 still trace their lineage directly to the GDR's civil rights movements. Now there is a compromise envisioning that one third of the building will be used by the Civil Servants Federation, with the remaining two thirds left to a (yet to be established) "Foundation for Investigating the SED Dictatorship."

5-12-1998

The Bundestag leaps across the Spree. Federal Parliament President Rita Süssmuth performs the first ceremonial spade-digging for the Marie-Elisabeth-Lüders-Haus. The complex by Munich architect Stephan Braunfels forms the eastern end of the "Federal Ribbon" linked to the Reichstag building by a footbridge over the Spree. In around 600 rooms, the complex will chiefly include the central parliamentary library with a press documentation center and Bundestag archive. Costs: approx. DM 330 mill. Scheduled competition: end of 2000. Cf. February 2.

5-13 to 5-14-1998

On the occasion of the 50th anniversary of the Berlin Airlift, US President Bill Clinton visits the city. The official greeting by Federal Chancellor Helmut Kohl at the Sanssouci palace park in Potsdam is followed at 5:30 p.m. by a commemoration at the Schauspielhaus theater on Gendarmenmarkt. Afterwards, the celebration moves on to the Federal President's reception at Schloss Bellevue, followed that evening by a gala dinner in the Hotel Adlon. On the second day, Bill Clinton baptizes a modern transport aircraft from the U.S. Air Force to the name of "Spirit of Berlin."

5-14-1998

On Prerower Platz in Hohenschönhausen, in the midst of prefab housing projects, a cornerstone is laid today for an additional cinema multiplex. Once again, it will have nine theaters, and (again) 2,000 seats. At the request of the district government, the cinema center will have a multifunctional hall at its disposal with 500 seats for theater, musicals, concerts, or conventions. Developer: Ulrich Weber, Berlin. Architect: Helmut Sprenger. Investment: DM 45 mill. Opening: December 11, 1998.

Knife and Fork *Sabine Lenz, 1995*

They are an old couple, an everyday, conventional couple, one that stays together for the usual reasons. There is nothing special to say about them; it is a simple, digestible relationship, the way it happens over the course of time. Sometimes, out of habit, the fork becomes a little sharp or the knife a little cutting when they speak of times gone by–the knife's bread-slicing days or the cake excursions of the fork–but those hurts have been patched up a hundred times, and there are no dry crumbs left to discuss. Now they always go to dinner parties together; the knife keeps to the right side of the plate, the fork to the left, so that they experience the evening from different sides and have something to talk about afterwards. The roast was really steamed, says the knife, for example, and the fork asks, did you notice how hot the curry was? Their conversations mostly revolve around food, the way it is with old couples. And naturally they gossip about the other silverware on the table. The fork sneers: I think the soup ladle gets fatter every day, don't you? And the knife complains: I wish they had had cheese for dessert instead of ice cream by the spoonful. That's the sort of thing they say after mealtimes; nothing else occurs to them. Only rarely do shreds of longing still cling to them, remnants they vainly try to brush off onto each other. One of our kind used to cut book pages instead of pushing gravy, sighs the knife, while the fork laments, if only I didn't have such a crooked back, I could be a tuning fork today. Spilled upon and licked clean, they hang over the edge of the plate. Let's go back to the drawer, says the fork, it was a wild evening. The knife cleans his blade, and the fork washes herself between the tines before they lie down in separate compartments. Thanks for cutting the meat for me, says the fork as they fall asleep. The knife doesn't hear; his quiet snores cut through the silence.

5-14-1998

"Sinn und Form", form and meaning, are not made to parallel in the same kind of drawer, like knife and fork; this much is obvious in the exhibition arranged by Richard Sapper for the International Design Center (IDZ) in its new quarters in Oberbaum City, Friedrichshain.

5-17-1998

Starting today, photographer Ellen Auerbach exhibits in the Academy of the Arts. The roughly 150 pictures on display constitute a cross-section of her work; in addition, short films from the early Thirties are shown. The now 92-year-old artist, born in Karlsruhe, studied sculpture and was the private student of Bauhaus photographer Walter Peterhans. She emigrated in 1933 to Palestine, then went to London, and has lived in New York since 1944. She came to Berlin to attend the exhibit. Through July 7.

5-19-1998

Topping-out ceremony for a residential facility with eight 5-to-7-story houses and a total of 223 condominium flats on Emmentaler Strasse in Reinikkendorf. Developer: GEWOBAG. Architects: Garsztecki and Hartmann, Berlin. Investment total: around DM 65 mill. Completion: November 1998.

5-20-1998

Opening of an exhibit on the "Building of the Steglitz Gyroscope"–and so of one of postwar Berlin's biggest construction scandals–in the Schwarz Villa in Steglitz. The CDU caucus in the district assembly used its absolute majority to withdraw financing for this project. Thanks to the Heinrich Böll Foundation, which made DM 8,000 available for its completion, the exhibit came about in spite of the CDU's veto.

May

5-15-1998

Today this year's Berlin Theater Prize goes to Luc Bondy, longtime member of the Berliner Schaubühne. His most beautiful staging there was surely Mariveaux' "Triumph of Love." Cf. BBA '97, May 11.

5-15-1998

The Green League of Berlin presents a model courtyard designed and planted by garden planner Angeli Büttner. Address: Prenzlauer Allee 230, backyard.

5-15-1998

Marrying made pretty, Nr. 3 (the last): Heike Birkenfeld and Axel Strehlau celebrate an adventure wedding in the hippo house at the Zoological Garden; wet eyes all round.

5-16-1998

Reopening of the Delphi-Terrassen on Kantstrasse near the Theater des Westens and the new Ludwig Erhard House. The terraces were reconstructed according to Bernhard Sehring's original plans from 1927 using rediscovered fragments of pillars and walls. Reconstruction was commissioned by the Chamber of Industry and Commerce, which also assumed the construction costs of DM 1.9 mill. Landscape planning: HORTEC, Berlin. Operator: Café Quasimodo, Giorgio Carioti. 250 seats. The reconstruction of the "Kaisertreppe" (the "Imperial Stairway" demolished and encased in 1988) linking the Delphi-Terrassen with the Theater des Westens remains to be done.

5-16-1998

Therese Giehse, actress, cabaret artist, and interpreter of Brechtian characters, would have turned 100 today. With a birthday mixture of recitation and music, the event is celebrated at the Schaubühne on Lehniner Platz.

5-17-1998

Today songwriter Wolf Biermann is awarded the German National Foundation's National Prize. The foundation–whose executive board includes ex-Chancellor Helmut Schmidt, Saxon governor Kurt Biedenkopf, and the Alexander-von-Humboldt-Foundation's President Professor Reimar Lüst–was founded in 1993 at Weimar with the goal of helping both parts of Germany get closer culturally and spiritually. The prize has a cash value of DM 150,000. Cf. February 10.

5-19-1998

Opening for the third nation-wide "Monkey Terror Literature Festival" at Kastanienallee 85 in Prenzlauer Berg. For five evenings, 32 authors read "social beat literature."

Social Beat Literature *Gunnar Lützow*

Since the beginning of the Nineties, a "social beat literature" scene–which by now is made up of approximately 200 authors, small publishers, and magazine makers–has been protesting the disappearance of reality from literature. Along with a predilection for narrative and a spiritual affinity for honest blues and hard rock, with a naturally fluid borderline dividing social beat from the more rap-like "poetry slam" scene–broken biographies seem to be the hallmark of the participants. Hardly anyone from this scene, after graduating from school or getting a master's degree, managed to make a soft landing on the cushion of arts grants. Although there is one ex-model present (Nadine Berth from the chic "Amica" outfit), the typical social beat freak still has a background more like Enno Stahl (from Duisburg-Rheinhausen), or (like "Shanhai") has studied to be a streetcar conductor, or worked at a place like Helmsted municipal administration (like Bettina Sternberg).

139

Ruled out version of Sir Norman Foster

5-20-1998

Edzard Reuter becomes an honorary citizen of Berlin. The award is meant to honor his services to the city. Reuter's decision, immediately after the fall of the Wall, to move Daimler-Benz management functions to Berlin stimulated construction at Potsdamer Platz.

5-20-1998

With a festival for 3,000 guests, the completion of the Treptowers is celebrated today. Developer: Allianz-Versicherung. General contractor: Roland-Ernst-Gruppe. Architects: Gerhard Spangenberg, Berlin, Reichel & Stauth, Braunschweig, Schweger + Partner, Hamburg. In spite of the most beautiful setting, at the moment it is hard to find tenants. Cf. BBA '97, p. 98.

5-24-1998

As part of the rapid train line connecting Hanover to Berlin, the stretch of track from the Bahnhof Zoo train station to the station in the eastern part of the city known as 140 Hauptbahnhof" is opened up for inter-city travel. The high-speed stretch that goes to Hanover via Stendal should be fully ready for operation by September. For now, however, nothing but breakdowns: total collapse of logistics during today's schedule change, and at times eight trains are simultaneously stopped in front of red signals on the newly opened urban rapid transit tracks, while the platforms are overcrowded, and the waiting period sometimes lasts for hours. Hanging over everything is the new punctuality board.

5-25-1998

The FDP (Germany's liberal party) celebrates a topping-out ceremony for its headquarters on Reinhardtstrasse in the Mitte district. A building designed in 1910 by architect Clemens Pickel as a hospital is being renovated there for DM 38 mill. and supplemented by some new building segments. The facade is being restored in line with landmark protection regulations, and the interior is being largely gutted. One third of the building will be occupied by the party itself, with the remaining office and shop space rented out for other purposes. Architects: Hoffmann and Krug, Kiel. Scheduled completion: End of 1998.

5-26-1998

The Senate approves four of five site layouts on the 124 acres site "Alter Schlachthof" ("Old Slaughterhouse") on Landsberger Allee in Prenzlauer Berg, thereby creating binding legislation for the area already designated in June 1993

Foster's approximation to the "Fat Hen"

5-27-1998

The Bundestag's Building Commission reaches unanimity on transferring Bonn's Bundestag eagle to the Reichstag in a version with just a light haircut, thereby following the recommendation of Sir Norman Foster, who will now only have to implant a back into the eagle, since the parliamentary animal must now (unlike earlier) have to be visible from behind as well.

Present Federal Eagle by Behnisch

Eagle by Kurt Weidemann

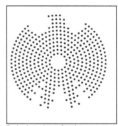
"Fat Hen" by Ludwieg Gies

Another trial by Sir Norman Foster

Design by Stauss

Design by Laeis, BBA favorite

5-21-1998

Opening of an exhibit in the Neue Nationalgalerie featuring works of Arnold Böcklin, Giorgio de Chirico, and Max Ernst. Under the title "Journey into the Unknown," it may be seen through August 10.

5-22-1998

The results of a restricted competition for the new building housing the Apostolic Nunciature on Lilienthalstrasse in Neukölln are announced. 1st prize: Dieter-Georg Baumewerd, Munich. The design envisions a 5-story complex divided into three sections with a glass-covered reception hall. Costs: DM 15 mill. Scheduled completion: end of 2000.

Eagle adorning the Federal Press papers

5-25-1998

"Die Berliner Ermittlung" ("The Berlin Investigation"), a variation on the play by Peter Weiss, is performed at the Hebbel-Theater, the Berliner Ensemble, and at the Volksbühne, staged by Esther and Jochen Gerz. Peter Weiss had collected voices from the Frankfurt Auschwitz trial (1963 to 1965) into eleven songs, following Dante's "Inferno." Jochen Gerz has picked the songs to pieces as quotes and put them in the mouths of 60 amateur actors whom he solicited in a letter-writing campaign, inaugurated into the production, and then allowed to appear in every conceivable medium as appetizers. Lots of daily chatter during rehearsal period, and misunderstanding during performances. Through June 1.

5-25-1998

Topping-out ceremony for the addition to the Federal Economics Ministry at the Invalidenpark in the Mitte district. The building will be finished by year's end. Architects: Baumann and Schnittger, Berlin.

as a development region. Over the next ten years, for around DM 2.5 billion, the urban development company "Stadtentwicklungsgesellschaft Eldenaer Strasse" (SES) plans to have a new urban quarter created there with 2,000 residences, a central park, and promenades. An initial building segment between Landsberger Allee, Hausburgstrasse, Thaerstrasse, and Ringbahn could be completed within two years. But there are still legal wranglings in the offing with three firms located in the area.

5-26-1998

In DAZ (German Architecture Center), an exhibit opens on the Italian architect Giuseppe Terragni (1904–1949). On display are around 20 models that students from the Hamburg Vocational College built as seminar projects following original plans. Terragni is regarded as a leading exponent of "Rational Architecture," and a major share of his buildings resulted from public commissions for the Italian Fascists. Through August 22.

The Eagle *Evelyn Roll*

In the first drawings of the Reichstag architect Sir Norman Foster, it did look a little like a puny chicken from the East—a kind of pan-German broiler, plucked and skinned like the whole land. The kind of federal German eagle, perhaps, that only an English "Sir" could invent in a fit of British black humor. Absolutely nothing left of "Soar High" (and certainly not of the "Red Eagle," heaven forbid). But then the representatives of the people rebelled. The delegates held up their fat hen from the fat Bonn years and formed an alliance "across party lines," an alliance to "save our heraldic animal." The fat hen, they said, was a kind of trademark of federal German parliamentary democracy, which should by no means be replaced by a newer, more modern, or even slimmer company logo. Inspection of the site later revealed, however, that the fat old two-dimensional eagle of Bonn days was unsuited to the Berlin republic. The fact is that in the Reichstag, it will no longer be nailed on the wall, but will hang free-floating, as it were, before the glass wall of the assembly hall, exposing even its previously concealed backside to the view of all. So now, whenever the very proper Sir Norman makes a state visit to Berlin, he brings along a new, fattened version of the eagle. And each time, the modest federal broiler looks more and more like the old fat hen. The whole thing has, of course, long since become a fine metaphor for almost everything, certainly for all the fat privileges and unaesthetic bloatings of our parliamentary system. After all, we wouldn't want them to be modernized, slimmed down, or even plucked with the move from Bonn to Berlin. Heaven forbid.

5-27-1998

The Berlin Senate decides to renovate and expand the Olympic Stadium to become a "multi-functional arena for professional soccer, gymnastics, and entertainment with 70–80,000 seats." A procedure for choosing investors must now be prepared, and a managing company found. The decision was preceded by five years of discussions, at heart revolving around the following problems: After the failure of the city's application for the Olympic Games in 2000, which naturally envisioned using the stadium and sporting arena as central game sites, the new campaign will be an application for soccer's World Cup in 2006. For this, Berlin has to prove that it has a football stadium living up to Fifa's strict standards; the number and style of seats as well as lighting conditions are among the current stadium's weak spots. Superimposed on this requirement is the necessity of preserving the weary landmark-

5-28-1998

Construction start for the "Tiergarten Dreieck" ("Tiergarten Triangle" in the district named after Berlin's large central park) on one of the largest inner city properties still unbuilt between

5-31-1998

Exactly on time for its 300th anniversary: the ancient art collection opens with a permanent exhibition on the main floor of the Altes Museum on the Museum Island. The exhibition unites precious objects previously split between east and west amounting to 1,100 exhibit pieces. Renovation of the Altes Museum, according to plans by architects Hilmer and Sattler, will not start earlier than 2003.

June 1998

Conclusion of the renovation work on the so-called Kurfürsteneck across from the Gedächtniskirche in Charlottenburg. The Dresdner Bank, builder and landlord, has invested around DM 60 mill. Architects: Novotny, Mähner and Associates, Berlin.

June 1998

To provide relief for Berlin's construction industry, the Berlin-Brandenburg branches of the Building Industry and the Professional Building Associations have reached an agreement with the Industrial Trade Union for Construction, Agricultural, and Environmental Workers on a DM 60 mill. program. The amount comes from a six per cent cut in contributions to the Berlin welfare fund, which is used to finance vacation pay and other social welfare benefits.

June 1998

The Bertelsmann conglomerate buys up the Berlin-Verlag publishing

6-3-1998

The Berlin Japanese-German Center moves into its new domicile in the Dahlem district on Saargemünder Strasse, corner of Clayallee. Architects: The firm RTW with Peter Billerbeck and Claus Reichhardt. Cf. BBA '97, April 24.

6-3-1998

Hung 55 centimeters lower, installed on traffic islands (Karl-Marx-Strasse), and adorned with the red dot that means it will be emptied at night and on Sundays—that's how the new, accessible, and time-saving mailboxes for drivers who refuse to leave their cars are being introduced. Nothing

protected ensemble. The owner is the federal government, which thus far (apart from handing over the property cost-free) has not been prepared to make any (additional) financial contributions, while the state of Berlin also lacks funds. The DM 400,000 study by Munich business consultant Seebauer concluded that (against expectations) at most one third of the costs (estimated at between DM 600 mill. and DM 800 mill.) could be privately financed. In principle, there were two alternatives: Building a brand new stadium just for soccer (on the site of the hockey stadium) while renovating the Olympic Stadium, or modernizing the Olympic Stadium into an arena equally suited for football or gymnastics. There are different suggestions on how to implement the latter option, now endorsed by this Senate resolution.

Stülerstrasse and Klingelhöferstrasse. Since July 1997, on the northern part of the site previously known as Klingelhöfer Triangle, just beyond Rauchstrasse, construction has been in progress on the five Nordic embassies that will be formed into an enclosed whole by a 16 m high curved wall: The larger, southern part of the property with a total area of 30,000 sq. m will be filled out with dense block construction grouped around a central, almost private "pocket park" (7,000 sq. m) only open to the public at specific times. Some of the prominent users have already been determined: Mexico's embassy and cultural center, the CDU's federal office, and the Federal Association of Private Building Loan Associations. The administrative buildings, rentalapartments, and condominiums will be built in accordance with the highest standards.

With the urban design contract concluded on May 20, 1998 between the state of Berlin and Berlin developer Groth + Graalfs, the developer commits to undertaking the most comprehensive traffic handling; in return, he is allowed to close off Corneliusstrasse and transform it into a promenade with sculptures. A total of 17 architects (most of them coming out of the 1997 Workshop—cf. BBA '97, July 1st) will build here. Total investment (without embassy buildings): DM 350 mill. Scheduled completion: early 2000.

June 1998

"Der Merkur" (subtitle: "German Journal for European Thinking") is going to hang out its shingle at the address of its Berlin editorial office. The rationale: "This was always the kind of journal that saw itself, and was seen, as a national platform for intellectual discourse. Or, better yet, let's put it this way: Merkur has always seen itself as a substitute platform for the main stage that was lost, that was never quite available, though we should by no means underestimate the intellectual charm of Germany's federal tradition... With this in mind, we intend to strengthen that essential counter-pole to the centrifugal pull of the provinces... Let's go there, and let's be there. Let us profit from the metropolis that Berlin may become in the future."

June 1998

"Flyer Updates" goes America. A New York edition of this little Berlin party and club magazine, which is distributed free, has started to appear in print, unfortunately only in New York.

house; company founder and boss Arnulf Conradi will remain in office. Wolf Jobst Siedler, manager of the Berlin Siedler Verlag publishing house, also part of Bertelsmann, retires. From now on, both publishing companies will be managed under their own names with a joint infrastructure, all under Conradi's aegis.

6-3 to 6-7-1998

A five-day "InnenStadt-Aktion" ("Down Town Action") against the "privatization and militarization" of public space at the hands of politicians and investors. From the activists' program: Wed., June 3, Alexanderplatz, 3 p.m.: boarding public squares, 5 p.m.: "Subjective feelings about security: Therapy of the paranoid masses." Thurs., June 4, Bhf. Friedrichstrasse railway station, 4 p.m.: "Safe and clean for the sake of metropolitan splendor." Women, bring cleaning utensils! Near the Tempodrom, 2 p.m.: "Intra-city mien [sic] fields to protect the government district."

stands in the way of their utilization by non-motorized postal customers—that is, apart from the separatist inscription "Auto mailbox" and the inability to deposit a letter from the sidewalk. The eight boxes that were put into service today are supposed to be followed by seven more.

6-4-1998

The long-awaited cornerstone laying took place for the AIDS hospice run by the society "Zuhause im Kiez" ("At Home in the 'Hood") on Reichenberger Strasse. Through May 1999, 21 separate apartments are supposed to be built to accommodate seriously infirm patients who cannot live alone, but do not need hospital treatment. Here they can receive care and medical supervision. Cf. BBA '97, January 9.

6-4-1998

Architects' Ranking has little to do with ranker or rankness. While such are matters of one's own capabilities the architect needs a little help from journalists to get to the top of the BauNetz (Building Network) Ranking List. The more he's written up, the more points he gets. Just how much sense—or non-sense—this kind of ranking makes is the subject of a discussion this evening at the German Architectural Center (DAZ). What still doesn't exist among the various ranking categories: The "Ground-Digging King" (for politicians), the "King for Chairing an Award Jury" (that crown would have to go to Max Bächer, for sure).

6-5-1998

"Philosopher encounters politicians" or "Intellect meets power." At the SPD's party headquarters in Wilhelmstrasse in Kreuzberg, Jürgen Habermas, philosopher and member of the Frankfurt School, meets Gerhard Schröder, the SPD's candidate for Chancellor in the upcoming federal parliamentary election, at the invitation of the Social Democracy Cultural Forum. The event's main theme, which both philosopher and politician broach during their speeches and discussion: "Drawing In the Other—For an Inclusive Politics."

6-5-1998

As of today, Spandau's public buildings find themselves gathered together in a little publication. Of the 13 buildings already completed or still being constructed between 1991 and 2001, almost all (with one exception), are day care centers and schools.

High Noon *Evelyn Roll*

Every day at noon for a number of weeks now, the philosopher Peter Sloterdijk has been frequenting the restaurant under the editorial offices of the Süddeutsche Zeitung. Probably no one recognizes him; he doesn't really look much like a philosopher. Besides, now everyone is always watching the table where Götz George has recently begun to hold court—a wonderful person too. Peter Sloterdijk always eats alone; usually he doesn't even have a book with him. Probably brought along some food for thought again. But he likes it when you look at him as you pass by, as if to say, I know who you are, I've even read you. That's the way it is in Berlin now, at least in Mitte.

You meet people, you know people, or maybe you don't; you greet people. And you like it—at least once you've lived here a while and your resistance to almost all the Berlin diseases has weakened. Yesterday, for example, George Tabori announced that he would be moving to Berlin in his old age, soon in fact, since he wants to write a piece for the Berlin Ensemble when Peymann comes. And now Gerhard Schröder: he moved into room 513 of the Willy-Brandt-Haus on Wilhelmstrasse with a picture of Max Uhlig, saying he didn't want to wait until the government moves, he wants to start governing from Berlin right away.

In the rest of the world it's been considered chic for a long time now, and soon it'll probably become fashionable here as well: not to have to think of any excuse at all to move to Berlin. And on Monday evening, they turned on the lights in the dome of the Reichstag. Just as an experiment. Looks great.

6-8-1998

Planwerk Innenstadt Berlin (Downtown Berlin Planning Works), this time from a different perspective. The IHK, BFW, and BBU (the acronyms for the Chamber of Commerce and Industry, the State Association of Independent Housing Companies Berlin/Brandenburg, and the Association of Berlin-Brandenburg Housing Entrepreneurs) issue an invitation to a discussion in the former Staatsrat (GDR executive council) building. Dr. Peter Ring explains "The Regional Economic Potential of the Downtown Planning Works," Gesine Giseke presents "An Open Space Concept for Downtown," Dr. Wulf Eichstädt supplies a "Feasibility Study on the Instrumental Sector—Urban Economic Part," Prof. Dr. Rudolf Schäfer presents the part of the feasibility study dealing with building law,

6-4-1998

Topping out ceremony underneath the Radio Tower for the fourth and final construction segment in the project to widen the Trade Fair Convention Center, following plans by O. M. Ungers and Partners. Cf. main section.

6-5-1998

Cornerstone laying on, around, and above an old bank safe. Following the Dresdner Bank's move to Pariser Platz, the "Stilwerk Design Center" is now being built on an area cleared for it along Kantstrasse. Because of the site's statics, the bank's safe has to stay where it is, so that the office building with 21,000 sq. m. of retail space will be erected around it. Architects: Novotny, Mähner + Associates, Berlin, and Studio & Partners, Milan. Scheduled completion: autumn 1999. Investment total: approx. DM 300 mill.

6-6-1998

The Staatsbibliothek (State Library) has acquired the (still uncollated) papers of the operetta composer Paul Lincke and is celebrating this event today with music in the interior courtyard of its building on Unter den Linden and with a small exhibit in the Lessing Hall.

6-6-1998

Opening of the exhibit "Dürer—Holbein—Grünewald" at the Kulturforum, with 185 Renaissance drawings (and not only by these three masters) from the engraving collections in Basel and Berlin. Through August 23.

6-7-1998

German Film Prize awarded, at the Brandenburg Gate of all places. Berlin's drivers are annoyed. As anticipated, the gold film ribbon for the best movie goes to the "Comedian Harmonist" by Joseph Vilsmaier, the top-drawing German film this year.

6-8-1998

Friedrichstrasse—Reading Mile! The bookstore chain Hugendubel, previously represented in Berlin only on Breitscheidplatz, today opens an additional branch on 1,500 sq. m. at Rosmarinkarree in the Mitte district. So now (for example) when it rains, it should be possible to keep reading from the Gendarmenmarkt all the way through to the Friedrichstrasse train station. First a few pages at Kiepert, the next few—be careful with that wet coat! —at Hugendubel, and the rest at Dussmann's. From there, it's not too far until you reach the safety of the rapid transit train, newspaper in hand.

and Dr. Reinhard Giehler speaks about "Traffic Planning Framework Conditions for Implementing the Planning Works." Familiar voices—the voice of Senate Building Director Prof. Barbara Jakubeit and of the State Secretary for Urban Development Hans Stimmann right into the background.

6-9-1998

Their plays have names like "Shopping & Fucking," "I Licked a Whore's Deodorant," or "Knives in Hens." By contrast, the director and dramaturge sport bourgeois names, Thomas Ostermeier and Jens Hillje. For their production of David Harrower's "Knives in Hens," in the barracks of the Deutsches Theater, both men today are getting the DM 15,000 "Friedrich Luft Theater Prize" awarded by the Berliner Morgenpost newspaper. Together with Sascha Walz and Jochen Sandig, these two whiz kids of the theater scene will be taking over the management of the Schaubühne am Lehniner Platz in the year 2000; just today, the contract was signed.

As far as building is concerned, expectation management is king in Berlin. The new year won't be much different from the old in that respect—the cranes come and go, competitions begin expensively and fizzle out. No one is shocked anymore. Sometimes the architectural sponsors even still hold their symposia. A little slaughter of ideas here, a little white lie there, and everywhere a little budget swindle. As long as everyone plays by the rules and doesn't do anything like shoot over the roofline, no one really gets upset anymore.
Thea Herold, 1-7-1998

6-10-1998

The German Trade Union Federation DGB announces that it will not be moving to Berlin. Trade unionists and politicians react with dismay. Klaus Landowsky, the leader of the CDU group in Berlin's parliament, characterizes the decision as "the opposite of solidarity—scandalous and ahistorical."

6-10-1998

Start of demolition work on the former guest house of the SED Central Committee on Wallstrasse in the Mitte district, in order to make room for the new Brazilian embassy. As of autumn 2000, 10 diplomats and 40 administrative staff from Brazil's old embassy in Bonn and from consulates in Cologne and Berlin will be moving in. Construction: Deutsche Grundbesitz Management GmbH. Architects: Pysall, Stahrenberg, & Partners, Berlin.

6-10-1998

Youth Senator Ingrid Stahmer (SPD) presents a study on the voting behavior of Berlin youth. 4,400 young people of voting age were polled: In the east, 41% of those in school and 36.6% of apprentices are not going to vote; in the west, the corresponding numbers are 34.2 and 31.4%. More than 20% of east Berlin apprentices want to vote for the right-wing parties NPD, DVU, or Republikaner, whereas only 6.7% of the secondary school students are voting for the right. In the west the share of right-wing voters is significantly smaller. We'll have more accurate data on September 27 (election day).

6-11-1998

Cornerstone laying for an exclusive, privately run senior residence with 90 apartments on Passauer Strasse in Schöneberg. Developer: Tertianum Management AG ("for residence and living in the third part of life"). Architects: Hilmer and Sattler, Berlin. Construction cost: DM 70–80 mill. Rental price: starting at DM 5,600 per housing unit. Anticipated completion: early summer 2000.

6-12-1998

Opening of the Painting Gallery at the Kulturforum in Tiergarten—a major event after more than 10 years of planning, including five years of construction. The interior is dominated by daylight and velvet in different colors. And by especially good air. Orderly decorated walls, the chance to get reacquainted with pictures that looked quite different while displayed in Dahlem. Closed on Mondays. Architects: Hilmer and Sattler, Berlin. Cost: DM 285 mill. Cf. main section.

6-15-1998

This is the year for centennial birthdays. And they're celebrated as they happen. Today the Academy of Arts starts an exhibit commemorating the 100th birthday of Hanns Eisler, whose precise date of birth was 7-6-1898. On display are autographs, theater and film posters, photos, letters, sheet music, programs, and records. Listening is also possible, using recorded documents from the Academy's Eisler Archive. Through August 2nd.

June

6-10-1998

Public swearing-in ceremony for military recruits in Berlin Mitte. The place: Within sight of the "Platz vor dem Roten Rathaus" (the square in front of Berlin's city hall), with Karl-Liebknecht-Strasse cordoned off. The players: Recruits and police versus counter-demonstrators. The instruments: brass band, military tattoo, water cannons against whistles, chanting choruses, loudspeaker wagons. From out of the various throats: Intoning of the swearing-in oath in unison—collective scanning of slogans. The officials: Eberhard Diepgen, mayor of Berlin: "The Bundeswehr is always welcome in Berlin" —Jürgen Trittin, executive spokesperson for Alliance 90/The Greens: "We have succeeded in preventing a public swearing-in ceremony, the place is a mobile barracks square under police protection." The weather: Initially good, later heavy rain, on both sides. Reactions: Eberhard Diepgen gets praise from all sides, and Jürgen Trittin scolding.

6-11-1998

The Russian historian Ilya Urilov, with the support of the SPD in the district of Wedding, has come out in favor of reconstructing a grave in Wedding's mausoleum where Julius Martov and five other members of the Mensheviks, Russia's moderate Social Democrats from the Twenties, lay buried. The burial sites of the politicians forced into exile by the Bolsheviks were destroyed by the National Socialists, and all the records about their situation were destroyed. Today the rebuilt grave is being dedicated. Among those present is the former mayor of Moscow, Gavril Popov.

6-11-1998

Thomas Flierl, 40 years old, Ph.D, nonpartisan, and manager of the Cultural Office in the Prenzlauer Berg district at the beginning of the Nineties, is elected to the office of Building Councillor of Mitte, which fills the gap left by Karin Baumert's recall the month before.

6-12-1998

Opening of an exhibit by the Dutch architect Herman Hertzberger in the German Architectural Center (DAZ). In four pavilions—arranged thematically according to whether they are schools, office buildings, theaters, or urban designs—models, sketches, drawings, and photographs provide an overview of the most recent work by the architect who (among other things) participated in the master plan for the Rummelsburger Bucht. Through August 22.

6-12-1998

The World Cup in soccer gets going, with the opening game matching Brazil against Scotland (2:1). But football fever doesn't really reach Berlin until June 16, when Germany plays against the USA (2:0).

6-15-1998

Test run for lighting the Reichstag dome. In addition to normal nighttime illumination, what's at stake here is the light that twelve 1,000 watt bulbs are able to cast into the city for a distance of up to four kilometers with the help of the dome's mirrored funnel. Present at the creation of "let there be light"—the Bundestag Building Commission, which is still blinking critically.

143

6-16-1998

Berlin's Senate passes a development plan for the area (over 25 acres large) where the Ministerial Gardens were once located between Leipziger Platz and Pariser Platz. Through the year 2000, seven offices representing the following states will be built here: Brandenburg, Hesse, Mecklenburg-Eastern Pomerania, Lower Saxony, Rhineland-Palatinate, Saarland, and Schleswig-Holstein. Current residential utilization and a child day care center are being integrated into the development plan.

6-17-1998

Topping-out ceremony for the "Quartier an der Museumsinsel" ("Accommodations on the Museum Island"); special guest: ex-Foreign Minister Hans Dietrich Genscher. Developer: Hanseatica and Deutsche Grundbesitz GmbH. Architects: Steffen Lehmann, Karl-Heinz Camman, Berlin. Construction cost: DM 180 mill. Completion: March 1999. Cf. BBA '97, June 12.

6-18-1998

Today, on the occasion of the 50th anniversary of the Main Federation of the German Construction Industry, the "Construction Industry House" is dedicated at Kurfürstenstrasse 129 in Schöneberg. The process of moving in has been completed, and a staff of 70 now works in the main business office here, as well as in the Federation's two auxiliary business offices in Brussels and Bonn. Architects: Schweger + Partners, Hamburg.

6-18-1998

Cornerstone laying for a residential and commercial building on the Reinhardtstrasse, corner of Luisenstrasse. Prominent tenants for the future "House on Karlplatz" will include the CDU Economic Council's federal business office and the state representative for Berlin-Brandenburg. Developer: Züblin Projektentwicklung GmbH, Stuttgart. Architect: Walter A. Noebel, Berlin. Construction cost: DM 27 mill. Completion: 2000.

6-19-1998

As of today, four bronze busts stand in a semicircle on the square in front of the Deutsches Theater. Portrayed here are the theater's four artistic directors, Otto Brahm (1894–1903), Max Reinhardt (1905–32), Heinz Hilpert (1934–45), and Wolfgang Langhoff (1946–63).

6-20-1998

For the third time now, "SiteSeeing Berlin" looks out on Berlin's construction sites — in 1,300 scheduled events, all tolled. New here: each of the eleven weeks has a different motto. Plus: Now there is also a "Showplace Brandenburg." Through September 5.

6-22-1998

Edge city housing colonies, the new residential concept for Berlin, now also available in southern Lichterfelde. Today a decision was reached in an urban design competition for 3,280 residences on an area 37 acres large between the rapid transit

6-23-1998

"My landlord has my last shirt" is (for anyone who dares to look) what it says on the little blackboard that covers the holy of holies (and nothing more) on the (actually naked) streaker hired for advertising purposes. A stroke of genius from the advertising agency TBWA, to sell affordable office space for the real estate firm Königsstadt-Terrassen. And if you take a second look, you'll see this local phone number: 030/443 31 50.

6-24-1998

Topping-out ceremony for buildings added on to the Mark Twain Primary School at Auguste-Viktoria-Allee 95 in Reinickendorf. The following will be built: an athletic hall and two wings having 23 classrooms, department rooms, and a media center. Architects: Hundertmark + Ketterer, Berlin. Completion: 1999. Costs: DM 26.5 mill.

6-18-1998

Topping-out ceremony for the Neue Hackesche Höfe (New Hackesche Courtyards) on the corner of Rosenthaler Strasse and Dirksenstrasse. Here, grouped around three courtyards, there will be twelve six- to seven-story houses with retail and commercial space as well as 114 residences and an underground garage. Unlike the historic Hackesche Höfe across the street, these new courtyards will not be accessible to the public. The houses' formal language recalls Aldo Rossi, which is certainly no accident, since the architects Götz Bellmann and Walter Böhm were at one time the Italian star's contacts in Berlin. Developers: Wohnungsbaugesellschaft Mitte and Bassmann Bau AG. Construction cost: DM 125 mill. Completion: Early in 1999.

6-18-1998

Opening of an exhibit entitled "BerliNetwork: Transportation Routes in the Capital City" in the Tiergarten Pavilion.

6-19-1998

Topping-out ceremony for the "Zehlendorf Forum" on Teltower Damm. The office and commercial building offers 1,500 sq.m of retail and 1,700 sq.m of office space. Developer: Trigon; Berlin. Architect: Jan Bassenge, Berlin. Construction cost: DM 40 mill. Completion: October 1998.

6-19-1998

The end of renovation work in the "Yellow Quarter" on Neue Grottkauer Strasse in Hellersdorf is celebrated with Brazilian sounds. The Sao Paulo planning office Brasil Arquitetura brings an exotic note into these prefab housing projects with its designs for facades and residential settings.

line right-of-way and Osdorfer Strasse, previously used for American troop maneuvers close to the city limits. The owner is the Railroad Property Management Ltd. (EIM, for „Eisenbahn Immobilienmanagement GmbH"), represented by Haberent Grundstücks GmbH. Prize winners: Florian Beigel, London (1st prize), Daniel Libeskind, Berlin and Ernst Mayr, Vienna (2nd and 3rd prize); all three prize winners will be rewarded with construction jobs. The urban design contract obligates the award-giver to build five child day care centers, a primary school, afterschool youth centers, and playgrounds worth DM 200 mill. In the middle of the residential neighborhoods, a park about 155 acres large is supposed to be built. Scheduled construction start: Early 2000. Expected completion: 2005. Cost framework DM 1.6 billion.

The awful German language *Mark Twain*

A person who has not studied German can form no idea of what a perplexing language it is. One is washed about in it, hither and thither, in the most helpless way; and when at last he thinks he has captured a rule which offers firm ground to take a rest on amid general rage and turmoil of the ten parts of speech, he turns over the page and reads, "Let the pupil make careful note of the following exceptions." For instance, my book inquires after a certain bird — (it is always inquiring after things which are of no sort of consequence to anybody): "Where is the bird?" Now the answer to the question — according to the book — is that the bird is waiting in the blacksmith shop on account of the rain. Of course no bird would do that, but then you must stick to the book. Very well, I begin to cipher out the German for that answer. I say to myself: "Regen" (rain) is masculine — or maybe it is feminine — or possibly neuter — it is to much trouble to look now. Therefore, it is either der (the) Regen, or die (the) Regen, or das (the) Regen, according to which gender it may turn out to be when I look. Very well — then the rain is der Regen, if it is simply in the quiescent state of being mentioned, without enlargement or discussion — Nominative case; but if this rain is laying around, in a kind of a general way on the ground, it is then definitely located, it is doing something — that is, resting (which is one of the German grammar's ideas of doing something), and this throws the rain into the Dative case, and makes it dem Regen. However this rain is not resting, but is doing something actively — it is falling — to interfere with the bird, likely — and this indicates movement, which has the effect of sliding it into the Accusative case and changing dem Regen into den Regen. Having completed the grammatical horoscope of this matter, I answer up confidently and state in German that the bird is staying in the blacksmith shop "wegen (on account of) den Regen." Then the teacher lets me softly down with the remark that whenever the word "wegen" drops into a sentence, it always throws that subject into the Genitive case, regardless of consequences — and that therefore this bird stayed in the blacksmith shop "wegen des Regens."

6-24-1998

"Berlin—Capital City Without Power," a discussion that is part of the series "Capital City Talks" in Schinkel's Schauspielhaus on Gendarmenmarkt. As so often happens, Paris—as the city where the nation-state wields power—is held up as the standard for Berlin. Invited as guest and advisor: Alfred Grosser, Parisian political scientist and pioneer of Franco-German relations. His summary: A "Berlin Republic" is nonsense; an accretion of power by Berlin is ruled out by the Federal Republic's federal structure. One could complain about the need for a "civic sensibility" uniting east with west, and which would suit Berlin quite well, although

6-25-1998

"Architects as Designers," an exhibit in the Contemporary Museum at the Hamburger Bahnhof, prepared by the Kunstgewerbemuseum (Arts and Crafts Museum), which owns most of the items on exhibit. 200 beautiful objects, familiar and unfamiliar, by 120 architects. Through August 30.

6-25-1998

Prize awarded to "Architects as Designers." Joseph Paul Kleihues, Berlin's renowned star architect, gets the chance to build kiosks, waiting stations, telephone booths, toilets, benches and other places to sit, rubbish containers, tree bark protectors, poles to keep cars off the sidewalks, as well as bicycle parking places along the "splendid boulevard" Unter den Linden. The exhibit, together with the works of the 113 competitors who were less successful, can be seen beginning July 7th in the foyer of the Senate Building Administration, on Behrenstrasse 42 in the Mitte district.

6-26-1998

Cornerstone laying for a parking lot site between Leibnizstrasse and Wielandstrasse, near Kurfürstendamm. Architects: Hans Kollhoff and Helga Timmermann, Berlin. The project has a circuitous history: A winning design in a 1984 competition, revised in 1989, that very same year made more difficult because of a building plan resolution passed by the District Assembly, slowed down because the exact same resolution was rescinded in 1995, that same year taken under wing, but then inundated by protests from neighborhood residents, the object of serious negotiations in 1996 between the city's financial building administration and investors, secured using partial building permits in December of the same year, and ultimately confirmed in March 1997 when Berlin's administrative court rejected a law suit. The controversial design consists of two severe-looking bars on two-story rows of supports; hence

6-27-1998

Airlift Week at Tempelhof airport: Berlin celebrates the 50th anniversary of the Airlift. On June 25, 1948 the Berlin Blockade began, and it ended on May 12, 1949. General Lucius D. Clay, then the American military governor in Germany, succeeded in doing what nobody deemed possible: For 462 days, a city of two million was supplied by air. What the Americans called "Operation Vittles" was dubbed "Operation Plainfair" by the Royal Air Force and "Rosinenbomber" ("Raisin Bombers") by Berliners. Some statistics: 277,264 flights brought 1,831,200 tons of

6-27-1998

Opening of the Allied Museum on Clayallee in Zehlendorf, on the grounds of "Outpost," once the movie theater for the American armed forces. The museum is exhibiting the history of the Western powers and Berlin between 1945 and 1994. In a certain way, or maybe not, the counterpart to the Surrender Museum in Karlshorst, which documents the Soviet contribution to liberation from Nazi rule. A photo archive of the Airlift from out of the thousands of exhibit pieces that were publicly and privately donated to the collection; the most sensational piece is a 430 m long tunnel pipe that the Americans used to tap the East Berlin phone network, including the dynamite cable to blow it up in an emergency.

there was hardly any opportunity for this to take shape thus far, given the government's tardiness in moving out of Bonn. Professor Grosser's hope: That Berlin might contribute to a long overdue admission on Germany's part that it is, after all, a nation of immigrants. However, he did not think much of the shallow formula "multicultural."

6-24-1998

Today, as a preview of the "Berlin Building Exhibition 1999," an exhibit opens in the Garbaty cigarette factory in Pankow. Through July 19. There is a shortage of affordable single family homes in Berlin, which is why the city Senate has sponsored the program "Ownership Strategy 2000." "Building Exhibition 1999" will put on display the first 400 out of 8,000 houses to be built on five areas in Weissensee and Pankow. They are supposed to be models for suburban housing colonies where space is limited. Cf. BBA '97, November 12.

6-26-1998

Opening of a small exhibit at Aedes East showing the latest state of planning and implementation of the Ludwig Erhard House, just before its opening in September. In addition, Nicholas Grimshaw presents Industrial Design from his London office, beautifully displayed in "free-standing airline luggage" cases that simultaneously serve as means of transportation, exhibition pieces, and samples from the very same Industrial Design's repertoire. Grimshaw flew in on a private jet for a short visit, then Grimshaw spoke at the Aedes Lectures about what's ecological.

6-26-1998

"Image of an Epoch and Black Hole: The Sixties," a podium discussion among architects from eastern Berlin and western Berlin, sponsored by the Berlin Chamber of Architects in their very own chambers.

the name "Leibniz Kolonnaden" ("Leibniz Colonnades"). Both buildings stand parallel to the Kurfürstendamm, and they form the boundary around a city square that is 100 m long and 30 m wide reaching from Leibnizstrasse to Wielandstrasse. 103 residences, a child day care center on the 6th floor, and an underground garage with 360 parking spots will be built. Investors: Hanseatica Unternehmensgruppe, IVG Immobilien GmbH, and West Project & Consult. Cost: DM 170 mill. Scheduled completion: 2000.

6-26-1998

Opening of an exhibition entitled "The Roman Trail —Artistic Investigations into the Relevance of Antiquity" in the "Haus am Waldsee." On display are works by 24 artists from different European countries who, as part of a multi-annual project, have embarked on a search for discovered or invented traces of Roman antiquity in modern Europe.
Through August 16.

goods to Berlin (60% coal, 30% food, 10% industrial goods, e.g. all the parts for an energy plant); up to 300 machines were in the air simultaneously, and they arrived via three air corridors in five levels on top of each other, landing every 90 seconds. When Tempelhof and Gatow weren't big enough, Tegel airport was built within 92 days. The Airlift stands as the greatest logistical achievement of the century. The Allies, occupying powers before the blockade, became protective powers, and have remained so ever since. Bill Clinton recalled this during his visit to Berlin on May 13. Helmut Kohl wasn't present in June.

6-27-1998

Exhibit on the 50th anniversary of the Deutsche Mark at the Federal Printing Press on Kommandantenstrasse in Kreuzberg. The currency reform ordered by the Soviets on the "territory of the Soviet occupation zone in Germany and in the greater Berlin region" on June 23, 1948—together with the prompt introduction, as a countermeasure, of the Western mark on June 24 —are part of the Berlin Blockade's prehistory. The history of both currencies is on display. Through August 28. Also in August, the Federal Printing Press will begin test runs for Euro coins. By 2001, it will have to complete 20 % of German first usage, which comes to 2.4 billion coins and an unknown number of bills. Production of the DM will be halted early in 1999.

145

6-28-1998

Bridge across the Klosterstraße in Spandau. The 270 ton bridge is part of the rapid transit line link to the Spandau railway station, which is supposed to be opened in December.

6-28-1998

Home ownership initiative by the "Wohnungsbaugesellschaft Stadt und Land" ("Town and Country Residential Building Society") in Altglienicke. Today the Society, which has built 2,400 residences south of the Mohnweg, is opening a model row house on the new Ruben-Wolf-Strasse. 64 additional ones are to follow. For a purchasing price of between DM 400,000 and DM 520,000 the buyer can help determine the layout of his apartment. About a third of the houses will be getting solar installations and basins for collecting rainwater. Architect: Eckart Schmidt, Berlin.

6-30-1998

Topping-out ceremony for the new building housing the Max Planck Society's Institute for the Biology of Infectious Disease and the Rheumatism Research Center. The U-shaped 6-story building is going up on the home grounds of the Charitéhospital in the Spreebogen (the arc-shaped area along the Spree river bend connecting the Tiergarten and Mitte districts), with an overall ground plan measuring 21,000 sq. m. The Institute is dedicated to high-level research in the field of molecular biology; with special sections for security-level-3 laboratories, and microscopy. Keeping animals is intended. Client: Max-Planck-Gesellschaft zur Förderung der Wissenschaften e.V. (Max Planck Society for the Advancement of Science), Munich. Architects: Deubzer and König, Berlin. Total construction cost: DM 105 mill. Estimated date of completion: end of 1999.

6-30-1998

As of today, the Berlin-Spandau Shipping Canal in the area between the Humboldthafen and Westhafen ports can be fully navigated again. This section of the canal, which was once part of the border zone, was renovated and widened, and its 150 year-old embankment stones were cleaned and mostly (up to two thirds) reused. The construction cost for the 4.5 km stretch came to DM 15 mill.

Late June

In the course of work being done on streetcar tracks between the Hackescher Markt and Alexanderplatz, arched cellar vaults from the early 18th century Garnisonskirche (Garrison Church) are exposed. The objects discovered are to be exhibited in the Museum des Alten Berliner Garnisonsfriedhofs (Museum of the Old Berlin Garrison Church) on the Kleine Rosenthaler Strasse.

This summer is misery. Late autumn temperatures prevail; you walk through the Tiergarten chilled to the bone by a harsh wind. You go down Potsdamer Strasse rain-soaked like a poodle. You float down the Spree, or even up it, on the deck of a steamer filled with people, and the sun is eternally absent. You'd think you were on the river Lethe, where everything is colorless and incorporeal. The ghosts on deck rattle their teeth; a dead waiter passes around the cognac. Gray, gray, gray. And still the sun stays away. Indeed, this summer is misery.
Alfred Kerr, July 31, 1898

7-1-1998

Wilmersdorf embarks on new pathways for fighting unemployment. Starting today, the Dutch firm Maatwerk will be looking for jobs for 927 welfare recipients from the Wilmersdorf district. By the end of the year, Maatwerk is promising, 240 of the former welfare clients should be breadwinners earning their keep. If employment continues beyond the trial period, the district government will reimburse Maatwerk DM 6,000 per person.

7-1-1998

Topping-out ceremony for an annex to the Justice

7-2-1998

For Americans, freedom rests on the backs of horses. And so it's only too normal that the objective sculpture "The Day The Wall Came Down" by American artist Veryl Goodnight should be showing five horses jumping over remnants of the Berlin Wall. Military—, American and German, is participating in the equine transport. Ex-President George Bush is there for the dedication. Jumping point: right next to the Allied Museum on Clayallee.

7-2-1998

Starting today, the exhibit "Lyonel Feininger Gelmeroda—New York" in the Neue Nationalgalerie charts the German-American painter's pathway from New York to Gelmeroda in Thuringia and back again. Curator Roland März takes works by different artists from the 19th century as well as by companions of Feininger and places them alongside 137 paintings in the Neue Nationalgalerie. Through October 11.

6-28-1998

"Architecture Day," the worthy initiative of the Berlin Chamber of Architects, takes place for the third time. On Sunday, architects give tours of their new buildings in Berlin.

6-29-1998

First ground-digging ceremony for the British Embassy, Wilhelmstrasse 70, right behind the Hotel Adlon. The firm of Michael Wilford and Partners, London, had won the 1995 competition with its design for an "open" house. A large gate is carved into the stone facade, and in one of the interior courtyards visitors take an open stairway leading them into the public "white zone" on the first above-ground floor with its winter garden, exhibit spaces, and conference hall. Six stories, 9,000 sq. m overall floor space. The construction cost amounting to DM 75 mill. will be financed via a private consortium of the construction firm Bilfinger + Berger. The scheduled date for moving the embassy from Bonn to Berlin: Autumn 1999.

6-30-1998

Today, the state of Berlin has cancelled its contract with the Bewag electric utility company for maintaining and servicing electric street lighting. From now on there will be open bidding to find a private service company that can carry out the necessary work at more affordable rates. Still unaffected by this privatization is the servicing of 46,000 gas lamps, a job that remains in the hands of another public utility, Gasag.

Early July

In the Official Gazette of the European Union, Berlin's Building Administration publishes a notice announcing that up to ten commissions will be granted for writing up reports offering the city professional advice about how to make comprehensive repairs on the Olympic Stadium. To be continued.

Early July

A new book is out on the market, a 564-page lexicon containing all the maps of Berlin that made it to market by 1920. The oldest is from 1652. Published by Gebrüder Mann Verlag.

Ministry building on Hausvogteiplatz in the Mitte district. The extension supplements a building ensemble consisting of three old buildings (used as fashion houses before the war) and a prefab building. The entire block is currently being renovated for a total of DM 142 mill. according to plans by architects Eller & Eller, Düsseldorf. Scheduled completion: Mitte 1999.

7-2-1998

BMW branch opened in Weissensee, Gehringstrasse 18–22. For DM 30 mill., a 20,000 sq. m large automobile service center is being built. Architects: BETEK Bau- und Energietechnik GmbH, Munich.

7-2 to 7-5-1998

Temporary Gardens the Second: For three days, 24 garden installations by landscape architects, students, and artists "enrich, supplement, explicate, shift, and develop" the image of the city around and about the Marx-Engels-Forum. After three days they go under the hammer.

7-2-1998

Courtly discourteousness in Berlin: more and more construction projects are trying to ennoble themselves using connections to the Court. For example, between Jannowitzbrücke and Moritzplatz, where the cornerstone is being laid today for the Annenhöfe (Courts of Anne). 400 residences, 4,000 sq. m of retail space, 5,000 sq. m offices, and an underground garage with 250 parking places are being built on the 12,000 sq. m construction property. Developer: Bayerische Hausbau. Architects: Kny and Weber, Berlin. Investment total: DM 190 mill. Scheduled completion: 1999 (first construction segment), 2001 (total complex).

7-3 to 7-5-1998

Berlin's city estates celebrate their 125th anniversary. At one time (starting in 1873) bought up piece by piece as a way of removing sewage water, then entrusted with social welfare responsibilities (like finding shelter for endangered persons, creating jobs, and providing city facilities with cheap provisions), today their future doesn't look rosy. In the city's northeast and south, the estates are doing business at too great a loss. In spite of that, around 50,000 visitors come to the birthday party on the Kleinziehten Estate (Dahme-Spreewald).

7-3-1998

1 p.m., and after 37 years Friedrichstraße can again be traveled along its entire length. Neither border controls nor construction sites impede vehicular progress, if traffic jams can be ignored.

7-3-1998

Cornerstone laying for 270 condominiums, 52 row houses, and a child day care center at Britzer Garten in Tempelhof. Construction along the edge of the block is being done by Frankfurt architects Braun & Voigt, while the setback construction is being planned by VEBA Immobilien Baupartner GmbH. Developer: Deutsche Grundbesitz Management GmbH, Frankfurt and VEBA Immobilien, Bochum. Investment total: approx. DM 125 mill. Scheduled completion mid-2000.

7-3-1998

Before and after. Erected in 1936 and documented for a photo album that each athlete got as a gift, photographed in 1997/98 one more time by Markus Ziegler from the same

7-3-1998

In the quarters of the NGbK and of the Kreuzberg Art Office, it says "Please Smile." And they are smiling, from out of a selection from the roughly 300,000 negatives in the archive of the Mathesie photo studio on Adalbertstrasse. 48 years of Kreuzberg history, a photographic socio-portrait. Appropriately: The studio has been closed since 1993, replaced by a Chinese fast food restaurant. Even the dogs common to this part of the city will find something to make them happy: portraits of the darling quadrupeds, at dog's-eye height, plastered all over the district.

7-4-1998

There are two reasons why a two-day celebration is starting today on the former grounds of the locomotive manufacture Borsig in Tegel: First of all, a topping-out wreath will be raised above the "Halls at the Borsig Tower". Over five historic manufacturing halls will be turned into a shopping and leisure center, and along the

7-6-1998

As of today, a 14 m high, five meter wide, 120 ton granite slab, leaning against the building for the Norwegian embassy, symbolizes Norway's mountain landscape in the mountain-starved district of Tiergarten. For a while, this landscape symbol, estimated to be 900 mill. years old, will continue to be disturbed by the din of a modern construction site. Only by mid-1999 will the five Nordic embassies between Budapester Strasse and Hofjägerallee have their diplomatic peace and quiet restored.

7-10-1998

The Coca-Cola Erfrischungsgetränke AG (Coca Cola Refreshment Company) and Tishman Speyer sign a 10-year rental contract for more than 8,500 sq. m of commercial space in the Quartier 205 (O. M. Ungers and Partners) on Friedrichstraße. The beverage manufacturer's move from its previous home in Hohenschönhausen should take place by the end of October.

7-10-1998

Together with Federal Foreign Minister Klaus Kinkel and Mayor Eberhard Diepgen, French Foreign Minister Hubert Védrine lays the cornerstone for the French embassy on Pariser Platz. But construction won't really start until after winter, and completion is

July 1998

The Humboldt University has restored every doctoral title rescinded on political or racial grounds under the Third Reich and the GDR. On the other hand, it was decided not to take back honorary titles granted for political reasons during this period. Since November 1996, a commission under the direction of the HU's First Vice-President, Konrad Gröger, has been investigating politically motivated withdrawals of doctorates during the Nazi and GDR periods.

Mid-July

After 150 years, "Spitta + Leutz", the artists' and office supply store frequented by all of Berlin's architects and located in Wilmersdorf near Fehrbelliner Platz, is forced to declare bankruptcy.

July

perspective: the Olympic Village in Elstal at the gates of the city. The photos are on exhibit in the library of the Berlin Chamber of Architects, Karl-Marx-Allee 78. On-site tours through the grounds (not otherwise open to the public). Through August 2.

7-3-1998

Topping-out ceremony for a model project by the youth aid organization "Building the Future" ("Zukunft Bauen e.V.") at Langhansstraße 74 in Weissensee. For a year now, 20 apprentices training to become painters, electricians, and masons have been working on the DM 18 mill. project, where (in addition to businesses and residences) supervised residential projects and the business office of "Building the Future" will be moving in.

street there will be a new building with offices and a hotel. Architects: Claude Vasconi, Dagmar Groß, Paris. Developer: Herlitz Falkenhöh AG. Scheduled completion: Early 1999. In addition, "One Hundred Years of the Borsig Grounds" will be celebrated—as befits Borsig's status, with a world record-breaking model train track over 400 m long.

7-6-1998

"In Roman cities, the forum was one of the most important public squares. There is where citizens went to talk and to find out what was new—about life, about major change, about the future. Something similar may also be said of the Audi Forum in Berlin." This is the explanation we're offered in the quadratic brochure on the role of the Audi Forum, inaugurated today on Friedrichstrasse 83. There are big things to report. Berlin is the second site for this exclusive entrepreneurial debut; the first one—how could it be otherwise?—is in New York, Park Avenue, near Central Park. Renovations cost: DM 6.5 mill.

7-9-1998

A settlement saves the American Business Center on Checkpoint Charlie from bankruptcy. More than 100 creditors, mostly construction firms and engineers (but also including the Siemens conglomerate), take a loss of approx. DM 23 mill. Three of the five construction projects could be completed; the other two will be tackled by 2000 at the earliest. Cf. BBA '97, p. 40 ff. and September 27.

7-9-1998

Beginning today—and after their departure for an absence lasting into the next century had already been announced earlier this year—120 masterpieces from the Alte Nationalgalerie are presented on tissue coverings on the upper floor of Schinkel's Altes Museum at the Lustgarten. Here the works will enjoy a congenial artistic refuge until August 1999, when they will become nomads again until their old domicile is restored.

scheduled for the year 2001. The architect is Christian de Potzamparc (also the architect of the Cité de la Musique in the Parc de la Villette), who will, for the first time, build in Berlin. Cf. BBA '97, May 22.

7-13-1998

Start of renovation work for the fountain on Ernst-Reuter-Platz in Charlottenburg. Berlin's Water Works utility company will be sharing half of the roughly DM 3 mill. cost.

July 1998

"Native Sounds" ("Heimatklänge"), the annual world music festival in the Tempodrom, ring out for the last time in Tiergarten. The Tempodrom is forced to close; its new neighbor, the Federal Chancellory, is simply getting too close for comfort. This month, too, another performance site, Huxley's New World, is shutting its gates in the Hasenheide.

Mid-July

The architects RKW, Düsseldorf, are commissioned with the development on the grounds of the International Trade Center on Friedrichstrasse by Wohnungsbaugesellschaft Mitte or WBM. Two blocks closing the edge of Friedrichstrasse are planned at the foot of the existing high-rise, which shall accomodate a hotel, office and retail space, restaurants. Preferred date for construction start: 1999.

7-13-1998

After more than two years of preparation, around 150 European scientists are meeting in Berlin in order to start the "Berlin Ozonexperiment— BERLIOZ," the largest German experiment to date in the field of atmospheric environmental research. On selected days (with extreme temperatures) from today through August 9 (and in addition to all the routine daily measurements), research airplanes, kite balloons and high-tech measuring instruments will be deployed to gather a variety of data on the formation and migration of summer smog in Berlin and Brandenburg. The project is supported with DM 7.75 mill. from the Federal Ministry for Education, Research, Science, and Technology, and the results will be incorporated into the formulation and implementation of environmental policy measures for reducing damage to the ozone layer.

In order to keep from perishing of boredom, meetings are organized here on all sides. One merry congress follows another. First came the writers. They celebrated a banquet, at Adlon and Dressel in Treptow. Then came the lawyers. Their congress was well attended, a thousand men with their wives, sisters-in-law, and female cousins. They celebrated a banquet, at Adlon and Dressel in Treptow. Now the women's suffragists have come. Not only from Germany, but also from America, Armenia, France, even Friedenau. They are celebrating a banquet, at Adlon and Dressel in Treptow. Thus a common, unifying thread runs through all these meetings with their differing objectives.
Alfred Kerr, September 18, 1896

Mid-July

The Austrian writer Elfriede Jelinek decides that she is going to have her plays premiere with the Berliner Ensemble.

7-14 to 7-17-1998

The 200 m long rerouting of the Spree channel along Spreebogen river bend is concluded. For two years, the Spree flowed 70 m away from its own river bed. As part of the Tiergarten tunnel construction project, the Spree bed was used as an open construction pit,

7-19-1998

First Sunday in a whole series of weekends where inline skaters get to romp around on a car-free John-Foster-Dulles Allee. Through August 23, the boulevard that runs parallel to the "Straße des 17. Juni" ("17th of June Street" commemorating the East German uprising of 1953 and traversing the Tiergarten park from the Technical University to the Brandenburg Gate) will still be providing runners with a 1 km open track, including hurdles and ramps.

7-22-1998

Prenzlauer Berg has become wealthier to the tune of one Alpine attraction. A viticultural footpath installed for DM 900,000 makes it possible to experience the mountainous structure originating in Barnim and its Ice Age geological shifts. The path starts at the street "Am Prenzlauer Berg," heads along the slope's border on a plank pathway to reach a height of 103 meters, surmounts a 14 meter abyss, and then leads directly to a playground in the Spree river valley.

7-24-1998

3sat starts a new film series featuring television premieres and entitled "Snapshots of Berlin." The first program is called "plus minus zero," was filmed by Eoin Moores, and relates a story set on the Potsdamer Platz construction site.

7-25-1998

Opening of a new building for the Konrad Adenauer Foundation in Tiergarten, attended by Federal Chancellor Helmut Kohl. The center of the three-story building is a lecture hall with 199 seats. The foundation's staff members who will be working in Berlin, together with the executive office for foundation management, are going to be accommodated on the building's office floor with its 25 rooms. The establishment, which is close to the CDU and will hold on to its main office in St. Augustin near Bonn, will mostly be using the Berlin premises (located right next to the CDU's new federal headquarters) for conventions and

7-26- 1998

The Hamburg office group gmp—the firm of Gerkan, Marg and Partners—does not emerge as the winner in a European-wide competition for the building meant to house both the Brandenburg and Mecklenburg-Eastern Pomerania state delegations to the Bundesrat (Germany's upper house of parliament). The first prize goes instead to Mai, Zill and Kuhsen, Lübeck. But because the design by gmp corresponds better to the developer's views about the building's function, it becomes the blueprint that will be implemented, against the judgment of the jury.

7-14-1998

At the 18th discussion that is part of the series "Stadtprojekte" ("Urban Projects") in the German Architecture Center, models for combating social division in the city are contemplated. There was unanimity among the participants—Peter Strieder (Berlin city Senator for Urban and Environmental Affairs), Thomas Mirow (Economics Senator in Hamburg), Ingeborg Junge-Reyer (District City Councillor for Health and Social Welfare in Kreuzberg), as well as one representative each from the Tenants' Association and the Turkish League in Berlin-Brandenburg—on one future policy: Residential quarters management should intervene routinely in district structures. But there was no unanimity, of course, on who should assume this responsibility, or on whose behalf. Still, over the next three years around DM 2 mill. will be available for the managers of residential quarters to set up and run their offices.

since the deployment of a shield-burrowing machine proved impossible. On a 1.50 m thick, 10,000 sq. m large floating concrete base at a depth of 17 m, conduits are now in place for four long-distance railway tracks, two rapid city transit rails, and a four-lane road. They are covered by a vaulted ceiling that is itself protected from water pressure and the external impact of heavy objects by two layers of sand, then by a 3 cm thick steel plate, and (on top of that) a 50 cm thick stratum of rubble.

7-16-1998

Construction start on the "Railway Overpass North-East," a bridge construction between Mettmannplatz and Kruppstraße in the Tiergarten district, which is supposed to link the future Lehrter Central Railway Station with the metropolitan rapid transit line ring. Two 4.7 m tracks are supposed to run alongside a stretch barely 570 m long crossing the Perleberger Bridge. Initially, 13 pier supports are installed. Completion is scheduled for the year 2000.

7-19-1998

Tupper parties, those legendary affairs for decades now, are being expanded by adding a new target group. Today the first gay and lesbian coffee klatsch excursion ever to be escorted by a Tupperware consultant gets underway in the Brandenburg locality of Langerwisch. We gather from the press that about a hundred tour guests (in what was surely a maxed-out heightened mood, compared to your average excursion) became victims of the irresistible sales pitch.

7-20-1998

Today, the first staff members at the headquarters of the German automobile sales division for Daimler Benz are moving into the new building designed by Rafael Moneo on Potsdamer Platz. A total of 700 people will be working in the new quarters, and 200 new jobs are being created. The division used to have its seat in Stuttgart.

7-23-1998

Happy Birthday to Götz George, who turns 60 and on whom Berlin retains its hold.

7-23-1998

Construction start for an office complex with Inter City-Hotel at the newly designed Ostbahnhof railway station in Friedrichshain. Investor: Deutsche Immobilien Leasing GmbH. Property owner: DB-AG. Architects: Lamm Weber Donath, Stuttgart. Investment total: DM 95 mill. Anticipated completion: 2000.

educational events. The program start in August. Architect: Thomas van den Valentyn, Cologne. Construction cost: DM 24 mill. Construction time: 2.5 years.

7-25-1998

The first, and probably the only, Berlin art parade. Organized by David Reuter, the manager of the workshop "Play and Stage" at the College of the Arts. Subdivided into a nighttime and daytime procession through the Prenzlauer Berg and Mitte districts, scenarios of "life stations" are staged at different stations along the street, largely unnoticed by the Berlin public.

7-27-1998

Five months after construction started, the BVG (Berlin's metropolitan transport authority) celebrates a topping-out ceremony for the new Mendelssohn-Bartoldy-Park subway station on Potsdamer Platz. Architects: Hilmer and Sattler, Munich/Berlin; cost: DM 20 mill.

7-27-1998

Peter-Klaus Schuster, director of the Alte Nationalgalerie on the Museum Island since 1994 and Dieter Honisch's successor at the Neue Nationalgalerie in the Kulturforum since 1997, leaves for Munich after ten years of working in Berlin. At his new home he will henceforth hold the office of General Director for the Bavarian State Painting Collection. The "Friends of the Nationalgalerie" grant him a departing wish and purchases a little painting by Adolph Menzel: the artist's foot.

7-28-1998

Today BOTAG (Bodentreuhand- und Verwaltungs-AG, a real estate trustee) introduces its plans for renovating two storage buildings at the Eastern Harbor. The former egg refrigeration house (1929) and the granary (1913) belonging to BEHALA are supposed to be converted into office buildings. The star attraction here is the kind of "virtual" landmark preservation intended for use on the egg refrigeration house. Since the facade has practically no windows, its present appearance will be captured on the glass facade planned for the building using a silk screen technique. The landmark preservation authority has not yet given the project its seal of approval. Planned investment: DM 160 mill. 38,000 sq. m of office space. Anticipated completion: end of 2000.

7-31-1998

The new bridge over the Landwehrkanal, which links Potsdamer Platz (and the future Tiergarten tunnel) with Schöneberger Ufer, is officially opened and baptized under the name "George C. Marshall Bridge." For construction purposes, the portions of the streets along the embankment within the crossing region were lifted 2 meters. Architects: gmp, Hamburg/Berlin. Construction cost: DM 14 mill. Until the Tiergarten tunnel is completed, this bridge will mostly be serving traffic going back and forth to the construction site on Potsdamer Platz.

Late July

Studio Hamburg, the largest German production and studio enterprise, buys the television studios in Adlershof that once belonged to the GDR TV station DFF. As a tenant, the firm is already using a portion of the studio. Essential renovation work will take five years and cost between DM 40 mill. and DM 50 mill.

7-31-1998

Little epilogue to the secondary residence tax: The time limit was postponed two months until today, not only in order to give owners of second domiciles enough time to register a change of address, but also in order to structure the legal clauses in a way that makes them idiot-proof. Among other things, this should help secure an exception to the rule so that prison inmates don't get summoned to the tax-collector's office because of their cozy second home. This way, residential havens for women also get to be tax-free. All thanks to sagacious foresight.

8-7-1998

The new Jafféstraße is finished. The construction project "Street 240" resulted from the trade fair convention center's southern expansion. Construction has been taking place since 1995 on the 1.4 km segment of the street between Heerstrasse and Messedamm. A wall 800 m long to protect against noise pollution has been erected between the new street and the rapid transit line. Karolingerplatz is also getting noise pollution barriers. 290 oaks were planted along both sides of the street between the auto and bicycle lanes.

8-7-1998

"Dance in August" takes place for the tenth time, this year for the first time in cooperation with all of Berlin's opera houses. International choreographers and teachers work together with young Berlin dancers in a number of workshops. The festival's most sensational hits are guest performances by the Nederlands Dans Theater, but they also in-

8-10-1998

The Alice Salomon College of Social Work and Welfare Education, Germany's largest, takes its 1,300 students and 150 instructors and moves from Schöneberg into its new house at Hellersdorf on Alice-Salomon-Platz 5. Architect: Bernhard Winking, Hamburg (cf. main section). Berliner Alice Salomon (1872–1948) studied political science, was one of the first women in Prussia to receive a doctorate, and founded the "German Academy for Women's Social Work and Education" in 1925. During the Third Reich the school was forced to close, and Alice Salomon had to give up all her public posts. She emigrated in 1937 to New York. Her old office quarters at the Schöneberg college will now be set up as an archive and documentation center on the social work profession and the women's movement.

August 1998

Advance notice: As of next school year, foreign languages will start getting taught as early as the third grade. Almost half of all the elementary schools in East Berlin and roughly a third in West Berlin will be taking part in the reform project. Most schools have opted for English as the first foreign language, twenty schools will be offering French, and Russian is the only language with no takers.

July   August

Late July

Now that the asbestos has been removed, the demolition of the Kudamm-Eck (Kudamm Corner) between the Kurfürstendamm and Joachimstaler Straße in Charlottenburg can begin. Opinion has it that putting up a new 40 m high building (following plans by gmp, Hamburg) would offer a better solution, all round, than the current structure, Berlin's very first "shop-in-shop," built in Berlin by Werner Düttmann in 1969–1972.

Late July

Start of reconstruction and renovation work on the Kulturbrauerei ("Culture Brewery") in Prenzlauer Berg. The Treuhand-Liegenschaftsgesellschaft (the real estate company for the trustee organization that privatized East German industry) has given out all of the building commissions. For around DM 100 mill., on 25,000 sq. m, there will be a multiplex cinema — hotly contested by the owner of the nearby Colosseum cinema complex, Artur Brauner — as well as a small arts stage, a market hall, supermarket, offices, and galleries. In May 2000 the work should be done. The various legal disputes still underway one may count on delays.

August 1998

The Lilienthal-Karree (Lilienthal Square), built in 1926 on Segelflieger-damm in Johannisthal with 162 houses that are now in need of renovation, was taken over by Bauwert GmbH. Also included in the independently financed modernization concept are plans to transform the attics into apartments. The homes will later be offered for sale at a price of DM 3.400 per square meters of residential space.

8-3-1998

"transArchitectures: Cyberspace and Emergent Theories" is the name of a presentation starting today at the architectural gallery Aedes East. Using videos, web sites, and panels, the exhibit demonstrates ways of applying conceptional techniques to architecture. Participating exhibitors from all over Europe. Through August 22.

clude "Not Garden" by Stephen Petronio and "Hanging Man" by Ctibor Turba. The successful festival received financial support from the Berlin city Senate and the Capital City Culture fund.

8-10-1998

First ground-digging ceremony on a 14 acres site between Lindenstrasse, Axel-Springer-Strasse, Zimmerstrasse, and Charlottenstrasse in Kreuzberg. Although the development plan process has not yet come to an end, a partial permit was granted for the Charlotten-Karree on Kochstraße, so that work on this area near Berlin's center can be completed quickly. For the time being, six apartment and commercial buildings with greenery in their courtyards are being built here. Architect: Thomas Spiegel, Hamburg. Developer: Investment group Röder/ debis. Estimated cost: DM 300 mill. The cross commemorating Peter Fechter, who bled to death after being shot on the border strip in 1962, had to give way to the construction in progress.

8-10-1998

StattReisen Berlin e.V. now offers guided tours through Neukölln, from Rathausvorplatz to Hermannplatz. Today, the first reconnaissance of Neukölln takes place, in order either to confirm or deny the horrifying report that the weekly new magazine "Spiegel" published about this largest of all Berlin's districts.

Mid-August

The Italian mobile home season on Schlossplatz in Berlin-Mitte gradually comes to an end as the summer recedes. The district council would like to get rid of the most temporary of all temporary users in the controversial heart of the city.

8-13-1998

On the 27th anniversary of the building of the Wall, a memorial is dedicated on the cemetery grounds of the Sophien-congregation on Bernauer Strasse, in order to keep alive the memory of the 938 victims who died on the intra-German border. There was a great deal of controversy about the site, the design, and the dedication to be inscribed on the memorial. At this cemetery (where more remains of the Wall than anywhere else), there now stands (next to tombs in ruins) a series of steel walls towering up high and surrounding a seven meter long section of the "death strip" delineated in the background by the Wall, with the "light line" (a stretch of mined turf where East German guard towers tracked down potential escapees under glaring searchlights). The written inscription at the entrance designates the dead as "victims of Communist tyranny." So far, funds are lacking for a documentation center that is supposed to round out the

Such noble walls… *Heinrich Wefing, 1998*

No sooner raised to the status of memorial, this section of the Wall was given all the consolations of landmark conservation. Holes were mended in its porous prefabricated parts (actually intended for the construction of farm silos); the GDR concrete of downright mediocre quality was either secured or replaced. At some point (that much should be clear), this Eastern product would get turned into a Western work. Sand grain by sand grain inventoried, rendered permanent, more chic than ever, the Wall may be still authentic in its outline, but materially just a copy. Standing offside a bit, like the corridor sets pushed aside after a thoroughly ill-advised exhibit, a couple of untouched panels of Wall are still hanging around. And how much more miserable, more authentic too, they seem, painted over with graffiti caricatures in loud colors. A rank growth of shrubs swarms up along their freely chiseled, long-since rusted iron reinforcement rods.

8-13-1998

The cult cinema theater "Notausgang" ("Emergency Exit") on Vorbergstraße 1 in Schöneberg, whose very existence has frequently been threatened since it started operating in 1914, has now been renovated for DM 150,000 and is opening today with a new interior and an Ingrid Bergmann retrospective.

August 1998

The Berlin company "Systema-Logistik" is given the contract for well finishing the biggest federal buildings in Berlin, the Paul-Löbe-Haus, the Marie-Elisabeth-Lüders-Haus, and the Jakob-Kaiser-Haus. The architecture firm, founded just seven years ago, won out in international bidding, and the Federal Building Company awarded a contract worth millions (though a more precise figure is not given).

8-15-1998

The Gloria-Palast, a traditional cinema with a turbulent history, must close for good today. The first cinema palace under this name (based on designs by Ernst Lessing and Max Bremer) was built into the Romanische Haus (Romanesque House) by

8-18-1998

Renovation work is completed in the Kunsthof in Oranienburger Strasse 27, directly adjacent to the new synagogue. Under the direction of Roland Ernst, the residential and industrial courtyard dating from the mid-19th century has been carefully restored by Rüdiger Reisig (Büro Civitas). Everything that could be preserved was carefully treated: the old windows, the floorboards, the cobblestones in the courtyard and especially the parquet floor in the main story of the front building which monument protectors consider to be the oldest in Berlin. The Kunsthof will contain galleries, studios, bookshops, a pantomime school, an agency for art mediation and even part of the University of Hildesheim. The reason: the Faculty of Cultural Education discovered that its students and professors spend most of their time in Berlin, so it is setting up a college in Berlin.

8-18-1998

The district council of Berlin-Mitte decides to forbid any election posters "in public parks and areas that are important for the city as a whole". Areas affected: Pariser Platz, the area in front of Brandenburg Gate, Unter den Linden from Universitätsstrasse to Schlossbrücke, Bebel-platz, Gendarmenmarkt, Volkspark am Weinberg, Monbijoupark, Marx-Engels-Forum and Pappelplatz.

8-18-1998

Topping-out ceremony for the Protestant geriatric centre Berlin (EGZB) at Reinickendorfer Strasse 61 in Wedding. Work has been in progress here since February on a building with 132 beds in which older citizens can be cared for as residents. A day clinic with 140 beds is already operating. Client: EGZB; architects: Baumann und Schnittger, Berlin; construction costs DM 76 mill. Completion is planned for April 1999.

memorial site. It shall be located in the parish house belonging to the Lutheran Reconciliation Congregation, whose church once stood on the Wall strip and was only blown up by border troops in 1985.

8-14-1998

The neighborhood cinema "Astra," located on the corner of Sterndamm in Johannisthal and running as a moving picture house since 1928, has been renovated for DM 6.5 mill and opens today with five new theaters all the modern conveniences.

8-14-1998

Topping-out ceremony for a new wood storage hall in Spandau, constructed entirely out of wood. According to the architect, the hall measuring 50 x 100 m is the largest of this kind in Europe. The roof consists of 27,000 boards that, 35 mm wide, were nailed together edgewise. It rests on 16 wooden supports that are loosely arranged in concrete feet. Architect: Thomas Schindler, Berlin, statics: Pichler engineering firm, Berlin, clients: Bernd-Michael and Hartmut Bauer (Bauer Holz/Bauer Syrsch). Cost: DM 4.5 mill.

8-15-1998

A new elementary school with an athletic hall on Drorytrasse in Neukölln is handed over to its users. The elementary school is laid out for 450 schoolchildren and prepares handicapped children for integration; the same is true of the athletic hall. The new buildings were constructed in the interior of a block, close to the dense residential area along Niemetzstrasse. The commission for the school resulted from winning a competition in 1992. Architects: BACKMANN + SCHIEBER, Berlin.

Franz Schwechten in 1926 and furnished with chandeliers, silk damask, and an orchestra pit for 40 musicians. In 1943 the house was totally destroyed, but by 1948 a makeshift cinema of the same name was opened on the Kurfüstendamm. Four years later, in January 1952, the Gloria-Palast moved to its current site — a house by Siegfried Feher and Gerhard Jäckel only half-finished at the time — where it was dedicated in splendor. Here is where the Berlin film festivals took place. Altogether, the Gloria-Palast played a mayor role in German cinematic history during the Fifties. The box office and the impressive staircase were preserved during the last renovation, and because they are landmark-protected, it is hoped that they will survive the house's scheduled conversion into retail space. Client: 58. Hanseatische Grundbesitz-Gemeinschaft, Hamburg, conversion: Cleve, Schilling, architects, Berlin; completion: end of 1998.

8-18-1998

International mathematicians' congress in Berlin with 3,500 participants. For the first time for 94 years, academics from a hundred countries (and publishers, software companies and industrial representatives) are meeting in Germany again. Until August 27. And there is a small parallel exhibition in the Ludwig Erhard Haus in Hardenbergstrasse in Charlottenburg with the title "(Innovation)3 — Mathematics and Art in Modern Architecture".

August 1998

Speaking of mathematicians: the statistics report that 49,000 people have moved from Berlin to the surrounding area, the number of people moving to Berlin was 29,800 less than the number moving away. As a result of the tax on the second residence, 7,800 registered their main residence in Berlin, which led to tax income of DM 42.9 mill., although DM 55 mill. was expected and the population fell by a total of 32,200.

8-18-1998

Decision in the competition for the Hessian state representation building. From 536 designs, the jury selected the entry by the Frankfurt architects Michael Christl and Joachim Bruchhäuser. The new building will be built in the former ministerial gardens in Berlin-Mitte where many federal states will have their representations.

8-20-1998

Topping-out ceremony for the conference centre of the Friedrich Ebert Foundation on the corner of Hiroshimastrasse and Hildebrandtstrasse in the new/old diplomats district in Tiergarten. The Foundation was founded in Berlin in 1925, but its headquarters will remain in Bonn. The new "Foundation building" aims to cooperate with the SPD education centers in the new federal states and to establish itself as an international encounter center. Besides office and seminar rooms it will also contain a conference hall for 1,000 persons. Architect: Volkhard Weber, Berlin. Costs: DM 53.2 mill.

There is no sky over this city, and whether the sun shines at all is questionable; at any rate, you only see it when it blinds you as you're trying to cross the street. They complain about the weather, but there is no weather in Berlin. The Berliner has no time. He always has something planned, he calls up and arranges meetings, arrives at appointments rushed and a little late—and has a great deal to do. In this city they don't work—they toil. (Here, even pleasure is work: you spit into your hands beforehand and expect to get something out of it.) The Berliner is not industrious; he is always wound up. He has quite forgotten why we are here in the first place. Even in heaven—assuming Berliners go to heaven—he would have "something planned" at four. The Berliner hurtles through his day, and when it is done, it was trouble and work, nothing more. You can live seventy years in this city without the slightest advantage for your immortal soul.
Kurt Tucholsky, 1919

Mid-August

A 3.5 sq. m pane came loose from Jean Nouvel's famous glass facade at the Galeries Lafayette and fell onto the department store's canopy and the street below. The single-layer safety glass then shattered into single shards; and because of that, the Mitte District

8-21-1998

Today was the topping-out ceremony in the Spandau Quartier Maselake Nord for the complex "Am Wasserbogen", where 218 apartments in the 2nd rental subsidy scheme and 53 owner-occupied apartments are being built. The developer is KG für Warenhandel Goetsche + Granobs, which has invested DM 95 mill. Architects: Grobe + Grobe, Berlin.

8-22-1998

The long night of the museums, for the fourth time and with ever-increasing success (150,000 visitors, 35 museums and 20 collections, innumerable guided tours, readings, concerts, performances).

8-23-1998

Beginning of the new school year and the German spelling reform. The

8-24-1998

The new school building at Ahrensfelder Chaussee 41 in Falkenberg, a part of Hohenschönhausen, is completed. Hohenschönhausen is the urban district with the largest number of new school buildings since the fall of Communism. The Barnim Upper School for 800 pupils is built "in the style of farming villages in the Mark", i.e. of semi-circular brick buildings set in a circle into which even the two sports halls with their auxiliary rooms are integrated. Architects: Stefan Scholz in Bangert Scholz, Berlin; construction costs: DM 63 mill.

8-25-1998

First ground-breaking for the headquarters of KSA - Kommunaler Schadensausgleich. KSA is an insurance institution in the east of Germany which serves 7,928 members (urban districts, towns, communities, savings banks, special purpose associations, water and land associations etc.) on a self-help basis. The central offices are being built in Berlin-Hohenschönhausen at Konrad-Wolf-Strasse 92/93, although KSA is not active in Berlin. The design envisages a comb-like building structure, with the street front integrated into the alignment of the old block edge buildings. The existing chestnut copse will be preserved, and a small public park will be developed in the center of the block on an area of 4,400 sq.m. Architects: Suter + Suter GmbH, Berlin; general contractor: INTERTEC, Berlin; construction costs: DM 26 mill. (first building phase). Planned completion date: end of 1999.

8-26-1998

The WISTA Business Center (WBC) opens on the Adlershof science estate. This building with 25,000 sq.m of floor space, which is particularly designed to stimulate the integration of scientific research and the economy and is so far the only building here to be built without subsidies, will be occupied in September by the department of Computer Science of the Humboldt University—temporarily, until the planned university buildings have been built. Architects: Dörr, Ludolf, Wimmer, Berlin. Cf. main section.

8-26-1998

Once every three years: the Rolling Stones in the Olympic Stadium. Fireworks and rain. The Olympic Stadium more beautiful then ever. The music as eternal as ever. Repetition of the concert on September 13 in the Waldbühne. Cf. BBA '96, August 17, 1995.

Office is saying, there's really no danger posed to passers-by on Friedrichstraße. It is therefore decided not to cordon off the sidewalk, but instead to wait a while and trust in fate; otherwise, the entire facade would have to be renovated.

Mid-August

The restoration of the west wing of the Pergamon altar (10 m high, frieze 120 m long and and 2.30 m high, from around 170 BC) has been concluded. Cost so far: DM 2 mill. Expected total cost through the year 2001: DM 5 mill. The Pergamon Museum takes in 900,000 visitors annually.

August 1998

Turnkey completion: The mid-sized business Weckbacher from Dortmund is put in charge of planning, delivering and installing the "general master key facility" (in German, that's one word: "Generalhauptschlüsselanlage") for the Reichstag. 10,000 cylinder locks are going to be installed, and 50,000 keys will be handed out in March 1999.

8-21-1998

"Concrete slab buildings for the next generation", exhibition of the results of the Independent Design Academy of European Architecture, abbreviated as DEA Studios 1-5. Until September 5 in Schlegelstrasse 26/27 in Berlin-Mitte.

8-22-1998

From today, the Swedish photographer Bernard Larsson shows a selection of 200 pictures he took in the 1960s "of the whole city and the people in their distress". His photographs of the death of Benno Ohnesorg went around the world. The documentary pictures of great and small are hung on barriers amidst the classical sculptures in the Friedrichwerder church. Until November 29.

212 spelling rules have been reduced to 112, the 52 rules for commas have dwindled to 9.

8-24-1998

Spandau continues to grow. In "Quartier Pulvermühle" on Goldbeckweg in Haselhorst the GSW residential association celebrated the completion of the building shell for 569 apartments under the 1st and 2nd subsidy scheme. Planned completion: October 1999. Two kindergartens and a multi-purpose building will round off the estate. Architects: Behrend and Stutzer, Berlin and Benedict Tonon, Berlin.

8-24-1998

Start of the event "Metropolis—Urban Scenery for a Global Future", for which 70 students from 25 cities of the world came to Berlin at the invitation of the urban development Senator, Peter Strieder. A student from the Philippines commented: "I'd like our cities to be as green as Berlin. Once I thought that only buildings mattered, but that has changed." Closing event on August 29.

8-24-1998

Topping-out in the underworld: the first section of the trunk railway tunnel, named Hannelore after the wife of the current German Chancellor and running to the north of Potsdamer Platz, is completed in skeleton. Work on the section to the south of Potsdamer Platz will begin in about one year. The tunnel route, which is about three and a half kilometers long, is being dug alternately by open excavation and subterranean drilling. It is part of the underground north-to-south connection which will one day (planned date: 2003) cross the overground east-to-west connections at the new railway junction at Lehrter Bahnhof. Developer: Deutsche Bahn Projekt Knoten Berlin.

8-26-1998

At 12 o'clock on the dot. The Spree returns to its old river bed. Pomp and ceremony. But the Berlin passenger boat "Kaiser Friedrich" is not there because the national boat "Seelöwe" represents the German nation. For two years the bed of the Spree was diverted, and now it flows over a 96 m long, 97 m wide and 18.5 m deep section of tunnel. A three centimeter thick metal panel separates the overworld from the underworld. Cf. June 14.

8-27-1998

First ground-breaking for the exhibition building of the German Historical Museum behind the Zeughaus. The last building to be personally wished by Chancellor Kohl. Architect: I. M. Pei. Calculated costs: DM 110 mill. Cf. BBA '97, January 17.

Late August

Before the festive opening of the "debis Area" on Potsdamer Platz at the beginning of October, these new buildings are getting draped with giant black-and-white photos. Twenty-one "Hanging Pictures" show Potsdamer Platz from the turn of the century through the war and post-war period up to the opening of the Wall. What looks much more exciting to visitors than the motifs on display is the technical challenge—the very attempt to mount these gigantic photos, on a transparent web of wires, some of them 1,500 sq. m large, and then to secure them against enormous wind resistance. Steel cable gets stretched from steel beams on the roof down to meter-high concrete blocks on the sidewalks. On opening day, 170 facade climbers from the Berlin firm "River and Mountain" will loosen the cables and roll up the photos.

8-28-1998

Topping-out ceremony for the long awaited sport complex of the sports club "Zehlendorfer Wespen 1911" at the corner of Benschallee and Lloyd-G.-Wellsstrasse. Costs: DM 14.4 mill.

8-28-1998

The "Haus für Kinder" is the first kindergarten completed in Staaken since 1989. 130 children in mixed age groups will be looked after there. Address: Am Wiesenweg 20. Architects: Augustin and Frank; landscaping: Horst Schumacher, Berlin: construction costs: DM 7 mill. to be borne by BEWOGE and Bauwert, the developers of the new estates.

Late August

Thomas Geissler, the species protection officer in Köpenick, sounds the alarm. Due to the renovation of the concrete slab buildings, bats will lose their winter quarters; in the tower building estates Salvador Allende I and II there were unusually large colonies of 300 to 400 bats. The gaps in the walls which the bats flew through are all to be sealed by the turn of the millennium. But the Senate expert on bats, Johannes Schwarz, has confidence in the skill of these night birds in looking for another place to hibernate. However, building

8-31-1998

Laying of the foundation stone for the new Spandau lock building. The new lock will be 115 m long and 12.5 m wide and will replace the old lock which has been out of service since 1993. Cost: DM 80 mill.; planned completion date: 2001.

8-31-1998

The British International School Berlin opens with 160 pupils in the former mansion "Gut Amalienhof" at Heerstrasse 465 in Spandau.

Late August

Attempts at rapprochement in the unequal partnership between Hohenschönhausen and Beverly Hills. The managers of the Rodeo Drive shopping mile offer the people of Hohenschönhausen their "Rodeo Drive Logo".

9-1-1998

The open space between Gorki Theater and Humboldt University will from now on be called "Platz der Märzrevolution von 1848" ("March Revolution of 1848 Square"). Berlin's city Senate had argued just long enough —with Ben Wargin (about the square) and with the district government (about the correct site)— to guarantee that they would not come up with a space worthy of the Revolution when its 150th anniversary rolled around in March. To our mild astonishment, we now learn from the press about the following design concept: "Two large lawns, surrounded by park paths, will be built, and in the middle will be the statue of composer Carl Friedrich Fasch, who founded the Singing Academy on May 24, 1791." Cf. March 18.

9-1-1998

The "House of Business" ("Haus der Wirtschaft") on Mühlendamm 21 celebrates a topping-out ceremony. October 1, 1999

8-27-1998

An attractive variation of a marriage. The lord mayor of Lichtenberg, Wolfram Friedersdorf (PDS) and the lady mayoress of Hohenschönhausen, Bärbel Grygier (PDS) symbolically celebrated the "marriage" of their two urban districts in the idyllic registry office by Obersee lake. Elegant clothes. Flowers for the bride. "We are already looking forward to our first shared administration building."

8-28-1998

Laying of the foundation stone for the state representation of the Free Hanseatic City of Bremen on the corner of Hiroshimastrasse and Reichpietschufer. The model shows a four-story rectangular block with representation and office stories and an eight-story single building linked to the adjacent buildings which will be used as a guest house. Architects: Léon & Wohlhage, Berlin; construction costs: DM 30 mill.

8-28-1998

Cinemas everywhere. Cinemas closing. Cinemas opening. Distinguished cinemas and local cinemas close, such as the "Venus" in Degnerstrasse and "Graffiti" on Ludwigkirchplatz, and on Kurfürstendamm the cinemas "Lupe 1" and "Gloria" (as reported). CinemaxX opens on Potsdamer Platz and in Landsberger Allee. Topping-out is celebrated for the CinemaxX centers in Hohenschönhausen and Marzahn. Because of CinemaxX, more people than ever before go to the cinema in Germany. 140 million tickets per year, for how many films? A reason to celebrate (but not until October) for Franz Stadler, who has shown film art for 25 years in "Filmkunst 66" in Bleibtreustrasse in Charlottenburg, and for the equally traditional Börse-Studiokino in Berlin-Mitte, which now opens after refurbishment and technical modernisation with 58 seats —as one of the smallest film theaters that does not belong to a cinema complex.

8-29-1998

90th birthday of the architectural historian Karl Junghans, known to many for his excellent work on Bruno Taut. After completing his studies in 1934, he was interned in Sachsenhausen for several years because of his political sincerity. After the GDR was founded, he was nominated to the German Building Academy in Berlin. His work mainly covered the theory and history of architecture.

8-31-1998

Karin von Welck is now the director of the Cultural Foundation of the federal states with its headquarters in Berlin. The foundation is empowered "to acquire works that are important and worthy of preservation for German culture, from Quedlinburger porcelain to the works of Joseph Beuys."

work is not permitted between October and March, because that is when the bats hibernate, and they would be shut in alive. Of the 16 species of bats which live in Berlin, the broad-winged bat, dwarf bat (pipistrellus) and nyctalus noctula hibernate in the concrete slab buildings, and less frequently the long-eared brown bat. For future cold seasons, the Friedrichshagen waterworks is being adapted to become the largest winter quarters for bats in Berlin.

September 1998

Now that the contract drawn up in 1995 between Peter and Isolde Kottmair and the TLG (the real estate branch of the "Treuhand" trustee agency that privatized East German industry) has been rescinded, the 27,000 sq. m large property on Leipziger Platz is up for sale again. The Kottmairs had planned an entertainment complex there (with the Cirque du Soleil among others) based on plans by Italian star architect Aldo Rossi, who died last year. Cf. BBA '97 September 5.

is the moving date set for the Federation of German Industry (BDI), the Federal Association of German Employers Associations (BDA), and the German Chamber of Industry and Commerce (DIHT). This meeting on the occasion of their joint topping-out ceremony is used by the top lobbyists for German business to confer with each other "about their economic and social policy demands for the coming legislate period." Architects: Schweger & Partners, Hamburg. Client: Groth & Graalfs, Berlin. Cost: DM 150 mill. Cf.BBA '97, August 27.

Thus Berlin is slandered *Ödön von Horváth*
The indictments heaped upon Berlin by the provinces can be grouped into the following categories:
1. **Berlin doesn't produce enough children.**
2. **In Berlin, there is nowhere to sit comfortably.**
3. **All our taxes migrate to Berlin and disappear under the table.**
4. **A young person can really only make something of himself in Berlin.**

9-1-1998

Decision: The future office for the state delegation representing Berlin in the federal government's upper house of parliament will be moving into the former directors' house at the Charité hospital, corner of Wilhelmstrasse and Dorotheenstrasse, just 300 m from the Reichstag. Renovation has begun on the 110 year-old house (which the state of Berlin owns); 29 office rooms, a large meeting hall, and a conference room are going to be installed. Renovation funds approved for the project: DM 4.8 mill. The two houses Berlin keeps in Bonn are being given up only with some hesitation: the first one in the summer of 1999, the other one in the year 2000. Their sale will bring in DM 7–8 mill.

9-2-1998

The Sony Center, the second biggest of the urban building blocks on Potsdamer Platz, celebrates a topping-out ceremony.

9-2-1998

48. Berlin Festwochen. Pars pro grosso modo: For Helen Levitt, grande dame of American photography, who like no one before observed the choreography of the street and banned "the decisive moment" (her idol Henri Cartier-Bresson) on film, a retrospective has been installed at the Festspielgalerie on Budapester Strasse. Until October 4.

9-2-1998

Wilmersdorfer Strasse is upgraded by the renovation of Peek & Cloppenburg (opening today), by a hotel being built across the street, by a new commercial building on the corner of Schillerstrasse (cf. Berlin's New Buildings 1997/98), and by subway entrances' redesign.

9-3-1998

Investment in Alexanderplatz as a business site: The Kaufhof department store (formerly Centrum-Warenhaus) was renovated, and today it opens as the "Galeria Kaufhof."

9-3 to 9-6-1998

Second Property Ownership Market in the Tent on Alexanderplatz, an event sponsored by the Senator for Construction, Housing, and Transportation.

9-4-1998

Topping-out ceremony for the commercial center "Manfred von Ardenne" in the Köpenick Innovation Park, which was founded in 1991. 20,000 sq. m of new space for offices, laboratories, and workshops will be created, and it is hoped that firms in the fields of materials and process technology will locate here. The district government as client invested DM 74.8 mill., with funds coming from the "Recovery East" project and from the state of Berlin. Architects: Ziltz and Partners, Berlin.

9-4-1998

At the Adlershof Science City, the accelerator facility named "Bessy II" officially goes into operation. Cf. main section.

9-5-1998

In Friedrichshain, the new municipal cultural house "Alte Feuerwache" ("Old Fire Station") has its opening.

9-5 to 9-11-1998

A Solar Week is sponsored by the 14 business associations in Berlin that jointly founded the initiative "Berlin Partners for Climate Protection."

9-8-1998

Cornerstone laying for a new building added to the Adlershof Science City (Wissenschaftsstadt Adlershof). On the grounds where the Academy of the Sciences was housed while the GDR was still a going concern, the Chemistry Department at the Humboldt University is getting a new home. The sizeable public investment has been justified on the grounds that the Adlershof is promoting to link research with teaching and business and thus will enhance career opportunities for students. Estimated construction cost: DM 99 mill. Scheduled completion: 2002.

9-9-1998

Cornerstone laying for the mega-construction project Lehrter Bahnhof. The railway station will be long and glassy, and it will run both above ground and underground. Glass-covered railroad platforms 400 m long running in an east-west direction (for ICE trains and urban rapid transit) will be encased above by two bridge constructions (for office use) and traversed below, at a depth of 17 m, by the tunnel pipes to be used for the north-south connection. Starting in 2003, 240,00 passengers and 110,000 people changing trains are expected each day. Design for the railway station's high-tech, five-level architecture: gmp, Hamburg/Berlin. Anticipated cost: DM 800 mill. Cf. BBA '96, main section. The anticipated total cost for Berlin's inter-city railway extension: DM 10 bill. On September 27 this year, after construction lasting six years, the DB (Deutsche Bahn) will inaugurate the high-speed line to Hanover (160 m/h).

On a 26,000 sq. m large, triangular area between Bellevuestrasse and the Neue Potsdamer Strasse, there will be seven buildings that trace the edges of the block, but without closing them off, and then inch ever closer toward the ellipsoid forum in the middle. Right on Potsdamer Platz, an office tower with 26 floors is shooting up to a height of 102 m. The 6,000 sq. m large steel-glass roof construction covering the forum will not be mounted until 1999; a mock-up on a 1:1 scale can be viewed next to the Info-Box. Architect: Helmut Jahn, Chicago. Developers: Sony, Tishman Speyer, Kajima (BEST Bellevuestrasse Development GmbH & Co. First Real Estate KG). Project development: Tishman Speyer Deutschland GmbH. Before next year is over, Sony will be moving its European headquarters to Berlin. Completion scheduled for 2000. Cf. end of April.

9-2-1998

Across from Potsdamer Platz: The CinemaxX movie theater center on Marlene-Dietrich-Platz, which is the largest in Germany and which (with its 19 theaters and 3,500 seats) is envisioned as a screening site for the Berlinale after 2000, has a grand opening with lots of celebrities. Cf. main section.

9-5-1998

Topping-out ceremony on the Marzahner Promenade: The first of many projects upgrading the urban quality along the 1.5 km long street is completed. On the 27,000 sq. m large site on Landsberger Allee near the Marzahn rapid transit station, a three-story entertainment center has been built with a multiplex cinema, a discotheque with two dance floors, 16 bowling lanes etc. Architects: Müller and Reimann, Berlin. Execution: Bautrako, Berlin. Investor and developer: Bavaria Immobilien Trading GmbH & Co. KG – LBD Fonds. Completion: Early 1999.

9-8-1998

The exhibit "Power of Age" has begun. Based on the lecture delivered in 1954 by Gottfried Benn — "Aging as a Problem for Artists" — young and old artists under the event-management of Bazon Brock experiment with this and that and not much else. In the Kronprinzenpalais Unter den Linden through November 1.

9-9-1998

The water frolics on Ernst-Reuter-Platz have been restored for DM 3,2 mill. Standing in front of 41 fountains at the square named after his father, Edzard Reuter greets the guests. Cf. July 13.

9-9-1998

Cornerstone laying for the future Indian embassy in the old diplomatic quarter, Tiergartenstraße 16–17. The 5,500 sq. m large property lies between the future site of South Africa's embassy building and the Baden-Württemberg state delegation. According to the mayor, 67 countries have already settled on a site for their diplomatic missions in Berlin. Architects for the Indian embassy: Léon & Wohlhage, Berlin, after their competition-winning design. Scheduled completion: 2000.

9-9-1998

Shooting has started on the movie "Sonnenallee," for which a section of the Wall is going be be rebuilt. Written and directed by Leander Haussmann, Detlev Buck, and Thomas Brussig, with Katharina Thalbach, Henry Hübchen.

9-10-1998

Cornerstone laying for the "Forum Neukölln" on Karl-Marx-Allee. The utilization concept for the 40,000 sq. m large shopping center (with shops ranging from Edeka groceries to Hugendubel books) will be enriched by the addition of a city library, a cinema center, and eventually a small swimming pool. Architect (named only for the outer looks): Bogan Johannsen, Hamburg. Client: KapHag and Bavaria, Berlin. Estimated cost: DM 250 mill. Scheduled opening: 2000.

9-10-1998

How many multi-story buildings can the city stand? While planners leisurely contemplate this question, the Tiergarten District Office and the investor Bauwert (which this year traded its Munich home office for a new one in Berlin) present their agreement to build a 23-story campanile with a marina in the midst of several 7-story office buildings along the shores of the Spree (Kaiserin-Augusta-Allee). The DM 200 million design is the outcome of a competition. Architects: WEP Effinger and Partners, Berlin.

11-9-1998

How many arcades can the city stand? Today at 11:00 a.m., the "Schönhauser Arcaden" celebrate their topping-out ceremony. The new shopping center with 90 stores — most of them already leased — is intended to bring new life to Schönhauser Allee as a shopping mile, and the businesses along the avenue have anticipated this day

15-9-1998

The Berlin district court decides in favor of the Advanta group in their eviction suit against the historic Hotel Kempinski on Kurfürstendamm. The legal conflict arose from unclear relations between the owners, managers, and the Thai investors who acquired the hotel. Only high financial securities can save the Kempinski.

9-15-1998

30 years of Mies' Neue Nationalgalerie: Sculptor Ulrich Rückriem clears the curtains from the windows (and the walls from the floor) in the upper exhibition hall, where he sets up an obstacle path for visitors in the form of 40 granite blocks whose unpolished surfaces are an exact match for the hall's polished granite slabs. The resulting impression left by this space can still be experienced through January 31, 1999.

9-17-1998

Topping-out ceremony for the "Bundesschlange" ("Federal Serpent") in Moabit. 718 dwellings for delegates to the Bundestag and federal employees are being erected not far from Bellevue palace. The dwellings in the 320-meter-long, undulating multistory building tend to be smallish (with rents running DM 15, 17, 19, and 21/sq. m), since many of the civil servants will keep their family homes in Bonn and live as "singles" in Berlin. Architect: Georg Brumiller, Berlin, clients: Deutschbau (510 housing units), Frankfurter Siedlungsgesellschaft (208 units), date of completion: August 1999.

17-9-1998

A nice gesture: the American ambassador John Kornblum has placed the U.S. Embassy headquarters on Neustädtische Kirchstrasse in Berlin-Mitte — heretofore a branch office — on equal footing with the embassy in Bonn. On September 1, 1999, the embassy in Bonn will officially close.

9-18-1998

Schönefeld airport: the association Flughafen-Holding Berlin sells 100% to the consortium "Flughafenpartner für Berlin und Brandenburg" (Airport Partners for Berlin and Brandenburg), consisting of the companies Hochtief Airport GmbH with 53.6 % of the shares (daughter firm of the construction company Hochtief), Flughafen Frankfurt Main AG (23.8 %), ABB Calor Schaltanlagen (12.6%) and the Bankgesellschaft Berlin AG (10%). Purchase price: DM 650 million plus DM 115 million assumption of debt. The large-scale airport with skywalks, designed by the Hamburg firm gmp, will cost DM 4 billion, with the consortium obligating itself to contribute DM 1 billion.

9-19-1998

Clubs United-Night in 18 locations, with a BVG bus-driver marathon on four routes beginning from Alexanderplatz.

9-17 to 9-18-1998

Twenty-fifth anniversary of the Deutsches Institut für Urbanistik (Difu), marked by a two-day conference with 300 participants from 60 European cities. Theme: Zukunfts-WerkStadt (FutureCity-Workshop).

Mid-September

The housing association WBG Marzahn has once again sold 610 dwellings (Wuhletalstrasse 2-68; Trusetaler Strasse 56-82) to the real estate firm HNW Duske with the obligation to renovate. The association has sold a total of ca. 3,500 dwellings, about 10% of its holdings, to intermediate buyers. Extensive legal protection for the tenants is guaranteed.

9-20-1998

Theodor Fontane is honored today, actually since the beginning of the year (many new publications, including his correspondence with his wife Emilie). Today is the

9-21-1998

The Chamber of Industry and Commerce opens its new building, the Ludwig Erhard Haus on Fasanenstrasse in Charlottenburg. Architect: Nicholas Grimshaw, London. Cf. main section.

9-23-1998

After a long period of construction, today is the topping-out ceremony for the 22-story high-rise over a low-lying structure on Kochstrasse in Kreuzberg. Renowned for its energy-efficient facade already before its completion (projected energy-usage reduction of 40 %), it has been selected as an "off-site project" for Expo 2000. The extension, built to accommodate the central offices of the housing association GSW (Gemeinnützige Siedlungs- und Wohnungsbaugesellschaft), comprises 24,500 sq. m

with all manner of artistic attractions. The new center extends over the S-Bahn tracks on seven steel arches spanning 40 m each. Architects: RKW, Rhode, Kellermann, Wawrowsky, Düsseldorf, client: Trigon Unternehmensgruppe, Berlin. Opening: March 4, 1999.

9-12-1998

10:00 p.m. Half a dozen men from the heavyweight transport company Stoppel maneuver a (nameless) coffee barge from ca. 1850 with a mast height of 20 m into the Museum of Technology on Trebbiner Strasse in Kreuzberg. There, the (much younger) Brandenburg tugboat "Kurt Heinz" is already waiting. On March 27 of this year, the cornerstone was laid for an extension building with an additional 12,000 sq. m of exhibition space, where the navigation and aviation divisions will be housed. The energy-optimizing design makes the building — scheduled to open in the year 2000 — an "off-site Expo 2000 project." Architects: MVT.

9-16-1998

The TLG (Treuhandliegenschaftsgesellschaft) will renovate the Kulturbrauerei in Prenzlauer Berg for DM 100 million and establish a multiplex cinema center there. Arthur Brauner had filed suit on account of the proximity to his Colosseum (cf. January). According to the TLG, ca. 66% of the 40,000 sq. m usable area in the Kulturbrauerei is already leased.

9-16-1998

Photographs of the buildings on view on the "Tag der Architektur" ("Architecture Day") are exhibited until October 9 in the offices of the Chamber of Architects on Karl-Marx-Allee 78 in Friedrichshain.

9-17-1998

Start of the Workshop Week for the "Freies Theater Berlin" on Koppenplatz, in and with the theater's rehearsal house. Through September 27, a total of 21 new productions will be presented, along with workshops and a podium discussion on the prospects for Berlin's independent theaters. The prelude: A "Theatriathlon," where four theater groups compete against each other in three rounds before a six-person jury of directors, critics, and authors.

9-20-1998

Twenty-fifth-anniversary Berlin marathon with a world record set by Ronaldo da Costa from Brazil and 25,000 participants under sunny skies. Unfairly eclipsed by the race: the 100th birthday of the Berliner Morgenpost (best wishes from the chroniclers).

100th anniversary of his death. Manuscripts, letters, pictures, writing instruments, and the so-called "Kaiserpanorama" as well as a model of the city and much more have been on view since September 10 in the exhibition "Fontane und sein Jahrhundert" ("Fontane and his Century") in the Märkisches Museum. Fontane himself, in Carrara marble, stands outside on a 2.5-meter-high pedestal.

usable area, of which 10,000 sq. m will be leased to other occupants. The extension is connected to the 17-story GSW high-rise from 1961. Architects: Sauerbruch Hutton Architekten, Berlin, cost: DM 180 million, date of completion: summer 1999.

Fontane turns seventy-five *Alfred Kerr*

Theodor Fontane is a tall, old man with narrow sideburns and a gray moustache. He strides down Potsdamer Strasse with a large scarf tied around his neck over his thick coat. He usually walks close to the buildings, since he has no desire to be stopped by the hundreds of acquaintances every inhabitant of the west encounters there daily. Not that he is unfriendly; it just isn't worth the trouble to exchange a few banalities and catch a cold in the process. He is very afraid of colds, which is why he always holds his famous gray-green scarf together in front with his hand. Beneath the hat, the kind, intelligent, large gray eyes gaze into the distance, and he walks with rapid steps, leaning slightly forward, going his way without stopping. ...A whiff of the good old days clings to the entire exterior of the man, even his clothing, down to the neckerchief and collar.

9-24-1998

Opening of the photonics center and a new center for gases on the grounds of WISTA in the science and research district Wissenschaftsstadt Adlershof, with three new buildings and three reconstructed old ones (18,000 sq. m total usable area). Cf. main section.

9-25-1998

Seventy-first meeting of the Stadtforum, this time focusing on the theme "Stadt für Frauen" ("A City for Women"), opportunities for emancipation in the metropolis. The program includes seven female speakers and is moderated by a man: Professor Dr. Rudolf Schäfer, legal expert for planning and building.

9-27-1998

Sunday evening, 6:00 p. m.: the historic election is decided, the new federal government will be led by the Social Democrats. Thirty-three parties were on the ballot. According to the preliminary prognoses, "everything went wrong for the CDU in the campaign"; "unity of person, program, and performance with the SPD"; "the Greens: five-mark debate and five-percent anxiety"; "the new course means a balancing act for the FDP"; "the PDS: to be or not to be"; "the DVU maneuvers, the NPD banks on terror." Official election results on Monday: 40.9 % for the SPD, 35.2 % for the CDU, 6.7 % for the Greens, 6.2 % for the FDP, 5.1 % for the PDS. A week later, it's decided: a red-green federal government will come to Berlin in 1999 and permit itself the luxury of bringing a cultural minister along. A sidelight: 60 registered voters in Berlin gave their votes to foreign residents in election sponsorships.

9-30-1998

September ends with art and more art: concurrently with the annual "art forum" (an art fair at the foot of the radio tower, presented this year for the third time until October 4), the Berlin Biennale opens its presentation of interdisciplinary "Glokales" (global + local). Exhibition sites include the Kunst-Werke on Auguststrasse, the old Akademie der Künste on Pariser Platz, and the Postfuhramt on Oranienburger Strasse. Curators are Nancy Spector from the Guggenheim Museum in New York, Hans-Ulrich Obrist from the Musée d'Art Moderne de la Ville de Paris, and Veni-Vidi-Vici curator Klaus Biesenbach from the Kunst-Werke in Berlin. On view until January 3, 1999.

The goal of all artistic endeavor in Berlin is to be tolerably pretty. It shouldn't exactly look crude and wretched, as if one didn't have it at all, but certainly there is no excessive artistic effort. It suffices to make a bit of a good impression; full-fledged art would be ridiculous. Besides, one would hear all kinds of disagreeable things from the citizens: waste … no other concerns … the taxpayers' money … in a time of social struggle … game-playing … and what have you.
Alfred Kerr, June 17, 1898

10-1-1998

132,000 signatures have been collected by opponents of the Transrapid magnetic railway in a petition which is handed over to Herwig Haase, the president of the Berlin parliament. Since 1997 the public petition has been fixed in the Berlin constitution as an institution of democracy; 90,000 signatures must be collected in a period of six months. After examination by the senate administration, the parliament will be obliged to hold a new debate on the controversial magnetic railway.

10-1-1998

The first underground train stops at the new overground station "Mendelssohn-Bartholdy-Park" in good time—one day before the opening of the Potsdamer Platz development and three months before the date which was originally scheduled. This 169th underground station in Berlin provides a rail

10-1-1998

"Oberbaum City" in Friedrichshain. Where light bulbs were once built, light can now enter house 4, the third of six buildings, after two years of renovation work. As the heart of the complex with its facades from the industrial development era of the 19th century, which are listed architectural monuments, it will house not only offices but also cafés, restaurants, shops and galleries. A special feature is the fountain of Slovenian tuff stone at the center of the inner courtyards. Architects: Reichel and Stauth, Braunschweig; client: Sirius-Projektentwicklungsgesellschaft; investment volume: DM 1.3 billion. Scheduled completion of all renovation work: autumn 2000.

September   **October**

9-25-1998

The S-Bahn system continues to grow: a 3-km-long section of the line S 25 between Lichterfelde-Ost and Lichterfelde-Süd is reopened after 14 years.

9-25-1998

Opening of a small-scale multiplex cinema in Oberschöneweide. The "Kinowelt in den Spreehöfen" ("Cinema World at the Spreehöfe") consists of five movie theaters, built into factory halls on the banks of the Spree under historic preservation. The project is managed by Kinowelt-Medien AG, well-respected for the cinema "Kant-Kino" in Berlin.

9-26-1998

The exhibit "Sensations" —with a large share of controversial, high-impact works by media-savvy young British artists—opens as part of the Hamburger Bahnhof festival. The works exhibited belong to the private collection of the British advertising agency Saatchi. Through January 1999.

9-29-1998

Ground-breaking for additional dwellings for federal employees, this time in Wilmersdorf. In the project "Wohnen am Preussenpark," 144 small apartments in seven stories are being built for commuters from Bonn. Architect: Hinrich Baller, Berlin, with Doris Baller-Piroth for landscape planning. Client: Haberent Grundstücks GmbH, Berlin, estimated cost: DM 55 million.

9-30-1998

Cornerstone-laying for the most controversial of all projects in downtown West Berlin: the "Neue Kranzler Eck" will now grow upward as a 16-story slab (55 m high, 160 m long) between Kurfürstendamm and Kantstrasse. Architect: Helmut Jahn ("A Whiff of Chicago"), investor: Deutsche Immobilienfonds AG (Difa), cost: DM 660 million, projected date of completion: mid-2000. Cf. January 19.

10-1-1998

The inner city development plan of the Senate is no longer the only one of its kind. The four neighboring districts of Hohenschönhausen, Lichtenberg, Marzahn and Hellersdorf are developing their own separate concept for the "eastern city", which they aim to complete in April 1999. The contract with two Berlin planning consultant offices is signed today. Cost: DM 150,000.

10-1-1998

The industrial estate "Gewerbe im Park" in Mahlsdorf is officially handed over after the five-year building phase. A third of the 32 acres of the estate is occupied by trees, bushes, flowers and water decorations. Architects: Fischer and Fischer, Cologne; developer: Gewerbe im Park GIP, Düsseldorf; clients and owners: Deutsche Immobilien Fonds AG(DIFA), Hansa Invest, Iduna/Nova, Pensionskasse Nordrheinische Ärzteversorgung; cost: DM 250 mill.

10-1-1998

Construction of the new media centre for the SAT.1 TV station was delayed for months by an intrusion of groundwater but now, at last, the topping-out is celebrated. The center extends from Jägerstrasse to Taubenstrasse in nine structural sections with an area of 33,000 sq. m and combines new and historic buildings. Architects: Dieter Hoffmann and Frank Uellendahl, Berlin, cost: approx. DM 250 mill.

transport connection for the "Daimler City". The transparent steel and glass structure has been built around the existing overground rail and gives a free view to all sides. Architects: Heinz Hilmer and Christoph Sattler, Munich/Berlin; execution planning: Architekturbüro Hans-Peter Störl, Berlin; client: Berliner Verkehrsgesellschaft (BVG); cost: DM 20 mill.

10-2-1998

Opening of the Hotel Marriott in the historic heart of Köpenick opposite the palace. Architects: Auer and Weber, Stuttgart; construction costs: DM 64 mill.

October 1998

A new interior for the ground floor area of Schinkel's Altes Museum. The Milan architects Giuseppe Caruso and Agata Torricella recreate the room layout designed by Schinkel by using free-standing square columns, which define the space and at the same time serve as information media and light sources.

10-2-1998

Opening of the debis complex at Potsdamer Platz. 19 new buildings, ten streets and a central piazza have been built on an almost vacant plot within four years. 3,945 guests of honor and about 900 journalists—including three from the Bauwelt Berlin Annual—are treated on a cold and windy morning to a glass of warming Grappa and the event-managed version of an official ceremony. Speeches by Jürgen Schrempp, Manfred Gentz, Eberhard Diepgen and Renzo Piano, punctuated by brief quotations on Potsdamer Platz and followed by an unparalleled concerted action by the Tölz boys' choir and the "Prinzen" pop group ("Wir sind das Volk"). Missing person: Edzard Reuter, who was not invited. We will remember the umbrellas which were given out for free, and which were gladly accepted in spite of the rain-free weather. The police were in groups of four, each carrying an umbrella; fork lift truck drivers were alone, with an um-

10-3-1998

The Brücke Museum shows works by the group of artists "Der Blaue Reiter". Until January 3, 1999.

Early October

After two years of building work, the large residential complex at the junction of Am Steinberg and Prenzlauer Promenade in Weissensee is completed. The 558 apartments are not only notable for their brightness, they are also individual in their spatial design. The building also contains a small shopping arcade with about 25 shops. Architect: Johann Friedrich Vorderwülbecke, Berlin; cost: DM 320 mill.

10-5-1998

An exhibition in Reinikkendorf town hall commemorates the 100th anniversary of the most modern industrial complex in Europe at the time, the Borsigwerke factory estate in Tegel. Until November 11.

10-5-1998

The Innovationszentrum für Umwelttechnologie (innovation center for environmental technology, UTZ), which works particularly in the areas of preventive technology, decontamination techniques and environmental services, opens on the WISTA estate in Adlershof. Architects: Eisele, Fritz, Bott, Hilka, Begemann, Darmstadt; developer: WISTA-Management GmbH. Cf. main section.

10-5-1998

Flat sharing atmosphere in front of the hedgehog mascot. 20 years ago about 70 left-wing groups in Berlin combined to form the "Alternative Liste" (AL). After their wild beginnings they now form a normal regional association of the Green political party.

10-7-1998

Laying of the foundation stone for the "Estrel Convention Center Berlin". Germany's largest hotel, the Hotel Estrel at Sonnenallee 225 in Neukölln, is building a congress centre with a capacity of up to 6,500 places. Architect: Andreas Bodem; developer: Ekkehard Streletzki; investment total: DM 45 mill.; scheduled completion: July 1999.

10-8-1998

The insurance company Provinzial celebrates its topping out ceremony at the corner of Ku'damm and Bleibtreustrasse. The combination of a new structure and building alterations is planned to provide both shops and dwellings. Architects: Moratz & Stolze, Berlin; developer: VGH Provinzial Lebensversicherung, Hanover; investment total: DM 50 mill.; scheduled completion: 1999.

10-8-1998

An anniversary. 75 years ago the first plane with a pilot and two passengers left Tempelhof Airport bound for Munich. The airport that now serves 15 airlines began with two wooden huts and a number of flying machines. But now its future is uncertain—it may become superfluous when the planned large airport Berlin-Brandenburg International (BBI) opens. Cf. June 26.

10-9-1998

Rita Süssmuth opens the exhibition "Art and Parliament" in the Reichstag building. 17 mainly German artists who have influenced the art scene since 1945 present their proposals for the design of the Reichstag, including Sigmar Polke, Georg Baselitz, Anselm Kiefer, Gerhard Richter, two former East German artists, Bernhard Heisig and Carlfriedrich Claus, the American artist Jenny Holzer and Christian Boltanski who lives in France. All the works deal with themes from Ger-

10-12-1998

The actor Bernhard Minetti dies in Berlin at the age of 93. For decades he was a member of the ensemble of the Schiller-Theater in Berlin, which was closed in 1993. His last stage appearance was on 11th September in Brecht's "Arturo Ui" with the Berliner Ensemble. The funeral is held on October 21.

10-14-1998

In the Chinese Garden in Marzahn Senator Strieder, the Senator for urban development, unveils a stone pagoda. The Chinese architect Jin Bo Ling gives information about the design of the rest of the garden, which is scheduled for completion in 2000.

10-15-1998

The industrial complex at Rheinstrasse 45/46 in Schöneberg celebrates its 100th anniversary. The factory was built for Carl Paul Goerz in 1897/98 by the architects Paul Egeling and Waldemar Wendt in the Neo-Gothic and

brella on their fork lift truck; high society guests carried their own expensive umbrella in their left hand, the free umbrella in their right... Within the first three days, over a million visitors explore the complex of 68,000 sq. m which provides Berlin with 600 apartments, 120 shops, 30 restaurants and 19 cinema theaters. Investment total: DM 4 billion. Cf. the main sections of BBA '97 and '98.

10-3-1998

"Life is a building site"—at any rate this is so for the construction workers at Potsdamer Platz. An exhibition in the Info-Box created by students from the Technical University (TU) and College of Arts (HdK) documents the life and work of the "building site people."

The desire to destroy, so widespread at the moment that it can be exploited for advertising purposes, is remarkably compatible with a veritably colonial will to build. If this magnificent city possesses any seductions, they are certainly not those the city itself considers seductive. But it exerts other attractions that are very effective, and one of its main charms doubtless lies in its mute, dogged struggle for a spacious existence, beyond the arrogance and the surge of phrases. Berlin is a poor antidote for melancholy.
Siegfried Kracauer, 1931

man history. Until December 11. Cf. BBA '97, March 13 and February 18.

Mid-October

Art at Checkpoint Charlie again. The Berlin artist Frank Thiel has set up large format photographs of a Russian soldier and an American soldier face to face—as a reminder of the time shortly after the Berlin Wall was built in 1961.

Mid-October

Arguments flare about whether the Hungarian Embassy at the corner of Unter den Linden and Wilhelmstrasse should be listed as an architectural monument. Both this building and the Polish Embassy at Unter den Linden 70/72 were classified as outstanding examples of the modern GDR style of the 1960s. Now, permission is given after all for the Hungarian Embassy to be demolished. Hungary's interest in having a worthy representation in the German capital is judged more important than the preservation claim.

Neo-Renaissance style. Now, after extensive renovation work, it appears in a new splendour. Photographs of the industrial monument by Jens Knigge can be seen from October 16 to 30.

10-18-1998

In the series of cultural events "Berliner Lektionen", the renowned American architect Richard Meier (Museum für Kunsthandwerk, Frankfurt/M. 1985) gives a lecture on the subject "The role of architecture in a new Europe."

10-22 to 10-24-1998

Specialist fair for ecological building and techniques in Kreuzberg.

10-22-1998

An exhibition on the route modernisation plans of the German railway board Deutsche Bahn AG is opened in the Deutsches Architekturzentrum. Until December 11.

10-23-1998

The scene is Gendarmenmarkt in Berlin-Mitte. A parked car explodes, a young woman falls down, flames shoot several meters into the air…the Tagesspiegel newspaper reports that Berlin is becoming established as the "capital of the detective film". It is the place where most detective films are made in Germany.

10-23-1998

Film again. This time the scene is the underground railway between Zoo and Hansaplatz. Through the window, underground passengers can experience a cinema for 30 sec-

10-26-1998

The exhibition "Best of European Cities" opens in the Red Town Hall. The cities of Amsterdam, Berlin, Hamburg, London, Munich, Vienna, and Zurich present themselves and their approaches to the solution of urban development tasks for comparison.
Until November 20.

10-26-1998

Topping-out for the new representation building of the federal state of Thüringen in Mohrenstrasse 64. Architect: Worschech + Partner, Erfurt; developer: Free State of Thüringen; investment: DM 21 mill.; scheduled completion: May 1999.

10-28 to 10-30-1998

Full steam ahead: the international transport technology fair "Inno-Trans '98" and the world congress for high speed rail travel, "Eurailspeed '98" take place in Berlin.

10-29-1998

The new business center is opened in the "Gewerbepark am Borsigturm" in Tegel. Architects: Walter Rolfes and Partners, Berlin. Cf. BBA '97, main section.

Late October

Construction begins on the triangular plot of the Lenné-Dreieck: Between Tiergarten and Sony, the building of the Association of Public Banks in Germany (VÖB) and the German Rural Districts Council (DLT) will be built. The nine-story building will be characterised by glass and aluminium. An exterior escape staircase will break up the strictly geometrical form. Architect: Edwin Effinger, Berlin; cost: DM 35 mill.; scheduled completion: 2000.

10-30-1998

In memory of Arthur Eloesser, a memorial stone is erected on the Jewish cemetery in Weissensee in honor of the writer, dramatist and critic who died in Berlin 60 years ago.

10-30-1998

The 1998 architecture prize of the Bund Deutscher Architekten Berlin (BDA) is awarded. The winners are the architects of the kindergarten No. 9 in Karow-Nord, José Paolo dos Santos, Porto and Barbara Hoidn, Berlin, and the architects of the memorial "Gleis 17" (Platform 17) on Grunewald station, Nikolaus Hirsch, Wolfgang Lorch and Andrea Wandel, Frankfurt.

In my youth, I had no particular affection for my native city — I considered everywhere else in the world more beautiful, warmer, more lovable. Berlin only became home to me when I began to lose it in the unceasing flood of new inhabitants, when it began to live for the day and against the past, without memory, without tradition, without obligation, an ungainly young giant with all the ugliness of too-rapid growth, immoderate in its sense of self, immoderate in work and above all in a grasping, indiscriminate hedonism.
Arthur Eloesser, 1919

10-19-1998

Even before its completion, the new bridge for the S-Bahn urban railway at Kablower Weg in Köpenick collapses. The bridge, which was to replace two old bridges in need of renovation and repair, should have been completed on October 26.

10-21-1998

Topping-out ceremony for the extension building for the German standardization institute (DIN) on Budapester Strasse. The ten stories high building is named after the Berlin scientist Alexander von Humboldt. Architects: Johannes Heinrich, in Bassenge, Puhan-Schulz, Heinrich, Schreiber, Berlin; cost: DM 60 mill.; scheduled completion: November 1999.

10-21-1998

On Invalidenstrasse the old German government celebrates its last topping-out ceremony. The new building will house the Ministry of Transport. Architect: Max Dudler, Berlin; cost: DM 172.4 mill.; completion: August 1999.

onds. For a distance of 600 metres, 900 projectors are installed on the side walls of the underground tunnel and project 30 pictures per second — computer-synchronized with the speed with which the train is travelling. The project "Metro-Cinevision" opens today with a Charlie Chaplin clip. Inventor and pioneer: Jörg Moser-Metius; costs: DM 4.5 mill.

10-24-1998

The film director Peter Greenaway stages Darius Milhaud's "Christoph Kolumbus" at the Deutsche Staatsoper. Today is the premiere.

10-24-1998

The cultural centre, Werkstatt der Kulturen, a meeting place for more than 180 nations, celebrates its 5th anniversary with a great party. The building in Wissmannstrasse in Neukölln offers musical, theatrical, dancing and literary programmes with participants from a wide range of countries.

Mid-October

The "Wintergartenquartier" at Friedrichstrasse station has found an investor. From the middle of 1999, Züblin Projektentwicklung GmbH proposes to begin construction work on the 10.700 sq. m complex. Eight to ten construction sections are planned in which different architects will execute their projects. Investment total: DM 300 mill.; scheduled completion: 2001.

10-27-1998

Removals. Today the Senate decides that the Berlinische Galerie will move to the Schultheiss brewery building in Kreuzberg. Since the gallery moved out of the Martin Gropius building last year because of alteration work on the building, the collection has been stored in packing cases on the land of the former brewery. It is to move into the renovated building complex in 2001. Architect: Frederick Fisher, Los Angeles.

10-29-1998

The Israeli ambassador Avi Primor presents the design for "Israel's most beautiful embassy in the world". It will be built on a plot measuring 9,000 sq. m on Auguste-Viktoria-Strasse in Schmargendorf. The buildings of the Protestant social care institute Diakonisches Werk will be demolished from January 1999, the listed historical villa built for Herrmann Schöndorff, a distinguished Jewish businessman, will be integrated into the new project. The Israeli architect plans to redesign the facade of the villa, with the new building of sandstone and copper leaning slightly towards the old building. In front of the largely glazed facade, six pillar-type stone elements will be set up as a reminder of the six million murdered Jews. Architect: Orit Willenberg-Giladi; cost: DM 20 mill.; scheduled completion: 2000.

10-29-1998

Opening of the "Forum Zehlendorf" on Teltower Damm. Visitors enter the new shopping center through a hall-type entrance which leads into a glass-covered inner courtyard where the customer can buy a wide variety of goods. Architect: Jan C. Bassenge, Berlin; cost: approx. DM 40 mill.

10-30-1998

Topping-out for an apartment building at the junction of Uhlandstrasse and Kantstrasse. Developers: Beko Projekt; investment total: DM 26 mill.; scheduled completion: April 1999.

10-30-1998

Topping-out for the Dorint-Hotel Schweizerhof in Budapester Strasse in Tiergarten. The hotel aims to continue old traditions and thus attract both the "old" and "new" elite of Berlin. Cf. March 27.

Late October

Life is more difficult for protectors of archaeological relics than for their architectural colleagues. The excavations on Schlossplatz have been neglected since 1996 for financial reasons — experts claim that the site will soon be a case for nature conservation. They would love to resume their research and to construct a viewing tower which would give visitors a direct overview of the excavation site.

10-30-1998

Rudolf Scharping, new German Minister of Defence and politician lacking a lucky star, undertakes his first official act in Berlin: he precedes the 4th Berlin military music festival.

10-30 to 11-1-1998

The Technical University is holding a symposium on the subject "Architecture and Exile. German-language emigration and the transformation of the modern age (1933-1945)."

10-31-1998

"Paradise Lost" — the Neue Nationalgalerie offers an extensive exhibition of works by Paul Gauguin to commemorate the 150th anniversary of his birth. Until January 10, 1999.

11-3-1998

The German civil servants' association (Deutscher Beamtenbund — DBB) is planning a new DBB Forum (architect: Karl-Heinz Schommer; construction costs: DM 120 mill.) between Französische

11-6-1998

Wolfgang Stresemann, twice director of the Berlin Philharmonic Orchestra and the son of the Foreign Minister, Gustav Stresemann, dies at the age of 94. His autobiography bears the title "Zeilen und Klänge" (Lines and sounds). Many obituaries, but no one can express the important role this upright man played for Berlin.

11-6-1998

Topping-out for the extension to the future German Foreign Office on Werderscher Markt in Mitte. The new structure has been built in front of the old building of the former Reichsbank, which for 30 years was the seat of the Central Committee of the GDR. It is the first topping-out ceremony in Berlin for the Foreign Minister Joschka Fischer, who will carry out his duties in Honecker's former office. Architects: Thomas Müller and Ivan Riemann, Berlin; cost: DM 163.3 mill.; planned occupation date: autumn of 1999.

11-10 to 11-22-1998

12th Jewish cultural festival. Under the title "Wiener Melange", the subject is the cultural exchange between Vienna and Berlin with exhibitions, concerts, theater, readings and much more.

11-11-1998

Opening of a new hospital with 355 beds in Lynarstrasse in Spandau. The new building (172 m long, 18 m wide and 26 m high), with its six-story facade with red facing bricks, fits in with the old hospital buildings. Architect: Robert Wischer, Berlin; construction costs: approx. DM 150 mill.

11-18-1998

Will the German Chancellor rule on a building site? In view of the relocation report presented today by the Minister of Building, Mr. Müntefering, we must probably say yes because building work on the government buildings is behind schedule. Gerhard Schröder will therefore be able to start work in Berlin in the autumn of 1999, not in April as planned, and "his" Chancellery building will only be ready for occupation at the end of 2000.

11-18-1998

There will also be delays in Berlin's "development zones" such as the "Water City" on the upper Havel and the new science estate in Adlershof. Today, the city parliament cancelled all funds planned for 1999 to limit the city's budget deficit.

11-18-1998

The documentation center of the Shoah Foundation set up by Steven Spielberg is to be located

Mid-November

New high class places to live in the capital city — for those who can afford it — are Potsdamer Platz and the Tiergarten-Dreieck (owner-occupied flats up to 250 sq. m in size, purchase price DM 6,000 – 12,000 per sq. m). The new expensive apartments are in great demand. Cf. October 2 and May 27.

Mid-November

40th anniversary of the Galerie Brusberg. The gallery, which Dieter Brusberg founded on November 9, 1958 in Hanover, celebrates with the exhibition "Wegzeichen". Brusberg has been on Ku'damm in Berlin since 1982. He has a special interest in classical Surrealism and painting in the GDR. Until January 30, 1999.

11-20-1998

The second new hospital building to be opened in November. In a symmetrical two-wing building, the Behring hospital in Zehlendorf now has space

11-23-1998

"The fall of the key" — at the handing over of the keys to officially open the Federal President's Office, State Secretary Wilhelm Staudacher drops the key handed over by the Minister of Building, Mr. Müntefering. After the initial scare, the ceremony in the new building with 150 employees and 400 guests of honor — including the Federal President — continues normally. The relocation of the Federal President's Office signals the start of the relocation of the government to the new capital. Cf. main section.

11-25-1998

The second great appearance in Berlin, at 9.30 in the morning: "As you could say, Ich bin ein Berliner" — the German Chancellor Gerhard Schröder opens his first cabinet meeting in the former GDR State Council Building with this statement of allegiance to the new German seat of government.

Strasse, Behrenstrasse and Friedrichstrasse. The "Haus der Demokratie" is also to be integrated into the ensemble of five buildings and completely renovated. To this end, all tenants have now been given notice of immediate termination. In their place, the national trust for the historical evaluation of the Communist dictatorship is to move into 2/3 of the building. But the occupants do not want to give up the building, which they regard as a symbol of the citizens' resistance in the GDR. Cf. May 11.

11-6-1998

Laying of the foundation stone for the senior citizens residence "Wilhelm-Eck" between Hotel Adlon and the British Embassy on Pariser Platz. Over a dual pedestal story there will be four upper stories, and a total of 72 flats. Architect: Gustav Peichl, Vienna; client: Prinz zu Hohenlohe-Jagstberg & Banghardt-Beratungsgesellschaft.

11-6-1998

The S-Bahn urban railway officially opens its new workshop in Grünau. In just 14 months, one of the most modern plants of its kind has been erected in this complex. General planning: Peter Altenkamp, Berlin; construction costs: DM 50 mill.

Early November

The Jewish congregation of Adass Jisroel is planning a new synagogue in Tucholskystrasse 40 in Mitte. The old synagogue was pulled down by the GDR in 1966. Now an eight metre high octagonal glazed building is to be built here, and in addition to the synagogue it will have a kindergarten, instruction rooms and a Mikwe, the Jewish bath. Architect: Christian Dierkes, Berlin; construction costs: DM 2.5 mill., which the Senate and the national government are being asked to bear.

11-14-1998

Alterations to the 30 year old shopping center in the Märkisches Viertel are complete — today is the opening. Investor: Hammerson GmbH; cost: DM 40 mill.

11-17-1998

Topping-out for a new primary school and sports hall in Rudow-Süd. The elongated, two-story building will accommodate about 450 pupils. Architect: Anne Rabenschlag, Berlin; cost: DM 14 mill., scheduled completion: for the school year 1999/2000.

in the Jewish Museum — this is announced by the museum director, Michael Blumenthal, and the German government's cultural administrator, Michael Naumann. Spielberg founded the foundation with the earnings from the film "Schindler's List", and he has now collected video recordings worldwide with reports by about 50,000 Holocaust survivors. To represent and support the Spielberg project in Germany, the first office of the foundation outside the USA is opened this week.

11-19-1998

Alterations to a former furniture store in Bismarckstrasse in Spandau are completed. Today the building is officially handed over to the Kant grammar school as an extension. Alteration plans: Spandau planning authority; alteration costs: DM 4.2 mill..

11-19-1998

Winter comes to Berlin.

for six new wards. The glass-covered, bright inner courtyards with olive trees are designed as recreation areas for the patients. Architects: Gottfried Böhm and Peter Pawlik, Cologne; cost: DM 117 mill.

11-23-1998

The Prussian cultural foundation "Stiftung Preussischer Kulturbesitz" (SPK) has a new president. The former general director of the Deutsche Bibliothek in Frankfurt, Klaus-Dieter Lehmann, was unanimously elected. He was the sole candidate for the post after lengthy haggling about the candidature. He plans to carry out thorough reforms in the SPK, to reduce the number of hierarchical levels and set up a uniform infrastructure. The alterations to the Museum Island and the reform of the Staatsbibliothek are also areas that are due for attention.

11-28-1998

And last of all…at the end of November, a second glass panel falls from the facade of the Galeries Lafayette — at the same corner where the first panel fell in August. This time the building authority sealed off the pavement, and over the next few days all the glass panels are dismantled and subjected to a test.

The Viceroy's Last Visit *Hubert Spiegel*

At the branch office of the Federal Chancellery in Berlin, "Am Schloss-platz 1," the viceroy of Chancellor Helmut Kohl looked out the window—the same window from which the East German head of state had formerly gazed at the Palast der Republik. Hands clasped behind his back, he stood at the window and saw what Erich Honecker had seen before him, what Helmut Kohl should have seen but never did, and what Gerhard Schröder would now see when his cabinet convened for the first time at the round table in the great room, the Diplomaten-saal. He saw the center of Berlin with the eyes of the old GDR, and the sight of it made his heart ache.

The viceroy had prepared everything with care. He had made contacts throughout the entire city. It hadn't been easy for him, for to someone from Bonn, the heavyweights in Berlin seemed incredibly provincial. He had soon learned to despise Berlin municipal politics. How quickly the city would have changed once the chancellor had arrived here! But the chancellor remained in Bonn. Not once did the cabinet of Helmut Kohl take their places in the Diplomatensaal of the Staatsratsgebäude. Was it because of the imposing round table around which Honecker used to assemble the diplomats of the Warsaw Pact on special occasions? Or was it because of the chairs the viceroy himself had fetched from the cellar of Bonn's Schaumburg palace? Sometimes he himself was surprised at how well the desks, armchairs, and sofas from Schaumburg harmonized with the old furnishings of the Staatsratsgebäude. Had the GDR and the Federal Republic in fact retained a greater aesthetic affinity than political relations would have

12-1-1998

A decision has been made on the renovation of the Olympic Stadium. According to a resolution of the Senate, the stadium will be converted into a multi-functional arena on the basis of plans by the architects gmp, von Gerkan, Marg and Partner, Hamburg. But the concept still needs to be revised: box seats and emergency escape routes are missing. And the investors and the operating company have not yet been found (selection process up to June 15, 1999), and the financing is still not clear: DM 100 mill. will be contributed by the German government, the remainder of the necessary DM 538 mill. must be borne by private investors. Renovation work is scheduled to begin in May 2000. Cf. May 27.

12-10-1998

After a third round of discussions, the building committee and district council decide in favor of the construction of a high rise on the area of Funkturm Fairgrounds. Architect: O. M. Ungers, Cologne/Berlin. The tower is to be 150 metres high and in a circular segment form.

12-11-1998

Topping-out ceremony for Ferdinandmarkt in Lichterfelde-Ost. On an area of 6,500 sq. m a shopping center is being constructed in which the market stalls that have been there since 1908 will again find their place—under a glass roof. Client: Thomas Degenhardt; investment volume: DM 30 mill.; scheduled completion date: June 1999.

12-17-1998

The German eagle has landed in Berlin. With the rear newly designed by Norman Foster, it now flies into the plenary chamber of the Reichstag building. Cf. May 27.

12-30-1998

Ten minutes past noon—the official opening of the new Spandau station. The 200 meter long glass vaults (architects: gmp, von Gerkan, Marg and Partners, Hamburg; cost: DM 120 mill.) begin immediately beyond the recently completed bridge over the Havel. They cover a total of six platforms: for the ICE trains, the S-Bahn lines S 5 and S 75 and the regional train lines RB 13, RE 4 and RE 5. For travellers, it is easy to change, even to the underground (U7) and the buses. Spandau station has been cut off from the S-Bahn system since September 17, 1980. With the new section from Pichelsberg to Spandau, the S-Bahn network has grown by a further 4.9 km. A total of 21 km of S-Bahn lines have been opened this year

led one to suspect? The viceroy had developed the habit of asking himself such questions. Following the viceroy through the building, it suddenly seemed to the visitor as if he, the viceroy, were treating him like someone looking for a house, someone viewing a building for sale. The viceroy himself, a fine gentleman in his prime, appeared to the visitor like a man fallen on hard times through no fault of his own, forced by cruel fate to sell his family home.

The viceroy stepped back from the window and traversed the imposing Diplomatensaal with short steps, reaching for his waistband where his keys hung on a small silver chain. Carefully he locked all the doors behind him, and once it happened that he left the visitor behind him in a large hall, having first requested his patience for a moment.

When the viceroy opened the room that he had previously entered alone, the visitor found himself peering into a windowless cabinet. It was lined in its entirety with white goat leather, on which countless fluttering doves of peace were stamped in gold. The precious wall covering had been a gift of the Mongolian Republic to the East German head of state. The viceroy had probably spent many hours in this extraordinary room. In a strange way, the empty, useless room, apparently created solely to accommodate the white goat leather of Mongolia, seemed to him like the secret heart of the building. In his solitude, he suddenly realized what he had become in the course of time: the viceroy of a capitulated province.

12-3 to 12-6-1998

Tickets were sold out even before posters announced the dance theater event: Pina Bausch's "Masurca Fogo" in Berlin.

12-3 to 12-6-1998

"Europe—a dream or a nightmare?"—this question is discussed by literary figures from 16 European countries in the House of the Cultures of the World.

12-4-1998

Anniversary. The Free University Berlin (FU) was founded 50 years ago today.

12-10-1998

The relocation of the government continues. With the dedication of the building at Behrenstrasse 21/22, Bavaria is the first of the 16 federal state representations to move to Berlin.

12-17-1998

After issuing demolition permission for the Hungarian Embassy, the Senate now feels compelled to do the same for the building of the old Polish Embassy, which is classed as a testimony of GDR architecture and a "building of the highest importance for urban development and monument preservation". The reason is the decision by the Polish association of architects in favour of a new embassy building to plans by the Polish architectural office of Marek Budzynski. Cf. mid-October.

12-18-1998

After a gap of 31 years, a tram travels across the "Alex" again. The new route from Mollstrasse via Alexanderplatz to the Hackescher Markt is officially opened today (routes 5, 6, 8, 15 and N92). Cf. main section.

alone (Westkreuz–Spandau, Tegel–Hennigsdorf, Lichterfelde Ost–Lichterfelde Süd), which means that the system has grown to a total of 321 km and 161 stations. The next major project of Deutsche Bahn is closing the gap on the Nordring in Berlin by the year 2002.

12-31-1998

New Years Eve, Hotel Adlon offers from the world's longest frozen champagne bar Laurent Premier at 15 DM a glass. The 35 year old ice artist and learned cook Christian Funk had the necessary 60 tons of ice transported on tractor trucks to Brandenburg Gate, where he began construction in spite of mild temperature. Ice art, so the master, "has to be monumental, oversized and unforgettable". Like Berlin so to speak.

Credits

Literature
122 Peter Fürst, Schnitzeljagd Berlin–New York,
Munich 1998, p. 16
123 Hans Unverzagt (Günter Plessow), Was es hat,
unpublished typoscript, 1998
123 Wilhelm Hausenstein, Eine Stadt auf nichts
gebaut..., Berlin 1984 (new edition), p. 11
125 Sulpiz Boisserée, Tagebücher I, 1808–1823,
Darmstadt 1978, p. 185
126 Carl Zuckmayer, Drei Jahre,
in: Theaterstadt Berlin, Berlin 1948, p. 87f
127 Wolf Biermann, Warte nicht auf beßre Zeiten,
quoted from a live recording in his apartment, CBS 1973
129 Evelyn Roll, Ein Gedicht über die Reling. In: Ecke
Friedrichstraße (ed. by E. Roll), Munich 1997, p. 30
132 Wilhelm Hausenstein, Eine Stadt auf nichts
gebaut..., Berlin 1984 (new edition), p. 24
132 Adolph von Menzel, Brief an C. W. Arnold, quoted
from Paul Ortwin Rave, in: Berliner Almanach 1948,
Berlin 1948
133 Michael Jeismann, Große Zähmung der Stofftiere,
in: Frankfurter Allgemeine Zeitung, 31.9.1998
134 Peter Fürst, Schnitzeljagd Berlin–New York,
Munich 1998, p. 54
135 Ilja Ehrenburg, quoted from Wolfgang Kil, Das Tor
zum Osten: Berlin, in: Last Exit Downtown. Gefahr für
die Stadt (ed. by Michael Mönninger), Basel, Berlin,
Boston, 1995 p. 20
137 Andreas Nachama, zum 80. Geburtstag seines
Vaters, in: Der Tagesspiegel, 4.5.1998
138 Gad Granach, Heimat los! Augsburg 1997, p. 74
139 Sabine Lenz, Messer und Gabel,
in: Neue Zürcher Zeitung, 4.2.1995
139 Gunnar Lützow, Eher erdig als elitär,
in: Berliner Morgenpost, 19.5.1998
140 Evelyn Roll, Der Adler,
in: Süddeutsche Zeitung, 4.2.1998
142 Evelyn Roll, Ecke Friedrichstraße,
in: Süddeutsche Zeitung, 17.6.1998
142 Thea Herold, Auf Wiedersehen im 21. Jahrhundert,
in: Süddeutsche Zeitung, 7.1.1998

144 Mark Twain, The awful German language,
Recklinghausen 1996, p. 5f
146 Alfred Kerr, Wo liegt Berlin? Briefe aus der Reichs-
hauptstadt. 1895–1900, Berlin 1997, p. 403
148 Alfred Kerr, Wo liegt Berlin? Briefe aus der Reichs-
hauptstadt. 1895–1900, Berlin 1997, p. 199
150 Heinrich Wefing, Sind so edle Mauern...,
quoted from: Pompeji der deutschen Teilung,
in: Frankfurter Allgemeine Zeitung, 13.8.1998
151 Kurt Tucholsky, quoted from: Der Berliner zweifelt
immer (ed. by Heinz Knobloch), Berlin 1977, p. 346f
152 Ödön von Horváth, quoted from: Der Berliner zweifelt immer (ed. by Heinz Knobloch), Berlin 1977, p. 486
154 Alfred Kerr, Wo liegt Berlin? Briefe aus der Reichs-
hauptstadt. 1895–1900, Berlin 1997, p. 5f
155 Alfred Kerr, Wo liegt Berlin? Briefe aus der Reichs-
hauptstadt. 1895–1900, Berlin 1997, p. 395f
156 Siegfried Kracauer, Berliner Nebeneinander.
Ausgewählte Feuilletons 1930–1933
(ed. by Andras Volk), Zurich 1996, p. 17
157 Arthur Eloesser, quoted from: Der Berliner zweifelt
immer (ed. by Heinz Knobloch), Berlin 1977, p. 346
159 Hubert Spiegel, Letzter Besuch beim Statthalter...,
in: Süddeutsche Zeitung, 5.11.1998

Photos
Erik-Jan Ouwerkerk
122, 124 (2x), 125, 128, 129 (3x),130, 131 (3x), 134 (3x),
143 (3x), 145 (2x), 146, 149 (2x), 150, 151, 152 (2x), 153,
154
127 Wolfgang Hilse, quoted from
Berliner Zeitung, 2.2.1998
133 MERIAN Berlin, June 1998
136 SONY Berlin/Edinger (1x), SONY Berlin
137 Ullstein Verlag, Berlin
139 IDZ, Norbert Kersten, 1998 (2x)
140 all ill. from: Der Tagesspiegel, 14.5.1998
141 Groth + Graalfs; Simulation WISTA, Berlin 1998
155 Berliner Morgenpost, 2.10.1998
156 Advertisement in: Berliner Morgenpost, 2.10.1998
157 from: Süddeutsche Zeitung, Magazine "jetzt", Nr. 28

Berlin's New Buildings 1997/98

According to our present feeling, the expansion of a metropolis must be unlimited, Otto Wagner stated about one hundred years ago. Berlin keeps building, so the list of Berlin's new buildings does not become any shorter even in this third edition. On 15 pages it brings together about 400 projects. Since 1996 we have listed about 1,400 buildings, and the metropolitan city of Berlin has grown by about the size of a small town during this period. The fact that Mitte, Pankow, Köpenick and Weissensee, where the cranes still turn fastest, fill the largest number of columns in the list is due to the cooperation of the districts and the various departments which have supported our work for the first time this year. Without Ms. Erfurt, Ms. Genz, Mr. Noppe, Mr. Prezewowsky, Ms. Strutzig and Ms. Wolter, who gave us the desired data on the buildings as far as this was possible within the strict confines of data protection, we would hardly have been able to compile this year's list.

The Association of Free Housing Enterprises Berlin/ Brandenburg also has a share in the success of the list of new buildings; we were able to use the association's yearbook as a source of information, and the members informed us of completed projects.

A special word of thanks is due to Ms. Dux of Bauwelt for ensuring that our appeals to architects and developers regularly resounded out of the pages of Bauwelt magazine. And finally, the same procedure as last year: those who were forgotten this year or who forgot themselves are hereby invited to take space in next year's volume, Bauwelt Berlin Annual 1999/2000. *Susanne Schöninger/Christoph Tempel*

Charlottenburg

Augsburger Strasse 35/Rankestrasse 26
Apartment and Commercial Building
Hasso von Werder and Partners, Berlin
Client: Bayerische Handelsbank AG, Munich
Corner building, 8 stories,
12 housing units, 3 commercial units
gross floor area 4.390 sq.m
Cost approx. DM 11,41 mill.
built October 1996–1998

Dahlmannstrasse 1–1A/Corner Gervinusstrasse
Apartment and Commercial Building
Karl Heinz Fischer, Berlin
Client: Karl Heinz Fischer, Berlin
Urban infill, 7 stories, neighboring house raised in height,
14 housing units, 1 commercial unit;
gross floor area 1.304 sq.m
cost DM 4,1 mill.
built December 1996–Sept. 1998

Grolmannstrasse 36
Apartment and Commercial Building
ELW, Eyl Weitz & Partner und Ursula Hüffer, Berlin
Client: Clarendon Nominees Ltd.
Block alignment, street front building,
7 stories, 2 commercial units, 6 office units, 7 housing units;
courtyard building, modernized and raised in height, 6 stories,
1 office, 20 housing units
cost approx. DM 15 mill.
built 1996–1998

Heilmannring 24 C
GEWOBAG-Offices
GEWOBAG with Garsztecki und Hartmann, Berlin
Client: GEWOBAG Gemeinnützige Wohnungsbau AG, Berlin
Office Building, 2 stories, out of prefabricated concrete slabs with green roof
gross floor area 757,46 sq.m
cost approx. DM 1,6 mill.
built April 1998–September 1998

Kurfürstendamm 30
Apartment and Commercial Building
Dan Lazar
Client: DEBEKO Immobilien GmbH & Co. Grundbesitz oHG, Eschborn
Block alignment, 8 stories,
12 housing units, 1 shop,
gross floor area 4.100 sq.m
cost DM 14 mill.
built 1996–1998

Passenheimer Strasse 10–20
Apartment Buildings
Planungsbüro Schwithz Aachen GmbH, Aachen
Client: Deutsche Bau- und Grund-stücks-AG, Bonn
7 houses, in north-south rows,
3 stories, 90 housing units
(4.680 sq.m total housing space) for Federal German Armed Forces personnel
cost approx. DM 13,4 mill.
built October 1997–end of 1998

Schillerstrasse 7
Apartment and Office Building
PTD plan team GmbH, Munich
Client: GFG Maison Schiller KG, Hechenberg
Urban infill, 7 stories, with courtyard building, 8 housing units
retail space 1.445 sq.m
gross floor area 3.958 sq.m
cost approx. DM 6,4 mill.
built 1997/99

Schlüterstrasse 31
Apartment and Commerial Building
"Palais Lintunen"
Kruse + Schütz, Berlin
Client: G. Nagel, Hamburg
Urban infill, 6 stories,
18 housing units, 6 commercial units, subterranean car park;
modernization of courtyard building overall gross floor area 2.600 sq.m;
cost (new building): DM 7 mill.
built mid 1996–May 1998

Stallupöner Allee 29–31
Apartment Building
Hansen & Wiegner & Eberl-Pacan, Berlin
Client: Diakonisches Werk Berlin-Brandenburg
5 urban villas, 2 stories + roof story,
28 apartments, subterranean car park
gross floor area 3.500 sq.m
cost approx. DM 6,3 mill.
built March 1997–April 1998

Tauentzienstrasse 7 B, c/ Nürnberger Strasse 9–11
Apartment and Commercial Building
EMW Eller Maier Walter & Partner GmbH, Berlin
Client: SYNODATA GmbH-EDV Systeme u. Co. Handels KG, Munich
High rise, 9 stories,
9 apartments, 1 shop
gross floor area 10.740 sq.m
cost approx. DM 43,7 mill.
built 1996–1997

Friedrichshain

Oderstrasse 25,26/Jessnerstrasse 47–53
Apartment and Commercial Building
Leopold Schaffhauser, Berlin
Client: Onnasch Baubetreuung GmbH & Co.
Corner building, 7 stories,
122 subsidized housing units,
1.659 sq.m retail space on ground floor
gross floor area 11.490 sq.m,
investment DM 50,5 mill.
completion June 1997

Wasserstadt an der Rummelsburger Bucht
(Information about urban concepts see Berlin's New Buildings 1996/97 in BBA 1997)

Quartier Stralau-Stadt

Friedrich-Junge-Strasse 1–4
Apartment Building
Winfried Brenne Architekten, Berlin
Client: WBF Wohnungsbaugesellschaft Friedrichshain mbH
5 stories, 45 housing units
completion end of 1997

Alt-Stralau 10–12
J. Wiechert, Berlin

Quartier Stralau-Dorf

Alt-Stralau 24, 25–27
Etzmann & Ettel, Berlin

Alt-Stralau 32
Horst Eckel, Berlin

Alt-Stralau 34
Primary School
Winfried Brenne Architekten, Berlin

Alt-Stralau 46
Birke + Partner, Berlin

Hellersdorf

Lyonel-Feininger-Strasse 1, 7
Peter-Weiss-Gasse 9
Kokoschka-Strasse 2, 4, 6, 8
Nelly-Sachs-Stasse 5
Apartment and Commercial Building
(Block 26a)
Dorner & Partner, Nagold
Client: MEGA AG, Berlin
Apartment and commercial building, 5 stories, 98 subsidized housing units
housing space 6.300 sq.m
retail space 1.950 sq.m,
cost approx. DM 23,1 mill.
built October 1996–April 1998

Lyonel-Feininger-Strasse 3, 5
Apartment and Commercial Building
(Block 26b)
Dorner & Partner, Nagold
Client: MEGA AG, Berlin
5 stories, 34 owner-occupied apart-ments for seniors, community space and diaconate on ground floor, planted inner courtyard, green roof
housing space 1.678 sq.m
retail space 170 sq.m
cost approx. DM 8,3 mill.
built October 1996–April 1998

Riesaer Strasse 94
Office Building
(section B and c)
R. Schüler & U. Schüler-Witte, Berlin
Client: Bezirksamt Hellersdorf von Berlin, Abt. Wirtschaft, Wohnen, Bauen u. Verkehr, Hochbauamt
U-shaped building complex, reinforced concrete skeleton, 5 stories, comple-ting the existing section A
gross floor area 10.457 sq.m
cost DM39 mill.
built January 1995–January 1998

Schönewalder Strasse 9
School Building
Rolf D. Weisse, Berlin
Client: Bezirksamt Hellersdorf von Berlin
Comprehensive primary and auxiliary school with full-day care,
building slab in clinker, 150 m long,
3 stories, gym hall(6 fields)
gross floor area 14.680 sq.m
cost approx. DM 60,4 mill.
built 1995–1997

Hohenschönhausen

Ahrensfelder Chaussee 41
Barnim-Secondary School
Stefan Scholz in Bangert Scholz Architekten, Berlin
Client: Bezirksamt Hohenschönhausen von Berlin represented by its building departement
Five-sided Secondary School with 2 gym halls. All buildings arranged within a circled wall,
gross floor area 14.667 sq.m
cost DM 63 mill.
built June 1995–June 1998

Edgarstrasse 18
Apartment Building
Kurt D. Schubert, Berlin
Client: Gründstücksgesellschaft Edgarstrasse 18 GbR, Lynarstrasse 1, Berlin
Urban villa, 3 stories, 12 housing units
cost DM 2,1 mill.
built June 1995–July 1998

Fennpfuhlweg 62–74 B
Apartment Buildings
Horst Hördt, Berlin
Client: A.R.T. Grund und Boden GmbH, Berlin
5 urban villas, 3 stories
40 housing units, 24 garages
cost DM 9 mill.
built December 1995–July 1998

Konrad-Wolf-Strasse 98
Apartment and Commercial Building
BUB - Service Baumanagement GmbH, J. Lange, Berlin
Client: Steffi Witt, Berlin
Apartment house with showroom for cars, 5 stories, 12 housing units
gross floor area 1.747 sq.m
cost approx. DM 4,3 mill.
built November 1995–July 1998

Landsberger Allee 315–345
Housing Estate "Weisse Taube"
**Planungsgemeinschaft Weber,
Klippel, Schulz & Partner, Berlin
Seifert Planung, Darmstadt
H. Klippel, Berlin
Klippel & De Biasio und Scherrer,
Berlin
Architektenkontor Thiemann +
Scheel, Darmstadt
Holm Becher, Berlin**
Client: Investorengemeinschaft
Apartment building, 5-6 stories, 1.166
housing units, 16 commercial units and
2 daycare centers
cost approx. DM 280 mill.
built 1995–1998

Malchower Weg 99–115
Apartment Building
J. Fr. Vorderwülbecke, Berlin
Client: Projekt GmbH & Co. &
Trifonds KG, Frankfurt/Main
3 apartment buildings, 107 housing
units
gross floor area 8.280 sq.m
cost DM 11,9 mill.
built December 1994–January 1998

Strausberger Strasse 10
Apartment and Commercial Building
Voskamp/Burgmayer, Berlin
Client: HOWOGE Wohnungsbaugesellschaft Hohenschönhausen mbH, Berlin
Block alignment, 34 housing units
gross floor area 3.167 sq.m
cost DM 8,1 mill.
built May 1997–May 1998

Weissenseer Weg 23–34
Car Market and Showroom
**Architektengemeinschaft Bassenge,
Puhan-Schulz, Heinrich, Schreiber,
Berlin**
Client: Renault Niederlassung Berlin
Exhibition hall with mezzanine
gross floor area 3.170 sq.m
cost DM 12 mill.
built June 1997–June 1998

Welsestrasse 32–34
Shopping Center "Welsegalerie I"
**Bähler-Koven-Hensel-Planungsbüro
GmbH, Berlin**
Client: D.D.C. Planungs-,
Entwicklungs- und Management AG,
Frankfurt/Main
Conversion of a small former cooperative store and restaurant into a shopping
center, 1 story high. The old shopping
hall was preserved, a public place was
created,
gross floor area 7.332 sq.m
cost DM 8,7 mill.
built January 1997–December 1998

Welsestrasse 56
Shopping Center "Welsegalerie II"
**D.D.C. Planungs-, Entwicklungs- und
Management AG, Frankfurt/Main**
Client: D.D.C., Frankfurt/Main
Conversion of a former service center
into a shopping center, 1 story high,
with super market, shops and
restaurants,
gross floor area 5.845 sq.m
cost approx. DM 3,9 mill.
built January 1997–August 1998

Wriezener Strasse 2–3
Apartment Building
Rolf D. Weisse, Berlin
Client: HOWOGE, Berlin
Extensions of an existing building, 4
and 6 stories, 25 housing units
gross floor area 2.517 sq.m
cost DM 6,5 mill.
built March 1998–November 1998

Wustrower Strasse 14
Office Building with Cinema Center
Helmut Sprenger, Hannover
Client: Prerower Platz/Wustrower
Strasse 14 GbR
4 stories, office space in 3 stories,
restaurants, shops and 9 cinemas
gross floor area 8.714 sq.m
cost DM 24,2 mill.
built April 1998–December 1998

Köpenick

Adlershofer Strasse 3 A–F
Apartment and Office Building
Jürgen Krüger, Berlin
Client: Adlershofer Strasse GbR, repr.
by Jenner & Partner GbR, Berlin
2 buildings, 4-6 stories high,
102 housing units, 1 commercial unit
gross floor area 6.250 sq.m
cost DM 17,8 mill.
built November 1996–Dec. 1997

Antoniuskirchstrasse 3–5
Old People's Center Oberschoneweide
GFA Hermann Korneli, Berlin
Client: Caritas Altenhilfe GmbH, Berlin
5 stories, 60 apartments for seniors,
1 apartment for care-taker
gross floor area 7.044 sq.m
cost DM 16,8 mill.
built May 1996–April 1998

Bohnsdorfer Strasse 14
Housing Complex
**Claus Winter, Berlin;
h+h Projektmanagement und
Bauleitung GmbH, Berlin**
Client: Renta-Concept GmbH,
Berlin/Josef Riepl Unternehmen für
Hoch- und Tiefbau GmbH, Berlin
7 urban villas, 3–4 stories + roof story,
73 housing units
gross floor area 4.858 sq.m
cost DM 12,4 mill.
built December 1995–end of 1998

Bruno-Wille-Strasse 2
Apartment Building
Rolf Eggenweiler, Berlin
Client: GbR Bruno-Wille-Strasse 2, bei
Kettler Liegenschaftenverwaltungs
GmbH, Berlin
Urban villa, 4-5 stories,
21 housing units
gross floor area 1.962 sq.m
cost DM 7,6 mill.
built October 1998–October 1999

Büxensteinallee 17
Apartment House
Albrecht & Partner, Munich
Client: GbR Alterum Immobilien-
entwicklungs GmbH, Berlin/
HuR Immobilien, Neuburg/Donau
3 stories, 10 housing units
gross floor area 630 sq.m
cost DM 1 mill.
built July 1997–August 1998

Dahmestrasse 9–11
Housing Complex „Seehaus
Grünauer Strand"
Hans Honigmann, Munich
Client: DEMOS Spreegrund Verwaltungsgesellschaft & Co. Bauträger KG
Palace-like ensemble at waterfront,
62 housing units
gross floor area 4.981 sq.m
investment DM 17,6 mill.
completion 1998

Deulstrasse 11/12
Apartment Building
Henningsen + Hürtgen, Berlin
Client: KÖWOGE Köpenicker Wohnungs-
gesellschaft mbH, Berlin
Urban infill and block completion,
street front building, 5 stories,
courtyard building, 3 stories,
37 housing units alltogether
gross floor area 3.059 sq.m
cost approx. DM 6,6 mill.
built March 1997–May 1998

Friedrichshagener Strasse 9
Wohnpark Halbinsel Köpenick
Peter Kopp Architekten, Stuttgart
Client: Hanseatica 5. Beteiligungs-
gesellschaft mbH & Co. KG, Berlin
Conversion of industrial area into
housing area with shopping center,
daycare center and infrastructure,
720 housing units, 23 commercial units
gross floor area 80.000 sq.m,
dwelling space 55.800 sq.m
built August 1996–March 1998

First building phase:
Apartment Building with 3 wings,
5-6 stories, 187 housing units,
subterranean car park
gross floor area 22.800 sq.m
cost DM 25,7 mill.
built August 1996–April 1998

Apartment Building, 5 stories,
130 housing units, subterranean car
park
gross floor area 16.000 sq.m
cost DM 19,6 mill.
built September 1996–Feb. 1998

Apartment and Office Building,
4–5–6 stories, 74 housing units,
9 commercial units, subterranean car
park
gross floor area 10.300 sq.m
cost DM 17,7 mill.
built May 1997–January 1998

Grünauer Strasse 3–15
Hotel Courtyard by Marriott
Auer & Weber, Stuttgart, Georg Döhrer
Client: GELIN Grundstücksverwaltungs
GmbH Immobilien KG
Hotel building, 5 stories, 190 units
gross floor area 23.400 sq.m
cost approx. DM 38,8 mill.
built May 1997–July 1998

Grünauer Strasse 35–39
Apartment and Commercial Building
Patzschke, Klotz & Partner, Berlin
Client: Wohn- und Büropark Grünauer
Strasse/Jürgen Treppner
Urban infill, 2 apartment and office
buildings, 4 stories, 12 housing units
each, 4 commercial units
gross floor area 3.015 sq.m
cost approx. DM 9,2 mill.
built October 1996–March 1998

Grünauer Strasse 66
Apartment and Commercial Building
Reichenecker & Klinski, Berlin
Client: GbR Grünauer Strasse 66 vertr.
durch B. Schlothauer/Stock &
Dr. Roose GbR
Urban infill, 5 stories, 15 housing units,
1 commercial unit
gross floor area 1.395 sq.m
cost DM 3,1 mill.
built May 1996–end of 1998

Grünauer Strasse 210–216
Parcel-Post Center
**Petra Kniepkamp in der Deutschen
Post AG**
Client: Deutsche Post AG, Bau- und
Immobiliencenter, Berlin
1 story-building with 30 gates
gross floor area 1.300 sq.m
cost DM 2,4 mill.
built August 1998–November 1998

*Helmholtzstrasse/Corner Nalepa-
strasse*
High School for
Social Security Economics
**Hilde Léon, Konrad Wohlhage,
Siegfried Wernik, Berlin**
Client: Senat von Berlin
Freestanding building, 5 stories,
extension of a historical school
building
gross floor area 8.600 sq.m
cost DM 38 mill.
built 1995–1998

Julius-Hart-Strasse 42
Apartment House
Thomas Kober, Berlin
Client: fsrg Planungs- und Bauträgergesellschaft
2 stories, 11 housing units
gross floor area 1.939 sq.m
cost approx. DM 2,5 mill.
built August 1997–end of 1998

Klarastrasse 8–9
Apartment and Commercial Building
Michael Zielinski, Berlin
Client: WuG Wohnungs- und Gewerbebau GmbH, Berlin
Block alignment, 6 stories,
40 housing units, 2 commercial units
gross floor area 3.670 sq.m
cost DM 7,2 mill.
built May 1996–end of 1998

Köpenzeile 12
Housing Complex
**Thomas Kober, Andreas Tannhäuser,
Berlin**
Client: Consul Bauträger GmbH, Berlin
3 single buildings, 2 stories high,
16 housing units, 1 commercial unit
dwelling space 1.243 sq.m
retail space 214 sq.m
cost DM 2,6 mill.
built August 1996–January 1998

Krampenburger Weg 41–45
Apartment House
Michael Lochner
Client: R. Marx/P. Baumgärtner GbR
2–3 stories, 14 housing units
gross floor area 1.567 sq.m
cost approx. DM 2,7 mill.
built March 1998–end of 1998

Lindenstrasse 25
Housing Complex
Manfred Vogel
Client: Klose Bauberatungs-GmbH
Buildings on open plan, 4-5 stories,
40 housing units
gross floor area 3.984 sq.m
cost DM 6,5 mill.
built February 1996–June 1998

Lindenstrasse 36/37
Housing Complex
Schreier Ing.-Büro
Client: Schreiber and Partners
Buildings on open plan, 1-2 stories,
24 housing units
gross floor area 1.870 sq.m
cost DM 4,3 mill.
built May 1996–May 1998

Lindenstrasse 45–47
(Berlin-Hessenwinkel)
Housing Complex
teambau GmbH, Berlin
Client: teambau GmbH
3 apartment buildings, 2–3 stories
each, 16 housing units
gross floor area 1.298 sq.m
cost approx. DM 2,8 mill.
built April 1997–January 1998

Löcknitzstrasse 19
Apartment Building
**Kunert + König Bauplanungs- und
Projektentwicklungsgesellschaft
mbH**
Client: Kunert + König
Corner building on open plan,
13 housing units
gross floor area 1.245 sq.m
cost approx. DM 2,3 mill.
built December 1996–end of 1998

Mathildenstrasse 4
Apartment Building
Jacqueline Bortfeld-Jungnitsch
Client: Vogt Grundstücksverwaltungs
GmbH, Berlin
Urban infill, 6 stories,19 housing units
gross floor area 1.750 sq.m
cost DM ca 3,8 mill.
built May 1995–March 1998

Möllhausenufer 14
Apartment House
**Kunert + König, Bauplanungs- und
Projektentwicklungs GmbH**
Client: Von Danwitz, Projektgesell-
schaft Wendenschloss GbR
3 stories, 10 housing units
gross floor area 1.622 sq.m
cost approx. DM 3,2 mill.
built August 1997–end of 1998

Nalepastrasse/Corner Helmholtz-
strasse
Photo-Lab
U. Peuker, Berlin
Client: Spree-Color Foto-Labor-GmbH
1-story hall, lined up by a 2-story
building
gross floor area 3.139 sq.m
cost approx. DM 5,6 mill.
built May 1998–end of 1998

Ostendstrasse 23–26/Slabystrasse
15–16
Technology and Innovation Center
Berlin-Oberschöneweide
Christian Möller, Frankfurt/Main
Client: BLEG Berliner Landes- und
Entwicklungsgesellschaft

House 1
Office high rise, 13 stories
gross floor area 5.330 sq.m
cost DM 32,8 mill.
built June 1996–December 1997

House 12
Office building, 4 stories
gross floor area 2.047 sq.m
cost DM 6,9 mill.
built September 1996–Dec. 1997

House 13
Office building, 4 stories
gross floor area 2.047 sq.m
cost DM 6,9 mill.
built August 1996–December 1997

Philipp-Jacob-Rauch-Strasse
Komplex Ludwigshöheweg I, Section A
Housing Complex
**Planungsgruppe Wittstock + Partner
GmbH, Berlin**
Client: V.I.A. Vertriebs- und
Konzeptionsgesellschaft für
Investment u. Immobilienfonds-
anlagen mbH, Berlin
6 apartment buildings, 2–3 stories
each, 48 housing units
gross floor area 3.848 sq.m
cost approx. DM 9,9 mill.
built October 1997–end of 1998

Regattastrasse 114–120
Apartment and Commercial Building
**hopro Bauplanung GmbH Berlin,
Weigert, Fuchs Hochbau GmbH,
Berlin, Nutt & Breuer**
Client: Konsum Projektentwicklungsgesellschaft Regattastrasse GbR, Berlin
Row building, 4 storie; 1-story hall for
supermarket, 36 housing units,
7 commercial units
gross floor area 5.111 sq.m
cost approx. DM 11,3 mill.
built November 1997–end of 1998

Regattastrasse 124
Apartment and Commercial Building
**Bypy-Ingenieurbüro, Berlin
Hein, Berlin**
Client: Fotoland Dienstleistungs GmbH,
Berlin
2 buildings, 3 + 4 stories, 11 housing
units, 4 commercial units
gross floor area 1.650 sq.m
cost DM 3,2 mill.
built October 1996–January 1998

Regattastrasse 137–139
Housing Complex
Ralf Becker, Berlin
Client: Gärtner & Partner, Berlin
3 urban villas, 2 + 4 stories,
35 housing units, 1 commercial unit
gross floor area 2.445 sq.m
cost approx. DM 6 mill.
built January 1997–April 1998

Regattastrasse 142–148
Housing Complex
Albrecht & Partner, Munich
Client: Alterum Immobilien-entwick-
lungs GmbH, Berlin/
HuR Immobilien, Neuburg/Donau
3 apartment and office buildings,
2 + 3 stories, 28 housing units,
4 commercial units
gross floor area 1.931 sq.m
cost DM 4,6 mill.
built January 1997–August 1998

Regattastrasse 166/Büxensteinallee
1–7
Housing Complex
**Werner Nierke, Marianne Miksch,
Berlin**
Client: GbR Regattastrasse 166 repr. by
Seefeld & Partner, Berlin
2 apartment buildings, 2 + 3 stories,
32 housing units
gross floor area 2.095 sq.m
cost DM 7,7 mill.
built July 1997–end of 1998

Scharnweberstrasse 16
Apartment Building
**Heinz Jopp, Schweinfurt,
Norbert Diepold**
Client: Plan concept GmbH/
Wiesner Bau GmbH
Block alignment, 3.5 stories,
20 housing units
gross floor area 1.598 sq.m
cost DM 2,5 mill.
built 1995–1999

Scharnweberstrasse 22
Housing Complex
Christine Weigl in Eukia, Regensburg
Client: Eukia Wohn- und Industriebau-
Baubetreuungs GmbH, Berlin
3 apartment buildings, 3 + 4 stories,
28 housing units
gross floor area 2.112 sq.m
cost approx. DM 3,4 mill.
built June 1997–January 1998

Strasse 330/Müggelseedamm
Apartment and Commercial Building
**Marie-Josée Seipelt/
Paul Dluzniewski, Berlin (design and
planning permission)
Schmidtlein, Stang, Assmann,
Würzburg (working drawings)**
Client: GbR MHF Grundbesitz GmbH /
Müggelseedamm Projektentwicklungs
GmbH
Complete block around a green
courtyard, 4 stories high, with
extensions above the flat roofs and
small courts and wells within the wings
to lighten kitchen and bathrooms,
165 housing units (71 subsidized)
dwelling space 10.818 sq.m
retail space 2.853 sq.m
gross floor area 18.066 sq.m
cost DM 38 mill.
built 1996–1997

Wassersportallee 17/19
Housing Complex
Albrecht & Partner, Munich
Client: Alterum Immobilien-
entwicklungs GmbH, Berlin/
HuR Immobilien, Neuburg/Donau
4 apartment buildings, 1–3–4 stories,
28 housing units
gross floor area 4.321 sq.m
cost DM 4,5 mill.
built November 1996–August 1998

Wattstrasse 1/Siemensstrasse 13–15
Apartment and Commercial Building
Henningsen + Hürtgen, Berlin
Client: KÖWOGE mbH, Berlin
Urban infill, 5–7 stories, 73 housing
units, 1 office space on ground floor
gross floor area 7.708 sq.m
cost DM 18,5 mill.
built September 1997–end of 1998

Weiskopffstrasse 18, 20, 22/
Wasserstrasse 1, 3, 5
Apartment Buildings "Wohnen an der
Spree"
Michael König, Berlin
Client: BOTAG Bodentreuhand- und
Verwaltungs AG, Berlin
2 apartment buildings, 2 stories and
1 staggered roof story, 51 housing units
gross floor area 3.668 sq.m
investment DM 19,5 mill.
built March 1996–May 1997

Wendenschlossstrasse

Wendenschlossstrasse 37, 39, 41/
Allendeweg 1, 3, 5/Am Amtsgraben 1/
Am Burggraben 2, 4, 6
(Block 1)
Apartment and Commercial Building
Maier, Voigt, Wehrhahn, Berlin
Client: Köpenicker Baugesellschaft
mbH; Berlin
6 stories, 127 housing units,
8 commercial units
gross floor area 14.600 sq.m
cost DM 25 mill.
built November 1995–August 1998

Allendeweg 8, 10, 12, 14, 16/
Am Amtsgraben 3, 10, 12
(Block 2)
Apartment Building
Buddensieg & Ockert, Berlin
Client: Köpenicker Baugesellschaft
mbH, Berlin
5 stories, 84 housing units
gross floor area 7.250 sq.m
cost DM 11,6 mill.
built November 1996– Sept. 1998

Wendenschlossstrasse 43/
Allendeweg 2, 4, 6
(Block 4)
Apartment and Office Building
Maier, Voigt, Wehrhahn, Berlin
Client: Köpenicker Baugesellschaft
mbH, Berlin
4–6 stories, 49 housing units,
3 commercial units
gross floor area 5.500 sq.m
cost DM 7,5 mill.
built September 1996–Dec. 1998

Wendenschlossstrasse 49, 51, 53/
Am Schlossberg 2, 4, 6, 8, 10, 12
(Block A1)
Apartment and Office Building
Lothar Bertolino, Berlin
Client: DCB Domicilbau GmbH, Berlin
6 stories, 100 housing units,
21 commercial units
gross floor area 15.600 sq.m
cost DM 21 mill.
built November 1995–May 1998

Wendenschlossstrasse 289–306
Gym Hall
**pgn consulting and engineering
GmbH, Berlin**
Client: YBG Yacht Berlin GmbH
1-story gym hall
gross floor area 1.623 sq.m
cost approx. DM 1,2 mill.
built January 1998–May 1998

Wendenschlossstrasse 289–306
Apartment and Commercial Building
**pgn consulting and engineering
GmbH, Berlin**
Client: YBG Yacht Berlin GmbH
5 stories, 26 housing units,
28 commercial units
gross floor area 11.034 sq.m
cost approx. DM 15,2 mill.
built April 1996–May 1998

Wendenschlossstrasse 412–416 A
Apartment Buildings
Von Sass & Weber, Berlin
Client: WIP Wintermayr & Partner,
Murnau
4 urban villas, 2–3–4 stories at
waterfront, 8 apartments each, with
privat marina
gross floor area 2.500 sq.m
cost DM 6 mill.
built June 1997–April 1998

Wendenschlossstrasse 462
Apartment House "Villa Köpenick"
**BRT Architekten Bothe-Richter-
Teherani, Berlin**
Client: City 7 b, Berlin
Urban villa, 3 stories, 10 housing units
gross floor area 961 sq.m
cost DM 7 mIll.
built 1996 April 1997

*Wilhelminenhofstrasse 50/
Mathildenstrasse 12*
Apartment and Commercial Building
Peter Voigt, Berlin
Client: KÖWOGE mbH, Berlin
Block alignment, 7 stories ,
42 housing units, 3 commercial units
gross floor area 2.950 sq.m
cost DM 11,5 mill.
built August 1996–January 1998

Kreuzberg

Lindenstrasse 9–14
Jewish Museum
Daniel Libeskind, Berlin
Client: Land Berlin, repr. by Senats-
verwaltung für Bauen, Wohnen und
Verkehr
Extension of the baroque palace of the
Berlin-Museum with E.T.A. Hoffmann
Garden on public grounds
gross floor area 15.500 sq.m
exhibition space 9.500 sq.m
cost DM 72,1 mill.
built 1993–January 1999

Reichenberger Strasse 129
Dwellings for People with Aids
Faber + Krebs, Berlin
Client: Reichenberger Strasse 129 GbR
Block alignment, 7 stories
gross floor area 1.942 sq.m
cost DM 4 mill.
completion 1998

Urbanstrasse 104
Apartment House
Backmann + Schieber, Berlin
Client: GbR Urbanstrasse 104
Infill in an existing block, roof stories
added, 10 housing units
gross floor area 700 sq.m
cost DM 2,1 mill.
built 1997–1998

Wrangelstrasse 79
Apartment and Commercial Building
Sadowski + Lebioda, Berlin
Client: Haas + Partner, Munich
Urban infill, 5 stories towards the street
and 6 stories towards courtyard,
8 housing units, commercial space on
ground and first floor
cost approx. DM 2,8 mill.
built January 1997–December 1998

Züllichauer Strasse 2
Apartment House "Stadtikone"
K. Meier-Hartmann, Berlin
Client: Dr. Will & Partner Grundstücksgesellschaft mbH, Berlin
6 storles wlth 2-story penthouse,
floor plan as quadrant, signaling the
street's end, 19 housing units
dwelling space 1.580 sq.m
cost approx. DM 8,7 mill.
built December 1996–March 1998

Lichtenberg

*Am Tierpark 31/
Alfred-Kowalke-Strasse 14*
Apartment and Commercial Building
hopro Bauplanung GmbH, Berlin
Bauherr:CRE Real Estate GmbH, Berlin
Corner building, 6 stories with 3
entrances, 45 housing units,
13 commercial units (shops,
restaurants, offices)
gross floor area 4.833 sq.m
cost DM 12,1 mill.
built July 1996–December 1998

Archenholdstrasse 37
Apartment Building
**IFAS Institut für Altbausanierung und
Stadterneuerung GmbH, Berlin**
Client: Schwörer Haus GmbH & Co,
Berlin
Urban infill, 7 stories, 18 housing units
cost approx. DM 2,1 mill.
huilt August 1996–January 1998

Fischerstrasse 1
Apartment and Commercial Building
**Atelier 33 Banse Döwe Schnapp,
Berlin**
Client: 5. Wohn- und Gewerbebau KG,
Pollux Grundstücks und Immobilien
GmbH & Co., Berlin
Block alignment, 6–7 stories,
25 housing units, 2 commercial units
gross floor area 2.900 sq.m
cost approx. DM 7,5 mill.
built 1997–1998

Güntherstr. 7
Apartment Building
**Planungs- und Ingenieursgemein-
schaft GmbH Kaltwasser-Lemke**
Client: Kaltwasser-Lemke GmbH,
Dormagen
5 stories, vaulted roof, extension of an
existing building, 14 housing units
gross floor area 1.070 sq.m
cost DM 2,5 mill.
built October 1997–end of 1998

Josef-Orlopp-Strasse 60–64
Revenue Authorities Lichtenberg
**Liepe & Steigelmann with Joachim
Mehlau and Harald Lindner, Berlin**
Client: BEG Grundstücks-und Verwaltungs GmbH + Co., Berlin
Street alignment with orthogonal wing,
5 stories
gross floor area 10.500 sq.m
cost DM 15 mill.
built May 1996–July 1997

Kurze Strasse 2
Apartment Building
Felix Fähnrich, Berlin
Client: TRANS-INNOVIA/
ARWOBAU mbH, Berlin
4 stories, 28 apartments for seniors
gross floor area 1.352 sq.m
cost approx. DM 4,6 mill.
built March 1997–March 1998

Liepnitzstr. 40/Corner Roedelstrasse 1
Apartment and Commercial Building
Ferger, Gossla + Partner, Berlin
Client: Grundstücksgesellschaft
Liepnitzstr. 40 bR, repr. by Kühnisch +
Partner, Berlin
Corner building at Seepark, supple-
menting an existing ensemble,
4 stories, 20 housing units (10 housing
units new), 2 commercial units
net floor area 1.579 sq.m
(621 sq.m new)
cost DM 3,6 mill.
built 1997–1998

Möllendorffstrasse 90b
Old People's Home
**Architektengemeinschaft Alte Fabrik,
Fr. Heyer**
Client: Dr. Hanne Unternehmensgruppe, Berlin
Block alignment, 4 stories,
68 housing units
gross floor area 4.258 sq.m
cost approx. DM 10 mill.
built 1997–1998

Nöldnerstrasse 3–7
Apartment and Office Buildings
Wöber & Partner, Berlin
Client: GbR Nöldnerstrasse 3–7,
repr. by Schlothauer, Berlin
Block alignment, 58 housing units,
shops on ground floor
cost approx. DM 14,2 mill.
built December 1996–January 1998

Römerweg 54
Apartment Building
Klaus Zell, Berlin
Client: Ingrid Zell, Hausverwaltung und
Immobilien GmbH, Berlin
Urban infill, 5 stories,
18 susidized housing units
cost approx. DM 5 mill.
built 1996–1998

Spittastrasse 6
Apartment Building
Bernd Willenbrinck, Dresden
Client: SW Baubetreuung GmbH,
Cologne
Urban infill, 5–6 stories,
11 housing units
gross floor area 1.485 sq.m
cost approx. DM 3,4 mill.
built March 1997–January 1998

Treskowallee 110
Office and Commercial Building
Augustin und Frank, Berlin
Client: GRUNDAG Grundbesitztreuhand
und Wohnbauten – Aktiengesellschaft
u. Co.; Grundstücksgesellschaft
Karlshorst Treskowallee KG
Freestanding corner building, 5 stories,
back part 2 storles,
62 commercial units
gross floor area 5.570 sq.m;
cost DM 13,5 mill.
built April 1997–March 1998

*Wasserstadt an der Rummelsburger
Bucht*

Quartier Rummelsburg I (West)
(in BBA '97 noted under "Friedrichshain")

social infrastructure:
2 day care centers
public green: approx. 55 acres

Urban design:
Klaus Theo Brenner, Berlin
Landscape design:
Thomanek & Duquesnoy, Berlin

Hauptstrasse 4–6, Hofgärten
Apartment Building
Pudritz + Paul, Berlin
Landscape design:
**Büro für Stadt/Landschaft,
Hermann Barges, Berlin**
438 housing units
built 1996/97

Hauptstrasse 4, Stadtpalais
Apartment Building
Pudritz + Paul, Berlin
Landscape design:
Pudritz + Paul, Berlin
106 housing units,
commercial space 2.200 sq.m
completion 1998

(End Rummelsburger Bucht)

Weitlingstrasse 43
Apartment and Commercial Building
Wolf und Kreis, Berlin
Client: Bewa Grund und Boden GmbH &
Co. Weitlingstr. 43. KG, Berlin
Block alignment, 4–5–6 stories,
12 housing units, 1 commercial unit
cost DM 2,7 mill.
built 1998

Wotanstrasse 29–31
Apartment Building
Leopold Schaffhauser, Berlin
Client: Onnasch Baubetreuungs GmbH,
Berlin
Urban infill, 6 stories,
49 subsidized housing units
gross floor area 4.621 sq.m
cost DM 7,7 mill.
built July 1996–May 1998

Marzahn

Ahrensfelder Chaussee 140–150 A
"Ahrensfelder Passage"
Shopping and Commercial Building
with apartments
PLS Planungsbüro Serrin, Berlin
Client: Grundwert Handelszentrum
GmbH und Co. Investitions KG, Berlin
3 stories, 48 housing units
investment DM 18 mill.
built 1995–1996

*Allee der Kosmonauten 151, 151 A–H/
Fichtelbergstrasse 5–15*
Commercial Center
Heinz Weisener, Hamburg
Client: Hesterberg und Leinberger
GmbH, Bremen
4–6 stories
investment DM 50 mill.
built 1995–1997

*Allee der Kosmonauten 198/
Bärensteinstrasse 22*
Commercial Center "Angerpark"
Heinz Weisener, Hamburg
Client: Hesterberg und Rolfes GbR;
Ellenstadt
2–3 stories
investment DM 10 mill.
built 1997–1998

Habichtshorst-Baufeld 55
(Development Area Biesdorf-Süd)
Row and Duplex Houses
**Veba Immobilien Baupartner GmbH,
Bochum, with Braun &Voigt and
Partners, Berlin**
Client: Veba Immobilien Baupartner
GmbH, Bochum
60 one family row and duplex houses
with 116 sq.m dwelling space each,
cost approx. DM 180.000 per house
built July 1998–December 1998

Havemannstrasse 4 A–10 A
Commercial Building
Lindner Roettig Klasing, Düsseldorf
Client: EGW Entwicklungsgesellschaft
Wohnumfeld GmbH, Düsseldorf
1-story shopping mall
retail space 800 sq.m
gross floor area 1.468 sq.m
investment approx. DM 3,6 mill.
built April 1997–April 1998

Hohenschönhauser Strasse 10
Canal Working Plant
ARBELOS GmbH, Berlin
Client: Berliner Wasserbetriebe
3 buildings (office building,
working plant, garage),
1–3 stories
investment approx. DM 9,9 mill.
built 1997–1998

Landsberger Tor
Sections 7.1/7.2
Apartment Building
**Hans Wolfhard Kaul Bürogemein-
schaft „Stadtarchitekten", Cologne**
Client: Nürnberger Versicherung
3–4 stories,
235 subsidized housing units
investment approx. DM 50,2 mill.
built 1997–1998

Landsberger Tor
Sections 9.1–3, 13.1–3, 15.4
Meyer, Georgije Nedeljkov, Berlin
Client: Bavaria, Berlin
Subsidized apartment buildings,
3–5 stories
investment approx. DM 112,7 mill.
built 1997–1998

Märkische Spitze
Building and Garden Market
KUBUS, Wetzlar
Client: Hornbach-Baumarkt AG, Berlin
1 story
investment DM 13,3 mill.
built 1996–1997

Märkische Spitze 7, 9, 11, 13
Furniture Stores
Wmb Wittmeyer Mertens Beier, Berlin
Client: Krieger Grundstücks GmbH und
Co. KG, Kreuzbruch
3 buildings, 3 stories retail space
investment approx. DM 42,7 mill.
built 1996–1997

*Mehrower Allee 18, 18 A–D, 20/
Walter-Felsenstein-Strasse 62, 64, 66/
Sella-Hasse-Strasse 51, 53, 55, 57/*
Housing Complex and Commercial
Building "Plaza Marzahn"
Baasner, Möller & Langwald, Berlin
Client: Gruppe Gädecke und Landsberg,
Plaza Berlin-Marzahn GmbH u. Co. KG,
Berlin
4 stories, 110 housing units
investment DM 20,3 mill.
built 1995–1997

Mehrower Allee 53 A
Apartment Building and Head Quarters
of the Berlin-Brandenburgische
Housing Co-op
Stefan Mücke, Berlin
Client: Berlin-Brandenburgische
Wohnungsbaugenossenschaft, Berlin
10 stories, 15 housing units,
1 commercial unit
gross floor area 2.381 sq.m
investment DM 7,7 mill.
built March 1996–April 1997

Oberweissbacher Strasse 7–9
Shopping Center "Tal-Center"
WM-Plan, Berlin
Client: Unternehmensgruppe Widerker,
Stuttgart
gross floor area 9.286 sq.m
investment DM 16,9 mill.
built 1996–1997

*Schackelsterstrasse/Am Waldberg/
Beruner Strasse*
Housing Complex
**SÜBA Consult Gesellschaft für
Bauplanung mbH, Berlin
with Michael Grunwald, Hohenheim**
Client: SGB SÜBA Generalbau, Berlin
Row and duplex houses,
66 housing units;
apartment and office building,
3 stories, 24 housing units
investment approx. DM 11,4 mill.
built 1996–1997

Wittenberger Strasse 66–74, 78, 80
Local Shopping Center "Zu den Eichen"
**Mahraun – Kowal – Heieis, Berlin
Fittkau, Bottrop**
Client: TM Immobilien- und Vermie-
tungs GmbH, Bottrop
50 commercial units
investment approx. DM 9,9 mill.
built 1996–1997

Mitte

Alte Jakobstrasse 76–80, 83, 84
Apartment and Office Building
**Neufert Mittmann Graf & Partner,
Cologne**
Client: Concordia Bau und Boden AG,
Cologne
Block alignment with high rise,
140 housing units
cost approx. DM 100 mill.
built July 1994–end of 1998

Charlottenstrasse 35/36
Apartment, Commercial and Office
Building "Charlottenpalais"
Patzschke, Klotz + Partner, Berlin
Client: GbR Dr. Leibfried und Patrick
Reich, Berlin
Historizing new architecture,
4 housing units, 2 shops on ground
floor, office space
net floor area 3.650 sq.m
built 1996–April 1998

Charlottenstrasse 62
Office Building "Dompalais"
Patzschke, Klotz & Partner, Berlin
Client: GbR Dr. Leibfried/
Bauwert GmbH, Berlin
Historizing new architecture,
1 housing unit, office space
net floor area 1.990 sq.m
built 1996–March 1998

*Chausseestrasse 25/
Zinnowitzer Strasse 1*
Office Building "Albingiahaus"
Holger Schmidt, Hamburg
Client: Schuhmacher & Co. Immobilien-
gesellschaft/Albingia Versicherungen
AG
Modernization and extension of a listed
building, 15 offices, 1 shop
gross floor area 6.250 sq.m
cost DM 21,6 mill.
built September 1996–April 1998

Chausseestrasse 26
Apartment Building with Shop
Holger Schmidt, Hamburg
Client: Schuhmacher Immobiliengesell-
schaft/Albingia Versicherungen AG
Urban infill, 9 stories, 14 housing units,
1 commercial unit
gross floor area 1.450 sq.m
cost DM 3,7 mill.
built 1996–April 1998

Dresdner Strasse 36–38
Apartment and Office Buildings
**Kny & Weber, Berlin (design)
KSP Engel, Kraemer, Zimmermann,
Frankfurt/Main, Berlin (working
plans)**
Client: Grundstücksgesellschaft
Dresdner Strasse, Berlin
Block alignment with wings,
4–7 stories, 145 housing units, 3 shops
gross floor area 14.280 sq.m
cost DM 25 mill.
built February 1996–1998 (last section
still under construction)

Friedrichstrasse 50
"Büro- und Geschäftshaus am
Checkpoint Charlie"
Lauber + Wöhr, Munich
Client: Checkpoint Charlie KG, Berlin
Block alignment, 8 stories, 6 shops,
32 office units
gross floor area 30.000 sq.m
cost DM 85 mill.
built March 1996–April 1998

Friedrichstrasse 191–193 A
Office, Apartment and Commercial
Building Quartier 108
Thomas van den Valentyn, Cologne
Client: DIFA Deutsche Immobilienfonds
AG, Hamburg
10 stories, 7 shops on ground floor,
34 office units, 42 housing units
gross floor area 25.284 sq.m
cost approx. DM 85 mill.
built January 1996– end of 1998

Kieler Strasse 1
Apartment Building
Heinz A. Musil, Munich
Client: Bayerische Städte- und
Wohnungsbau GmbH, Munich
7 stories with terraced roof,
66 housing units, subterranean car
park
dwelling space 4.407 sq.m
gross floor area 7.859 sq.m
cost approx. DM 13 mill.
built January 1997–November 1998

Kieler Strasse 2
Apartment Building
Heinz A. Musil, Munich
Client: Markt- und Kühlhallen AG,
Munich
6 stories with terraced roof,
24 housing units, subterranean car
park
dwelling space 1.269 sq.m
gross floor area 2.488 sq.m; cost
approx. DM 4,1 mill.
built January 1997–November 1998

Kieler Strasse 3
Apartment and Office Building
**Maedebach, Redeleit & Partner,
Berlin**
Client: Efficio GmbH, Berlin
Block alignment, 6 stories,
14 housing units, 4 commercial units
(2 offices, 2 shops)
gross floor area 1.602 sq.m
cost DM 3 mill.
built March 1997–May 1998

Kronenstrasse 8–10
"Kronenpalais"
Patzschke, Klotz and Partners, Berlin
Client: Bauwert GmbH, Berlin
Historizing new architecture,
net floor area 4.250 sq.m
dwelling space 590 sq.m
built April 1996–January 1998

Leipziger Strasse 51
Head Quarters of the East German
Savings and Transfer Bank Berlin
**HPP – Hentrich-Petschnigg & Partner
KG, Düsseldorf**
Client: DBM & debis Immobilien
Management Grundstücksbeteiligung
GmbH & Co. Projekt Spittelmarkt KG,
Berlin
High rise corner building, 20 + 9
stories, reinforced concrete skeleton,
curtain facade of metal, glass and
stone; 3 shops, 1 bank
gross floor area 27.890 sq.m
built 1996–end of 1998

*Markgrafenstrasse 37/
Taubenstrasse 30*
Science Forum Berlin at Gendarmen-
markt
Wilhelm Holzbauer, Wien
Client: ICM Center- und Facility
Management, Düsseldorf
Block alignment, 7 stories, the new
building neighbors the Berlin-
Brandenburgische Akademie der
Wissenschaften, central entrance hall,
restaurant and shops
office space 3.500 sq.m (1.–6. floor)
cost approx. DM 20.mill.
built April 1997–November 1998

Pariser Platz 1
Office Building
"Haus Sommer"
Josef Paul Kleihues, Berlin
Client: Rheinische Hypothekenbank,
Frankfurt/Main
4 stories, 14 single offices, exhibition
rooms, conference and representation
rooms
gross floor area 1.975 sq.m
built February 1996–February 1998

Pariser Platz 3
Office and Apartment Building
**Frank O. Gehry & Associates Inc.,
Los Angeles**
**Planungs AG Neufert Mittmann Graf
Partner, Cologne**
Client: Pariser Platz 3 Grundstücksgesellschaft mbH + Co. Bau KG, Berlin
4 stories, 30 housing units,
4 commercial units
gross floor area apts.
approx. 14.000 sq.m
gross floor area offices
approx. 6.500 sq.m
cost approx. DM 140 mill.
built 1996–1998

Pariser Platz 7
Office Building
"Haus Liebermann"
**Josef Paul Kleihues with
Norbert Hensel, Berlin**
Client: Harald Quandt Grundbesitz KG,
Bad Homburg
4 stories, 4 offices units, representation
rooms, conferece and exhibition rooms
gross floor area 2.035 sq.m
built February 1996–December 1998

*Reichstagufer 12, 14/
Dorotheenstrasse 84*
Press and Information Office of the
Federal Government in Berlin
**KSP Engel, Kraemer, Zimmermann,
Frankfurt/Main, Berlin**
Client: Bundesrepublik Deutschland
repr. by Bundesamt für Bauwesen und
Raumordnung, Berlin
Conversion of the listed post office
building; extended by a cubic building
for public function
gross floor area. 40.761 sq.m
cost DM 182 mill.
built 1996–   10/97 (1. BP);
            10/98 (2.BP);
            10/99 (3.BP)

Reinhardtstrasse 29
Apartment and Commercial Building
"Residenz am Deutschen Theater"
Krüger, Schuberth, Vandreike, Berlin
Client: GbR Reinhardtstrasse 29
Symmetrical plan with 3 freestanding
buildings: a 5-story cube in the middle,
2 identical wings, 7–8 stories, each
supplemented by 2 3-story wings.
Historizing architecture.
92 housing units, 21 commercial units
(8 offices, 16 shops), rehearsal of the
Deutsches Theater, subterranean car
park
investment DM 110 mill.
built October 1996–October 1998

*Robert-Koch-Platz 4/
Hannoversche Strasse 19–22*
Apartment and Commercial Building
"Luisen Carree"
Stefan Ludes, Berlin
Client: VEBA Immobilien AG, Bochum
Block alignment at Robert-Koch-Platz
through 2 buildings, 6 stories each,
76 housing units, 47 commercial units
gross floor area 28.869 sq.m
cost DM 80 mill.
built October 1996–August 1998

Scharnhorststrasse 28/28
Apartment Building
Heinz A. Musil, Munich
Client: Markt- und Kühlhallen AG,
Munich
6–7 stories, 1–2 terraced roofs,
123 housing units, subterranean car
park
dwelling space 6.911 sq.m
gross floor area 10.557 sq.m
cost DM 20,3 mill.
built January 1997–November 1998

Seydelstrasse 2, 4, 5/Beuthstrasse 7, 8
Apartment, Office and Commercial
Buildings
**HPP – Hentrich-Petschnigg & Partner
KG, Düsseldorf**
Client: DBM & debis Immobilien
Management Grundstücksbeteiligungs
GmbH & Co. Projekt Spittelmarkt KG
New urban block with orthogonal
wings, 8 stories:
3 office and commercial buildings,
1 apartment and office building,
1 historic building
gross floor area 22.205 sq.m

Wallstrasse 27
Office and Commercial Building
Ferdinand & Gerth, Berlin
Client: Grundstücksgesellschaft
Immelmannstrasse GmbH & Co.
Wohnanlagen KG, Berlin
6 stories, 7 office units
gross floor area 4.475 sq.m
built April 1995–July 1997

Wilhelmstrasse 67 A/Reichstagufer 7–8
ARD-Hauptstadtstudio Berlin and
Apartment Building
**Ortner & Ortner Baukunst,
Berlin/Wien**
Client: Bauherrengemeinschaft ARD
Hauptstadtstudio
gross floor area 8.843 sq.m (TV-studio),
2.152 sq.m (apartment house)
cost DM 57 mill.
completion September 1998

Neukölln

Alt-Britz 111–115
Housing Complex "Am Britzer Garten"
Arthur Numrich, Berlin
Client: BOTAG Bodentreuhand- und
Verwaltungs-AG, Berlin
U-shaped block, 4–6 stories,
90 housing units
dwelling space 6.500 sq.m
cost approx. DM 18 mill.
built June 1997–October 1998

Drorystrasse 3
Primary School and Gym Hall
Backmann + Schieber, Berlin
Client: Bezirksamt Neukölln von Berlin
Upraised row building as block
alignment, spanning over Drorystrasse
and attached to neighboring buildings;
within the block: gym hall, half buried,
green roof
gross floor area 8.901 sq.m
cost DM 26.7 mill.
built August 1996–August 1998

*Drusenheimer Weg 84–114 und
132–150*
"Töpchiner Dreieck" Duplexes
Becker, Geukes & Reinig, Berlin
Client: Stadthaus, Gesellschaft für
innovativen Wohnungs- und Städtebau
mbH, Berlin
13 duplex houses, 1,5 stories,
26 housing units,
each housing unit: dwelling space
approx. 100 sq.m,
cost approx. DM 370.000
built May 1997–February 1998

Karlsgartenstrasse 6, 7
School Complex with Duplex Gym Hall
**Assmann, Salomon und Scheidt,
Berlin**
Client: Bezirksamt Neukölln von Berlin
School building, 3 stories, doubled gym
hall
cost DM 33,9 mill.
built December 1995–August 1998

Oderstrasse 3 a
Gym Hall
Pysall-Stahrenberg & Partner, Berlin
Client: Bezirksamt Neukölln von Berlin
Tripled gym hall, steel structure with
roof lights
gross floor area 6.026 sq.m
cost DM 20,35 mill.
built December 1993–March 1998

Ortolanweg 88/Wendehalsweg 1–3
Housing Complex "Offensive Aging"
**Liepe & Steigelmann with
Gerlinde Berndt, Berlin**
Client: Berliner Bau- und Wohnungsge-
nossenschaft von 1892, Berlin
3 buildings, 3 and 5 stories,
30 subsidized housing units
(24 for elderly women and single
mothers, 6 for families)
cost DM 4,2 mill.
built 1997–1998

Berlin's New Buildings
1997/98

Gartenstadt Rudow
(information on urban design
see Berlin's New Buildings 1996/97
in BBA '97)

Elfriede-Kuhr-Strasse 11
Mobile Classrooms for Primary School
Hundertmark & Partner, Berlin
Client: Senatsverwaltung für Schulwe-
sen, Berufsbildung und Sport
Building structure of prefabricated
concrete slabs, 2 stories, 8 classrooms
(65 sq.m each)
cost approx. DM 1,6 mill.
built November 1996–July 1997

Elly-Heuss-Knapp-Strasse 49
(Block 32 /1. BA)
Apartment Building
**Schulze-Rohr/Ruprecht/Schlicht,
Berlin**
Client: GAGFAH, Berlin
Open block alignment with green roof,
4 stories, 32 housing units
gross floor area 3.186 sq.m
cost approx. DM 7 mill.
built 1997–1998

Lieselotte-Berger-Strasse 33
(Block 631) Apartment and Office
Building
**Schulze-Rohr/Ruprecht/Schlicht,
Berlin**
Client: GEHAG, Berlin
Open block alignment, 5 stories,
12 housing units, 2 shops
gross floor area 825 sq.m
cost approx. DM 1,8 mill.
built 1996–1997

Pankow

Arnouxstrasse 6–8
Apartment Buildings
Faskel – Becker, Berlin
Client: Dr. Upmeier Verwaltungs GmbH,
Berlin
2 apartment buildings, 4 stories,
38 housing units, subterranean car
park
gross floor area 3.470 sq.m
cost approx. DM 10,3 mill.
built March 1997–July 1998

*Arnouxstrasse 17/
Rosenthaler Weg 47–51*
Apartment and Office Building
Kammann und Hummel, Berlin
Client: CML Wohnbauten GmbH, Berlin
Block alignment, 5 stories,
47 housing units
retail space 420 sq.m
gross floor area 5.232 sq.m
cost approx. DM 9,6 mill.
built July 1996–February 1998

Arnouxstrasse 18
School with Gym Hall
Geske/Wenzel, Berlin
Client: Bezirksamt Pankow von Berlin
L-shaped school building, reinforced
concrete, clinkered, 4 stories
gross floor area 10.234 sq.m
cost approx. DM 33,2 mill.
built May 1997–August 1998

Aubertstrasse 11–21
Apartment Buildings
Engel & Zillich, Berlin
Client: CML Wohnbauten GmbH, Berlin
2 apartment buildings, 3–4 stories,
54 housing units
gross floor area 7.579 sq.m
cost approx. DM 12,7 mill.
built April 1997–July 1998

Beethovenstrasse 19
Apartment House
Carl-August von Halle, Berlin
Client: Baugesellschaft Degerloch mbH
& Co. KG, Stuttgart
Freestanding apartment house,
3 stories, 16 housing units
cost approx. DM 3,3 mill.
built September 1996–January 1998

Benjamin-Vogelsdorff-Strasse 4
Apartment Building
**A+A Architects Associates, Krefeld
(Entwurf)
Schwartinski, Hamburg
(1. Überarbeitung)
Sawka, Berlin (2. Überarbeitung)**
Client: commercial units Projektpla-
nungsgesellschaft für Gewerbebau +
Erschliessungen mbH, Munich
Block alignment, 6 stories,
30 housing units
gross floor area 2.520 sq.m
cost approx. DM 1,2 mill.
built July 1996–September 1998

Beuthstrasse 21
Apartment House
Karl-Michael Limberg, Berlin
Client: Bork and Partners Immobilien-
und Baubetreuungsgesellschaft mbH,
Berlin
5 stories, 10 housing units
cost approx. DM 1,9 mill.
built September 1997–March 1998

Blankenburger Strasse 135
Production and Office Building
R. Hohmuth, Erkner
Client: Raytek GmbH, Berlin
L-shaped building, 2–3 stories,
1 commercial unit
gross floor area 3.442 sq.m
cost approx. DM 5,8 mill.
built December 1997–Oct. 1998

Blankenburger Strasse 161
Car Sales and Repair Station
Michael Velde
Client: Peter Unger
1–story hall, 1 commercial unit
gross floor area 1.675 sq.m
cost DM 1,5 mill.
built 1998

Blankenburger Strasse 165
Commercial Building
H. Velde
Client: Berthold Schäfer, Heilbronn
1–story shopping center,
1 commercial unit
gross floor area 1.213 sq.m
cost approx. DM 1,1 mill.
built August 1998–end of 1998

Blankenfelder Strasse 50
Day Care Center
Barkow + Leibinger, Berlin
Client: ERGERO Grundstückserschlies-
sungsgesellschaft, Berlin
Day care center for 180 children,
2 stories
gross floor area. 1.053 sq.m
cost DM 2,5 mill.
built December 1997–July 1998

Breite Strasse 46–47
Hospital
Bayer and Partners, Berlin
Client: Caritas Krankenhilfe, Berlin
New wing to an existing hospital
gross floor area 6.720 sq.m
cost DM 38 mill.
built 1997–November 1998

Cunistrasse 40, 42, 44
Apartment Buildings
Claus GmbH
Client: CML Wohnbauten GmbH, Berlin
2 apartment buildings, 3 stories,
gross floor area 703 sq.m;
1 apartment building, 3 stories,
gross floor area 712 sq.m,
25 housing units alltogether
cost approx. DM 4,1 mill.
built June 1997–April 1998

Dietzgenstrasse 56
Apartment House
Schlimpert & Thaeter, Berlin
Client: CRE Real Estate GmbH
22 housing units
retail space 300 sq.m
gross floor area 2.050 sq.m
investment DM 9,9 mill.

Eschengraben 13–17
Apartment Building
Baesler, Schmidt + Partner, Berlin
Client: Bau-Herr 2. Verwaltungs GmbH
+ Co. Wohnen am Eschengraben 13–17
oHG., Berlin
Housing complex, 6 stories,
81 housing units
gross floor area 7.352 sq.m
cost DM 31 mill.
built June 1996–June 1997

Florastrasse 49–51
Apartment and Office Building
**Planungsbüro P+R, Reindt + Kreutel,
Berlin**
Client: Trigon Consult GmbH + Co.
Florastrasse KG, Berlin
Urban infill between the listed Pankow-
Rapid-Station and the neighboring
housing complex in Florastrasse,
5–6 stories, 28 housing units,
10 commercial units
gross floor area 4.184 sq.m
cost approx. DM 3,9 mill.
built December 1996–August 1998

Fontanestrasse 16
Subsidized Apartment House
Ralf Becker, Berlin
TIG Wohnbauten im Westend GmbH +
Co. Fontanestrasse 16 KG
10 housing units
gross floor area 550m²
investment DM 3,2 mill.

Friedrich-Engels-Strasse 12
Apartment and Office Building
H. Parschat, Berlin
Client: GEG Grundstücks-
entwicklungsgesellschaft, Berlin
Block alignment, 3–4–5 stories,
10 housing units, 1 commercial unit
net floor area 1.000 sq.m
cost approx. DM 2,7 mill.
built beginning of 1996–April 1997

Granitzstrasse 55–66
Administration of DB (German Railway)
"Netz"
**RKW – Rhode, Kellermann,
Wawrowsky, Düsseldorf**
Client: Deutsche Bahn AG, Objekt-
gesellschaft Herschel Verwaltungsgesellschaft mbH + Co. Vermietungs-
2 row houses, 5 stories, plus 1 slanting,
streched building, 7 stories
gross floor area 27.716 sq.m
cost DM 57 mill.
built December 1996–April 1998

Guyotstrasse 30–34
Apartment Buildings
Engel & Zillich, Berlin
Client: CML Wohnbauten GmbH, Berlin
3 apartment buildings, 4 stories,
gross floor area 786 sq.m each,
24 housing units alltogether,
subterranean car park
cost approx. DM 6,9 mill.
built January 1997–June 1998

Hadlichstrasse 19
Shopping Center
Planungsgruppe Grobe, Berlin
Client: MAP Liegenschaften GmbH,
Berlin
U-shaped 1–story buildingof reinforced
concrete, clinkered
gross floor area 4.577 sq.m
cost DM 7 mill.
built 1995–September 1997

Hauptstrasse 111
Apartment Buildings
Thomas Schindler
R & W Immobilienanlagen
9 houses with tenant's gardens,
2,5 stories each, 54 housing units
(12 subsidized, 42 privatly financed)
gross floor area 6.343 sq.m;
investment DM 20 mill.
completion autumn 1997

Heinrich-Böll-Strasse
Subsidized Housing Complex
**Architekten Arbeitsgemeinschaft
Winfried Brenne – Joachim Eble,
Berlin**
Client: GSW, Gemeinnützige Siedlungs-
und Wohnungsbaugesellschaft Berlin
mbH
Row houses, 4 stories (within the 2.
building phase of Heinrich-Böll-
Housing-Estate);
exemplary project for ecological
building: 32 housing units, net floor
area 2.028 sq.m;
215 housing units in all
built November 1996–May 1998

*Jean-Calas-Weg 15–21,
Rupertweg 17–19,
Vienweg 172, 100, 124, 134, 174, 82,
Triftstrasse 9–41*
Client: GbR Arge Nord Pandion GmbH &
Co. Grundbesitz KG und
Otremba Grundbesitz Verwaltungsgesellschaft mbH, Berlin
15 urban villas, 3–4 stories each, 209
housing units;
1 building as block alignment along
Triftstrasse, 3–4 stories, 46 housing
units, 13 commercial units
gross floor area 36.838 sq.m
cost approx. DM 63 mill.
built 1997–1998

Jean-Calas-Weg 15
Engel & Zillich, Berlin

Jean-Calas-Weg 16, 17, 18,
Klaus Meier-Hartmann, Berlin

Jean-Calas-Weg 19
Müller & Keller, Berlin

Jean- Calas-Weg 20, 21, 22
Klaus Meier-Hartmann, Berlin

Rupertweg 17–19
Klaus Meier-Hartmann, Berlin

Triftstrasse 9–41
Monika Krebs, Berlin

Vienweg 72
Engel & Zillich, Berlin

Vienweg 82
Müller & Keller, Berlin

Vienweg 100, 124,134
Engel & Zillich, Berlin

Vienweg 174
Klaus Meier-Hartmann, Berlin

Kabelitzweg 3/Corner Schönholzer Weg
Apartment and Commercial Building
Hans Otto Bols, Berlin
Client: DOM Bau GmbH, Berlin
Corner building, 2,5 stories,
12 housing units, 1 commercial unit
gross floor area 630 sq.m
cost DM 2,4 mill.
built May 1997–May 1998

Kalvinistenweg 40
Apartment House
Hans-Jürgen Mücke, Berlin
Client: Hinz und Höhne, Berlin
3 stories, 16 housing units
gross floor area 1.216 sq.m
cost approx. DM 2,5 mill.
built March 1997–June 1998

Kalvinistenweg 117
Apartment House
Hans-Jürgen Mücke, Berlin
Client: Dr. Upmeier Verwaltungsgesellschaft mbH, Berlin
Row house, 2 stories
gross floor area 836 sq.m
cost DM 2,8 mill.
built March 1998–beginning of 1999

Kastanienallee 118
Apartment House
Martin Baldus
Client: Dergfort GmbH, Berlin
Freestanding apartment house,
4 stories, 15 housing units
cost approx. DM 2 mill.
built August 1997–May 1998

Kavalierstrasse 28 A
Apartment House
**Fundata Bauengineering + Consulting
GmbH, Berlin**
Client: Kopleder and Partners
6 stories, 12 housing units
gross floor area 1.149 sq.m
cost approx. DM 2,1 mill.
built November 1996–December 1998

Mathieustrasse 12
Day Care Center "La Cigalle"
**Musotter Poeverlein Architekten,
Berlin**
Client: ERGERO Grundstücks-
erschliessungsgesellschaft, Berlin
Day care center for 100 children,
2 stories
gross floor area 1.162 sq.m
net floor area 992 sq.m
cost DM 3,3 mill.
built August 1996–May 1997

Neumannstrasse 69–72
Apartment and Commercial Building
GRS Reimer & Partner GbR
Client: R. Zündorf & H. Abels GbR
Block alignment, 6 stories,
59 housing units
retail space 2.470 sq.m
gross floor area 8.088 sq.m
cost DM 15 mill.
built 1997–1998

Parkstrasse 32/34
Apartment and Office Building
**Planungsbüro Putzmann & Putzmann
with Hubert Kroll, Martin Putzmann,
Nicole Berganski, Berlin**
Client: Reconwert Projekt-
entwicklungs- und Grundstücks-
verwertungsgesellschaft mbH, Berlin
Block alignment, 5–6 stories,
12 housing units, 1 commercial unit
gross floor area 1.448 sq.m
cost DM 3,1 mill.
built October 1997–Dec. 1998

Pestalozzistrasse 1, 1A, 1B
Apartment Building
U. Kötler + B. Dorendorf
Client: GbR Pankowbau
Subsidized building, floor plan on circle
segment, 6 stories, 29 housing units
gross floor area 2.489 sq.m;
investment DM 12. mill.

Pestalozzistrasse 2
Apartment and Office Building
csz Ingenieurconsult GmbH, Berlin
Client: Ostprojekt, Landesentwick-
lungs- und Baumanagement GmbH,
Berlin
Block alignment, 6 stories,
14 housing units, 2 commercial units
gross floor area 1.632 sq.m
cost approx. DM 3,4 mill.
built December 1996–Nov. 1998

Petitweg 20
Day Care Center
Schmiedeskamp + Petrzika, Berlin
Client: ERGERO Grundstückserschlies-
sungsgesellschaft, Berlin
2–story day care center for 100 children
gross floor area 1.147 sq.m
cost DM 2,5 mill.
built June 1997–February 1998

Robert- Rössle-Strasse 10
Laboratory
**Dieter Husemann, Claus Wiechmann,
Braunschweig**
Client: BBB Biomedizinischer For-
schungscampus Berlin-Buch GmbH
H-shaped building complex with 2 lab
wings, 3 stories high;
1 administration building linking the
wings, 4 stories high,
10 commercial units
gross floor area 5.040 sq.m
cost approx. DM 20,6 mill.
built February 1997–Sept. 1998

*Rosenthaler Weg 14–16/Guyot-
strasse 36–38/Nantesstrasse 81–83*
Apartment Building
Engel & Zillich, Berlin
Client: CML, Berlin
Block alignment, 5–6 stories,
99 housing units
gross floor area 11.042 sq.m
cost DM 17,5 mill.
built August 1996–January 1998

*Rosenthaler Weg 59–63/Cunistrasse 9/
Arnouxstrasse 16*
Apartment and Office Building
Kammann & Hummel, Berlin
Client: CML, Berlin
Block alignment, 5–6 stories,
65 housing units, subterranean car
park
retail space 691 sq.m
gross floor area 7.413 sq.m
cost DM 13,4 mill.
built August 1996–March 1998

*Schillerstrasse 2–3,
Waldowstrasse 22/23*
Subsidized Apartment Building
Winfried Brenne Architekten, Berlin
Client: GSW, Gemeinnützige Siedlungs-
und Wohnungsbaugesellschaft Berlin
mbH
Steet-lining buildings (within the 2.
building phase of Heinrich-Böll-
Housing-Estate), 4 stories,
experimental project for ecological
building,
63 housing units, 3 commercial units
net floor area 4.536 sq.m

Schillerstrasse 4–6, Waldowstrasse 32A
Subsidized Apartment Building
Joachim Eble – J. Kalepky
Client: GSW, Gemeinnützige Siedlungs-
und Wohnungsbaugesellschaft Berlin
mbH
Street-lining buildings (within the 2.
building phase of Heinrich-Böll-
Housing-Estate), 4 stories,
experimental project for ecological
building,
42 housing units, 2 commercial units
net floor area 3.288 sq.m
built March 1995–October 1997

Schönerlinder Strasse 48, 49
Building Market
Karl Peter Betz, Mannheim
Client: Bauhaus AG, Mannheim
Commercial building, 2 stories,
1 commercial unit
gross floor area. 9.545 sq.m
cost DM 11 mill.
built April 1998–December 1998

*Schönholzer Weg 3 A/
Corner Beethovenstrasse*
Appartment House
Eckart Ruff, Stuttgart
Client: Baugesellschaft Degerloch mbH
& Co. KG, Stuttgart
Freestanding apartment house,
2 stories, 12 housing units
cost approx. DM 1,1 mill.
built May 1996–January 1998

Schützenstrasse
Day Care Center
Freitag-Hartmann-Sinz, Berlin
Client: GbR ARGE Nord
2 stories
gross floor area 1.134 sq.m
cost DM 3 mill.
built July 1998–December 1998

Tiriotstrasse 8, 10, 12
Apartment Buildings
Weiss & Faust, Berlin
Dr. Upmeier Wohnungsbau
3 freestanding apartment buildings,
3–4 stories each, 30 housing units
gross floor area 1.823
investment DM 10,2 mill.
completion spring 1998

Tschaikowskistrasse 54
Apartment House
Preikschat & Partner, Berlin
Client: Borchardt Immobilien-
gesellschaft, Berlin
4 stories, 10 housing units
gross floor area 1.043 sq.m
cost DM 2 mill.
built May 1996–February 1998

Uhlandstrasse 12
Apartment and Commercial Building
Norbert Jokeil
Client: Hans Rehms, Düsseldorf
Block alignment (5 stories)
with courtyard house (3 stories)
in reinforced concrete,
8 housing units each
cost DM 4,8 mill.
built December 1997–Dec. 1998

Wiesenwinkel 17
Day Care Center
DGI Bauwerk GmbH, Berlin
Client: Bezirksamt Pankow von Berlin
Vaulted building in reinforced concrete,
2 stories
gross floor area 1.126 sq.m
cost DM 6,2 mill.
built September 1996–Oct. 1998

Wolfshagener Strasse 135
Apartment and Office Building
F. A. Kohn, Bremen
Client: Pebo Verwaltungs GmbH,
Bremen
Block alignment (6 stories)
with courtyard house (5 stories),
20 housing units, 1 commercial unit
gross floor area 1.825 sq.m
cost approx. DM 3,3 mill.
built September 1996–April 1998

Prenzlauer Berg

Ahlbecker Strasse 12
Apartment Building
M. P. Burgmayer, Berlin
Client: Mössner Bauträger- und
Verwaltungsgesellschaft mbH,
Stuttgart
Urban infill, 8 stories, 20 housing units
gross floor area 1.927 sq.m
cost DM 5,6 mill.
built 1994–April 1997

Ahlbecker Strasse 17
Apartment Building
Becker-Zang + Mitelach, Berlin
Client: GmbH & Co. Immobilienbesitz
KG Berlin
Urban infill, 8 stories,
33 housing units (5 apartments for
seniors)
gross floor area 2.360 sq.m
cost DM 6,2 mill.
built 1995–November 1997

Bernhard-Lichtenberg-Strasse 9, 10
Apartment and Commercial Building
**Häussler und Wörner,
Schwäbisch Gmünd**
Client: Omega Immobilien GmbH & Co.
KG, Stuttgart/GG -Grundfonds
Vermittlungs GmbH, Berlin
Urban infill, 6 stories,
48 housing units (38 subsidized),
5 commercial units
gross floor area 4.977 sq.m
cost approx. DM 15,8 mill.
built 1994–October 1997

Greifswalder Strasse 136, 137
Commercial Building
Suter und Suter, Berlin
Client: Hengst Filterwerke GmbH & Co.
KG, Berlin
Medical Care Center with extension for
offices and exhibition rooms, 5 stories
gross floor area 4.846 sq.m
cost DM 11,5 mill.
built 1995–February 1997

Greifswalder Strasse 209
Apartment and Commercial Building
**Feddersen, von Herder and Partners
Winkelbauer, Berlin**
Client: WIP Wohnungsbaugesellschaft
Prenzlauer Berg mbH
Urban infill, 6 stories,
12 housing units/commercial units
dwelling space 1.000 sq.m
cost DM 2,5 mill.
built 1997–1998

Grellstrasse 35
Subsidized Apartment and Commercial
Building
Arnim B. Schnörr, Berlin
Client: CITY 7b, Berlin
Urban infill, 7 stories,
17 housing units, 1 commercial unit
gross floor area 1.160
investment DM 6,7 mill.

Kollwitzstrasse 4
Apartment Building
**Feddersen, v. Herder and Partners
Winkelbauer, Berlin**
Client: WIR – Wohnungsbaugesellschaft
in Berlin mbH
Urban infill, 7 stories,
12 housing units, 2 commercial units
gross floor area 1.200 sq.m
cost DM 3,1 mill.
built 1996–1997

Kollwitzstrasse 70/Wörther Strasse 33
Apartment and Office Building
Alfred Grazioli, Berlin
Client: GbR Kollwitzstrasse 70/
Wörther Strasse 33 bei Dr. Speck
GmbH, Berlin
Corner building, 5 stories,
28 housing units, 3 commercial units,
subterranean car park
gross floor area 3.630 sq.m
cost DM 10,2 mill.
built 1995–1997 (14 months)

Paul-Heyse-Strasse 1/
Danziger Strasse 207, 209
Apartment and Office Building
**Planungsbüro Siegmund,
Soden/Taunus**
Client: Harbisch and Partners GmbH,
Cologne
Corner building, 8 stories,
69 housing units, 3 commercial units
gross floor area 3.160 sq.m
cost DM 8 mill.
built 1994–June 1997

Schönhauser Allee 78/80
Shoping Center with Offices
"Schönhauser Allee Arcaden"
**RKW + Partner,
Düsseldorf/Berlin/Frankfurt**
Client: TRMF Grundstücks-
entwicklungsgesellschaft mbH + Co.,
Berlin Allee Arcaden KG
Shoping center with glass roof,
90 shops on 3 stories
gross floor area 59.000 sq.m
cost DM 107 mill.
built April 1997–March 1999

Schönhauser Allee 123
Cinemaxx "Colosseum"
**me di um Architekten
Jentz, Popp, Roloff, Wiesner + Partner,
Hamburg**
Client: GbR A. und T. Brauner
Modernization of the listed movie
theater "Colosseum", 9 new cinemas,
shops and offices
net floor area 9.450 sq.m
cost DM 60 mill.
built April 1996–December 1997

Schönhauser Allee 181
Apartment and Office Building
**Feddersen, v. Herder and Partners
Winkelbauer, Berlin**
Client: WIR – Wohnungsbaugesellschaft
in Berlin mbH
Urban infill at block corner,
5–6 stories, 45 housing units,
1 commercial unit
dwelling space 4.000 sq.m
cost DM 10 mill.
built 1996–1997

Schwedter Strasse 15
Hotel
Jörg-Wido Wodtke, Berlin
Client: IVF Immobilienverwithtlung und
Anlagenberatung mbH, Reutlingen
Urban infill, 8 stories,
hotel with 53 rooms
gross floor area 1.586 sq.m
cost approx. DM 4,5 mill.
built 1994–September 1997

Schwedter Strasse 44, 46
Apartment and Commercial Building
**Günter Stahn, Berlin
und RCAP Coenen, Cologne**
Client: SSB Stadtprojekt Betreuungs-
Betriebe GmbH & Co. KG, Cologne
Urban infill, 8 stories,
78 housing units, 3 commercial units,
subterranean car park
gross floor area 3.692 sq.m
cost approx. DM 14,4 mill.
built 1995–October 1997

Storkower Strasse 160/
Landsberger Allee
"Forum Landsberger Allee"
Office and Commercial Center with
Hotel
**RKW – Rhode, Kellermann, Wawrowsky,
Düsseldorf**
Client: Bauwert GmbH, Berlin
Ensemble of 3 building parts, up to 10
stories,
net floor area 36.000 sq.m
(10. 000 sq.m shops, 20.600 sq.m
offices, hotel: 161 rooms)
built April 1996–April 1998

Storkower Strasse/
Rudolf-Seifert-Strasse/
Franz-Jacob-Strasse
Local Center "Storkower Bogen"
Hascher + Partner, Berlin
Client: MC City-Center Beteiligungs
GmbH & Co. Berlin Storkower Strasse
KG, Düsseldorf
8 buildings grouped around a central
place with 13-story gate-house,
14 housing units,
offices, shops and service space
gross floor area 35.000 sq.m
cost DM 120 mill.
built 1993–1997

Wichertstrasse 14–15
Apartment and Office Building
Tiemann + Scheel, Düsseldorf
Client: Commerzial-Bau GmbH & Co. KG,
Düsseldorf
Urban infill, 8 stories,
20 subsidized housing units,
subterranean car park
retail space 1.600 sq.m
gross floor area 4.387 sq.m
cost approx. DM 9,9 mill.
built 1994–1998

Reinickendorf

Am Borsigturm 40–54
Commercial Park at Borsigturm
Walter Rolfes + Partner, Berlin
Herlitz Falkenhöh AG
Block structure with inner courtyards,
4 stories
gross floor area 13.000 sq.m
net floor area 9.700
cost DM 34 mill.
built 1997–1998

Gorkistrasse 205–215
Housing Estate "Am Park Wittenau"
Hans Honigmann, Munich
Client: DEMOS Spreegrund Verwaltungsgesellschaft & Co. Bauträger KG
48 row houses and half duplexes,
6 housing units,
gross floor area 10.541 sq.m
investment DM 33 mill.
built spring 1997–end of 1998

Karolinenstrasse 9–10
Apartment House + "Alte Waldschänke"
**Feddersen, v. Herder and Partners,
Berlin**
Client: Karolinenstrasse
Grundstücksverwaltungsgesellschaft
L-shaped block, 3 stories, 42 housing
units; restaurant for 90 persons
cost DM 11 mill.
built 1996–December 1998

Lindauer Allee 39 A–C
Apartment Building
Hentschel + Oestreich, Berlin
Client: GSW, Berlin
Block alignment and infill of a housing
estate from the 50ties, 5–6 stories,
35 housing units
gross floor area 4.540 sq.m
built 1997–1998

Veitstrasse
Apartment Buildings with Commercial
Units
Norbert Stocker
Client: Herlitz Falkenhöh AG
Part of the urban project "Am Borsigturm", apartment buildings, 5 stories,
208 housing units
retail space 223 sq.m
gross floor area 16.433 sq.m
investment DM 69,1 mill.
completion autumn 1997

Schöneberg

Ansbacher Strasse 17/19
Apartment and Office Building
**Grashorn + Grashorn-Wortmann,
Berlin**
Client: Hallesche Nationale, Stuttgart
Conversion, Aufstockung und
Modernization and upraising of a 1970
apartment and office building,
7 office stories, 6 housing units
cost approx. DM 10 mill.
built 1996–1998

Fregestrasse 19–20
Day Care Center
Bender Glass Architekten, Berlin
Client: Bezirksamt Schöneberg von
Berlin - Hochbauamt
Freestanding extension of an existing
day care center within a listed
Wilhelminien building ensemble
for 80 children, 3stories
gross floor area 900 sq.m
cost DM 3,5 mill.
built 1997–1998

Hauptstrasse 87
"Wüstenrot-House"
Jung & Schützger, Berlin
Client: Wüstenrot Bausparkasse
Urban infill, office building,
7 stories, subterranean car park
gross floor area 3.195 sq.m
cost approx. DM 10 mill.
built 1996–1998

Kolonnenstrasse 8/Corner Feurigstr.
Apartment and Office Building
**ELW, Georg Eyl & Partner with Laura
Wendt-Mieser, Berlin**
Client: Stadt und Land Wohnbauten-
Gesellschaft mbH, Berlin
Corner building as urban infill (part of
modernization area Crellestrasse/
Kolonnenstrasse), 7 stories,
10 housing units, 3 commercial units
(gross floor area 1.870 sq.m)
cost approx. DM 4,4 mill.
built March 1996 – May 1997

Kurfürstenstrasse 129
House of German Building Industry
Berlin
Schweger + Partner, Berlin/Hamburg
Client: Hauptverband der Deutschen
Bauindustrie e.V., Berlin
Block completion, reinforced concrete-
skeleton with curtain facade of greyish
green concrete stone, glass lamellas
towards Kurfürstenstrasse
gross floor area 3.506 sq.m
cost DM 20 mill.
built May 1996–April 1998

Luitpoldstrasse 2
Apartment and Commercial Building
Preikschat & Partner, Berlin
Client: Preikschat & Partner Immobilienmanagement und Co. Bauträger KG
Urban infill, 7 stories, 13 housing units,
1 penthouse, 1 commercial unit
net floor area 1.020 sq.m
cost DM 3 mill.
built August 1997–August 1998

Spandau

Buschower Weg 55–57
One-Family Houses
Udo Pohling, Berlin
Client: RPE Rentaco Projekt-
,entwicklungsgesellschaft mbH
Half duplexes, 2 stories, with 5 rooms,
112 sq.m dwelling space each,
16 housing units alltogether
investment DM 10 mill.
built 1996–1997

Flankenschanze 20/
Falkenseer Damm 22–28
Primary School
Heinz Bose im Hochbauamt Spandau
Bezirksamt Spandau von Berlin,
Abt. Bildung, Kultur und Sport
2 angled building wings with classrooms connected by 1 cylindric
entrance and community building
gross floor area 7.709 sq.m
cost DM 13,6 mill.
built September 1995–August 1998

Remscheider Strasse 39/
Corner Falkenseer Chaussee 234–235
Day Care Center
Heinz Bose, Hochbauamt Spandau
Client: Bezirksamt Spandau von Berlin,
Abt. Jugend und Familie
2-story corner building on circle
segment with sloping (partly green)
roofs
gross floor area 1.798 sq.m
built October 1996–December 1998

Spandauer Strasse 81–84
Day Care Center
Hochbauamt Spandau
Client: Bezirksamt Spandau von Berlin,
Abt. Jugend und Familie
3-story flat building for 120 children
(age from 1 through 6)
net floor area 1.690 sq.m
built 1994–1997

Strasse 341
Apartment Buildings
"Wohnen in Albrechtshof"
Michael Bensch, Berlin
Client: BOTAG Bodentreuhand- und
Verwaltungs- AG, Berlin

No. 1–3
"Wohnen in Albrechtshof 4"
2 duplex houses, 103 sq.m each;
3 urban villas, 6 housing units,
74 sq.m–120 sq.m each
cost DM 3,4 mill.
built March 1998–December 1998

No. 4/6
"Wohnen in Albrechtshof 3"
1 duplex house, 103 sq.m;
1 one-family house, 135 sq.m;
2 urban villas, 6 housing units,
74 sq.m–120 sq.m each
cost DM 2,6 mill.
built March 1998–November 1998

No. 18
"Wohnen in Albrechtshof 2"
3 duplex houses, 103/4 sq.m each;
1 urban villla, 6 housing units,
74 sq.m–120 sq.m each
cost DM 2,3 mill.
built March 1998–October 1998

Nr. 22/24
"Wohnen in Albrechtshof 1"
2 duplex houses, 116 sq.m each;
2 one-family houses, 143 sq.m each,
2 urban villas, 6 housing units,
75 sq.m–121 sq.m each
cost DM 3,6 mill.
built October 1995–December 1997

Wasserstadt am Spandauer See
(information on urban design
see Berlin's New Buildings 1996/97
in BBA '97)

Quartier Pulvermühle
Romy-Schneider-Strasse 3/5
Apartment and Office Building
Hentschel & Oestreich, Berlin
Client: GSW Gemeinnützige Siedlungs-
und Wohnungsbaugesellschaft mbH,
Berlin
U-shaped solitaire,5 stories,
40 housing units, 4 commercial units
gross floor area 8.830 sq.m
built 1996–1998

Landscape design
Quartier Pulvermühle:
Hafner & Jiménez, Berlin
(correction)

Quartier Havelspitze
section WA 5
Josef Paul Kleihues, Berlin
Client: Bavaria Objekt- und
Baubetreuungs GmbH/
Siemens Beteiligungs GmbH, Berlin
Housing for the elderly and
nursing-home
built 1996–1998

Am Wiesenweg 20
House for Children
Augustin und Frank, Berlin
Client: ARGE BEWOGE Bauwert, Berlin
3-story day care center for 130 children
net floor area 1.100 sq.m
cost DM 7,2 mill.
completion August 1998

Steglitz

Bassermannweg 17, 19
Apartment House "Largo"
Gert Eckel, Berlin
Client: Damian Freies
Wohnungsunternehmen, Berlin
Urban infill, 4 stories,
24 housing units, partly maisonettes,
subterranean car park
gross floor area 2.470 sq.m
cost DM 8,5 mill.
built 1996–1997

Berner Strasse 40 C-F
Apartment Houses
Hans Jürgen Juschkus, Berlin
Client: Dr. Dieter Kressner Baubetreu-
ungen-Eigenheimbau GmbH, Berlin
2 freestanding urban villas, 2–3 stories,
25 housing units
gross floor area 1.950 sq.m
cost approx. DM 5 mill.
built May 1996–October 1997

Hanielweg 13–19,
Malteser Strasse 150–158
Apartment Building
BSP **Klaus Baesler, Bernhard Schmidt,**
Martin Schwacke, Berlin
Client: Bau-Herr Zweite Verwaltungs
GmbH & Co. Hanielweg oHG
Ensemble of row houses and square
intermediate houses, 4–5 stories,
187 housing units, 1 commercial unit
net floor area 14.002 sq.m
cost DM 103,8 mill.
built Nov. 1995–June 1997

Kastanienstrasse 6–8
School and Gym Hall
Rolf D. Weisse, Berlin
Client: Bezirksamt Steglitz von Berlin
Block alignment as extension of
existing building, 3 stories, in yellow
clinker, transparent intermediate
building with entrance hall and
stairways, gym hall in steel and glass
gross floor area 3.390 sq.m
cost approx. DM 17,7 mill.
built 1995–beginning of 1999

Kundrystrasse 2
Apartment and Office Building
Klaus Wachsmann, Berlin
Client: West Kap Bauträger GmbH
Block alignment, 6–7–8 stories,
18 housing units, 1 commercial unit
dwelling space 1.540 sq.m
cost DM 5 mill.

Tempelhof

Greulichstrasse 3/5
Apartment House
Klaus Wachsmann, Berlin
Client: M. Brecht
Urban villa on open plan, 2–3–4 stories,
24 housing units
cost DM 5 mill.
built 1996–1997

Im Domstift 47–55
Housing Complex
Georg-Peter Mügge, Berlin
Client: Petrus-Werk GmbH, Berlin
Urban infill, winding row of 5 apartment
houses, 3–4 stories, 7–10 housing units
each (different shapes and sizes),
38 subsidized housing units
gross floor area. 3.278 sq.m
cost approx. DM 8,4 mill.
built 1996–1997

Lichtenrader Damm 132–160
Apartment and Commercial Building
Schulze-Rohr, Ruprecht, Schlicht,
Berlin
Client: GAGFAH, Berlin
3 block aligning separate buildings,
1 building with shops on ground floor,
101 subsidized housing units
gross floor area 11.760 sq.m
cost approx. DM 22,5 mill.
built 1997–1998

Manteuffelstrasse 5
Apartment and Commercial Building
André Savidis, Berlin
Client: GbR Berlin-Tempelhof Manteuffelstrasse 5
5–6 stories, 29 subsidized housing
units
gross floor area 2.353 sq.m
commercial space 381 sq.m
investment DM 14,6 mill.
completion mid 1997

Lichtenrader Damm 190
Day Care Center
Georg-Peter Mügge, Berlin
Client: Bezirksamt Tempelhof von
Berlin
Completion of the "Garden Town
Lichtenrader Damm" (competition
project), floor plan on circle segment,
massive walls towards north, glass
walls towards south, 100 places
gross floor area 1.287 sq.m
cost approx. DM 6,1 mill.
built 1995–1997

Oberlandstrasse 26–35
Office Building
MEP **Meyer - Enst and Partners**
Client: Becker & Kries
Finanzierungs-AG & Co.
Extension building for
Berlin UNION Film
gross floor area 2.000 sq.m
investment DM 4,8 mill.
built May 19978–March 1998

Tiergarten

Kulturforum am Kemperplatz
Painting Gallery Berlin
**Hilmer & Sattler with Partner
T. Albrecht, Munich/Berlin**
Client: Stiftung Preussischer
Kulturbesitz
Supplement to the Cultural Forum
Kemperplatz, integrating 1 listed
Wilhelminian building.The gallery
houses the collection of 15th through
18th century paintings of the Stiftung
Preussischer Kulturbesitz;
70 exhibition rooms grouped around a
central hall
gross floor area 28.000 sq.m
net floor area 24.000 sq.m
exhibition space 8.700 sq.m
cost DM 283 mill.
built 1991–June 1998

"Potsdamer Platz" debis Area
**Masterplan: Architektengemeinschaft
Renzo Piano Building Workshop,
Paris/Genua
Christoph Kohlbecker, Gaggenau**
Client: Daimler Benz AG
gross floor area above ground 340.000
sq.m;
gross floor area below ground 210.000
sq.m;
gross floor area offices 175.000 sq.m;
gross floor area housing 70.000 sq.m;
retail/restaurants 40.000 sq.m;
2.500 parking lots below ground;
1.500 parking lots above ground;
investment DM 4 Mrd.
building cost DM 2,7 Mrd.
built October 1994–October 1998
(A1 and B1 summer 1999)

Alte Potsdamer Strasse
Office Building (A1)
Hans Kollhoff, Berlin

Alte Potsdamer Strasse
Office Building (B1)
**Renzo Piano, Paris/Genoa,
Christoph Kohlbecker, Gaggenau**

Alte Potsdamer Strasse
Apartment Building (B3)
**Renzo Piano, Paris/Genoa,
Christoph Kohlbecker, Gaggenau**

Alte Potsdamer Strasse
Apartment Building (B5)
**Renzo Piano, Paris/Genoa,
Christoph Kohlbecker, Gaggenau**

Eichhornstrasse
Imax-Theater (B7)
**Renzo Piano, Paris/Genoa,
Christoph Kohlbecker, Gaggenau**

Eichhornstrasse/Linkstrasse
Apartment Building (B9)
Lauber und Wöhr, Munich

Linkstrasse/Brüder-Grimm-Gasse
Apartment Building (B8)
Richard Rogers Partnership, London

Linkstrasse/Eichendorff-Gasse
Office Building (B4)
Richard Rogers Partnership, London

Linkstrasse/Gneist-Gasse
Office Building (B6)
Richard Rogers Partnership, London

Marlene-Dietrich-Platz
Casino (D1)
**Renzo Piano, Paris/Genoa,
Christoph Kohlbecker, Gaggenau**
Big hall with 1.800 seats,
Varieté-Hall with 700 seats

Marlene-Dietrich-Platz
Musical-Theater (D2)
**Renzo Piano, Paris/Genoa,
Christoph Kohlbecker, Gaggenau**

Reichpietschufer/Schellingstrasse
debis Headquarters (C1)
**Renzo Piano, Paris/Genoa,
Christoph Kohlbecker, Gaggenau**

Reichpietschufer/Linkstrasse
Office and Commercial Building (C2, C3)
**Arata Isozaki & Associates, Tokio
with Steffen Lehmann, Berlin**

Voxstrasse/Eichhornstrasse
Grand Hyatt Hotel (A5)
José Rafael Moneo, Madrid
Hotel building, 7 stories, 350 rooms,
ball-room for 700 persons

Voxstrasse/Neue Potsdamer Strasse
Office Building (A4)
José Rafael Moneo, Madrid

Voxstrasse/Alte Potsdamer Strasse
Cinemaxx Center and Madison City
Suites (A2)
Lauber und Wöhr, Munich
19 cinemas with 3.500 seats alltogether
and 196 apartment suites
(see main section)

Spreeweg 1
The President's Offices
**Gruber + Kleine-Kraneburg,
Frankfurt/Berlin**
Client: Bundesrepublik Deutschland,
repr. by Bundesministerium für
Bauwesen, repr. by Bundesamt für
Bauwesen und Raumordnung
Oval building, 4 stories, clad in black
natural stone, glass covered inner
courtyard
gross floor area 18.806 sq.m
cost DM 94 mill.
built March 1996–November 1998

Tiergartenstrasse 35,
Headquarters of the Konrad-Adenauer-
Foundation
Thomas van den Valentyn, Cologne
Client: Konrad-Adenauer-Stiftung
e. V., St. Augustin
Solitaire with offices and conference
room, 3 stories, clad in travertine,
roof terrace
gross floor area 4700 sq.m
cost DM 24 mill.
built 1996–1998

Treptow

Am Treptower Park 40–42
Apartment and Office Building
Doss + Over, Mainz
Client: Konsumgenossenschaft Josef-
Orlopp-Strasse 30–32
Urban infill, 4 stories, roof story with
gallery, shops on ground floor, 36
housing units, subterranean car park
gross floor area 6.500 sq.m
cost DM 15,3 mill.
built December 1996–May 1998

Baumschulenstrasse 1A
Tennis Hall with Social Section
Stadler & Besch, Berlin
Client: TC Grün-Weiss, Berlin
2 tennis halls, 1-story wooden
structures connected by a 1-story
social wing in brick
gross floor area 1.745 sq.m
cost DM 1,2 mill.
built October 1997–May 1998

Bohnsdorfer Weg 85–86
Apartment Buildings
Elisabeth Rüthnick, Berlin
Client: DEGEWO, Berlin
Housing Complex of 3 urban villas,
2 stories each;
23 row houses, 77 housing units
cost DM 17,75 mill.
built October 1996–March 1998

Bruno-Bürgel-Weg 151
Riding-School
Ilona Meyer, Berlin
Client: Sportverein AdW
1-story hall for manège and stables,
2-story social section
gross floor area 1.800 sq.m
cost approx. DM 1,1 mill.
built May 1995–end of 1998

Büchnerweg 45
Apartment Building
Peter Träger, Berlin
Client: IBT Ingenieurbauträger GmbH,
R+ S Wohnbauten und Treuhand GmbH
GbR, Berlin
Block alignment, 5 stories, 19
subsidized housing units
cost approx. DM 4,2 mill.
built December 1995–January 1998

Buntzelstrasse 14
Super Market
Eberhardt + Deist GmbH, Eschwege
Client: Inge Radler, Bad Salzungen
1-story building with 1.084 sq.m gross
floor area
cost DM 1,2 mill.
built April 1998–November 1998

Elsenstrasse 26
Apartment and Commercial Building
**Feddersen, von Herder and Partners,
Berlin**
Client: Grundstücksgesellschaft
Elsenstrasse 26 bR, Berlin
Corner building with large courtyard,
70 housing units, 5 commercial units
gross floor area 5.347
investment DM 33,7 mill.
completion mid 1997

Elsenstrasse 87–96
Casino
SIAT, Munich
Client: Siemensstadt Gründstücksver-
waltungs GmbH, Berlin
1-story building with 1.000 sq.m gross
floor area
cost DM 3 mill.
built January 1997–June 1997

*Elsenstrasse 111–113/
Am Treptower Park 14*
Office, Commercial and Apartment
Building
"Shopping Center"
**Henne-Rödl + Dr. Braschel GmbH,
Stuttgart**
Client: Shopping Center
Am Treptower Park GbR, Berlin
Corner building, 6 stories,
35 housing units
gross floor area 31.330 sq.m
cost DM 110 mill.
built March 1997–December 1998

Engelhardtstrasse 18
Gym Hall
Chestnutt & Niess, Berlin
Client: Bezirksamt Treptow von Berlin,
Abt. Bildung und Kultur
1-story freestanding tripled gym hall
net floor area 2.063 sq.m
cost DM 15,5 mill.
built April 1996–December 1998

Friedenstrasse 6
Apartment House
Hans Berger, Berlin
Client: Berger Grundstücks-gemein-
schaft, Oberhausen
Block alignment, 5 stories,
10 housing units
cost approx. DM 1,7 mill.
built August 1996–January 1998

Gross-Berliner-Damm 75
Training Center TÜV-Akademie (for
techical security)
Lanz, Berlin
Client: Landos Immobilien GmbH,
Berlin
Training center, 3 stories,
with a 1-story hall
gross floor area 5.616 sq.m
cost approx. DM 10,3 mill.
built November 1997–Sept. 1998

Heidelberger Strasse 63/64
Office Building
CBF-IPRO, Berlin
Client: Heidelberger Srasse 63/64 GbR,
Berlin
Office building, 5 stories
gross floor area 6.025 sq.m
cost approx. DM 1,8 mill.
built December 1996–January 1998

*Hoffmannstrasse 23–26/
Fanny-Zobel-Strasse 23–49*
Apartment Block (Karrée A+B)
Wörle & Partner, Munich
Client: Grundstücksgesellschaft Am
Treptower Park GbR, Berlin
2 karrées, 6 stories each, 181 housing
units, subterranean car park
cost DM 31 mill.
built November 1997–August 1998

Hoffmannstrasse 27, 28/
Fanny-Zobel-Strasse 44–50
Apartment Block (Karrée E)
J.S.K. Architekten, Frankfurt/Main
Client: Grundstücksgesellschaft Am
Treptower Park GbR, Berlin
6 stories, 96 housing units
cost DM 17 mill.
built October 1997–July 1998

Kiefholzstrasse 221
Crematorium
Axel Schultes Architekten, Berlin
Client: Bezirksamt Treptow von Berlin
Freestanding building, 4 stories
gross floor area 9.340 sq.m
cost DM 60 mill.
built March 1996–November 1998

Köpenicker Strasse 19/20
Apartment and Office Building
Gerhard Seidler, Berlin
Client: LBB Landesbank Berlin
Corner building, 5 stories, 16 housing
units, subterranean car park
cost approx. DM 6,1 mill.
built April 1995–June 1998

Moississtrasse 10–18
Apartment Building
**Baywobau Baubetreuung GmbH,
Munich**
Client: Baywobau Bauträger GmbH +
Co. Hausbau KG, Munich
Block alignment, 5 stories,
78 housing units
cost DM 10,8 mill.
built November 1995–April 1998

Porzer Strasse 39, 41
Apartment Buildings
**Tim Heide und Verena von Beckerath,
Berlin**
Client: Bavaria Objekt- und Baubetreuungs GmbH, Berlin
2 clinkered cubes, 4 stories each,
8 subsidized housing units each
gross floor area 890 sq.m per house
cost approx. DM 1,2 mill. per house
built 1993–1997

Puschkinallee 6 B–D
Apartment Buildings
Regina Schuh, Berlin
Client: Grundstücksgesellschaft Am
Treptower Park GbR
3 urban villas with penthouses, 3
stories, 34 housing units alltogether
retail space 897 sq.m
gross floor area 2.895 sq.m
investment DM 18 mill.
completion beginning of 1997

Rudower Chaussee 3
Mobile Radio Exchange
Udo Matzat, Berlin
Client: Mannesmann Mobilfunk GmbH,
Berlin
2-story technical building with
70 m radio tower
gross floor area 789 sq.m
cost approx. DM 2,2 mill.
built March 1998–October 1998

Rudower Chaussee 5 (main address)
WISTA Adlershof

"East-West-Cooperation Center (OWZ)"
Fehr + Partner, Berlin
Client: WISTA-Management GmbH,
Berlin
Center for new enterprises from middle
and eastern Europe (branch of the
Innovation and Founder's Center, IGZ)
gross floor area 14.660 sq.m
cost DM 43,2 mill.
built June 1995–May 1997

Einsteinstrasse
"Bessy II" Electron Storage Ring for
Synchroton Radiation
**Brenner & Partner, Stuttgart in
Zusammenarbeit mit der Bauabtei-
lung der Max-Planck-Gesellschaft,
Munich**
Client: Bessy GmbH, Berliner Elektro-
nenspeicherring-Gesellschaft für
Synchrotronstrahlung mbH
Storage ring with 121 m diameter,
entrance hall, 2 stories, building with
laboratories and offices, 4 stories
gross floor area 22.681 sq.m
cost DM 70,6 mill.
built September 1994–Nov. 1997

Einsteinstrasse
"Innovation Center for Computer
Sciences (IZ)"
**CEPEZED bv, Delft, Niederlande
represented by DGI Bauwerk GmbH,
Berlin**
Client: WISTA Management GmbH,
Berlin
Building slab, 8 stories, with glass
atrium, 4 stories high
gross floor area 6.500 sq.m
cost DM 18,7 mill.
built December 1996–Sept. 1998

Etwaldstrasse
Innovation Center for Optics, Optoelectronics and Laser Technic
"Photonic Center 1"
**Sauerbruch & Hutton Architekten,
Berlin/London**
Client: WISTA-Management GmbH,
Berlin
2 office and lab buildings in form of
amoeba, 3 stories, reinforced concrete,
doubled glass facade
gross floor area 10.719 sq.m
cost approx. DM 38,4 mill.
built June 1996–April 1998

Etwaldstrasse
"Photonic Center 2 and 3"
**Ortner & Ortner Baukunst,
Berlin/Wien**
Client: WISTA-Management GmbH,
Berlin
2 reinforced concrete skeleton
buildings, 3 stories, ceramic clad,
front parts in glass
gross floor area 4.432 sq.m (center 2),
3.758 sq.m (center 3)
cost approx. DM 18,2 mill. (center 2),
15,2 mill. (center 3)
built September 1996– March 1998

Rudower Chaussee
"WISTA Business-Center (WBC)"
Office and Commercial Building
Dörr, Ludolf, Wimmer, Berlin
Comb-shaped building with 4 wings
and 3 intermediate glass halls, 5 stories
gross floor area 24.000 sq.m
cost approx. DM 40 mill.
built November 1996–Dec. 1998

Volmerstrasse
"Innovation Center for Environmental
Technology (UTZ)"
Lab and Office Building
**Eisele + Fritz + Bott + Hilka +
Begemann, Darmstadt**
Client: WISTA-Management GmbH,
Berlin
Meandering reinforced concrete
skeleton, 4 stories
gross floor area 24.000 sq.m
cost DM 118 mill.
built August 1996–October 1998

End WISTA Science City

Rudower Strasse 7
Double Gym Hall
Enzmann/Ettel, Berlin
Client: Bezirksamt Treptow von Berlin
Reinforced concrete building, 2 stories
net floor area 3.870 sq.m
cost DM 22,2 mill.
built September 1995–Aug. 1998

Spreestrasse 14
Hotel
Michellini , Berlin
Client: Klaus Mädige & Partner GbR,
Cologne
9 stories, 126 rooms
cost approx. DM 6,5 mill.
built May 1997–June 1998

Sterndamm 67, 67 A, 67 B, 67 C
Apartment and Office Building
Klaus Ethner, Darmstadt
Client: ABS Albert Baubetreuungs
GmbH, St. Ingbert
4 stories, 35 housing units
net floor area 1.425 sq.m
cost DM 9 mill.
built February 1997–April 1998

Sterndamm 69
Cinema "Astra"
Bau-ART, Düsseldorf
Client: Köhler & Specht GbR, Berlin
Conversion and extension (3 cinemas)
gross floor area 1.814 sq.m
cost approx. DM 4,3 mill.
built January 1998–August 1998

Tiburtiusstrasse 14
Day Care Center
Dietmar Doering, Berlin
Client: Bezirksamt Treptow von Berlin
2-story day care center for 110 children
(age 3 through 6)
cost approx. DM 2,7 mill.
built September 1997–Oct. 1998

Volmarstrasse/Keplerstrasse
Apartment and Office Building
**Christa Braum, Kronberg,
Dietzenbach**
Solitaire with atrium, 5 stories,
office space, 4 housing units
net floor area 8.025 sq.m
cost DM 15,2 mill.
built October 1996–August 1998

Waldstrasse 2, 3
Apartment and Office Buildings
Frank Jahn, Berlin
Client: Röding GmbH, Kürnach
Block alignment at corner, 3 stories,
21 housing units
cost approx. DM 4,8 mill.
built March 1996–January 1998

Winckelmanstrasse 70/
Haeckelstrasse 1
Apartment and Commercial Buildings
Pieper + Partner, Berlin
Client: Capitalis Liegenschaften GmbH,
Berlin
Block alignment at corner, 3 stories,
15 housing units
cost DM 3,2 mill.
built June 1996–January 1998

Wedding

Amsterdamer Strasse 11
School
Bezirksamt Wedding Hochbauamt
Client: Bezirksamt Wedding von Berlin
Block alignment, 5-story extension of
an existing school
cost DM 5,1 mill.
built March 1997–March 1998

Hochstrasse 23–27
Subsidized Apartment Building
Wolf und Kreis, Berlin
Client: BKatz Verwaltungsgesellschaft mbH & Co. Wohnpark am Humboldthain KG
Block alignment with courtyard
building, 7 stories, 200 housing units
gross floor area 13.892 sq.m
investment DM 94,7 mill.
built March 1995–January 1998

Iranische Strasse 2–4
Jewish Hospital Berlin
Service Building
Dietmar Kloster, Berlin
Client: Jüdisches Kankenhaus Berlin,
Stiftung bR
Reinforced concrete skeleton attached
to neighboring building, 4 stories, with
height and facade adapted from
existing building structures
gross floor area 3.900 sq.m
cost approx. DM 22,2 mill.
built June 1996–end of 1998

Lynarstrasse 27
Apartment House
Peter Pfundstein, Berlin
Client: Grundstücksgemeinschaft
Lynarstrasse 27 bR, repr. by
Rhombus GmbH, Berlin
Urban infill, 7 stories
gross floor area 1.506 sq.m
cost approx. DM 3,7 mill.
built 1997–1998

Müllerstrasse 170–174
Schering Operating Plant
Schering-Bauentwurf
Client: Schering AG, Berlin
Operating plant,10 stories, for the
development of pharmaceutica
gross floor area 6.200 sq.m
cost approx. DM 40,2 mill.
built June 1992–July 1998

Nazarethkirchstrasse 52
Apartment and Office Building
Hans-Jörg Engel, Berlin
Client: Deutsches Gewerbehaus GmbH;
Berlin
Urban infill, 6 stories,
4 housing units in the roof story
cost DM 5,5 mill.
built June 1996–May 1998

Seestrasse 28
German Cardiology Center Berlin
Nurses' Home and Foundation
"Elternhaus" (Parent's House)
Oskar Hillmann, Berlin
Client: Gesellschaft für sozialen
Apartment Building gemeinnützige AG;
Berlin
Urban infill, 8 stories
gross floor area 1.957 sq.m
cost DM 7,7 mill.
built August 1997–end of 1998

Sellerstrasse 1–15
Schering Operating Plant
Schering-Bauentwurf
Client: Schering AG, Berlin
Extension of the center for Galenics and
pharmaceutic development, 4 stories
gross floor area 5.250 sq.m
cost DM 32,5 mill.
built March 1995–February 1997

Sellerstrasse 1–15/Fennstrasse 50–52
Schering Operating Plant
Schering-Bauentwurf
Client: Schering AG, Berlin
Urban infill at Fennstrasse, 7 stories,
labs and office space
gross floor area 8.500 sq.m
cost DM 33,1 mill.
built March 1997–end of 1998

Weissensee

Neu-Karow (Karow-Nord)
(information about urban design
see Berlin's New Buildings 1996/97
in BBA '97)

Block 13, 15, 19, 20, 22
Achillesstrasse 51–75
Karow-Nord Center
Apartment and Office Buildings
Moore, Ruble, Yudell, Santa Monica
Faskel + Becker, Berlin
Ferdinand + Gerth, Berlin
Lunetto + Fischer, Berlin
Client: AQUIS Zweite
Verwaltungsgesellschaft mbH & Co.
Karow-Nord Center OHG
4 stories, 153 housing units,
83 commercial units
dwelling space 26.131 sq.m
cost DM 53,8 mill.
built December 1996–March 1998

Block 25
Zum Kappgraben 16, 18, 20,
Losebergplatz 1, Forkenzeile 7, 9, 11
Apartment Buildings
Neumeyer + Schönfeldt, Berlin
Eyl + Partner, Berlin
Nielebock + Partner, Berlin
Hermann + Valentiny, Berlin
Siedtmann + Grenz, Berlin
Seidel + Partner, Berlin
Thomas Sieverts, Bonn
Nüchterlein + Reck, Berlin
Client: AQUIS Zweite
Verwaltungsgesellschaft mbH & Co.
Karow-Epsilon OHG
4 stories, 225 housing units
dwelling space 15.774 sq.m
cost DM 42,2 mill.
built July 1996–September 1997

Block 26.1
Achillesstrasse 104, 106, 108, 110
Münchehagenstrasse 51, 53, 55, 57
Am Hohen Feld 127, 129
Apartment Buildings
Seidel + Partner, Berlin
Hierholzer + v. Rudzinski, Berlin
Axel Heueis, Berlin
**KSV Krüger, Schubert, Vandreike,
Berlin**
Client: AQUIS Zweite
Verwaltungsgesellschaft mbH & Co.
Karow-Lambda OHG
4 stories, 145 housing units
dwelling space 9.721 sq.m
cost DM 26,9 mill.
built June 1996–June 1997

Block 26.2
Achillesstrasse 76, 78, 80, 82, 84, 86
Forkenzeile 20, 22, 24, 26,
Apartment Buildings
Axel Heueis, Berlin
Hierholzer + v. Rudzinski, Berlin
**KSV Krüger, Schubert, Vandreike,
Berlin**
Seidel + Partner, Berlin
Client: AQUIS Zweite
Verwaltungsgesellschaft mbH & Co.
Karow-Zeta OHG
4 stories, 257 housing units
dwelling space 16.695 sq.m
cost DM 45,3 mill.
built July 1996–September 1997

Block 27
Achillesstrasse 112, 114, 116, 118, 120
Am Hohen Feld 124, 126, 128, 130
Münchehagenstrasse 65
and Block 27A
Am Hohen Feld 114, 116, 118, 120, 122,
Münchehagenstrasse 64
Hofzeichendamm 49
Apartment Buildings
Hierholzer + v. Rudzinski, Berlin
Lunetto + Fischer, Berlin
Moore, Ruble, Yudell, Santa Monica
Pysall, Stahrenberg + Partner
Seidel + Partner, Berlin
Client: AQUIS Zweite
Verwaltungsgesellschaft mbH & Co.
Karow-Kappa OHG
4 stories, 158 housing units
dwelling space 11.346 sq.m
cost DM 30,2 mill.
built December 1996–Dec. 1997

Block 29
Strömannstrasse 93, 95, 97, 99
Apartment Buildings
**HPP – Hentrich-Petschnigg & Partner,
Berlin**
Client: AQUIS Zweite
Verwaltungsgesellschaft mbH & Co.
Karow-Eta OHG
4 stories, 44 housing units
dwelling space 2.553 sq.m
cost DM 6,3 mill.
built October 1996–Sept. 1997

Block 30
Münchehagenstrasse 2–26
Hofzeichendamm 3–21
Forkenzeile 1, 3, 5
Strömannstrasse 96–104
Apartment Buildings
Neumeyer + Schönfeld, Berlin
Ferdinand + Gerth, Berlin
Hermann + Valentiny, Berlin
Client: Immobilienfonds
Karow-Theta GbR
4 stories, 335 housing units
dwelling space 23.301 sq.m
cost DM 57,4 mill.
built December 1996–Dec. 1997

Blocks 31.i, 31.0, 31.y
31.i: *Hofzeichendamm 23–33 a. 39–47*
      Münchehagenstrasse 28–38 u. 62
      Am Hohen Feld 115–123
31.0: *Münchehagenstrasse 40–50*
      Hofzeichendamm 35–37
31.y: *Münchehagenstrasse 52–62*
      Hofzeichendamm 39–47
      Am Hohen Feld 115–123
Apartment Buildings
Hermann + Valentiny, Berlin
Faskel + Becker, Berlin
Lunetto + Fischer, Berlin
Moore, Ruble, Yudell, Santa Monica
Nüchterlein + Reck, Berlin
Client: Immobilienfonds Karow-Iota
GbR
4 stories, 477 housing units
dwelling space 31.023 sq.m
cost DM 78 mill.
built December 1996–Dec. 1997

Block 33-Nord
Strömanstrasse 78–94
Row Houses
Projekt GmbH
Client: Industrie- und Wohnbau
Groth + Graalfs GmbH, Berlin
28 privatly owned apartments and
duplex houses
dwelling space 2.213 sq.m
built February 1997–December 1997

Block 33-South
Strömanstrasse 72–76
Sieverstorpstrasse 1A–3G
Row Houses
Projekt GmbH
Client: Industrie- und Wohnbau
Groth + Graalfs GmbH, Berlin
16 privatly owned apartments and
duplex houses
dwelling space 2.101 sq.m
built May 1996–August 1997

Block 35.1–3
Dreilinienweg 65–83
Sägebockweg 90–96
Sieverstorpstrasse 19–33
Row Houses
Projekt GmbH
Client: Industrie- und Wohnbau
Groth + Graalfs GmbH, Berlin
60 row and duplex houses
dwelling space 7.489 sq.m
built April 1997–July 1998

Block 37.1-Süd
Am Hohen Feld 78–100
Row Houses
Projekt GmbH
Client: Industrie- und Wohnbau
Groth + Graalfs GmbH, Berlin
12 privatly owned apartments and
duplex houses
dwelling space 1.310 sq.m
built November 1997–August 1998

Am Steinberg 2–8/
Brauhausstrasse 1–6/
Heinersdorfer Strasse 38A
Apartment Buildings "Akzent
Weissensee"
**Johann Friedrich Vorderwülbecke,
Berlin**
Client: Falk, Arnan, Gleich, Vorderwül-
becke Heinersdorfer Strasse 38A GmbH
& Co. Verwaltungs GbR
Block alignment, 13 freestanding
houses (8 stories) and 3 high rises,
563 housing units, 35 commercial
units, subterranean car park
net floor area 46.100 sq.m
cost DM 112,5 mill.
completion mid 1998

Bahnhofstrasse 41
Apartment and Office Building
hopro Bauplanung GmbH
Client: Konsumgenossenschaft Berlin
und Umgegend eG
Subsidized apartment and office
building, 2–4 stories, staggered,
on U-shaped floor plan,
31 housing units
gross floor area 3.923 sq.m
retail space 1.539 sq.m
investment DM 20 mill.

Berliner Allee 126/Lindenallee 1A, 1B
Apartment and Commercial Building
FUNDATA GmbH,
Ausführung BRÜCKEL GmbH
Client: GbR Berliner Allee 126 Corner
Lindenallee – repr. by Onnasch
Baubetreuung GmbH & Co
Corner building with tower, 6 stories,
35 housing units
gross floor area 3.089 sq.m
commercial space 365 sq.m
investment DM 17,3 mill.
completion May 1997

Gartenstrasse 1–5
Bischof-Ketteler-House,
Old People's Home
**Feddersen, v. Herder and Partners
Winkelbauer, Berlin**
Client: Neusser Gesellschaft für
Krankenpflege
Freestanding building, 3 stories,
120 beds
gross floor area 8.000 sq.m
cost DM 20 mill.
built 1996–1997

*Gustav-Adolf-Strasse 146–149,
Charlottenburger Strasse 89–91*
Apartment Buildings
Wolf R. Eisentraut, Berlin
Client: Kalisch & Kreiseler GbR
Block completion through 5-story
structures lining up with 3-story listed
buildings,
60 housing units, 3 commercial units
cost DM 10 mill.
built 1996–1998

Langhansstrasse 5
Apartment and Commercial Building
Atelier 33 und Michael Tappe, Berlin
Client: 13. Wohn- und Generalbau KG
Pollux Grundstücks- und Immobilien
GmbH & Co., Berlin
Block alignment, 2 courtyard buildings
with 6 resp. 2 stories,
24 housing units, 3 commercial units
gross floor area 2.000 sq.m
cost approx. DM 8,3 mill.
built 1997–1998

Langhansstrasse 7
Apartment and Office Building
Klaus Meier-Hartmann
Client: Langenhans Baubetreuungs
GmbH
Block alignment, 5 stories,
14 housing units, 2 shops
built 1996–1997

*Prenzlauer Promenade 47, 47 A, 47 B,
48/Treskowstrasse 30–34*
Apartment and Commercial Building
Bartels + Schmidt-Ott, Berlin
Client: Grundstücksgesellschaft
Dii-Fonds B 100
Closed block structure, 6–7–8 stories,
209 housing units (5 housing units for
seniors, 17 housing units with service)
commercial space 2.615 sq.m
gross floor area 15.883 sq.m
cost DM 58 mill.
built September 1995–January 1997

Seidenberger Strasse 1–33
Apartment Building
Gisela Schneidewind, Berlin
Client: GEWO Süd, Berlin
Upraising of a whole listed housing
estate from the 1920s,
42 housing units
built 1996–1998

Wilmersdorf

Bismarckallee 6
Urban Villas
Langer - Dörries - Honnef, Berlin
Client: G + S GmbH, Tuttlingen
2 freestanding buildings,
3–4 stories, 12 housing units
gross floor area 1.438 sq.m
cost DM 6 mill.
built 1997–1998

Bundesallee 208–210
Headquarters of the Investment Bank
Berlin
Stankovic + Bonnen, Berlin
Client: Investitionsbank Berlin (IBB)
Retrocession, conversion, extension of a
high rise from the 1970s
gross floor area approx. 18.000 sq.m
cost DM 95 mill.
built 1995–1998

Caspar-Theiss-Strasse 27–31
Temporary Hospital
**C. Flohr und Söhne GmbH u. Co.,
Cadolzburg**
Client: Martin-Luther-Krankenhaus
Betriebs GmbH, Berlin
Freestanding building composed of
prefabricated units, 2 stories, 100 beds
gross floor area 1.851 sq.m
cost approx. DM 2,3 mill.
built May 1998–July 1998

Emser Strasse 4–11
Apartment and Office Buildings
Nalbach + Nalbach, Berlin
Client: Henning, von Harlessem & Co.,
Berlin
2 office buildings, 4 apartment
buildings, 7–8 stories, 104 housing
units, subterranean car park
commercial space 6.606 sq.m in all
cost DM 42,4 mill.
built 1997–1998

Hohenzollerndamm 28
Privat Hospital with General Practices,
Apartments for Seniors
Arno Bonanni, Berlin
Client: JFK Projekt und Designs
Company GmbH u. Co.
Hohenzollerndamm 28 KG, Berlin
Corner building, 7 stories, 6 commercial
units, 31 apartments for seniors
gross floor area 1.751 sq.m
cost DM 5 mill.
built April 1997–July 1998

Hohenzollerndamm 183
Office Building
Maximiliano P. Burgmayer, Berlin
Client: Hohenzollerndamm 183
Grundstücksverwaltung GmbH & Co. KG;
Hamburg
Block alignment, 7 stories
gross floor area 11.279 sq.m
cost approx. DM 25,8 mill.
built 1997–1998

Hohenzollerndamm 208
Main Pump Station Wilmersdorf
Kurt Ackermann + Partner, Munich
Client: Berliner Wasserbetriebe
Transparent industrial hall with suction
room below ground
gross floor area 3.780 sq.m
cost approx. DM 40 mill.
(incl. machinery)
built 1994–1998

*Rüdesheimer Strasse 14–30/
Wiesbadener Strasse 66, 67*
Primary School at Rüdesheimer Platz
**ELW Eyl, Weitz, Würmle and Partners,
Berlin**
Client: Bezirksamt Wilmersdorf von
Berlin, Abt. Volksbildung
2-story extension and conversion of a
4-sided integrating primary school,
tripled gym hall for school and club
sports
gross floor area. 4.797 sq.m (Neubau)
cost DM 37,7 mill.
built October 1995–end of 1998

Sachsische Srasse 47
Apartment Building
Brückel GmbH, Berlin
Client: GbR Hotel Urbin repr. by
Onnasch Baubetreuungs GmbH, Berlin
Urban infill, 6 stories,
13 housing units, subterranean car park
gross floor area 1.970 sq.m
cost approx. DM 4,3 mill.
built November 1997–Dec. 1998

Zehlendorf

Finkenstrasse 23
Urban Villa
Langer-Dörries-Honnef, Berlin
Bauherr: G + S GmbH, Tuttlingen
Freestanding building, 2–3 stories,
5 housing units
gross floor area 653 sq.m
cost DM 2,8 mill.
built 1997–1998

*Glienicker Strasse 1/
Kohlhasenbrücker Strasse 14*
Housing Complex at Stölpchensee
Langer-Dörries-Honnef, Berlin
Client: NFS Projektbauträger GmbH,
Tuttlingen
Rebuilding of a listed ensemble of 4
buildings, completed through new
building substance at Kohlhasenbrücker Strasse, 15 housing units
gross floor area 1.852 sq.m
cost DM 7,5 mill.
built 1997–1998

Karl-Hofer-Strasse 7
Housing for Disabled People
**Feddersen, v. Herder and Partners
Winkelbauer, Berlin**
Client: Genossenschaft zur
Förderung musischer Erziehung
Angled building, 2 stories + roof story
gross floor area 1.606 sq.m
cost DM 6 mill.
built 1996–1998

Reichensteiner Weg 8–10
Urban Villa
Atelier Kroh GmbH
Client: GFG Gesellschaft für Grundbesitz
mbH
Freestanding building, 10 housing units
gross floor area 980 sq.m
investment DM 7 mill.
built spring 1997–end of 1997

*Teltower Damm 35/
Corner Gartenstrasse*
"Forum Zehlendorf"
**Architektengemeinschaft Bassenge,
Puhan-Schulz, Schreiber, Berlin**
Client: TRIGON Wohn- und
Gewerbebau GmbH
Urban infill on triangular site near
Rapid-Station-Zehlendorf,
subterranean car park
gross floor area 5.825 sq.m
net floor area 5.222 sq.m
commercial space 1.450 sq.m
office space 1.610 sq.m
cost DM 17,6 mill.
built November 1997–Nov. 1998

KREATIVE IDEEN -

Kompetente Partner.

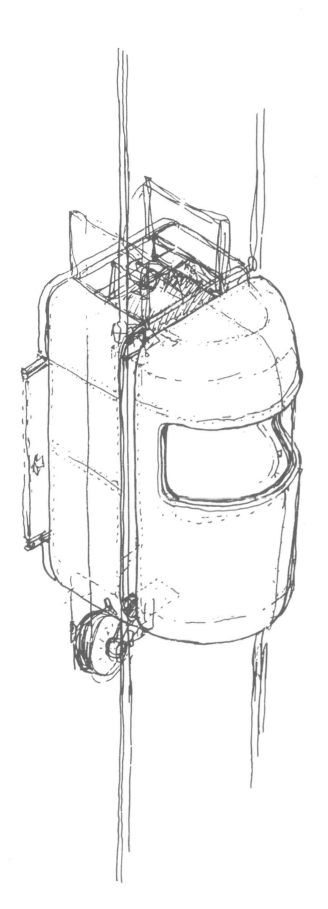

Am Anfang steht die Idee. Die Umsetzung
braucht Partner, die ihr Handwerk verstehen.

Das Ziel: Aufzugsdesign, das sich harmonisch
in die Architektur einfügt. Funktionalität, die
eine komfortable Erschließung des Gebäudes
gewährleistet.

Aufzug für das Ludwig-Erhard-Haus, Berlin

Fordern Sie uns – bereits in der frühen Planungs-
phase Ihrer Aufzugsanlage.
Damit Ihre Ideen Wirklichkeit werden.

OTIS – die Aufzugs- und Fahrtreppenexperten.

OTIS GmbH   Postfach, 13500 Berlin, Telefon 0 30 / 43 04-0, Telefax 0 30 / 4 32 30 12

■ Logistische Meisterleistungen für effizienteres Bauen

Der Unterbau des Ludwig Erhard Hauses, der auch eine geräumige Tiefgarage mit zwei Parkebenen beherbergt, ist im Gegensatz zu der luftig-leichten Stahlskelett-Konstruktion eine massive Angelegenheit: Hier lieferte die Readymix Beton Berlin-Brandenburg GmbH Transportbeton für die „weiße Wanne" und die Zwischendecken:

Es kam vornehmlich Beton der Güteklasse B 35 für die Bodenplatte, für Stützen und Wände sowie die Kellerdecke zur Anwendung. Für die Sauberkeitsschicht unterhalb der Bewehrung der Bodenplatte wurde Beton der Güteklasse B 10/ B 15, für die Innenbauteile B 25 geliefert. „Die Betonage im Allgemeinen war eher eine Routineangelegenheit", erinnert sich Torsten Schiller als der verantwortliche Vertriebsmitarbeiter bei Readymix an die Arbeiten, die auch bei Nacht ausgeführt werden

mußten. „Wirklich interessant war aber das ‚Ambiente' der Baustelle, da die Logistik haargenau stimmen mußte."

Was hier in aller Bescheidenheit als ‚Routine' heruntergespielt werden soll, war in Wirklichkeit eine logistische Meisterleistung. Galt es doch, allein bei der Betonage der Kellersohle, 2.500 m³ Beton am Stück einzubauen. Im Einsatz waren hierfür drei Betonpumpen und bis zu 40 Fahrmischer. Betrachtet man die Bedingungen, unter denen die Arbeiten reibungslos und vor allem fristgerecht ausgeführt werden mußten, erkennt man erst das ganze Ausmaß der Leistung. Da der Bauplatz eng von anderen Gebäuden umstanden ist, war kaum ein ausreichender Platz für die Betonpumpen und zum Manövrieren zu finden. Erschwert wurden die Arbeiten durch die Enge der Zufahrtsstraße, die ihrerseits kaum genügend Platz für die schwerbeladenen Fahrzeuge bot.

Die Art der Realisierung dieses Bauvorhabens ist ein gutes Beispiel für die Vision von Readymix, einen Vorsprung durch innovative Lösungen für das Bauen zu erarbeiten. Auf diesem Weg steht die Kundenzufriedenheit – das Erkennen der Kundenwünsche sowie die qualitätsbewußte und termingerechte Erfüllung der Anforderung – an vorderster Stelle. Dieses war auch das Credo für die herausragende Bauaufgabe des Ludwig Erhard Hauses.

An dem Ziel, mit neuen Lösungen das Bauen effizienter zu gestalten, arbeitet die Beton AG der Readymix-Baustoffgruppe täglich. Ein Beispiel dafür ist das Zentraldispositions-System für Transportbeton. Der Einsatz moderner Kommunikationstechnologie macht es möglich: jeder Auftragsabruf geht in der Zentral-Dispo „ReadyCall" ein, in der ein Computer über alle Auftragsdaten verfügt. Das Modul „ReadyCom" sucht die erforderlichen Fahrmischer, Pumpen, Lieferwerke und günstigsten Anfahrwege und optimiert die Daten. Vom Modul „ReadySat" werden Fahrzeuge, Fahrzeiten, Verzögerungen und Entladezeiten per Satellit erfaßt. Mit diesen Daten ist das System über die aktuelle Situation ständig informiert und kann die Disposition den Verhältnissen entsprechend sofort anpassen. Just-in-time wird noch präziser, der Bauablauf optimiert und die Effizienz der Bauleistung erhöht.

Die Readymix Beton Berlin-Brandenburg GmbH gratuliert allen, die an der Fertigstellung des Ludwig Erhard Hauses – dem neuen, futuristischen Kommunikations- und Service Zentrum für die Berliner Wirtschaft – beteiligt gewesen sind.

Readymix AG für Beteiligungen, Daniel-Goldbach-Str. 25, 40880 Ratingen, Tel.: 021 02/401-0, Fax: 021 02/401-601

LUDWIG ERHARD HAUS

DAS LUDWIG ERHARD HAUS
Das neue Kommunikations- und Service-Zentrum für die Berliner Wirtschaft

Überblick

Ludwig Erhard Haus
Fasanenstraße 85, 10623 Berlin

Gesamtnutzfläche:	22.000 m²
Büroflächen:	18.000 m²

Nutzung:
Kommunikations- und Service-Zentrum für die Berliner Wirtschaft
Mietbare Flächen zwischen ca. 300 und 800 m² Größe

Kommunikations-/ Ausstellungsflächen:	500 m²
Serviceflächen:	500 m²
Multifunktionaler Saal, 3fach teilbar:	450 Pers.
Kleiner Hörsaal:	100 Pers.
Restaurantbereich:	150 Pers.

Nutzung von 60 % der Büroflächen durch:
- **IHK** Industrie- und Handelskammer zu Berlin
- **BAO BERLIN** Marketing Service GmbH
- **VBKI** Verein Berliner Kaufleute und Industrieller e.V.
- **Berliner Wertpapierbörse**
- **Wirtschaftsförderung Berlin GmbH**
- **Technologiestiftung Innovationszentrum Berlin**

40 % der Büroflächen:
- Weitere wirtschaftsnahe Dienstleister

Infrastruktur:
Parkraum: 250 Stellplätze
Behindertengerechte Ausstattung des gesamten Gebäudes
Hervorragende Verkehrsanbindung: S-/U-Bahnnähe, Bushaltestellen, Taxi in unmittelbarer Nähe.

Information

Erstkontakt für Mietinteressenten:
IHK Berlin Hauptgeschäftsführung
Fasanenstraße 85
D-10623 Berlin
Tel.: +49-30-3 15 10-2 33
Fax: +49-30-3 15 10-1 15

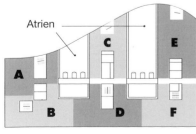
Atrien
Beispielhafte Büroetage

Hardenberg-Atrium

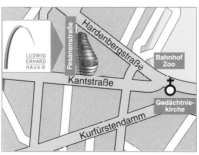
Blick auf das Börsenparkett

Im Herzen der City West, an der Fasanenstraße, steht das Ludwig Erhard Haus kurz vor seiner Vollendung. Der britische Architekt Nicholas Grimshaw hat es eindrucksvoll in Form und Funktion entworfen. Mit seinen 9 Geschossen, abgehängt in 15 bis zu 39 Metern aufragende Stahlbögen, seinen luftigen Atrien und transparenten Glasfassaden gehört das Ludwig Erhard Haus zweifellos zu den herausragenden Bauwerken der Hauptstadt. Aber auch unter ökologischen und ökonomischen Aspekten setzt das Ludwig Erhard Haus neue Akzente und erfüllt höchste Anforderungen an zeitgemäße Technologien:

- Die vergleichbar geringe Oberfläche reduziert Energieverluste.
- Natürliche Belüftung statt Dauerklimatisierung.
- Verglaste Atrien als Klimapuffer zu den Büros vermindern den Heizenergieverbrauch um ca. 30 %.
- Das Klimatisierungssystem für die Büros spart gegenüber konventionellen Systemen

25 % Kühlenergie und 80% Elektroenergie:
- Das in die Fassade integrierte Sonnenlenksystem optimiert die Tageslichtverteilung und reduziert die Kosten für künstliche Beleuchtung.

Insgesamt bietet das Ludwig Erhard Haus 18.000 m² Büroflächen für bis zu 800 Beschäftigte. Unterschiedlich große Mieteinheiten von 100 bis 3.000 m² ermöglichen eine multifunktionale Nutzung – vom Einzelbüro über sogenannte Kombizonen bis zum Großraumbüro. Die moderne Infrastruktur des Ludwig Erhard Hauses ist ganz auf die Anforderungen wirtschaftsnaher Dienstleistungen ausgerichtet:

So stehen 500 m² Kommunikations- und Ausstellungsräume sowie weitere 500 m² Serviceflächen zur Verfügung, außerdem ein multifunktionaler, dreifach teilbarer Saal für bis zu 450 Personen mit High-Tech-Ausstattung und Dolmetscherkabinen sowie ein kleinerer Hörsaal für 100 Personen. Der Restaurationsbereich entspricht mit seinen unterschiedlichen Angeboten von A-la-Carte bis Mittagsimbiß und Bar heutigen Ansprüchen an moderne Businessgastronomie.

Modernste Informations- und Leitsysteme gewährleisten schnelle Kommunikation und Transparenz und unterstreichen den Anspruch des Ludwig Erhard Hauses, mehr zu sein als nur ein Bürogebäude. Hier findet die Berliner Business Community ein adäquates Umfeld für intensive Begegnungen und Kommunikation. Im September 1998 wurde das Ludwig Erhard Haus offiziell seiner Bestimmung übergeben.

Sewage Pumping Station Wilmersdorf

A Reflection of Time

The function is the same, but the architectural ideas of any time have a different shape. Berliner Wasserbetriebe take much care of preserving their listed buildings and provide space for modern architecture.

Berliner
Wasserbetriebe are

http://www.bwb.de
E-Mail:pr@bwb.de

Berliner Wasser Betriebe

Switches for more comfortable living

A. JUNG GMBH & CO. KG
P.O. Box 1320
D-58569 Schalksmühle/Germany
Phone: +49-2355/806-0
Fax: +49-2355/806-254
E-mail: Jung-info@t-online.de
Internet: http://www.jung.de

Sales and Marketing Office for ASIA
JUNG ASIA PTE LTD
48, MacTaggart Road, #06-01
MAE Building
Singapore 368088
Phone: +65/2868816
Fax: +65/2864943
E-mail: Jungasia@pacific.net.sg

The timeless classical switch
range is now available in
black colour. Of course,
including all special devices
such as detectors, dimmers,
phone/fax/computer
sockets, key card holder,
room thermostats etc.

LS 990

Foto: Sharon Simonson

Sie stellte den Champagner weg

und zitierte aus der Ästhetik des Widerstands:
Nach dem Heizen der Tiegel, um vier Uhr morgens,
dauerte es drei Stunden, bis das Zinn geschmolzen war.
Robert war beeindruckt.

*„Zweiter Bildungsweg. Hätte mir nichts ausgemacht.
Aber daß er eine Membran nicht von einem Blimp
unterscheiden kann ...“*

So einfach gewinnt man eine internationale Designauszeichnung.

Das Schalterprogramm Gira E2 wurde vom Design Center Stuttgart im Rahmen des Internationalen Designpreises Baden-Württemberg 1998 ausgezeichnet.

Die einfachsten Ideen sind oft die besten. Gira E2 ist ein Schalterprogramm, dessen intelligente Technik sich hinter einem klaren, sachlichen Design verbirgt.

Ob Info-Display oder Tastsensoren, die sich auf unterschiedlichste Lichtszenen programmieren lassen – immer ist es die Reduktion auf das Wesentliche, die die Form bestimmt. Das überzeugte auch die Jury des Design Center Stuttgart.

Gira E2 ist also in der Tat eine ausgezeichnete Entscheidung.

Weitere Informationen erhalten Sie über den Gira Architekten-Service:
Tel. 02195/602-258
Fax 02195/602-427

Gira
Giersiepen GmbH & Co. KG
Postfach 1220
42461 Radevormwald
http://www.gira.de

**Gira.
Elektroinstallation
mit System.**

GIRA

Architekt: Richard Meier & Partners, New York/Los Angeles; Lichtplanung: J. Fisher, P. Marantz, New York und Francisco Labastida, Barcelona.

Museum für
zeitgenössische Kunst
in Barcelona.
Im Licht von Erco.

198
199

Barceló

ERCO

Die vierte Dimension
der Architektur.

Berlin hat Farbe verdient. Wo das Gesicht der Stadt für lange
Zeit erblaßt war, schaffen weiterentwickelte Bautraditionen
und moderne Architektur heute die Voraussetzungen für das
neue Leben in einer Metropole von morgen.

Die Anforderungen an die verwendeten Baustoffe sind
entsprechend hoch. Dauerhafte und bewährte Materialien sind
gefragt, die gleichzeitig modernen Ansprüchen genügen.
Zum Beispiel TECU®-Patina: Kupfer für Dach und Fassade in
einer zeitgemäßen Definition. TECU®-Patina ist von Anfang an
natürlich grün patiniert – eine Farbe, die nicht nur Berlin gut
zu Gesicht steht. Und alle bekannten positiven Eigenschaften
von klassischem Kupfer bleiben uneingeschränkt erhalten.

TECU®-Patina ist sofort und für immer grün –
dauerhafte und lebendige Farbe für Berlin
und andere interessante Orte dieser Welt.

immergrün

KM Europa Metal
Aktiengesellschaft
Postfach 33 20
D - 49023 Osnabrück

Internet http:// www.kme.de

Informationen zu
TECU®-Produkten
erhalten Sie über:
KME Technische
Kundenberatung
Bauwesen
Tel. (05 41) 321- 43 23
Fax (05 41) 321- 40 30

TECU®-Classic
TECU®-Oxid
 **TECU**®-Patina
TECU®-Zinn
TECU®-System-Schindeln

TECU®

Für Dachdenker.

Berlin`s Architecture
from the Birkhäuser Publishers

The pace of development in Berlin is truly dizzying: hardly a week passes without a foundation stone ceremony for a new building or a festive opening event in the city center. By the turn of the millennium the city will have undergone a complete transformation, a process to which almost all architects of international stature will have contributed.

Foreign Affairs
New Embassy Buildings and the German Foreign Office in Berlin
*Sebastian Redecke,
Ralph Stern (Ed.)*

240 pages, 60 color and
350 b/w illustrations.
24 x 33 cm. Softcover
sFr. 88.–
ISBN 3-7643-5618-9
Hardcover with jacket:
sFr. 108.–
ISBN 3-7643-5629-4
English / German

Chancellery and Office of the President of the Federal Republic of Germany
International Architectural Competitions for the Capital Berlin
*Annegret Burg,
Sebastian Redecke (Eds)*

240 pages, 40 color and
610 b/w illustratons.
33 x 24 cm.Softcover:
sFr. 78.–
ISBN 3-7643-5203-5
Hardcover with jacket:
sFr. 108.–
ISBN 3-7643-5204-3
English / German

Downtown Berlin
Building the Metropolitan Mix
*Annegret Burg,
Hans Stimmann (Ed.)*

224 pages, 90 color and
220 b/w illustrations.
24 x 33 cm.Softcover:
sFr. 88.–
ISBN 3-7643-5063-6
Hardcover with jacket:
sFr. 108.–
ISBN 3-7643-5062-8
English / German

BIRKHÄUSER

Birkhäuser – Verlag für Architektur

Postfach 133 · CH – 40 10 Basel · e–mail: orders@birkhauser.ch · http://www.birkhauser.ch

**Capital Berlin –
Central District Spreeinsel**
International Competition for Urban Design Ideas 1994

212 pages, 40 color and
310 b/w illustrations.
24 x 33 cm Hardcover
with jacket
sFr. 118.–
ISBN 3-7643-5041-5
English / German

Havenly Housing.

Redeveloping Waterfronts

WASSERSTADT

Nacht für Nacht
setzen Außenleuchten
von BEGA öffentliche
und private Bauwerke
ins rechte Licht.
Immer in so
vorbildlichen Formen,
daß sie das Auge
auch bei Tag erfreuen.
BEGA Leuchten gibt
es beim Elektro-
handwerk und im
Elektrofachhandel.

BEGA - Licht draußen.

BEGA

Mehr Licht.

FSB

FSB Franz Schneider Brakel
http://www.fsb.de
Telefon (0 52 72) 60 81 20
Fax (0 52 72) 60 83 00

Alle Formate,
alle Medien.
Kein Ärger.

Wohnungsbau-
gesellschaft
Friedrichshain
Ausstellung
Fotowettbewerb
Berlin-
Alexanderplatz
CACTUS 18/1
Plakat 130 g,
wetterfest

Digitale Prints
für Präsentationen,
Ausstellungen,
Werbung.

Bundesministerium
für Verkehr, Bau und
Wohnungswesen
Bundeshauptstadt
Berlin
Ständige Ausstellung
Hohlsaumlaminat matt
Druck 120 x 280 cm

Senatsverwaltung
für Bauen, Wohnen
und Verkehr
Internationale Wander-
ausstellung
148 x 60 cm
in Leuchtstelen

**Fachlabor für
Farbfotografie und
Digitale Medien**

BAAG
Berlin Adlershof
Aufbaugesellschaft
Dauerausstellung
im InfoCenter
Rudower Chaussee
Transparentpapier
Print 100 x 240 cm

Bundes-
baugesellschaft Berlin
Wanderausstellung
80 g Papier,
standkaschiert
auf Aludibond 2 mm
140 x 200 cm

Schöning & Ruh GmbH
Lützowstraße 100
10785 Berlin
Fon 030. 23 08 11- 0
Fax 030. 23 08 11-15
photolab@ccsberlin.de

Deutsches
Historisches Museum/
Alliiertenmuseum
Ständige Ausstellung
Transparentpapier Panel
Hohlsaumlaminat matt
90 x 350 cm

Partner für Berlin
Das neue Berlin
Internationale
Wanderausstellung
Kratzfestes Laminat
im transportablen
QuickScreen Messe-
system
90 x 220 cm

Außenwerbung
Digital Drucke
Fachvergrößerungen
Finishing
Großdias
Ilfochrome
Ilfocolor
Ilfojet
Iris Drucke
Kaschieren
Lambda Imaging
Laminieren
Leuchtkästen
Overhead Filme
Repros
Scans

Museum für NRW-Forum
Ausstellung VW Beetle
Acrylglas 4 mm,
versiegelt

Groth + Graalfs
Flughafen Köln / Bonn
Leuchtkasten
DIN A 0 quer

TRADITION UND
MODERNE

Berlin 1998. Rund um den Gendarmenmarkt hat die Bauwert-Gruppe drei außerordentliche Häuser fertiggestellt: **Dom Palais**, **Charlotten Palais** und **Kronen Palais**. In klassischer Architektursprache verbinden diese Bauten die Vorzüge der traditionellen Bauweise mit den höchsten Standards moderner Bürokultur.

Die exklusive Lage der Grundstücke in der neuen „alten" Mitte der Hauptstadt erforderte exklusive Lösungen. Und die neuen „Altbauten" bieten ein einzigartiges Ambiente: den stilvollen Hauch klassischer Eleganz mit großzügigen Raumhöhen, Sockelausbildungen und Stuckarbeiten in Verbindung mit den Annehmlichkeiten effizienter Büroflächenstruktur. Ideale Voraussetzungen für anspruchsvolle Repräsentanzen.

Die Bauwert-Gruppe hat mit den Projekten Dom Palais, Charlotten Palais und Kronen Palais einen weiteren konsequenten Schritt getan. Auf dem Boden unserer Erfahrungen mit der Sanierung repräsentativer Altbauten und den richtungweisenden Konzepten beim Neubau von Büro- und Geschäftshäusern verbinden wir Vergangenheit und Zukunft.

BAUWERT
ALLGEMEINE PROJEKTENTWICKLUNGS-
UND BAUTRÄGERGESELLSCHAFT MBH

DOM PALAIS
CHARLOTTENSTRASSE 62 · 10117 BERLIN
TEL. 030/20 26 2-0 · FAX 030/20 26 2-121

The New Berlin: Looking To The Future.

On the threshold of the new millennium the New Berlin presents its best perspectives. The new capital city combines urban density with a wide choice of accommodation and leisure-time activity, institutions, scientific facilities and cultural outlets. Be a part of this year-zero feeling right at the heart of Europe. At the junction between East and West – in Berlin Adlershof, for example.

Live and work hand-in-hand with research and development – experiencing innovation directly. With the mathematical and scientific institutes of the Humboldt University, the university

external research institutes and the innovative commercial companies, MediaCity Adlershof and last but not least with a green living environment, surrounded by shopping, leisure, sport facilities, school and kindergartens.

In Berlin Adlershof the vision of the city capital becomes a reality. Visit our information centre at Berlin Adlershof, Rudower Chaussee 25, or call us: +49 (0)30 21 49 09 03.

BESSY II
Electron Storage Ring

Berlin Adlershof
The City of Science and Technology

DAS NEUE Berlin
Eine Aktion der Berlin-Partner

Audi

VIAG Interkom

 Boehringer
Ingelheim

BVG

24 | 8 | 8 | 8 | Ankunft   Arrivals 1

www.audi.com

www.bosch.com

The book design is based on a concept by MetaDesign.

MetaDesign

Worldwide Corporate Design

Worldwide Corporate Design

Corporate Design
for VIAG Interkom

Corporate Design
for Boehringer Ingelheim

Corporate Design and Orientation System
for Berlin Public Transport

Corporate Design and Orientation System
for Düsseldorf Airport

Audi Homepage

Bosch Homepage

www.metadesign.com

MetaDesign Berlin
Bergmannstrasse 102
D-10961 Berlin
+49·30·695 79·200
fax +49·30·695 79·222
contact@metadesign.de

MetaDesign London
5–8 Hardwick Street
GB-London EC1R 4RB
+44·171·520 1000
fax +44·171·520 1099
Contact: Robin Richmond
robin@metadesign.co.uk

MetaDesign San Francisco
350 Pacific Avenue
USA-San Francisco CA 94111
+1·415·627 0790
fax +1·415·627 0795
Contact: Mark Goldman
mgoldman@metadesign.com

GELBES VIERTEL
BRASILIANISCHE ARCHITEKTEN WERTETEN EIN WOHNQUARTIER MIT LATEINAMERIKANISCHEM FLAIR AUF.

DER WEG

ROTES VIERTEL
DER CECILIENPLATZ – DAS ZWEITGRÖSSTE HELLERSDORFER ZENTRUM – ERHIELT DANK FARBIGER GESTALTUNG DER FASSADEN UND NEUER EINGANGSBEREICHE EINEN UNVERWECHSELBAREN CHARAKTER, DER EIN HARMONISCHES GANZES BILDET.

DURCH HELLERSDORF

FÜHRT ZU

BRANITZER PLATZ
INDIVIDUELLES, URBANES WOHNEN WAR DAS PLANUNGSPRINZIP BEI DIESEM NEUEN WOHNENSEMBLE. DIE MISCHUNG AUS WOHNEN, EINZELHANDEL UND DIENSTLEISTUNG SCHAFFT EINE EIGENSTÄNDIGE WOHN- UND ERLEBNISQUALITÄT.

STADTGESTALTUNG ALS INSTRUMENT ZUR AUFWERTUNG DER WOHNQUALITÄT IST IN HELLERSDORF LEBENDIGE WIRKLICHKEIT. HIER WURDE IN DEN LETZTEN JAHREN VIELEN QUARTIEREN EIN INDIVIDUELLES GESICHT VERLIEHEN. DAS RESULTAT KANN SICH SEHEN LASSEN. HELLERSDORF SETZT ZEICHEN.

KIENBERG-VIERTEL
SANIEREN UND MODERNISIEREN UNTER ÖKOLOGISCHEN GESICHTSPUNKTEN LAUTETE DER ANSPRUCH. DAS ERGEBNIS IST NATURNAHES WOHNEN IM GRÜNEN, BEI DEM DIE SCHONUNG DER RESSOURCEN BEISPIELHAFT PRAKTIZIERT WIRD.

NEUEN PERSPEKTIVEN

WOHNUNGSBAUGESELLSCHAFT HELLERSDORF mbH
ADELE-SANDROCK-STRASSE 10, 12627 BERLIN
TELEFON: 030/9 90 10, TELEFAX: 030/9 91 80 00

Bouwfonds bietet

• hohe Qualität
• gebündelte Kompetenz
• finanzielle Sicherheit

Bouwfonds - baut auf Menschen

Bouwfonds realisiert europaweit Bauprojekte, die sich einer großen Anerkennung erfreuen. Fachleute schätzen dabei besonders den hohen Qualitätsanspruch, die durchdachte Architektur und das sehr gute Preis-/Leistungsverhältnis. Unter der Bouwfonds-Federführung befinden sich in Berlin, Brandenburg, Sachsen, Sachsen-Anhalt, Nordrhein-Westfalen und Hessen zahlreiche Wohnprojekte in Realisation. Dahinter steht die Erfahrung der Bouwfonds Muttergesellschaft N.V. Bouwfonds Nederlandse Gemeenten, die bereits 1946 von niederländischen Gemeinden gegründet wurde. Getragen von der Idee, den Erwerb hochwertigen Wohneigentums für Familien zu ermöglichen, die sich nicht so ohne weiteres ein Eigenheim bauen können, entstanden durch den mittlerweile größten holländischen Projektentwickler 190.000 Wohneinheiten. Ein Erfolg, der für sich spricht!

 **Bouwfonds**
Bauentwicklung GmbH
Storkower Straße 101
10407 Berlin
Telefon 030/428 43 30